TURNING ON THE MIND

# TURNING ON THE MIND

## *French Philosophers on Television*

TAMARA CHAPLIN

The University of Chicago Press

Chicago and London

TAMARA CHAPLIN is assistant professor of modern European history at the University of Illinois at Urbana-Champaign.

The University of Chicago Press, Chicago 60637
The University of Chicago Press, Ltd., London
© 2007 by The University of Chicago
All rights reserved. Published 2007
Printed in the United States of America

16 15 14 13 12 11 10 09 08 07     1 2 3 4 5

ISBN-13: 978-0-226-50990-7 (cloth)
ISBN-13: 978-0-226-50991-4 (paper)
ISBN-10: 0-226-50990-7 (cloth)
ISBN-10: 0-226-50991-5 (paper)

Portions of chapter 2 previously appeared in "From Text to Image: Philosophy and the Television Book Show in France, 1953–1968," *French Historical Studies* 28, no. 4 (Fall 2005): 629–59, © 2005 the Society of French Historical Studies, and are reprinted by permission of Duke University Press. Portions of chapter 3 previously appeared in "Embodying the Mind, Producing the Nation: Philosophy on French Television," *Journal of the History of Ideas* 67, no. 2 (April 2006): 315–41, and are reprinted by permission of the University of Pennsylvania Press.

Library of Congress Cataloging-in-Publication Data

Chaplin, Tamara.
    Turning on the mind: French philosophers on television/Tamara Chaplin.
        p. cm.
    Includes bibliographical references and index.
    ISBN-13: 978-0-226-50990-7 (cloth : alk. paper)
    ISBN-10: 0-226-50990-7 (cloth : alk. paper)
    ISBN-13: 978-0-226-50991-4 (pbk. : alk. paper)
    ISBN-10: 0-226-50991-5 (pbk. : alk. paper)   1. Philosophers—France—
Interviews.   2. Interviewing on television—France.   I. Title.
    B2421.M377 2007
    194—dc22
                                                        2007014099

# CONTENTS

## ACKNOWLEDGMENTS

My research interests are born of the passions that have driven my professional careers—first as a ballet dancer and now as a Modern European historian. Three broadly interconnected questions have propelled my work: What does it mean, or is it possible, to embody the mind? What is the role of the intellectual in today's world? And what is the value of "high" culture to the masses? My related curiosity about the American academy's fascination with postmodern discourse and continental philosophy ultimately led me to the French television archives. The sources I found there became my laboratory; this history of the televising of philosophy in France is a response to the investigations I conducted there. It is also a product of my transition from artist to academic, an evolution that would not have been possible without the contributions of the many people who have helped bring this book to fruition. It is my great pleasure to finally thank them.

The inspired teaching of Geoffrey Fidler, Frederick Krantz, Claudia Clausius, Virginia Nixon, and the late Harvey Shulman at Concordia University's Liberal Arts College convinced me that I wanted to pursue a life in academe. At Rutgers University, my adviser, Bonnie G. Smith, provided a remarkable feminist model of scholarly discipline and intellectual *éclat*. I am deeply honored to have been her student, and thank her for her continued support and encouragement. Her admonishments to "keep writing" are burned in my brain. The semester I spent studying Foucault with Joan W. Scott was critical to my intellectual trajectory. From the start, Joan cajoled, reprimanded, pushed, and praised. Her enthusiasm for this project buoyed my spirits, and her pragmatism helped me keep heart and mind intact throughout the long dissertation process. This project began as a seminar paper in a course led by John Gillis. John has a rare passion for teaching and an even rarer capacity for caring about those who come under his tutelage. Working with him was a joy. I thank Matt K. Matsuda for sharing his brilliance—for meetings, coffees, dinners, stimulating conversation, insightful suggestions, and dazzling coaching. As he knows, I owe my first academic job, in part, to an enthusiastic rehearsal conducted in his Greenwich Village studio. Jennifer Jones is a remarkable teacher and friend. Her lyrical mind has kept me spellbound. Edward Berenson permitted me to audit courses at the Institute of French Studies at NYU and provided me with research support during my semester as a visiting scholar there in 2005. I am indebted to Herrick Chapman for his quiet humor and keen insights and for serving as an outside reader on this project, and to Christian Baudelot for teaching me about the inner sanctum of the French educational system, for sharing his experiences in it during a tour of the École normale supérieure, and for introducing me to Alain Badiou.

In 2002 I joined the Department of History at the University of Illinois at Urbana-Champaign. I thank Peter Fritzsche for hiring me when the ink was barely dry on my Ph.D., and for providing me with the chance to begin my academic career in the company of a set of outstanding scholars. My mentor, and now chair, Antoinette Burton has shaped my subsequent intellectual development more than any other person. She is awe-inspiring. Antoinette reminds me every day that it is possible to be both an exceptional scholar and a compassionate, rigorously principled human being. I thank Harry Liebersohn, Kristin Hoganson, John Randolph, Behrooz Ghamari-Tabrizi, Dana Rabin, Fred Hoxie, Mark Steinberg, Diane P. Koenker, Maria Todorova, Leslie Reagan, Clare Crowston, Siobhan Summerville, Jean-Philippe Mathy, and especially Adam Sutcliffe, Mark S. Micale, and Carol Symes for welcoming me into life in the academy. The Department of History staff is wonderful, and I am grateful for their efficient and cheerful ministrations. My students keep me inspired about the path I have chosen, and remind me that history becomes meaningful when we understand how it has relevance for our lives today. I strive to remain open to all that they have to teach me, even as I seek to transmit what I know to them. I am blessed to have worked with Mihaela Gainusa, Irina Gigova, Max Follmer, Frankie Sturm, Rachel Sims, Jessica Smith, Elana Goldbaum, and particularly Brendon Stark (all those e-mails!), and Cory Collman, whose friendship I cherish and who did a brilliant job formatting the images in this book.

In France, I would like to extend my deepest gratitude to Christine Barbier-Bouvet (adjointe, Consultation des fonds audiovisuels at Inathèque de France) for her efforts on my behalf. I am indebted to Inathèque for providing me with a home away from home during my sojourns into their archives. SLAV 67 has my name metaphorically inscribed on it. My special thanks to secretary Myriam Fleury, and to archivists Rachel Denoeud and Sylvie Fégar and technician Bruno Canlet. Their assistance was, and is, invaluable. For granting me special access to collections, and extraordinary favors, I would also like to thank Jean-Michel Rodes, director of the Institut national de l'audiovisuel (INA), Michel Raynal (Consultation des fonds audiovisuals), Valérie Chaumelle-Serrus (Collecte du dépôt legal), Denis Maréchal (Lundis de la BNF), Claire Mascolo (Documentation écrite), and Véronique Clavier (Photothèque). I would futher like to acknowledge INA, UNESCO, and the Centre national de documentation pédagogique (CNDP) for enabling me to illustrate this book with images from their collections.

Among the most pleasurable aspects of my research (besides, of course, watching hours of mind-blowing TV) were the interviews I conducted in France. I shall never forget an hour with Pierre Dumayet in his little study piled with books, nor his wave through the café window outside Radio-France the following day; Pierre-André Boutang picking up the phone a half-dozen times to make other contacts for me during our dialogue; tea beside the Bastille with Jean-Claude Bringuier; a tour of Yves Jaigu's sixteenth-century apartment; Alain Badiou pointing up from his office at the ENS to Althusser's apartment and whispering, "That's where he killed her, you know." For their time, insights, and patience with my awkward French, I am also indebted to Jean-Noël Jeanneney, Luc Ferry, André Comte-Sponville, Michel Cazenave, Jean Cazeneuve, Laure Adler, Denis Huisman, Alain Etchegoyen, Isabelle Veyrat-Masson, Jérôme Bourdon, and Jean Beaujean. Between 1998 and 2000, from my tiny sixth-floor flat off the rue Mouffetard the rooftops of Paris were my constant companions. When I needed more articulate friends, I turned to Caroline Mertens, John Wright, Kelly Roughton, Cynthia Cervantes (and all her babies!), Matia Karrell (ballet classes), Marta Pragana-Dantes (pancakes), Sylvie and Philippe Midy, and, more recently, Thierry and Anne Pech, whose generosity provided me with an apartment during my final summer of research in 2006.

The French government granted funding for this project in the form of a Bourse Chateaubriand. I also received support from the

government of Québec's FCAR (Fonds pour la formation de cherch-
eurs et l'aide à la recherche), the Woodrow Wilson Foundation's Charlotte W. Newcombe Doctoral Fellowship for Research in Ethics, and a
five-year Excellence Fellowship from Rutgers University. The Research
Board at the University of Illinois at Urbana-Champaign afforded me
a vital semester of Humanities Released Time, and financed several
crucial research trips to France. The History Department at UIUC
provided an additional semester off. I am beholden to all of these
organizations and institutions for their invaluable assistance. At the
University of Chicago Press, I am indebted to my anonymous readers,
and to Anita Samen, Margaret Mahan, and especially my remarkable
editor, Alan G. Thomas. I am nothing short of blessed to be working
with all of you.

No book is ever finished without the unstinting support of a close
circle of friends and family, and mine has been amazing. I thank Richard Jobs and Carla MacDougal for shared meals, phone calls, and advice. Roxanne Panchasi accompanied my academic growth, literally
from day one. She is a gifted scholar, and I treasure her friendship.
Adam Sutcliffe remains dear from afar, as do Ellen Hoffman, Kather-
ine Panter-Roland, Tobi Panter, Catherine Hollis, Kelly Gates, Sabine
Rohr, and Abudi Zein. They make my life richer. Marie Leger—her
irrepressible spirit, deep compassion, inquisitive mind, and ability to
get insanely silly (pooking, anyone?)—made life in the corn and soy
a joyous adventure. I thank my brother Daniel for inspiring me to be
a better human being and for reminding me to relish each moment
because life is precious. I regret that this project has kept me farther
from my brother Scott than I might have hoped. My mother, l. tarin
chaplin, and my father, Anton S. Chaplin, and his wife Jean taught
me in very different ways that the life of the mind is a marvelous and
miraculous thing, but one that must always be balanced by the life
of the heart. My mother nurtured my work as she has nurtured me.
Her sharp mind and insatiable curiosity (not to mention her skills
with shorthand) opened creative windows on this project. Many years
ago my father abandoned the completion of his own Ph.D. in order to
support our family. He has been my staunchest fan during these final
years of writing, and I am so very proud that I can finally say to him,
"Hey Dad, I'm done!"

Finally, I want to express my thanks to the two people who have
lived with this book, in very different ways, since its inception: the
first is my dear friend (and INA archivist) Rachel Denoeud. You have

truly been my personal archival angel—digging up obscure sources, sending me articles, e-mailing those important facts that I could not access from this side of the ocean, translating, transcribing, listening, advising, suggesting—your generosity is boundless, as is my gratitude. The second is Andrew Matheson, the man with whom I spent almost seventeen years of my life. Whatever the future brings, I thank you for loving me so well for so long. To say that I am grateful for the time that we shared doesn't even begin to cover it.

CNCL        Commission nationale de la communication et des libertés
CNDP        Centre national de documentation pédagogique
CNE         Comité national des écrivains
CNRS        Centre national de la recherche scientifique
CSA         Conseil supérieur de l'audiovisuel
ENA         École nationale d'administration
ENS         École normale supérieure
FEMIS       Fondation européenne de l'image et du son
FEN         Fédération de l'éducation nationale
FLN         Front de libération nationale
FR3         France Régions 3
GRECE       Groupement de recherche et d'études pour la civilization
            européenne
GREPH       Groupe de recherche sur l'enseignement philosophique
HEC         École des hautes études commerciales
IDHEC       Institut des hautes études cinématographiques
INA         Institut national de l'audiovisuel
IPN         Institut pédagogique national
LA SEPT     La Société d'édition de programmes de télévision
MRP         Mouvement républicain populaire
OAS         Organisation de l'armée secrète
ORTF        Office de radiodiffusion et télévision française
PCF         Parti communiste français
PS          Parti socialiste
RDF         Radio diffusion française

| | |
|---|---|
| RDR | Rassemblement démocratique révolutionnaire |
| RPF | Rassemblement du peuple français |
| RTF | Radiodiffusion et télévision de France |
| RTS | Radio-télévision scolaire |
| SFIO | Section française de l'Internationale ouvrière |
| SFP | Société française de production |
| TDF | Télédiffusion de France |
| TFI | Télévision française 1 |

# Portrait of a Philosopher

Gaston Bachelard. From
"Portrait d'un philosophe,"
1 December 1961.

I. INTERIOR KITCHEN. NIGHT.
*A dimly lit room in the Fifth arrondissement, Paris, 1961. . . . Click. A*
*gentle hum. On the table, a small black and white television blooms*
*to life. Close-up of the screen. . . .*

2. TELEVISION SCREEN. FULL FRAME.
*The camera scans the angled wall of a shabby room, shelves rise to the*
*ceiling, crammed to bursting with books, papers, tumbled files, jour-*
*nals. The image pans downward, seizes on a figure in the far corner*
*and zooms in. Behind a desk sits an old man. His balding forehead*
*is set off by a halo of fine white hair, his tufted eyebrows thrust for-*
*ward over sparkling eyes. Deeply wrinkled skin, bulbous nose, white*
*mustache, a mouth hidden beneath a cascade of frothy beard; the face*

"Portrait d'un Philosophe," *Cinq Colonnes à la une,* Channel 1, 1 December 1961,
INA. All translations and script transcriptions are my own unless otherwise indicated.

*of Sophocles, or Santa Claus. Now he's shifting forward. His craggy hand arches across the desk. He settles. His bones ache. The man in the chair is Gaston Bachelard, French philosopher. He tilts his head, turning toward the sound of a voice.*

3. CLOSE-UP ON BACHELARD.

VOICE (*off screen*): Is there a precise definition of a philosopher?

BACHELARD (*quavery*): I gave one once, when I taught, but . . . I've lost it (*grins slyly*) . . . Why do you want one, heh? It is a professor of wisdom, as we used to say. . . .

VOICE (*off screen*): I'm going to ask you one of those general questions that annoy you so much . . . are philosophers superior to other men?

BACHELARD: We're not God the Father, you know . . . No, no, no, life and the life of the mind are not mutually exclusive . . . you want absolutely to stick the label of philosopher on me as if I'm some sort of dreamer separated from all the real difficulties of life . . . (*musing*) it is a popular idea about philosophers—but, no, it must be rectified.

4. FADE TO BLACK.

# Televising Philosophy in Postwar France

In 1951, the eight o'clock nightly news covered Jean-Paul Sartre for the first time. By the end of the twentieth century, more than 3500 programs dealing with either philosophers or their work had aired on French television.[1] Even after the partial privatization of the state broadcasting system in the 1980s, philosophy continued to be a regular component of TV in France. The mere existence of these shows—which have brought the most difficult and abstract of disciplines to the French public for over fifty years—challenges our assumptions about the incompatibility of elite culture and mass media, and belies the argument that television is inevitably anti-intellectual, a menace to democracy, culture, and moral values, and the archenemy of the book *tout court*.[2]

In this book I argue that a history of the televising of philosophy in France is crucial to understanding the struggle over French national identity in the post–World War II period. The source of this struggle was a series of challenges to France's historically confident view of itself—from the experiences of German occupation and collaboration during the Second World War to the processes of decolonization, modernization and globalization that followed. It was in this context that France's humanistic literary tradition came to compete with and accommodate itself to an increasingly visual modernity. The fascination expressed by French citizens with televised philosophy, and their obsession with both the dangers and the opportunities posed by what Guy Debord has famously called "the society of the spectacle," are inextricable from a set of hopes and anxieties about what it means to be French in a modernizing world.[3]

No history of the post-1945 French state can be understood without attention to its administrative, institutional and cultural apparatus. In the second half of the twentieth century the French state embraced the technology of television not simply to "educate, inform, and entertain" the public—in the words of the national broadcasting administration—but as a tool in the service of nation building.[4] The Fourth Republic established a monopoly over the audiovisual field, initially in order to counter a print media that had been delivered into the hands of the left following the widespread purges that marked the end of WWII. What began as a political maneuver grew into a strategy for containing dissent and controlling national consumption not just of news but also of the cultural legacy that was understood to be constitutive of French national identity itself. As we shall see, the work of philosophy on television demonstrates with particular clarity how the state project of visualizing "Frenchness" reified for popular consumption an image of national superiority at a time when France's international stature was declining.

Following the Liberation from German occupation in 1944, France was eager to refashion itself as a nation of resisters and to regain a place in the global balance of power. When the state turned its focus to philosophy in the decade after the war, it did so in part because French existentialism was generating international interest. In philosophers the state found a valuable form of cultural capital that could assist in the nation's symbolic reconstruction. While cognizant that early TV exerted little influence beyond national borders, television producers recognized the medium's potential to confirm French greatness to domestic audiences. By the 1950s, broadcast coverage of philosophers like Sartre, Albert Camus, and Simone de Beauvoir was carefully deployed by a politically cautious television administration as a visible sign of French renewal. Eschewing political controversy, early TV footage presented philosophers almost exclusively as literary celebrities. They were depicted as cultural jet setters, winning literary awards, attending theater openings, or besieged by paparazzi as they scurried to and from glittering social events. Through news clips, theater reviews, and even obituaries, state television promoted philosophers as national icons, making them the corporeal synecdoche for a specifically French form of national glamour and intellectual power.

At the same time, the French state was dealing with the debacle of the Algerian War (1954–62). The eight-year battle to keep Algeria French, which destroyed the Fourth Republic and brought de Gaulle to power, became one of the bloodiest examples of decolonization on record. By the time Algeria was finally granted independence in 1962 under the terms of the Evian Accords, the stakes of national and cultural redemption for France were high. After the Algerian War, the forces of American hegemony, globalization, and political and legal integration in the European Union made the definition and cultural acquisition of "Frenchness" all the more important. Philosophy was identified in postwar France as a tool to grapple with these needs, and to inculcate not only the capacity for autonomous critical thinking but also for ethical reflection into the very core of French identity.[5] In this context, a committed group of intellectuals, educators, and television professionals saw state-directed television—with its unique aptitude for colonizing the intimate spaces of the private sphere—as an innovative means for philosophy's dissemination. Cloaked in moral responsibility, philosophers were summoned before the cameras and requested to perform to a modern *agora,* that of the ever-expanding national television audience.

The history of televising philosophy in France shows how arguments over the constitution of French identity have played out over the airwaves for more than fifty years. But I also want to make an argument about the history of philosophy in contemporary France. We cannot understand the markedly public role that philosophy came to play in French society during the late twentieth century, or the renewed interest in political philosophy in the early twenty-first, unless we appreciate the work of television. TV coverage of great teachers like Gaston Bachelard, Georges Canguilhem, Jean Hyppolite, and Vladimir Jankélévitch also reminds us that contemporary French philosophy has been more influenced by French academic institutions, and less unified around a specific cadre of master thinkers (Sartre, Foucault, Derrida, etc.), than Anglo-American audiences typically believe.[6]

French philosophy on television emerged as a means both to cover and to counter a complicity of silence—silence about Vichy, Algeria, the Gulag, the Holocaust, racism, women, AIDS, and, to a degree, the failure of a republican democracy to adapt to the changing demands of a modern, multicultural world. Drained of political valence, philosophy on TV during the 1950s and '60s served as an abstract symbol of French cultural regeneration. In this forum it promoted a universalizing, patriarchal vision of French republican superiority. And in so doing, it participated in a national project of denial, one that effaced French responsibility for discrimination, injustice, and violence. It was only when televised philosophy began to acknowledge its own silences and, in the aftermath of 1968, to *demand* its own ethical orientation that we see a dramatic shift. By the 1970s, French TV became one of the most visible platforms for the restoration of philosophy's political, social, and ethical utility. While this process invariably masked new prejudices, within two decades a broad public came to understand philosophy as an unparalleled tool for social judgment, but also for personal enlightenment and self-transformation. The craze for *le philo* that swept France during the 1990s (evidenced not only by TV coverage but also by print media and philosophy cafés) and the revival of political and moral philosophy that followed need to be understood not as effects of fashion (the common explanation) but rather as the product of a historical shift in philosophy's public role—one inseparable from the influence of the small screen. This shift has also traced a political course, with philosophy moving roughly from left to center-right. Primed by the "end of ideologies" and the fall of communism and, more recently by the rise of global terrorism, philosophy in its contemporary incarnations as "self-help" and neoliberal theory offers the French public increasingly conservative answers to a world unmoored.

### Tearing Down the Ivory Tower

In what follows, I set out to engage a wide range of scholarship that has to date remained largely disconnected. For too long, French historians of ideas have kept the intellectual and the sociocultural separate, isolating intellectual developments in an ivory tower. There has been ample attention to the role of print culture in the construction of national identities, but few scholars of nationalism have considered the effects of the audiovisual media on this important field.[7] Examinations of the relationship between intellectuals and television invariably sidestep a direct analysis of programs.[8] Philosophical reflections on the media are likewise theoretically based and inevitably ahistorical.[9] French histories of television are mainly administrative or political.[10] To be sure, TV research has been hindered not only by scholarly prejudices but also by problems of access. In France, the fragile stock on which much early programming was recorded has never been recopied and is unavailable to view.[11] It is partly for this reason that few historical monographs have focused on the programs themselves.[12] Indeed, this book—one of the first works of television history to extensively analyze actual broadcasts—would not have been possible without the generous assistance of the French television archives (the Institut national de l'audiovisuel), whose technicians transferred dozens of shows to tape specifically for this project. There is a substantial literature on French cultural policy, but the genre of philosophical TV slips through the net.[13] Although French visual culture has stimulated a considerable body of research, this scholarship tends to divide neatly between works focused on high culture and those that take popular culture and "the masses" as their subject.[14] Philosophical television necessarily tests this stance, denaturalizing the boundaries that often separate the two fields.

How are philosophers defined in postwar France? Since the nineteenth century the route that customarily leads to the practice of philosophy in France has been competitive entry into the École normale supérieure (ENS), followed by the successive mastery of a nationally defined corpus of philosophical texts and the passing of the *agrégation,* an exam taken after years of intensive postsecondary study that opens the doors to careers in teaching and, ultimately, to the universities and elite institutions of the French state.[15] But if the educational trajectory appears invariable, delimiting the field remains a difficult task—not least because one can be publicly identified as a philosopher *without* having pursued this path.[16] In addition, during the twentieth century a growing number of intellectuals (from the sociologist Pierre Bourdieu to the anthropologist Claude Lévi-Strauss) passed the prestigious philosophy *agrégation* only to pursue careers in other disciplines. Breadth of scholarly production can further complicate matters. From Plato to Aristotle, Rousseau, Locke, Hume, Nietzsche, Wittgenstein, Heidegger, Arendt, Sartre, and beyond, philosophers have addressed political and social issues as well as epistemological and ontological ones. And in France, as elsewhere, individuals are identified differently depending on which parts of their oeuvre are valued at any given time—a fact that reminds us that the designation "philosopher" has no stable meaning outside of specific historical contexts.[17]

New debates about the definition and attribution of the title "philosopher" were provoked in the postwar period by the emergence of a figure that Pierre Bourdieu has called *le philosophe journaliste* (the "philosopher- journalist").[18] While not without historical precedents, this figure, epitomized first by Sartre, challenged the structures that regulated the selection and consecration of the philosophical corps by confronting the boundaries that, since the nineteenth century, had come to separate academic philosophy from the more public worlds of literature, theater, journalism, and—later—film, radio, and television. By the 1970s, the intellectual and commercial impact of such activity, particularly on TV, had become increasingly controversial, for in exercising its own systems of intellectual sanctification, TV effectively "produced" new philosophers and both created and legitimized competing forms of philosophical thought. It is because I am interested in this process of cultural production (and not only its intellectual validity—or lack thereof), that I use the terminology employed by television itself to define the players and determine the parameters of the genre. However, since much of the argument advanced here applies to intellectuals in general (and since philosophers also function, and are referred to, as "intellectuals," "public intellectuals," "committed intellectuals," "writers," and "thinkers"—a practice I follow, as well), why should this category be favored as a group apart? Quite simply, because the French themselves have done so. In the aftermath of WWII, philosophers were produced in France as the repositories of a specific type of cultural capital. And it was via their status as "philosophers" that they were understood as the symbolic apex of the French intellectual elite, an elite that was (and continues to be) predominantly male.

My book's cast of characters illustrates that, notwithstanding Simone de Beauvoir, the philosophers who gained recognition in postwar France are nearly all men. This gender imbalance reflects the contemporary field; female philosophers (like female intellectuals in general) are absent mostly because their numbers were few.[19] Their television appearances are correspondingly scarce (and hence their place in my story is limited). When female intellectuals *are* featured on French TV, it is often as the consorts of their more celebrated male partners (with Beauvoir paired, of course, with Sartre, and Kristeva with Philippe Sollers). And here again, there are denominative ambiguities. Despite her standing as the dominant female intellectual of the postwar era, Beauvoir, an *agrégée* in philosophy, is often introduced as a novelist or feminist. Among the contemporary French feminist "philosophers" typically recognized in the American academy—Luce Irigaray, Hélène Cixous, Michèle Le Doeuff, and Julia Kristeva—it is the latter two that are identified as such on French TV, but only Irigaray and Le Doeuff are philosophers by training.[20] Kristeva is a psychoanalyst and linguist, and Cixous, a writer. It is not until the late 1970s that we see female intellectuals consistently presented on television in their own right—although even then it is often in broadcasts related to "women's issues"—whether explorations of concepts like love and desire, or strictly political discussions pertaining to feminism. This is a development that clearly merits further research. Barring the odd exception, television appearances by female philosophers where gender questions are not at issue are rare before the 1990s. Despite this evolution, insofar as French philosophy (not to mention its televisual representation) is concerned, gender equity has yet to be achieved.

( · )

This book draws on hundreds of hours of TV footage, numerous personal interviews, and almost four thousand program summaries, as well as a vast range of original documents, from press releases and administrative, governmental and private records, to viewer's letters, audience statistics, and newspaper and magazine articles. My aim is to map discourse onto media practice, integrating intellectual history into popular culture, and analyzing the actual contents of French philosophy on television against the complex historical specificity of an era. In this I am building on Raymond Williams's insistence that modes of communication are "a major way in which reality is continually formed and changed."[21] I want to resituate Williams's theoretical critique in an identifiable historical context and to show that if we are to fully understand the ways in which both ideas and images are vested in national histories, we ignore the medium of television at our peril.

### Making High Culture Popular

An overview of more than fifty years of French television history reveals the presence of philosophy and philosophers in a startling array of genres. These include literary talk shows, cultural magazines, portraits within a documentary series, isolated specials, television news, obituaries, educational programming, religious broadcasts, political debates, variety shows and film reviews, series dedicated entirely to philosophy as such, and even—amusingly—sitcoms (notably, *La Philo selon Philippe* ["Philosophy according to Philippe"], a comedy produced in the 1990s and set in a high school philosophy class that was the French equivalent of the American series *Beverly Hills 90210* or the

Canadian *Degrassi High*). Consequently, in this book I am interested not only in how TV covers philosophy qua philosophy but also in the ways in which—and to what ends—it has featured philosophers within other mise-en-scènes.

This vast corpus of programs is but one example of the French broadcasting system's commitment to bringing high culture to the French nation. The history of the televising of philosophy in France is inextricable from a distinctively French commitment to cultural diffusion, one enshrined in state policy in the constitution of 1946 and formalized through the creation of a Ministry of Culture in 1959. Notwithstanding the fact that TV—because of its political potential—was consigned to the jurisdiction of the Ministry of Information (and not Culture), the debates shaping French cultural policy in the postwar period directly affected attempts to televise philosophy, and they are worth clarifying here. For when culture is comprehended as both a historically contingent construct and a social process, these debates can be seen for what they were: not simply expressions of aesthetic preference or intellectual affinity, but rather politically mobilized attempts to control the social sphere and, in so doing, to shape both the remembrance of the French past and the presentation of its future.

During the Fourth Republic and the early Fifth, the social process of cultural production was linked to one of "cultural democratization." Cultural democratization was originally understood largely as an issue of *access*, in which the key government task was to bring high cultural forms (what Herbet Gans calls "taste culture," i.e. the practices, goods, and ideas generated within the arts and the media broadly defined—including literature, theater, music, and architecture), into direct contact with the French public.[22] It has been argued that such politically prescribed cultural intervention is a fairly recent phenomenon in France. Nevertheless, the French state has a long tradition of supporting a wide range of cultural endeavors, from the practices of patronage that promoted artistic and musical creation within the royal courts, to the funding of watershed cultural projects—such as the construction of the Paris Opera (1875) and the Eiffel Tower (1889)—undertaken during the Third Republic.[23] In the 1930s, the Popular Front government gave greater attention to popular culture and initiated a process of institutional consolidation later appropriated by Vichy conservatives in the 1940s. During the war, ventures like the École des cadres (leadership school) at Uriage and Albert Ollivier's Jeune France (Young France), sought to promote national cultural renewal, on the one hand supporting innovative youth projects and on the other introducing the nation's youngest members to the country's revered cultural patrimony.[24]

To many of its early proponents, television's unprecedented ability to provide widespread access to works of high culture (and in the unintimidating setting of one's own living room, no less!) was a critical part of its attraction. However, following the student revolutions of 1968, the inherent value of the "major works of humanity" (as specified in the 1959 founding decree of André Malraux's Ministry of Culture) was increasingly challenged by "cultural omnivores"—proponents of culture understood in its wider anthropological or sociological sense who, harking back to their Popular Front forebears, rejected "cultural *democratization*" in favor of what they called "cultural *democracy.*"[25] In their view, the state's charge was not one of providing access to "taste culture" (also known as "cultured culture") but rather of supporting a profusion of cultural forms, wherein *all* cultural practices (highbrow, middlebrow, and lowbrow) were understood to be of equal worth, and in which people had a right to engage with whatever cultural manifestations they preferred.

Under the influential tenure of Jack Lang (minister of culture from 1981 to 1986 and again from 1988 to 1993), conflicts between proponents of taste culture and the advocates of cultural democracy were eclipsed in France by the emergence of a new cultural policy matrix, dominated by the culture industries and focused on the global cultural economy. But, as apparent from the backlash among a certain cluster of the intellectual elite against what had become known as *le tout culturel* (an expression referring to the economic process whereby Lang rendered everything cultural), underlying tensions remained.[26] In some ways, the concern for French "cultural exceptionalism" that now dominates French cultural policy debates can be seen as a compromise between champions of taste culture (cultural democratization) and those supporting a vision of culture more broadly understood (cultural democracy), in which both come together to preserve national cultural autonomy. In 1994, television became an explicit part of this argument when France successfully fought to get the European Union to strengthen protections for the audiovisual domain at the Uruguay round of the General Agreements on Tariffs and Trade (GATT) negotiations in Marrakech. Advocates of cultural exceptionalism claim that cultural goods are *not* goods like any others, but rather should be exempt from the rules governing free trade in order to safeguard the sanctity of national cultural identities (by refusing, for example, to allow foreign television or cinema unrestricted access to national markets). For the French, the impact of these debates is enormous—indeed, nothing less than their power to control, define, and perpetuate a distinctive national presence both within Europe and on the global stage is at stake.

## Too Little Time and Nothing to Show

Television's temporal and structural constraints are often considered inimical to complex intellectual thought. Appearing in 1994 on the program *Le Cercle de minuit,* philosopher Olivier Postel-Vinay fumes, "Socrates would have subscribed to the idea that television constitutes a grave menace to the city." Why? Because, he states, "the power of a spirit like Socrates requires time for expression."[27] Sociologist Pierre Bourdieu concurs. "Is it possible to think fast," he asks in *On Television,* his polemic against the medium, without thinking "in clichés?"[28] Television, in this view, is by definition hasty and superficial; it craves "cultural 'fast food'—predigested and pre-thought" and so requires its protagonists to promote their work in formulaic sound bites. When it comes to philosophy, such arguments hinge on two principal assumptions.[29] The first, clearly, is that the process of "philosophizing" takes time. The second is that, given philosophy's abstract nature, there is nothing to show. Both these stances take for granted that the relationship between television, time, and the image is mainly structural and not historically constructed. When a historical perspective *is* employed—often in a problematic, because reductive fashion—the emphasis is on duration: since older programming formats tended to run longer, so the argument goes, they must have been better—at least insofar as philosophy is concerned.[30]

A return to the archives complicates this picture. True, during French television's early years, longer, simpler production formats, fewer participants, and slower editing styles, not too mention a heavily didactic agenda and more patient audiences, all supported the kind of sustained production conducive to the televising of complex thought. And, not surprisingly, the retreat of the public model, the introduction of commercial advertising (in 1968), and the rise of the entertainment ethos posed challenges for the televising of philosophy. Indeed, by the 1990s the effects of privatization were epitomized when, in an attempt to woo audiences used to fast-paced editing and flashy graphics, an array of short-format philosophy programs appeared, often lasting no more than fifteen or even five minutes—as in the ironically titled *Pas si vite!* (Not So Fast!). It would be ridiculous to deny that serious philosophical scholarship demands tremendous temporal investment, or that uninterrupted airtime benefits philosophy's televised transmission. Yet numerous examples, from Michel Foucault's fifteen-minute discussion of *The Order of Things* on *Lectures pour tous* in 1966, to Jean-François Lyotard's equally brief interrogation of the role of the intellectual in the media on *Tribune Libre* in 1978, show that substantive philosophical exchange *can* take place on the small screen in a limited period of time. Further, even in the new market-oriented audiovisual environment, in which the short format is king, uninterrupted, full-length programs on philosophy continue to be produced. In other words, both the temporal requirements of the discipline and the negative effects of historical change on those requirements have been overestimated.

The question "Can one learn philosophy from TV?" posed to philosopher André Comte-Sponville on a 1994 broadcast called "Why is Philosophy So Popular?" provides another example of how queries about philosophical television are often framed in ahistorical terms.[31] I am more interested in the historical circumstances that made it possible for the French to feel that one either *should* or *could* learn philosophy from television in the first place. Yet in response to Comte-Sponville's reply, "Not unless one is already schooled in the discipline," it is worth noting that by the 1990s a remarkably large part of the French public *was*. Instruction in philosophy has been a mandatory subject in the *classe terminale,* or final year of French secondary studies, since 1874. The popularity of philosophy in France during the late twentieth century was premised on the democratization of education.[32] As Comte-Sponville observes, "In the 1950s, maybe 5% or 6% of the population had completed studies in philosophy to the level of the *baccalauréat* [the French equivalent of a high school diploma]. If 70% of the French population has a *baccalauréat* today, it means that 70% of French adults have studied philosophy."[33] The success of philosophy on French television is also a product of this historical shift.

In *What is Philosophy,* Gilles Deleuze and Felix Guattari assert that "philosophy is the discipline that involves *creating* concepts."[34] Philosophy deals in abstractions. This being so, does it have a visual dimension? "*No!*" philosopher and former minister of education Luc

Ferry told me emphatically—despite his regular appearances on television.[35] Both Yves Jaigu, former president of the radio station France Culture (1975–1984) and Jean-Noël Jeanneney, former president of Radio France (1982–1986) took the same position, arguing that on TV, language is trounced by the power of the image. All these men insist that when it comes to philosophy, radio is a superior means of transmission.[36] In contrast, philosopher Alain Badiou is convinced that philosophy is fundamentally embodied, and hence visual. As he informed me, "we can say what we like, but philosophy, singularly because it is *not* uniquely *un savoir* [a body of knowledge], needs a figure of transmission that is not simply a book and is not merely abstract speech . . . Socrates was corporeally present."[37] In this book I likewise claim that due to the performative nature of their discipline, founded on the Socratic dialogue and rooted in an embodied oral practice, philosophers are in fact uniquely suited to the demands of television. It is my fascination with the relationship between abstract thought, visual representation, and corporeality that has drawn me to study the presence of philosophy on television, rather than on radio—despite the latter's rich concurrent history. Yet such claims for a rapport between television, philosophy, and embodiment also require historicizing, since this connection necessarily carries historically particular effects. While philosophers may "embody" their oeuvre on French TV (incarnating philosophy as practice), there is no doubt that by the 1970s, in response to the growing impact of the audiovisual field on the commercialization of intellectual goods, they were increasingly lured onto the small screen simply to sell books.

Historical specificity has, of course, exerted pressures on the public functions of philosophers throughout the French national past. It is now commonplace to note that in France, intellectual celebrity (as illustrated by Voltaire, Diderot, or Rousseau) can be traced to the Enlightenment, and that the French concept of the "committed" public intellectual (the *intellectuel engagé*) took its modern form during the Dreyfus Affair at the end of the nineteenth century.[38] Since at least that time, France has understood itself as "a country whose republican ideology, to a large extent, is grounded on the necessity of the secular priest as mediator and representative."[39] This vision, also articulated in Julien Benda's *La trahison des clercs* (Treason of the Intellectuals,1927), presumes that particular interests—be they politically, racially, nationally, or economically motivated—are morally incompatible with intellectual concerns. Media mastery threatened this mythic vision of intellectual objectivity. As mentioned earlier, television encroached upon the networks (first universities, then publishing houses) that traditionally legitimized French intellectual power.[40] Media personalities emerged as important cultural actors, exercising unprecedented influence over the development of the intellectual field. By the late 1970s, TV had become a formidable advertising tool. To give just one example, during the weeks following Vladimir Jankélévitch's 18 January 1980, television appearance on the book show *Apostrophes*, the seventy-six-year-old French philosopher sold thirty thousand books—more than he had over the course of his entire career. But if the medium privileged some, it ignored others. It is little wonder that television quickly became the target of opprobrium among those it dispossessed of control, authority, and prestige.[41]

For many, philosopher Bernard-Henri Lévy personifies the negative impact of television on the intellectual field. Much caricatured for his poetic good looks, shock of black hair, and unbuttoned white shirts, Lévy soared to prominence in the mid-1970s as the poster boy of the movement known as the New Philosophy. By the end of the twentieth century, despite sharp criticism of his work, he had been featured more times on television than any philosopher except Sartre. Lévy's image is invariably summoned by anyone who would reject the medium wholesale. Here, the seductive power of Lévy's charismatic performance is extended to a critique of the television image itself—read as both hypnotic and inherently deceptive. Interestingly, however, television coverage of other philosophers—notably Jankélévitch and Bachelard (men who incarnate the stereotypic ideal of the sage)—has met with uniformly positive, even adoring responses. Indeed, Bachelard's case illustrates the ways in which TV has become a valued philosophical tool in post-1945 France. The 1961 interview with the philosopher portrayed in my prologue captured an unprecedented 83% of the viewing public.[42] The clip became a television classic, so much so that by the end of the century excerpts from it had been rebroadcast more than twenty times in France.[43] The fact that in this instance the philosopher's image reinforced rather than undermined his intellectual legitimacy reminds us that the seductive power of the television image is not the problem. At issue is what is done with that power, and why?

While a plethora of factors necessarily affect the production and reception of philosophical television, as we so easily forget, it is not television per se but its commercially driven demands—for variety, spectacle, stimulation, and entertainment—that often thwart intellectual exchange. The history of philosophy on French television provides remarkable instances of the discipline in action and has produced powerful new forms of philosophical iconography. Is all that passes for philosophy on French TV good? Of course not. But can one "do" philosophy on television? This book unequivocally responds in the affirmative.

## Audience Reception: "It's for You to Ponder!"

Before I am accused of overstating the significance of philosophical programming and the highbrow tastes of French TV audiences, let me address a tenacious (and as yet unacknowledged) question: What did the post-WWII French public make of these shows? The simple answer is that we do not know because there were no carefully conducted reception studies.[44] We can, however, uncover clues. In Jacques Tati's 1958 film *Mon Oncle,* a meditation on modern consumer society, plump, well-coiffed Mme Arpel and her balding, bespectacled husband carefully set their Noguchi-style plastic and steel conical chairs on the patio of their hypermodern suburban open-floor plan home (in which, as Mme Arpel is proud of informing her guests, "everything communicates"), and, clicking a nifty remote control towards an unseen television, settle down to watch the evening broadcast. Classical music swells. A baritone voice announces: "Tonight, as every night, at the same time, we bring you the television program of Professor Platoff!" Breathless pause. "Today's subject? *'It's for you to ponder!'* [*'A vous de réfléchir!'*]." Fade to black. Tati has chosen precisely the style of programming embodied by the televising of philosophy as the target for his pithy, tongue-in-cheek assessment of the contrast between modern society and the rapidly disappearing world of dusty village squares, fruit vendors, yapping dogs, and lazy afternoons. The brief scene offers a hilarious critique of bourgeois taste, snorting at the pretentious aspirations of French public TV and hinting that, for all their self-importance, both M. and Mme Arpel and the programs they watch are more than a little absurd. In the larger scope of the story, the contrast between Mme Arpel and her bumbling, charmingly inept brother, M. Hulot (played by Tati), a man bewildered by the sterile exigencies of modern life, succinctly captures some of the cultural contradictions that persistently trouble the genre of philosophical television—and by extension, cultural programming at large. Mme Arpel's enthusiasms aside, "everything" in this speedily changing postwar world clearly did *not* communicate with everything else. Not everyone in postwar France liked philosophy on TV, and not everyone watched it.

Proponents of public programming consistently bewail the fact that throughout its history, cultural television has struggled to capture and keep its audiences. Still, while it may be true that ratings for philosophy broadcasts dropped as channels and programming options proliferated (from the high of 83% in 1961, cited above, to lows in the single digits by the 1990s), such statistics—and the industry responses they motivated—need to be interpreted with care. Percentage shares may have fallen since the sixties, but adjusting for the overall increase in television viewers, philosophy's TV audiences in the ensuing decades actually expanded appreciably. By the mid-1990s, an apparently meager 2% to 3% of the market still translated to upwards of 500,000 TV spectators per show. More interestingly still, despite low market shares, by the end of the century the number of broadcasts featuring philosophy multiplied dramatically. This push to produce more programs in a genre that was failing to capture large audiences is certainly a paradox worth examining. Lacking reception studies, I draw on survey data, ratings, published opinions, and private interviews in order to generate insight into public responses to these shows. Overall, however, my approach is unabashedly top-down. My justification is straightforward: the fact that philosophical television not only endured but actually increased over time attests to France's continuing commitment to shaping its citizenry via this genre. It is this commitment, rather than a necessarily speculative assessment of either audience reception or the capacity to capture ratings, that supports the historical focus on cultural production undertaken here.

## A Genre Transforms: Fifty Years of Philosophy on French TV

The audiences for televised philosophy have grown, and the production of philosophy broadcasts has certainly increased since their first appearance in the early 1950s. The constitution of the public and, in parallel, the content, form, and intent of the shows have also changed. Targeting both complete collections and individual programs (on Jean-Paul Sartre, Gaston Bachelard, and Michel Foucault, among others) my chapters trace these transformations. Chapters 1 and 2 examine the celebratory, abstract, and politically cautious approaches to philosophy that characterized the 1950s and '60s. Chapter 3 serves a transitional role, propelling the narrative forward via a series of educational and cultural experiments in philosophical programming across the break that was 1968 towards the market-driven, politically strident, morally charged engagement that typifies the genre from the mid-1970s through the end of the century. Chapters 4 and 5 work to historicize the period from 1974 to the present while exploring the nature of that later engagement, investigating both its commercial and ethical dimensions. The book focuses successively, in other words, on the cultural politics of early television news coverage of philosophers as playwrights and literary celebrities; the 1950s transition from text to image in the television book show (and the first discussions of philosophy as a discipline); educational programming and decolonization in the 1960s; media celebrity, economics, cold war politics, and the New Philosophers in the 1970s; and, through an analysis of philosophy programs on Heidegger and the Holocaust, the national ethical crisis epitomized by the Klaus Barbie trial in 1987, the first trial for crimes against humanity conducted in France. My conclusion examines the historical context behind the vogue for philosophy that brought eight new program collections on the discipline to the French small screen during the 1990s.

To fully appreciate what the televising of philosophy has done, and continues to do, in shaping postwar French national identity, we must resist addressing it as a purely cultural rather than historically produced phenomenon. Such a project requires that we jettison assumptions about the fundamentally anti-intellectual nature of television and encourages us to rethink philosophy itself—asserting that the content of the discipline is indivisible from the new media forms in which it has found expression. The stakes of this investigation are vast: the issues it raises strike at the heart of our understandings of the role of education in democratic societies, of the relations between high and popular culture, and of the effects of the media on the intellectual field. This study also engages critical questions about the very survival of national identities in a globalizing world. The production of philosophical television in France is a rich arena for historical research because it is the fruit of a unique relationship between a governing ideology, an administrative structure, a cherished cultural heritage, a radically transforming national public, and a blossoming technological and artistic field. Our story begins with visual documents and two very short questions: Why France? Why television?

# The Cultural Politics of Philosophical Celebrity, 1951–1968

On a wintry evening in January of 1954, almost half the inhabitants of the tiny village of Viffort (population 250) could be found gathered in a classroom at the local primary school. The building dated from the 1880s, a vestige of the Third Republic's efforts to extend free and compulsory primary education throughout the nation. In the corner, an iron stove gave off a vague aura of heat as the day's ration of firewood burned to ash. An odd assortment of chairs (brought in for the comfort of the elderly) augmented the standard-issue wooden benches. The walls were hung with children's drawings, prize-winning compositions, and multiplication tables. More men were on hand than women, and more young people than old, but all categories of age, sex, and profession—from manual laborers and farmers to local shopkeepers—were nevertheless represented. Some were regulars; others dropped in from time to time, attracted by an exceptional event. The evening's agenda had been well publicized. Fliers were posted in the local café, outside the bakery, at the greengrocer's. Teachers announced the schedule in school, and children carried the news home to their parents. Even the local policeman took part; he proclaimed the night's program through a tiny bullhorn as he made his rounds, alerting the villagers. Arriving on foot, by bicycle, or in specially organized school buses, the townspeople braved the cold night to congregate in a shabby classroom where—under the guidance of a teacher or rural organizer charged with moderating the debate that followed—they would "see television."

Viffort, located some hundred kilometers from Paris, was not unique. By 1954 almost two hundred villages had organized and equipped

Local policeman announcing
the evening *télé-club* schedule, 1954. (Photo UNESCO–
Cassirer. Reproduced by
permission of UNESCO.)

the societies for popular education that became known as *télé-clubs*.
Intended as a replacement for its financially troubled precursor the
*ciné-club,* the *télé-club* was inaugurated when Roger Louis, a former professor and acting delegate for the association Peuple et culture
(People and Culture) convinced the Philips company to loan televisions
to five communities in the department of the Aisne for a series of trials.[1] The experiments proved successful, and by the end of 1952 there
were 42 *télé-clubs* in existence. The *télé-clubs* were among those postwar movements that sought to extend throughout French society the
republican ideals of "equal access for children and adults to instruction, professional training, and culture" inscribed in the Constitution of 27 October 1946.[2] Their structure was relatively simple. Lo-
cals banded together to purchase a television set, and the minimal fees
charged for entry eventually reimbursed investors. TV sets were usually installed in classrooms in the public schools (which contributed
to their purchase and benefited from their use during school hours).
With the assistance of national associations aimed at promoting popular education, including Peuple et culture, the Ligue de l'enseignement
(Teaching League) and Travail et culture (Work and Culture), villages
located teachers to lead debates that followed the broadcasts, arranged

informational workshops for the public, and developed a network of related activities.[3] Collectively organized in 1952 as the Fédération nationale de télévision educative et culturelle, the clubs communicated with the state television administration, the Radiodiffusion-télévision française (RTF), sending programming requests, issuing a constant stream of opinions regarding content and scheduling, and ultimately proposing to produce their own shows for national broadcast. By 1955, in collaboration with UNESCO (an organization founded to promote world peace, specifically committed to advancing the study of philosophy), the initiative resulted in a series of programs and a sociological survey intended to respond to the question, "Can television constitute an effective means of popular education?"[4] The answer (a heavily qualified yes), the inquiry, and the *télé-club* project it addressed are symptomatic of a longstanding state commitment to public enlightenment that was also pivotal to the televising of philosophy.[5]

While France was not alone in developing communal viewing associations, the "formation of the television viewer by the *télé-club*" was quickly claimed as "a properly French initiative, one that is now extending to other countries, including Great Britain, Italy, and Japan".[6] If the *télé-clubs* proved a fleeting phenomenon (they disappeared by the mid-1960s, when many people had installed TV sets in their homes), such comments suggest that from its earliest incarnation French television was understood—at least among select groups—as a

*Télé-club* meeting at the village school, 1954. (Photo UNESCO–Le Fauconnier. Reproduced by permission of UNESCO.)

Guided discussion following the broadcast at a *télé-club* meeting. (Photo UNESCO–Le Fauconnier. Reproduced by permission of UNESCO.)

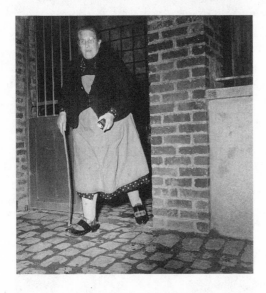

Returning home after a *télé-club* gathering, 1954. (Photo UNESCO–Le Fauconnier. Reproduced by permission of UNESCO.)

medium primed to shape French national identity. The clubs evoke a clutch of concerns about culture, education, democracy, public access, and state involvement central to the development of television in postwar France. Though not always clearly defined, these concerns were reflected in the distinctly didactic character of the state broadcasting system, contributed to the emergent interest in televising intellectuals, and laid important foundations for the televising of philosophy.[7] But if the *télé-clubs* and their educative agendas are anecdotally suggestive, it nevertheless remains difficult to understand how *philosophers* first became objects of interest on French TV. To begin to do so, we need to take into account three intricately layered stories: the development of French television, the history of philosophy in modern France, and the fraught relationship between intellectuals and the state in the aftermath of WWII.

## Specifically French: Philosophy and National Identity

Philosophers and philosophy hold extraordinarily prominent positions within French culture. France has historically been spared the anti-intellectualism evident in modern American society; Sartre and Beauvoir provide archetypal models of the virtually cult status French intellectuals often acquire. The import of philosophy within contemporary France stems from an intellectual tradition dating at least from Descartes. However, although much Western and most Continental philosophy finds its roots either in or in resolute response to Cartesian rationalism, this common reference gives rise to widely divergent national practices. Further, neither philosophers nor philosophy have acquired a similar mass appeal in North America, Britain, or elsewhere in Europe (not even—despite its rich philosophical heritage—in Germany).[8] Why—and how—has philosophy come to hold such particular significance within French culture?[9] In what ways did this status contribute to French attempts to televise the discipline?[10]

( · )

In the first decades of the twentieth century, Victor Delbos remarked that "French philosophy, taken as a whole and also in the diversity of its doctrines, seems to have a certain physiognomy proper to itself."[11] Such claims for philosophical specificity form a muted refrain that has long accompanied discussions of the discipline in France.[12] This "certain physiognomy" is discursively constructed in the processes of self-reflection (memoirs, essays, historical overviews) that document the French philosophical tradition. It is also culturally constituted though a series of salient relationships: between philosophy and French political culture, between philosophy and French education, between philosophy and French literary life, and—especially since the Dreyfus affair—between philosophy and the figure of the engaged intellectual. Indeed, whether this specificity is objectively verifiable (i.e., "Is there something 'truly French' about French philosophy?") is less important than what the very existence of the claim expresses about the cultural and social processes that imprint an emphatically national character on what has long been considered a universal subject.

The birth of French philosophy is often attributed to the moment in 1637 when René Descartes decided with his *Discourse on Method* to respond in French—rather than the Latin that was de rigueur at the time—to Montaigne's *Essays,* themselves written in French.[13] Cartesianism's stress on the primacy of the subject, on consciousness, transparency, and the mind/body problem foreshadows many of the key philosophical debates of our own era. The *Discourse* also contains the seeds of four themes that—with remarkable consistency, and despite considerable shifts in content and method—continue to be recognized as principal traits of French philosophical disquisition: a penchant for clarity (with its attendant stepchild, vulgarization); a richly diverse literary style; a proclivity towards autobiography; and a sustained interest in practical morality. Each of these attributes ultimately influenced the development of philosophical television in France.

"French philosophers," wrote Lucien Lévy-Bruhl in 1899, "as a rule are desirous of making themselves accessible to all. Descartes set the example."[14] Descartes' decision to write in the vernacular gave his work a wider audience and contributed to the cultural cachet ascribed to the language. By the end of the seventeenth century, French was not only considered the idiom of the educated; it was also, according to Diderot, "the language of truth."[15] Even after Diderot's belief in French as "the clearest, most direct, and therefore the most rational of languages" had lost ground to eighteenth-century epistemology, linguistic clarity continued to be invoked as a defining characteristic of French philosophical thought.[16] Thus, when the nineteenth-century historian Hippolyte Taine described Hegel's idea of nature as emerging "from amidst myriad hypotheses, among the impenetrable shadows of the most barbarous of styles," he was implicitly contrasting the heavy Germanic philosophical style against that of its "purer" French cousin.[17] Almost a century and a half later, the French philosopher André Comte-Sponville remarked, "Anyone among your friends can read Pascal, Montaigne, or Descartes, but Hegel's *Phenomenology of Spirit,* or Kant's *Critique of Pure Reason* are another matter entirely."[18] And the conceit persists that what Nietzsche termed "beautiful French clarity" is a characteristic attribute of philosophy in France. Its survival in the face of the charges of linguistic obscurantism often aimed at structuralism, poststructuralism, and deconstruction merely reinforces the power of this perceptual bias.

In their quest to reach popular audiences, French philosophers have frequently produced accessible versions of their scholarly works.[19] Efforts at democratizing the discipline multiplied following the rise in literacy that succeeded advances in education during the nineteenth century.[20] Accordingly, Auguste Comte's *Introduction to Positive Philosophy* offers a simplified variant of his six-volume *Cours de philosophie positive* (1830–1846). Henri Bergson gave substance to his claim that "there is no philosophical idea so profound or subtle that it cannot or should not be expressed in language accessible to all" by publishing a rudimentary synthesis of *Matter and Memory* in his more straightforward *Mind-Energy*.[21] Sartre's essay "Existentialism and Humanism" popularized many of the central ideas expressed in his dense tome *Being and Nothingness*. More recently, Jean-François Lyotard's *The Postmodern Explained*, and even André Comte-Sponville and Luc Ferry's *La sagesse des Modernes*, provide epistolary encapsulations of their more erudite oeuvre. Interestingly, one of the common critiques against the televising of philosophy is that it vulgarizes an inherently complex form of thought. Yet, the historical record demonstrates that vulgarization has been an integral part of the French tradition, the fruit of a sustained interest in popularizing philosophy. Advocates of cultural television merely built on this custom. The French bent for clarity and readability further facilitated their work. This is not to say that vulgarization has been without critics. Debates continue over whether even "accessible" philosophy can be popularized (particularly on TV) without doing violence to the thought it represents.[22] Nevertheless, the practice of vulgarization has become increasingly central to the French philosophical field. The televising of philosophy was a crucial part of this process.

French philosophers are known for the unusually broad range of genres—stretching well beyond the standard philosophic treatise—in which they've expressed their ideas. Flexibility in French philosophical forms is evident in everything from essays (a form perfected in the work of Montaigne and Pascal and taken up in the twentieth century by Alain), to fiction, theater, and journalism (Voltaire's *Candide*, Camus's *Caligula*, Mounier's *Esprit*). Autobiography, from Rousseau's *Confessions* to Sartre's *The Words*, holds a special place in this pantheon of genres. French philosophy frequently places the authorial subject at the center of its theoretical reflections. This tendency towards self-scrutiny both heightens public fascination with the individuals who are its object and creates moral imperatives of its own. Comte-Sponville remarks, "In opposition to the German tradition, which is more speculative and systematic, the autobiographical dimension is an integral part of [French] philosophical reflection. You know, Hegel said somewhere, 'that in my system which resembles me is false.' "[23] In contrast, in the seventeenth century, Descartes proposed the *Discourse* as "an autobiography," and it was his individual particularity that was used to establish the universal validity of his observations and experience.[24] This French tendency to link philosophy and philosopher sometimes erupts in controversy, as visible in the debates over Heidegger's politics that split the French intellectual field in the 1980s.[25]

French philosophy's autobiographical tradition lent itself easily to fresh incarnations (documentary biographies, interviews, and publicity appearances) compatible with the virgin technology of television, whose focus on personality was critical to its appeal. And yet, Régis Debray overstates the case when he claims that the celebrity-philosopher is a post-1968 creation attributable to the rise of television and the demise of the university, publishing, and journalism.[26] Long before the appearance of electronic media, philosophers—from Rousseau, Voltaire, and Diderot to Comte, Cousin, Bergson, and Alain—were objects of popular acclaim whose celebrity was often generated as much by individual personality as by scholarly production. Rousseau was recognized in the streets. Indeed, his reputation was so extensive that he was subsequently dubbed *un philosophe médiatique* (a mass media philosopher).[27] That said, during the twentieth century, by reproducing the classical opposition between the *intellectuel mondain* (worldly intellectual), characterized by Brunetière, Barthes, or Bernard Henri Lévy, and the *intellectuel savant* (learned intellectual), incarnated by Durkheim, Bourdieu, and even Debray after '68, television exacerbated longstanding debates about the proper purview of the French philosophical field.

A final trait evident in discussions of the discipline has been French philosophy's enduring concern with practical morality. Under the influence of Renaissance humanism, moral authority gradually shifted from the religious to secular domains. And moral competence carried political weight.[28] Philosophers, who used reason as an access to truth, assumed new power. By the eighteenth century, the *philosophes* were defined through their moral capacities. The entry for *philosophe* in Diderot and d'Alembert's *Encyclopédie* (1752–82) declares, "Other men are carried by their passions, without their actions being preceded by reflection. These are the men who walk in the shadows; whereas the *philosophe* even in his passions acts only after reflection; he walks at night, but he is preceded by a flame."[29] It is worth clarifying that this emphasis on ethical reflection does not necessarily translate into the production of moral philosophy, strictly defined.[30] For if we disregard studies in the sociology of morals, or in pedagogical, religious, scientific, economic, literary, political, or medical domains, barring a few key exceptions (Bergsonism, Sartrean existentialism, or, more recently, the work of Vladimir Jankélévitch, Paul Ricoeur, or Emmanuel Levinas), French philosophers have not been widely known for their work in this area.[31] The writings of the eighteenth-century French *moralistes* and their modern-day equivalents usually pertain to topics that fall under the category of popular philosophy, that is, practical wisdom for living (*Lebensweisheit*) or general guidance about the conduct of life.[32] Not inconsequentially, these concerns continue to be particularly suited to the interests of television audiences. Indeed, it was in part philosophical television's fascination with basic ethical questions in the 1980s and early '90s that contributed to the revival of interest in Levinas's thought at the end of the century.[33]

When the Enlightenment fostered the exercise of private reason in the public sphere, it furnished a meaningful link between the French philosophical tradition and French political culture. The idea that reason unhindered is within the lawful purview of the public sphere is central to all democratic notions of freedom—including the freedom of the individual, of the press, and of the audiovisual media.[34] Of course, the eighteenth-century public sphere was profoundly elitist: "public opinion" was the product of the literate and the propertied. The contradiction between a growing belief that the exercise of reason in the public sphere was both a fundamental human capacity and a natural right, and the actuality of an authoritarian social and political structure inhibiting the exercise of these rights and capacities, sought resolution in revolution.[35]

The French Revolution provided the framework for the public use of reason within a republican nation by bonding two competing eighteenth-century models of citizenship: a generalized model understood abstractly as civil equality before the law (defined through common rights and obligations), and a limited active model produced by the possession and exercise of political rights and participation in governance.[36] The salient dimension of this merger of civil and political models of citizenship for the development of the cultural role of French philosophy is that in establishing general political rights legislating the public use of reason, education became a national imperative. As the

Swiss pop-philosopher Alain de Botton observes, merely increasing the number of voters will not increase the wisdom of their choices: "What you really have to do is increase the wisdom of every person who is voting." [37] Education would enable the newly enfranchised citizenry to employ their reason in making informed, free, and responsible political decisions. Philosophy was the discipline that would guide them in this task. And in the return to order that followed the upheaval of the French Revolution, the French state founded the École normale supérieure (ENS), an institution that would guide the educations of the majority of France's philosophers well into the twentieth century. [38] A decade and a half later, Napoleon decreed (in a ruling dated 19 September 1809), that in all French lycées "there shall be a year of philosophy." During this year, for eight hours a week, "the students shall be instructed, either in Latin, or in French, in the principles of logic, of metaphysics, of morals, and on the history of the opinions of the philosophers." [39] With this edict the infrastructure was established that created, over the course of the next two centuries and after much reform and modification, the academic foundation for a general television audience educated in the fundamentals of philosophy.

Recent scholarship has done much to challenge interpretations that read the Enlightenment unambiguously out of the "high literature" of the *philosophes* and the French Revolution just as unambiguously out of the Enlightenment. [40] But it is not overly audacious to plead for a relationship between the classic Enlightenment call for the emancipation of reason implored in Kant's *Sapere aude,* "Dare to know!" the formulation of the *Declaration of the Rights of Man and Citizen,* and the emergence of a tradition of televising philosophy in France. Justification lies not in the argument that the works of the *philosophes* single-handedly instigated revolution or dominated social change, but rather in the ways these works contributed to more subtle transformations in the growth, constitution, and education of a newly politicized, literate public.

Twentieth-century French philosophy would not be what it is if not for the influence of the "three H's"—Hegel, Husserl, and Heidegger— and the "three masters of suspicion"—Marx, Nietzsche, and Freud. [41] Still, there are several factors that, taken as a whole, are particular to the French tradition. From its diversity of literary styles and special emphasis on subjectivity and autobiography, to its custom of vulgarization and popularization, to its predilection for clarity and interest in practical wisdom for living, French philosophy exhibits a series of traits that render it uniquely suited to the parameters of the television medium. By incorporating philosophical instruction into secondary education, the French state ensures a widespread, if basic, familiarity with the discipline among its public. French political culture, by anchoring philosophical education into its conception of citizenship, contributes to this disposition. As "engaged intellectuals" expected to speak out on issues of public concern, philosophers have long maintained a strong presence in the French media. Yet despite the presence of social imperatives demanding their participation, as well as national predispositions favorable towards both philosophy and cultural television, it took time for the subject and its practitioners to develop a presence on the small screen. Indeed, given the complicated politics controlling the growth of French television, it is perhaps unsurprising that the earliest coverage of philosophers eschews the controversial domain of ideas, capitalizing instead—as my analysis of broadcasts on Sartre and Camus shall shortly illustrate—on their celebrity status in the worlds of literature and theater. To better comprehend this development as well as the constraints placed upon it, we need to turn to the troubled relationship between intellectuals and the state following the Second World War.

## French Intellectuals and Postwar Politics

When the Allied forces liberated Paris from four years of German occupation in August 1944, the fractured nation embarked on a frenzied path of self-renewal. Between the end of the war and the early 1950s, 7037 accused collaborators were sentenced to death for treasonous activities, 4397 in absentia.[42] Over 50,000 individuals, mostly Vichy government employees, were officially investigated. Numerous others were subjected to less formal acts of retribution. Although all sectors of French society were exposed to charges of collaboration, the purging of the intellectuals was particularly harsh.[43] The anti-Semitic writer Robert Brasillach was included amongst the 791 accused collaborators who were eventually executed.[44] Brasillach's offense was distinctly textual: his published ideas, opinions, and assertions were deemed criminally influential. "There are words," wrote Simone de Beauvoir, "as murderous as gas chambers."[45] Not since the Dreyfus affair had the public responsibility of intellectuals been subject to such zealous attention. For Brasillach and his contemporaries, the powerful relationship between word and action was asserted with a sudden, stunning force.

The most contentious aspect of the postwar purge of the intellectuals lays in the fact that intellectuals undertook it themselves. In so doing they underscored the political power of language, simultaneously reaffirming their own importance and extending their range of influence throughout postwar society. Intellectual purges, both legal and covert—as in the blacklisting of pro-Vichy writers undertaken by the Comité national des écrivains (National Writers' Committee, CNE)— also effectively redefined the cultural and political landscape.[46] The intellectual Right was reduced to veritable silence for almost a decade. When it reemerged during the cold war, it was no longer dominant but gradually found new strength within the growing Gaullist movement that periodically lashed out against Fourth Republic politics. By the 1950s, the political terrain split roughly three ways. Expelled from the postwar tripartite coalition government in 1947, the Parti communiste français (French Communist Party, PCF) staked out the far left. The Section française de l'Internationale ouvrière (French Section of the Workers' International, SFIO), the primarily Christian democratic Mouvement républicain populaire (Popular Republican Movement, MRP), and other advocates of a neutral European "third way" (including Sartre and Emmanuel Mounier, with their journals *Les temps modernes* and *Esprit*) were just left of center.[47] The Gaullists, particularly the short-lived Rassemblement du peuple français (Assembly of the French People, RPF), and after 1955 the followers of Pierre Poujade, along with the radicals and the old right-wing Independents, were slowly expanding their hold on the center and the right. These competing tendencies were enmeshed in the struggle for political supremacy. Throughout the 1950s, debates over decolonization further polarized an already contested political turf. The intellectual imperative towards political commitment was powerfully reaffirmed, but the focus was no longer on the humanist vision of abstract reason and principled morality described by Julien Benda in his 1927 *Treason of the Intellectuals*.[48] Now it was the refusal to enter social debate, not the intellectual's acceptance of political partisanship, that constituted the treasonous act.

France emerged from World War II in shambles. Economically devastated and politically fragmented, the country turned to culture to resurrect national pride. Writers were recognized as an increasingly valuable form of cultural capital. "Now a second-class power," writes Beauvoir, "France exalt[ed] her most characteristic national products with an eye on the export market: *haute couture* and literature."[49]

In the midst of this postwar cultural ascension new hierarchies were established. Philosophy soon dethroned literature as the discipline of choice. The literary and theatrical works that survived this reversal were often impregnated by philosophical visions. (The philosophical subtext in the novels and plays of Camus and Sartre as well as that visible in the works of Eugène Ionesco, Samuel Beckett, and Jean Genet comes to mind.) Existentialism became an intellectual and cultural sensation. Jean d'Ormesson expressed the climate of the times well:

> Immediately after the war and for several years thereafter, philosophy carried incomparable prestige. I don't know if I can describe now, at this distance, what it represented for us. The nineteenth century was, perhaps, the century of history; the mid-twentieth century seemed dedicated to philosophy, [. . .] literature, painting, historical studies, politics, theater, and film were all in philosophy's hands.[50]

The sense that philosophy's star was rising was further reflected in the realm of journalism. From their posts at the reigning review *Les temps modernes* (whose original editorial committee included Sartre, Beauvoir, Maurice Merleau-Ponty, Raymond Aron, Michel Leiris, Jean Paulhan, and Albert Ollivier—later director of television programming from 1959 to 1964), at the Catholically inclined *Esprit* (under the direction of Mounier), and at the daily paper *Combat* (edited by Camus), philosophers dominated the postwar press.[51] Meditating— much like d'Ormesson—on this transformation of the cultural field, Mounier comments:

> A whole era was coming to an end, the dazzling era of post–World War I literary flowering; Gide, Montherlant, Proust, Cocteau, Surrealism—this display of fireworks was falling back silent on its own ashes. It had sprung forth as a marvelous expression of its times. It had not brought mankind the torch of a new destiny. [. . .] Literature at its most gratuitous had dominated the preceding generation. The one that followed was to commit itself more intimately to spiritual, philosophical and political quests.[52]

Radio and television provided new possibilities for the expansion of intellectual authority. Sartre's written apologia for the literary professions (published as "What is Literature?" in the spring of 1947 in *Les temps modernes*) validates the public role of the writer and emphasizes the importance of intellectual engagement with the emergent audiovisual media. Here Sartre insists that the critical task of "conquering the virtual public" requires writers to "learn to speak in images."[53] His own interaction with the new technologies began towards the end of the war. In 1944, Sartre read his text "La république du silence" ("The Republic of Silence") on the radio.[54] Two years later, he could be heard on the air discussing "the liberty and responsibility of the writer."[55] However, Sartre's nascent commitment to new media was not widely shared.[56] During the 1940s and '50s, most philosophers (comfortably established within the press, publishing, and the universities) were either indifferent towards or dubious about television. The concept of TV as a cultural emancipator did not yet concern them, and when they did consider it, they saw the medium as a creeping symptom of a mass modernity that had yet to arrive. In their view, culture resided in the book, the theater, the concert-hall, the museum, or even the cinema, but not on the small screen. Many philosophers were heavily involved in politics, yet radio and, especially, television—notwithstanding a few exceptional broadcasts—generally appeared politically quiescent, a fact supporting suspicions that these media were not (or not yet) technologies requiring serious intellectual consideration.

In the 1950s, French television was in the midst of tremendous experimentation. Two communities of interest shaped most broadcast coverage: (1) television professionals (i.e. those involved in production, development, and diffusion), the majority of whom tended to enthusiastically embrace the view supported by proponents of the *télé-clubs,* in which the technology was understood as an unparalleled instrument for social enlightenment; and (2) the state politicians charged with administering the broadcasting system, most of whom made little use of television in the early 1950s and, when they did, viewed it with mild suspicion, as a more or less benign presence whose potential powers were to be observed but not yet entirely controlled—although this attitude changed rapidly once de Gaulle returned to power in 1958.[57] When it came to televising philosophers, these two communities had contradictory effects. Television professionals, eager to exploit philosophers' status as cultural celebrities, often sought their participation. But government reticence in the face of political opponents meant that the state broadcaster was cautious in its coverage.[58] Consequently, early French TV largely avoided featuring philosophers as political actors, skirting both their intellectual engagements and their strictly philosophical work and focusing instead on their production within the (seemingly) less divisive realms of theater and literature. Thus, the early years of the televising of philosophy were shaped by paradox. In one sense, the climate was restrictive; analysis reveals a steady increase in political control and raises important questions about media access.[59] In another, these years were driven by impulse and inclination—improvisation, ingenuity, and invention were the order of the day.

### "Inform, Educate, Entertain": The Early History of French TV

The first experiments in television broadcasting began in France in the 1930s, but the French were slow to employ the new technology. There were several reasons for this hesitancy.[60] Radio absorbed the majority of state resources, and the French government was reluctant to shoulder the financial burden of developing national networks for television broadcasting. Television programming costs were prohibitive, and program output correspondingly low. Poor distribution combined with minimal offerings provided little incentive to purchase the new product. Further, television sets were priced beyond the means of a general public whose modest living standards, especially in the 1930s and 1940s, conspired against the acquisition of luxury goods. Ideological influences also factored in; elites in particular were skeptical of television, perceiving it as a harbinger of mass culture and Americanization.[61]

With the outbreak of war in Europe in 1939, French television ceased transmission. During the German Occupation of France, television broadcasts were reintroduced under German direction with operations functioning from the tiny studios of Paris PTT Vision. Expanded in 1942 (by order of General Thiele, commander-in-chief of the Wehrmacht in Berlin) and officially launched in November of 1943, Fernsehsender Paris—the only station in Europe to broadcast during the war—was a collaborative affair. The Germans financed productions, the French enlarged the studios at rue Cognac-Jay (incorporating the site of the old Magic-City music-hall), and Kurt Hinzmann, an enterprising (and secretly Francophile) former assistant director of German programming, oversaw the enterprise.[62] Wartime broadcasts avoided controversial political topics (a propensity that outlasted the war). Under Hinzmann's guidance, Fernsehsender Paris produced a cultural carnival of programs: cabaret, music-hall song and dance numbers, ballet, marionettes, acrobats, clowns, and art expositions

Early RTF *mire* (test screen), 1953. (Reproduced by permission of the Institut national de l'audiovisuel.)

filled the small screen. Designed to raise military morale, the shows were also broadcast to over one hundred sets specially installed in Parisian hospitals where wounded German soldiers were receiving treatment. Hinzmann's efforts were not intended to survive the German withdrawal. On 17 August 1944, Hinzmann received orders to destroy the production studios and dynamite the Eiffel Tower (the location of the principal television transmitter). He balked. Two days later he fled Paris in a truck obtained through clandestine contacts with the French Resistance and went into hiding. Although pursued by the Gestapo, Hinzmann managed to avoid capture. He returned to Paris on 15 December 1946 and participated in the postwar development of French television until 1950. Thanks to his obstinate refusal to demolish the fruits of so much labor, the infrastructure of French television remained intact.[63] The studios at Cognac-Jay survived the war and (in concert with studios constructed later at Les Buttes-Chaumont) became the home of French television after the Liberation.[64]

French broadcasts resumed—airing on only one channel (Channel 1)—on 1 October 1945. The provisional government established an absolute monopoly over the newly reconstituted Radiodiffusion française (RDF). This was not just public, but culturally ambitious, politically controlled state TV, a fact that differentiated the French model sharply from Great Britain's more professionally and politically autonomous British Broadcasting System (BBC) as well as from the privatized commercial system emerging in the United States. The establishment of the state monopoly over the audiovisual sector was also conceived as a direct rebuke of private print journalism, whose corrupt past was linked to a collaborationist press and the recently discredited Vichy regime.[65] The ties forged between government and television in the immediate postwar period had a powerful influence on the subsequent development of the medium. Their short-term impact was less obvious. Despite the sale of some one thousand TV sets in Paris, in 1947 Channel 1 still aired a mere twelve programming hours a week. (By way of comparison, in 1939 BBC television was already broadcasting for twice as long.)[66] French interest in the nascent technology was confined primarily to a discrete circle of engineers within the electronics industry.

In 1949 the RDF was transformed into the RTF, or Radiodiffusion-télévision française, and the overbearing bureaucratic structure that would later weigh so heavily on the state broadcaster began to take shape.[67] While the centralized administrative model put in place in 1949 underwent successive modifications—notably conversion in 1964 into the Office de radiodiffusion et télévision française—its basic configuration continued as a fixture of successive governments until the ORTF's ultimate dissolution in 1974. The year 1949 also witnessed the adoption of a new broadcast definition standard of 819 lines—a choice that complicated program exchange with the rest of Europe and one that was later adjusted to the 625 lines in use today.[68] Educational programming was authorized by government decree in 1951 and developed separately—as will be discussed in chapter 3—under the aegis of the Institut pédagogique national (National Pedagogical Institute, IPN). Much early TV aired live (35% in 1948), which both distinguished it from cinema and added to the sense of wonder it evoked among audiences.[69] TV host and reporter Pierre Tchernia recalls, "In the years between 1949 and 1952, children actually approached me in the street and asked, 'Do you recognize me?' because they thought that I could see them!"[70] Understood as a transparent access to truth, television inspired awe in television professionals as well. "Television enlarges our field of vision to the limits of the human universe," gushed producer and TV host Étienne Lalou in his 1957 book, *Regards neufs sur la télévision* (A Fresh Look at Television). He continued, "It abolishes all frontiers, those of ignorance, of fear, of superstition, and of suspicion, as well as of language, history, and geography. It is par excellence an instrument of rapprochement, in all senses of the word!"[71] Lalou's bright-eyed enthusiasm (which calls to mind contemporary descriptions of the internet) was reflected in the RTF's triple objective, clearly articulated by Jean d'Arcy, director of television programming from 1952 to 1959. "Our goals," d'Arcy proclaimed, "and you know them well, are *to entertain, to inform, to educate.*"[72]

During the 1950s French audience demand slowly grew as televisions installed in cafés and *télé-clubs* introduced the medium to a wider viewing public. Live coverage of the Tour de France in 1948 and the highly publicized 2 June 1953 coronation of Elizabeth II direct from England did much towards raising awareness and awakening curiosity about the new technology among potential audiences throughout France. However, the public presence of television was still minimal in the late 1940s and early 1950s, so that significant influence on French society during this period is doubtful. Indeed, in 1958 fewer than 10% of French households could boast a TV set of their own.[73] Nonetheless, within the industry this was a time of euphoric discovery; the men and women responsible for creating television broadcasts rapidly defined new styles, genres, and prototypes that sought to master the medium's unexplored potential. Journalists like the "four Pierres" (Dumayet, Desgraupes, Tchernia, and Sabbagh) and directors like Claude Barma, Marcel Bluwal, and Jean Prat—all destined for major TV careers—cut their teeth on the sound stages of Cognac-Jay and Les Buttes-Chaumont.[74] This epoch gave birth to the award-winning book program *Lectures pour tous* (Reading for All, 1953), which proved instrumental in promoting philosophers on TV; to the variety show *36 Chandelles* (36 Candles, 1952); to Igor Barrière and Étienne Lalou's groundbreaking medical series *Médicales* (Medical Check-Up, 1954); to the history drama *La caméra explore le temps* (The Camera Explores the Past, 1956); and the newsmagazine *Cinq colonnes à la une* (Banner Headlines, 1959). Under the influence of television news— itself an important new genre—the first political shows (such as *Face à l'opinion* [Confronting Public Opinion], 1954 and *Faisons le point* (Taking Stock, 1955) were also developed in the mid-1950s.

Television news made its official debut in France on 2 October 1949.[75] At first, it failed to attract much attention. To most people it seemed inconceivable that the medium, limited as it was to a restricted network of viewers, could ever rival radio—let alone the printed press. In fact, when television professionals Pierre Sabbagh, Wladimir Porché, Jean Luc, and Jean d'Arcy submitted a request for permission to develop a news program to the minister of information in 1948, the document was returned with an indulgent marginal note: "Let the kids play in the courtyard so they'll leave us in peace!"[76] The first broadcasts were filmed either in 16mm by the news team or in 35mm by France-Vidéo—the image archive created by La presse filmée française (the French Cinematic Press).[77] Because synched sound was not yet possible (the first sound cameras were not developed until 1953–54), the silent image of the film was televised to the accompaniment of voiceover (voix off or V.O.) delivered live by an unseen journalist. By the mid-1950s, images from the newsroom itself, peopled first by a series of journalists (among them Pierre Dumayet, later a producer and host of Lectures pour tous) and then by an anchor, became an increasingly important component of the show. From this time forward the journalist, anchor, host, or speakerine (a program presenter, usually female, like the charming and popular Jacqueline Joubert) was poised to challenge the intellectual as the public voice of knowledge and power.

If a program was neither filmed as it aired nor recorded on the kinescope (a precursor to contemporary video, which involved filming a television screen during the live broadcast), then the conducteur (technically referred to in English as the "rundown," meaning program summary or outline) remained the sole archival record of the show.[78] Newscasts aired from the small studio at Cognac-Jay. Technical conditions were rudimentary: one studio, several armchairs, two fixed cameras, and a small central control room. Until June of 1953, all news programming was interrupted over the summer months, usually resuming in mid-September. In the early years either foreign news clips or excerpts from the Cinematic Press regularly augmented French television news. Thanks to the development of lighter, portable equipment, better recording and transmission devices, and the use of helicopters, broadcasting from remote places became a viable option and quickly improved coverage. Field pieces were shot with three amateur cameras and two vehicles—one being a jeep recuperated from army surplus by the head of news programming, Pierre Sabbagh, following his return from the French colonial conflict in Indochina.[79]

Owing largely to its regular live broadcasts, by 1953 television was acknowledged as surpassing cinema newsreels as an audiovisual news source.[80] That same year, public reactions to the televising of Parliament's deliberations during the presidential elections that brought René

Coty to power, piqued government interest in the medium.[81] Although responses to the broadcasts were mixed, politicians were awakening to television's political potential.[82] In grudging acknowledgment of TV's growing influence, Parliament decreed in December of that year that television should become a major public service and voted to finance the enlargement of the facilities at Cognac-Jay and the building of new installations at Buttes-Chaumont. However, as the medium's ideological impact became apparent, the drive to control content increased. When news was removed from the auspices of TV programmers to the authority of a state-appointed director of information in 1954, it was clear that surveillance of television broadcasts had tightened. Operating in a notoriously unstable political context (the Fourth Republic averaged one government each six months over the span of fourteen years), RTF directors Wladimir Porché and Jean d'Arcy carefully avoided possible political entanglements by concentrating their energies on culture and education; television news itself focused on these areas. Particularly during the early years, "hard" topics were eluded, and ludic subjects—mostly social happenings and artistic, literary and cultural events, with the occasional nod to foreign affairs—dominated news lineups.[83] And it was on these broadcasts that television first began its romance with the discipline of philosophy.

### Entertainment Tonight? The Philosopher as Cultural Celebrity

Television craved celebrity; philosophers, in their roles as literary stars, playwrights, cultural icons, and even as the subjects of eulogistic obituaries (a genre examined in chapter 2), fit the bill. Literary prizes and other honors consistently brought philosophers to the attention of television news audiences.[84] When Bachelard was awarded an honorary doctorate in the presence of Queen Elizabeth in 1956, the evening news ran the United Press footage relayed from London.[85] Bachelard was televised again in February 1960 when he was presented with the Prix Paul Pelliot.[86] And when Laureate Raymond Aron, winner of the Prix des ambassadeurs for his sociological study *Paix et guerre entre les nations* (1962) was fêted in October of 1962, the evening news took note.[87] TV also covered authors whose prize-winning works took philosophers as their subjects. Thus, Paulette French received the Prix Hachette et Larousse for her study of Camus, and television news deigned it deserving of airtime.[88] High cultural honors such as the

Nobel Prize were clearly newsworthy. *Les actualités françaises* proudly presented Camus's acceptance of the award in Sweden in 1957.[89] Back in Paris, when journalists spied Camus in the stands at a soccer match at the Parc des Princes, cameras immediately turned his way. The Nobel laureate was declared "the pride of France" and was asked to offer his opinion on the game; somewhat bemused, Camus pronounced the Swedish soccer commission better equipped than he to speak to the issue, and declined to answer.[90] Sartre's 1964 repudiation of the prestigious award—on the grounds that commitment can be undermined by accolades—constituted a veritable media event. The first television broadcast announced him as winner.[91] The second two reports covered the scandal of his refusal.[92] Sartre speaks to journalist Thierry de Scitivaux in defense of his choice in the latter clip. The images of Sartre and Beauvoir exiting a car surrounded by photographers, of Sartre lighting a cigarette, and of Sartre and Scitivaux conversing as they cross a street filled with cars became staple footage of the famous philosopher. Nobel laureates possessed so much cultural capital that anniversaries of their achievements also attracted regular notice. For example, in 1963—six years after he had received the prize—TV news paid tribute to Camus's former triumph.[93] Two years later, several retrospectives again featured the original coverage of Camus receiving the award.[94] And a full decade after his win, the news ran yet another commemorative story: "Ce jour-là: Camus Prix Nobel" ("On that Day: Camus Nobel Prize").[95]

Responses to this neophyte form of intellectual publicity varied. Bachelard's reaction to media attention was purely pragmatic: the problem was that it interrupted one's work. Within hours of the announcement that he had been awarded the prestigious Prix national des lettres in November of 1961, the philosopher was inundated by attention from the press and broadcast media. The normally solitary Bachelard found the barrage of reporters overwhelming. "For the last fifteen days," he wrote, "I've been living an impossible life. [. . .] The journalists come to interview me. [Yesterday] it lasted from nine-thirty in the morning until half past noon, and then again from 2:30 to 5:00 p.m. There were seven people in my little room—youths—very nice young people. But they smoked so much, and this morning I'm still feeling poisoned by it. And my correspondence is so behind. [. . .] I don't know where to turn!"[96]

Others responded more acerbically. In December 1954, when Beauvoir received the Prix Goncourt for her novel *The Mandarins*, the

Camus receives the Nobel Prize. From "Interview de M. Albert Camus, Prix Nobel, 1957," 23 October 1957.

The Nobel Prize. From "Interview de M. Albert Camus, Prix Nobel 1957," 23 October 1957.

Sartre refuses the Nobel Prize. From "Le refus de Sartre," 23 October 1964.

television news announced the tidings.[97] Beauvoir offered insight into her feelings about the broadcast in her memoir *Force of Circumstance*. Although she admitted to accepting the prize to boost book sales, she expressed disdain towards the media's penchant for publicity. "I fail to see in what respect the decision of the Goncourt jury can be said to have created an obligation on my part towards the television, the radio and the press," she wrote. "Furthermore," she continued, "with the best will in the world, or the worst, publicity disfigures those who fall into its hands. In my view, the relations a writer entertains with the truth make it impossible for him to acquiesce to such treatment; it is quite enough that it should be inflicted on him by force."[98]

French television became a crucial instrument in the politically selective promotion of philosophers as media celebrities, cultural icons, and especially—as I discuss below—playwrights, in the decades following the war. Television's visual dimension was critical; most early coverage avoided the contentious terrain of ideas and was exclusively iconographic, rendering philosophers into symbolic forms of French cultural capital. By marking certain intellectual achievements (like the Nobel Prize), postwar TV reflected the state's desire to reinstate French cultural superiority. By avoiding others (existentialism—for reasons discussed in the next chapter—was noticeably absent), the state television administration asserted its control over the shapes these visions took.

## The *Dramatique en direct:* Television as Tradition

Early television regularly drew on the French classical heritage in order to anchor technological innovation in historically respected traditions. The television book show—which soon became a major platform for the televising of philosophy—became one of the enduring examples of this practice. The creation of programs dedicated to philosophy during the 1960s was another. However, the development that best characterized the decade of the 1950s was the live theater broadcast, the so-called *dramatique en direct*.[99] Airing on Tuesday nights when the national theaters were dark, these programs brought the classical repertoire—from Molière and Racine to Shakespeare—to the French small screen. Sometimes faulted on aesthetic grounds, the shows were nevertheless popular with a surprising range of viewers. (According to a 1955 UNESCO *télé-club* study, more than sixty percent of rural viewers reported appreciating filmed theater.)[100] Director of programming Albert Ollivier's decision to broadcast Aeschylus' *The Persians*—complete with music by Prodomidès and a full chorus—in 1962 (a project about which he was so excited that he personally appeared on the air twice to promote the show in the week preceding its broadcast) epitomized the pedagogical ambitions of the times. Director Claude Santelli mused, "Whether it was seen in private homes or in bistros, there was no doubt; the next day almost everyone in France was talking about *The Persians*." Of course, "There was only one channel," as producer and host Pierre Tchernia wryly notes, "Either you watched *The Persians,* or you didn't watch anything."[101]

The success of the *dramatique en direct* confirmed the interest of French audiences in televised theater. In addition to broadcasting its own versions of the classical repertoire, French televsision also reviewed and publicized standard theatrical productions. When television newscasts were deemed insufficient to handle the growing volume of theatrical and cinematic tidings, new television collections with names like *Page Théâtre* (Theater Page), *Les Trois Coups* (Three Hits), *Les Spectacles de la semaine* (This Week's Shows), and *Gros plan* (Close-Up) offered novel venues for those working in the theatrical vein. Since Sartre and Camus were both prodigiously active in writing, adapting, and producing works for the theater in the decades following the war, it was just a matter of time before television turned its cameras their way.[102]

## From Stage to (Small) Screen:
## Jean-Paul Sartre and Albert Camus

The very first mention of a philosopher on French television was made in a 1951 news broadcast covering the soirée held to honor the hundredth performance of Sartre's *The Devil and the Good Lord* at the Théâtre Antoine.[103] The play, which was set at the time of the Peasant's Revolt in Germany during the Reformation, revolves around Goetz, a nobleman's bastard, professional soldier, and remorseless killer who engages in evil for evil's sake. Disgusted that his actions go unnoticed in a world where evil abounds, Goetz reverses his stance, not out of reverence for a just God, but in anger at God's absence and dedicates himself to a life of peace, love, and community. Perversely, his efforts bring more evil than good to the peasants he tries to aid. The play illustrates the moral message crucial to Sartre's philosophy: that good and evil are inseparable. Sartre asserts that in the absence of God man must confront his responsibility for his freedom and acknowledge that—even in a nihilistic and amoral universe—his choices have ethical consequences. Written the year before Sartre began a brief flirtation with Stalinist communism, *The Devil and the Good Lord* also functions on a political level: it represents Sartre's rejection of a vision of a neutral Europe equally independent of the United States and the Soviet Union.[104]

Running without interruption from June 1951 until March 1952, *The Devil and the Good Lord* was the major success of the theater season. Television celebrated the event. The program rundown reveals that the news clip opened with a shot of Pierre Brasseur (who played the lead), in his dressing room. He wiped the sweat from his brow, drank a glass of water, and loosened his collar. The camera cut to a long shot of Brasseur leaving his loge in evening dress. Beyond him an image of Camus's lover, the actress Maria Casarès who co-starred, could be glimpsed on the poster mounted in the lobby. A jump cut to an elegant dinner given in honor of the occasion at the Hôtel Claridge

offered an opportunity to display the Parisian "in-crowd." Michel
Etcheverry and Henri Nassiet approached via the artist's entrance. In
the grand ballroom Juliette Gréco, Arletty, Jean Marais, and Philippe
de Rothschild mingled to the strains of a Moroccan orchestra. Waiters
filed in and the camera made a panoramic sweep of the packed room.
The entire effect was undoubtedly sparkling and glamorous, intimat-
ing elegance, style, and affluence. But the philosopher was noticeably
absent from the footage.

Sartre produced a wealth of theatrical works throughout the
1950s. *Kean* premiered in 1953, and *Nekrassov* in 1955—the same
year *No Exit* opened in revival; 1957 saw the Polish production of *The
Flies,* and 1959 the Paris debut of *The Condemned of Altona.* Yet,
despite television's apparent predilection for the stage (as discussed below, Camus's plays drew consistent interest), following the coverage
of *The Devil and the Good Lord,* the medium mostly steered clear
of Sartre until the early 1960s.[105] And save one incidental reference
(in an interview with the actor Serge Reggiani in 1959), television ne-
glected to review Sartre's theatrical efforts again until 1963.[106] Given
his formidable reputation and public presence, only the complex dialogue between Sartre's politics and those of the governments controlling broadcasting can explain his extended absence from the small
screen at this time.

( · )

French television largely ignored politics, both national and international, in favor of less weighty topics throughout the 1950s.[107] The
cautious political practices of TV administrators during the Fourth
Republic intensified under Gaullist rule. De Gaulle's ascension to
power (under contested circumstances spurred by the crisis in Algeria,
where the indigenous population was rebelling against French colonial domination) brought the 1959 ruling that transformed the RTF
into a public institution of an industrial, commercial character under
the authority of the minister of information. In theory a public service monopoly, the RTF and later the ORTF—until its 1974 demise—
increasingly functioned in practice as a direct extension of the French
government. Personnel were regularly appointed by the Gaullist regime
and removed or replaced with startling regularity if they failed to tow
the party line.[108] Suspicious of opponents, de Gaulle quickly cultivated a tighter relationship with the state broadcaster, purportedly to

combat what he saw as a press dominated by the intellectual left in the wake of post-Vichy purges.[109] An avid viewer, de Gaulle carefully mastered the performative demands of the medium (often to brilliant effect) and was renowned for his charismatic screen presence. Fears about the unstable political climate triggered by the stresses of the Algerian war magnified concerns over program content, especially in television news.[110] Growing governmental vigilance reflected mounting tensions over decolonization, the proposed 1962 constitutional amendment (which made the presidential office subject to direct election by the people), and the escalating cold war. Successive ministers of information (André Malraux—briefly—followed by Roger Frey and then Alain Peyrefitte, who remained in office from 1962 to 1966) were charged with TV's regulation and expected to privilege topics deemed important and to suppress those thought "problematic." [111] The installation of a direct line linking the minister's bureau to that of the director of television testified to de Gaulle's desire for more state control.[112] The consequences were visible in news reporting; the smilingly relaxed delivery of early television journalists was replaced by a more professional and sober style. Censorship was endemic. A review article from the London *Times*—republished without commentary in *Le monde* in 1960—minced no words: "[French television news] is a performance seen through rose-colored glasses, where the smallest disagreeable aspects of reality are hidden from view." [113]

Sartre's support for revolutionary movements and his anti-American, anti-imperialist beliefs kept him at odds with the French government throughout the 1950s and '60s.[114] His four-year identification as a communist fellow traveler (1952–56) and his radical politics led to rifts with colleagues and further incensed the government.[115] Throughout the late 1950s he railed against the injustices of colonial rule—often in the pages of *Les temps modernes*.[116] In August of 1960, Sartre added his name to the "Manifesto of the 121," protesting against military conscription in the Algerian war. The signatories were prohibited access to radio or television. Yet when additional sanctions against the group were proposed by the Council of Ministers, Sartre's growing reputation convinced General de Gaulle to famously advise, "You do not imprison Voltaire." [117] However, if Sartre's international celebrity protected him, it also made him a target. October of 1960 saw five hundred war veterans parading up the Champs-Elysées yelling, "Kill Sartre!" [118] On 19 July 1961 and again on 8 January 1962, Sartre's apartment at 42 rue Bonaparte was bombed, reportedly by members of the Organisation de l'armée secrète (OAS)—an extremist group determined to keep Algeria under French control. The second of these events, which destroyed the apartment upstairs, attracted television coverage.[119] On both occasions, Sartre was unharmed.

While Sartre's politics clearly put him at odds with state-controlled television, by 1963 the effects of his growing celebrity and a temporary lull in his political activism (brought on by the end of the Algerian war) shifted his relationship with the Gaullist government and made television coverage of the philosopher and his work once again permissible. Lest the change seem too dramatic, it should be noted that television, following its customary pattern, focused almost exclusively on Sartre's literary and theatrical exploits, thus retaining the political upper hand. Throughout the mid-1960s, TV once again depicted Sartre—often with Beauvoir at his side—as a glamorous jet-setter. Television cameras tracked the famous man from Prague to Venice to Paris, promoting his plays or cinematic adaptations of them (like Vittorio de Sica's 1963 *The Condemned of Altona,* starring Sophia Loren and Maximilien Schell).[120] Sartre's plays were also produced—in the tradition of the *dramatique en direct*—for television. Michel Mitrani's 1965 version of *No Exit,* featuring Michel Auclair, Judith Magre, and Evelyne Rey in the principal roles, proved particularly memorable.[121] Mitrani's formidable staging captured the work's suffocating sense of entrapment and irreversibility. The broadcast was an unequivocal success. In 1967, French TV reporters from the review show *Cinema* caught up with Sartre at the Venice Film Festival, where he was promoting a film based on his novella *The Wall.*[122] During this broadcast, Luchino Visconti also defended his cinematic adaptation of Camus's *The Stranger,* starring Marcello Mastroianni, against the critics. In 1968 both Sartre and Beauvoir appeared in a documentary portrait of the Guatemalan writer, diplomat, and winner of the 1967 Nobel Prize in Literature, Miguel Angel Asturias.[123] And in the same year, reviews of a revival of *The Devil and the Good Lord*—seventeen years after its premiere—once again found their way to the small screen.[124] As before, Sartre was absent from the footage.

( · )

Camus proved less politically problematic than Sartre for the French audiovisual administration. Of course, because he died in an automobile accident in 1960 when television was still in its infancy, broadcast coverage of Camus was largely retrospective. Even so, unlike coverage of Sartre, programs with or about Camus aired without interruption throughout the 1950s and '60s. Like those of his cohort, however (and in keeping with TV's apolitical bent), these shows focused primarily on Camus's theatrical works. In 1957, his second play, *Révolte dans les Asturies*[125]—written more than two decades earlier—was reviewed on the book show *Lectures pour tous*.[126] By 1959, Camus had gleaned considerable attention from television cameras for his stage adaptation of Fyodor Dostoevsky's *The Possessed*. Camus had been working since 1953 on the massive project, which reduced the 900-page novel to three and a half hours, three acts (including twenty-two scenes), and twenty-three characters. The complex plot traces the career of Nikolay Stavrogin, a nobleman afflicted by spiritual nihilism. Stavrogin indulges in crime and debauchery, marries a disabled woman he does not love, and ultimately commits suicide. The core issues of the drama—nihilism and the question of suicide—were major preoccupations in Camus's thought at the time. The play's opening on 30 January 1959, to mixed reviews, was considered such a major event that André Malraux (minister of culture) and Georges Pompidou (then director of de Gaulle's cabinet, later president of France, 1969–74) were in attendance. Camus, who was—not incidentally—an attractive and elegant man, was televised discussing this project on three separate occasions. The first was a brief appearance on the evening news.[127] The second was lengthier, consisting of a twenty-minute interview on *Lectures pour tous*.[128] The third, a 12 May 1959 program entitled "Albert Camus" broadcast in the series *Gros plan*, would be his last.[129]

"Albert Camus" was a thirty-five-minute special that provided the lengthiest footage of Camus ever committed to film. Images culled from the program continue to figure in retrospectives on his life. The brainchild of director Pierre Cardinal, *Gros plan* was structured as a half-hour show in which an important celebrity (usually an actor or playwright) spoke alone to a camera. Interpolated into the resultant monologue were excerpts from films that shed light on the character and personality of the guest. Technically, the focus on an individual, and particularly on the face shot in close-up, reflected an aesthetic that fascinated French television directors throughout the 1950s and early '60s. The close-up was implicitly invoked not as something to interpret but rather as a lucid access to truth. Thus, Cardinal insisted, "What is most important is the face, for the simple reason that it is the only thing that appears as large as life on television."[130] As will be seen in chapter 2, *Lectures pour tous* also was utterly invested in this perspective. Although Camus purportedly wrote "a very fine text" for the program, Cardinal ultimately chose to cut the scripted sequences, opt-

Production shot, 1959: Camus and Cardinal. (Photo INA–Daniel Fallot. Reproduced by permission of the Institut national de l'audiovisuel.)

ing instead for those moments when Camus spoke extemporaneously. Confessional intimacy revealed in close-up was the order of the day.

Greek masks drift across the screen and disappear into the dark. When the light lifts, the camera gazes out from the stage into the empty audience across the dim expanse of a theater. Footsteps break the silence. A man emerges from the horizon; he slowly makes his way down the center aisle, takes off his coat, and places it carefully across a chair. "What?" he asks, responding to a silent question as he turns towards the camera, "Why do I do theater? Umm, well—I've often asked myself—and the only response that I've come up with until now will probably seem discouragingly banal to you. It is simply that the stage of a theater is one of the places in the world where I am happy." Perhaps, however, this is less banal than it seems, Camus reflects, since "happiness, after all, is an original activity today, and the proof is that we

From "Albert Camus," 12 May 1959.

have a tendency to hide ourselves in order to exercise it." [131] From the outset, the commentary takes a philosophical turn. As Camus speaks, he approaches the stage until the camera flips, and suddenly we seem to be viewing the space through his eyes. "The theater is a monastery," he muses, "the agitation of the world dies outside it; inside, a community of monks works together for a single goal, to celebrate the office that will be celebrated for the very first time." With Camus, we get a bird's-eye view of the stage. The scene is set. An actor enters, and the play begins.

As the program continues, Camus's monologue is interspersed with excerpts of Michel Bouquet and Catherine Sellers (with whom Camus was romantically involved at the time) performing in his adaptation of *The Possessed*. Turning smoothly from one topic to the next, Camus speaks successively of the work that goes into producing a play, of the importance of décor, of the relationship between theater and literature, and of the dangers that menace the theater's continued vibrancy. The excerpted scenes, undoubtedly chosen for their dramatic tension, functioned as publicity for the play, which, although considered a success, was suffering financial woes. From the discussion of theater Camus meanders into an extended musing on his preference for actors over intellectuals: "What I am trying to say is that I prefer the society of theater people, virtuous or not, to those of my intellectual 'brothers.' Not only because, as it is known, intellectuals (who are rarely likable), manage to like each other only with difficulty—no—rather because in the society of intellectuals, I have the impression of always feeling guilty. I always feel as if I'm infringing on the rules of the clan." The show is a meditation in which Camus's outlook on theater provides the fabric through which is woven his outlook on life: "It's generally said that the theater is a place of illusion, but I don't believe that at all. It is society that is the place of illusion [. . .] and you will find fewer histrionics on stage than in society. Take one of those people we see in a room filled with generals and put him on the stage under 4000 watts of light—you'll find him naked. The people on stage confess, in a way, and declaim their true identities. I always know people better if they play another character. [. . .] Believe me, to live in truth, *jouez la comédie* [*act!*]." Camus's comments self-consciously disassociate him from a "rarely likable" (and politically problematic) social group ("intellectuals"), while at the same time suggesting that by placing himself "on the stage under 4000 watts of light" (television), he is declaiming his true identity. "Albert Camus" aired on 12 May 1959, just months before his tragic death.

( · )

Like Sartre, Camus became a public figure in the aftermath of World War II, but both his provincial origins and his politics contrasted starkly with those of the educated Parisian elite that formed his intellectual coterie. Born into a working-class family in Algeria in 1913, Camus and his brother lost their father to the First World War and were raised by their mother, a cleaning woman. Advancing with the aid of competitive scholarships from public school to the University of Algiers, where he studied philosophy, Camus was a stellar example of the successful application of the educational reforms of the Third Republic to the colonial project. Denied a teaching career because of tuberculosis, he organized an avant-garde theater group in Algiers in 1935 and began working as a journalist in North Africa and Paris. During this time he spent two brief years as a member of the Communist Party. Between 1937 and 1941 Camus wrote the works that established his international reputation: a novel, *The Stranger;* an essay, *The Myth of Sisyphus;* and a play, *Caligula.* It was in these that he elaborated his concept of the absurd—the inescapable paradox that is man's desire for reason in the face of "the benign indifference of the world."[132] World War II brought Camus to Paris, where he became active in the Resistance. For three years he wrote for the clandestine paper *Combat,* becoming the newly licit journal's editor-in-chief after the war—a post he abandoned in 1947 to dedicate himself to artistic pursuits. At the Liberation (out of opposition to the death penalty and on the urging of François Mauriac, with whom he otherwise had little in common), Camus signed a plea to General de Gaulle for clemency on behalf of Robert Brasillach—despite his personal antipathy towards the collaborator and his work. His writings testify to the ethical positions on which he based his politics: *Neither Victims nor Executioners* and *The Rebel,* published in 1946 and 1951 respectively, condemned Stalinism and distinguished the act of revolt from its perversion in totalitarian revolutions that invoked doctrine to justify murder. Camus's defense of liberty against the oppression of totalitarian ideologies and his advocacy of a negotiated solution to the crisis of the Algerian war ultimately resulted in a permanent rupture with Sartre and the progressive left.

By the end of the 1950s, Camus had established his reputation as a moralist who, by his own proclamation, was ill at ease with politics. Unable to reconcile his love for his native Algeria and his profoundly French identity, Camus withdrew into a much-criticized silence.[133] "I am not a political man," he wrote in January of 1956; "my passions and my tastes call me to places other than public tribunes. I go there only from the pressure of circumstances and the idea I sometimes have of myself as a writer."[134] Interestingly, Camus's political reticence may have endeared him to the increasingly conservative governments controlling television programming.[135] The minister of information (and head of television) Alain Peyrefitte averred, "If you are politically faithful to Camus, it is difficult to see how you could commit yourself to a specific political party."[136] It was Camus's moral authority more than his political convictions that captivated his public.[137] And it was precisely this combination of moral rigor and political restraint that rendered Camus (unlike Sartre) consistently attractive to television programmers, audiences, and the government alike.[138]

( · )

Suspicious of their political affinities, the French government kept a sharp eye on the television coverage of philosophers throughout the Fourth Republic. Not counting a handful of broadcasts, philosophers' political interventions—a pivotal component of their television activity by the late 1970s—were notably absent. Through the end of de Gaulle's presidency in 1969, Raymond Aron was the only philosopher conveying distinctly political messages given consistent access to the small screen, largely—as evident in the next chapter—because his own sympathies lay closest to those of the parties in power. Aron's appearances were mainly confined either to book shows or newsmagazines, both programs with more political leeway than the tightly controlled television news. During the same period, Sartre had the rare distinction of being the only philosopher linked to political incidents on the TV news: first (as mentioned earlier) as a result of the bombing of his Paris apartment, and then in 1966 when he was shown (but not heard) participating in a debate about Vietnam.[139] Not surprisingly, the only interview footage ever shot with Sartre specifically for television (a 1969 conversation with Olivier Todd on the newsmagazine *Panorama,* in which the philosopher virulently denounced American atrocities in the massacre at Song My), aired after de Gaulle's resignation.[140] Sartre's presence on the program attested to his belief that the ORTF, and especially the television news, had liberalized following de Gaulle's departure.[141] The fact that political coverage of Sartre appeared on the TV news more than a dozen times between 1969 and 1971 suggests that he was right.

## A Perilous Freedom?

In "What is Literature?" Sartre maintains that although vested political interests control the media, even intellectuals of the opposition need to court its dominion. Interestingly, he fails to note the degree to which the party in power determines not only whether but also how such courtship is possible. Since politics writ large was at first virtually absent from and then highly controlled on French TV, and since politically invested intellectuals equated writing with action and considered the press—over which they exerted substantial control and influence—vastly preferable to television, the scant political coverage of philosophers on television in the Fourth and early Fifth Republic is not surprising. More curious is the fact that, given the administration's evident interest in philosophers, only thrice during the Fourth Republic was philosophy qua philosophy the actual focus of broadcasts. (Two of these programs, which aired within the context of the book show *Lectures pour tous,* will be analyzed in the next chapter).[142] However, philosophy, particularly as incarnated by Sartrean existentialism, posed ethical questions—offering moral guidance, but also implying judgment. Literature and drama, even when possessed of evident philosophical subtexts, invited less controversy. By featuring their cultural achievements, French television managed to capitalize on intellectual celebrity, selectively framing philosophers as symbolic embodiments of a carefully cultivated and often conservative notion of French cultural grandeur. In this process, television created new forms of intellectual publicity—with repercussions that would escalate beyond the wildest imaginings of those first broadcast on its shows.

By 1964, almost 40% of French homes contained TV's—an astonishing increase of 400% within a mere six years. More than 50% of those people without sets viewed programs regularly in other venues.[143] As the burgeoning economy coupled with advances in technology to make televisions an affordable purchase for working-class households, the collective dimension of reception was abandoned in favor of the intimacy of family viewing within the privacy of the domestic sphere. Cultural and popular programming continued—within limits—to be the designated realm for innovation and artistic freedom. The success of the *dramatique en direct* during the 1950s illustrates that French television regularly exploited the classical heritage, developing new genres but also building its own legitimacy on the back of established cultural forms. Television also began to explore new types of entertainment—variety shows, game shows, sports telecasts, and the first dramatic series—all the while gingerly skirting the controversial political arena. The political sensibilities of the creative artists (producers, directors, and cinematographers) who produced such programs were often on the left; hence attempts to "push the (political) envelope" were not uncommon. But the specter of government censure and the ever-present—and not unused—threat of dismissal provided constant pressure to conform.[144] For its part, the public denounced the state's repressive hold over the broadcasting system, a fact of which the government was not unaware. The creation of the second channel in 1964 opened debates over the merits of competition and was used to defend claims that the government was preparing to relax control over the state apparatus. In reality (and despite the expanded programming potential offered by Channel 2), the French television administration continued to operate as a uniform and highly regulated entity until the end of the 1960s.

( · )

If the eighteenth-century *philosophes* promoted the Kantian belief that "the public use of one's reason must always be free, and it alone can bring about enlightenment among men," the French Revolution made clear that "the public use of one's reason" on the part of "private persons" was both emancipating and intrinsically dangerous.[145] In the wake of Revolution, it devolved upon philosophy, newly integrated into a developing system of national education, to structure that perilous freedom, simultaneously expanding the spirit and controlling the choices it made. The manifold characteristics long associated with French philosophy—from its tendency towards clarity and literary diversity to its penchant for autobiography and interest in practical morality—in combination with a political culture that demanded both the democratization of reason and the socially engaged presence of intellectuals, produced a philosophical tradition uniquely suited to exploitation by the television medium. As we will see in chapter 2, philosophy's classical roots as a fundamentally dialogic, performative practice also suited it to the small screen. Meanwhile, early French television, supported by visions of the medium as a transparent reflection of reality, bolstered by audiences awed by the new technology, and protected from the competition of the private market by government monopoly, was both assured a public and guaranteed a level of temporal continuity (unimaginable in North America) that supported the kind of sustained argument that the televising of philosophy required. Yet while French television was understood as an instrument for the extension of national culture and education—hence amenable to the broadcasting of philosophy—it is equally clear that TV's potential was perceived (like enlightenment itself) as at once liberating and dangerous. Indeed, the rural *télé-clubs* that sprang up across France in the 1950s and early '60s were as committed to influencing television's audiences as they were to increasing them.[146] Operating under the imprimatur of the government agenda—to inform, educate, and entertain—and ever more politically guarded, the French television administration gradually tightened its grasp over the airwaves. Philosophers *and* philosophy, willingly and not, were increasingly caught in its visual grip.

# Philosophy and the Early
# Television Book Show, 1953–1968

In the decades following World War II, television laid siege to the culture of the book. However, with French television regarded less as a creative form in its own right than as a means for the transmission of the classical heritage, most early aficionados saw the medium not as a threat but rather as a boon to print culture.[1] Television would "spread the word"—heightening public awareness about important new publications, encouraging viewers to read, and bringing the rich legacy of the French humanistic tradition directly into the homes and heads of the nation's citizens. Few countries have worked as hard as France to merge the word and the image via the small screen. Indeed, between 1953 and 1989 alone, 106 series dedicated to literary programming sought to marry these disparate entities on French TV.[2] Since its inception, the format known as the *émission littéraire,* or television book show, has also provided one of the dominant platforms for the televising of philosophy in France.[3]

*Lectures pour tous* (1953–58) inaugurated the book show genre.[4] Along with Bernard Pivot's celebrated *Apostrophes* (1975–89), it remains widely recognized as among the most important in the field. While philosophy was but a small part of its purview, *Lectures pour tous* became the first television series to regularly feature the discipline and its practitioners.[5] Indeed, thanks to a confluence of factors, from its interview structure, to its hosts' magnetic conversational style, to its sustained rhythm and innovative camera work, the show inadvertently manifested the range of programming models that have distinguished the televising of philosophy throughout its history.

In this chapter I take up five broadcasts from *Lectures pour tous* (on Sartre, Camus, Bachelard, Aron, and Foucault) aired between 1955 and 1966. Examining first the earlier shows (including those on Sartre and Bachelard, as well as the 1960 Camus obituary) in terms of the fifties vogue for existentialism and the educational crisis in philosophy, and then the later shows (on Aron and Foucault) within the context of the Gaullist regime's active anti-Marxism and pursuit of French cultural grandeur, I identify several trends. First, as early as the 1950s, television began to emerge as a formidable advertising tool with an arguably positive impact on the expansion of the market in the chief intellectual commodity: books. Television hosts exerted new forms of intellectual and cultural control, offering, for example, exposure to a philosophy (existentialism) and a philosopher (Sartre) decidedly out of favor with the politics in power. Second, philosophers, faced with a state-regulated medium that requested their presence and, at the same time, socially motivated to speak out on issues of public concern, were suddenly charged to negotiate an audiovisual landscape whose terrain both exceeded their influence and challenged deeply held beliefs about the disinterested and commercially innocent nature of scholarly inquiry. Nonetheless, because philosophy exists as embodied performative practice—and hence could be observed "in action"—philosophers were well equipped to meet both the theatrical and the structural demands of the book show genre. While demonstrating how political considerations and screen charisma equally shaped media access, *Lectures pour tous,* during the fifteen years of its run, contributed to the postwar construction of French intellectual celebrity, launched an important public forum for philosophy, and became a legitimizing force in the field of French intellectual power—in so doing creating a potent (and increasingly contested) relationship between commerce and culture.[6] Whether it successfully molded mass audiences into the enlightened viewers envisioned by the state, however, was another question entirely.

## *Lectures pour tous* (1953-1968): Birth of a Genre

*Lectures pour tous* began broadcasting on 27 March 1953. Airing each Wednesday evening on Channel 1—until 1964 the sole French channel—the show enjoyed almost instant acclaim.[7] The fact that it was scheduled into an ideal time slot (originally appearing at 9:30 p.m., during French prime time) did not hurt.[8] After its first six months on the air and despite having not yet developed its characteristic visual style, the new program was commended by *La semaine radiophonique* as "lively and varied, neither pedantic nor pretentious."[9] At the end of its first season *Lectures pour tous* won the 1954 award for best new television show. Admittedly, the competition was not stiff. In 1953 the RTF was broadcasting a mere thirty-two hours a week (up from thirteen in 1948).[10] Initially audiences were small, but even if only 126,000 households boasted television sets in 1954, sets installed in cafés and the *télé-clubs* introduced the program to a constantly growing public. *Lectures pour tous* acquired a loyal following. By 1962 *Le monde* reported that the show regularly captured between 26% and 32% of the viewing public.[11]

Key to *Lecture pour tous's* success was the fact that it fulfilled with brio the RTF's triple agenda ("entertain, inform, educate"), an agenda fervently supported—as mentioned in chapter 1—by the RTF's influential director of programming from 1952 to 1959, Jean d'Arcy.[12] This agenda relied heavily upon a view of the new technology as a transparent vehicle for the democratization of French culture and emphatically *not* as a challenge to it. Indeed, television could only accede to the level of a legitimate cultural practice in France if it was able to be of service to the dominant—and ostensibly literary—culture.[13] Like the theater broadcasts discussed in chapter 1, the book show was the fruit of this belief. Yet, as the hosts and producers of *Lectures pour tous* quickly discovered, television would not merely transmit but also transform French culture. In the case of the book show, two elements were critical to this process: first the introduction of a new cultural mediator in the person of the television host, and second the impact of the physical image of the writer (or, in this case, the philosopher) on the reception of text. By wresting control of traditional avenues for the attribution of intellectual value and privileging the producer at the expense of the product, both factors challenged elite networks and generated tremendous controversy.

D'Arcy conferred *Lectures pour tous* on two ambitious young journalists, Pierre Desgraupes and Pierre Dumayet. Both men had worked in the artistic programming division of Radio diffusion française (RDF) and had also presented the radio news—Dumayet on *Actualités de Paris* and Desgraupes on *Paris vous parle*. Television news gigs soon followed. Their collaboration began in 1947, as co-hosts of a radio book show, *Domaine français*.[14] When the offer came several years later to create a television book show together, they jumped at the chance. They quickly discovered that they had similar perspectives on the new medium. Both had studied philosophy, first as *lycée* students under Georges Perret and later at the Sorbonne, where Dumayet had taken classes with Bachelard. Following the war, Desgraupes began preparing a diploma thesis on Descartes. Initially, both young men had resolved to take the *agrégation* in philosophy. Ultimately, however, both abandoned this plan in favor of gainful employment, first as print journalists and then at the RDF. Desgraupes later claimed that it was because they "communed in the religion of Perret" that their partnership blossomed.[15] Although readily disavowing elitist programming ("I'm not at all a fan of 'intello' TV," Dumayet informed me), Desgraupes nevertheless insists, "We were philosophers of radio, and then television" who "were necessarily drawn towards those shows where our studies could still serve us in some way."[16] Despite this penchant for erudite subjects, both men agree that "even the cultural shows we did, we sought to make as accessible as possible."[17] *Lectures pour tous* fit the bill beautifully and established their reputations in the field.

Typically shot live by the use of three cameras in the small third studio at Cognac-Jay, the show exhibited extremely simple production values: as producers and principal hosts, Dumayet and Desgraupes took turns sitting at a small table opposite their guests and posing questions.[18] In the beginning, they reported, no one really knew how to "do" television, so for the first few weeks they simply talked and let the cameras run.[19] The uninspired results ultimately led to the hiring of a new director, Jean Prat. Prat's youth (he was only twenty-six when he joined the team in 1955) reflected the youthfulness of the field: Desgraupes was thirty-five, Dumayet thirty. Like many new TV directors, Prat (the son of a railroad official) had trained at the Institut des hautes études cinématographiques (IDHEC). And like many, when he failed to break into film, he headed for television, widely acknowledged as the fastest route to the top. *Lectures pour tous* was Prat's first regular directing assignment. His inspired camerawork quickly transformed the program from what a reviewer called "a radio show of the 'blah-blah-blah variety' that has no business being on television," to one with a distinctive visual signature, reminiscent of Godard's new wave cinema.[20] Prat's style, dubbed *face à face* for its direct staging and serene tone, aimed to establish a sense of intimacy and inclusion that was close to confessional. Under his eye, reported television critic Jacques Mourgeon, "each program [attained] an almost esoteric significance [. . .]; literature became gesture."[21] Prat's approach proved so successful that even in his absence (guest directors were not infrequent) his aesthetic imprint endured.

The program opened with a presentation of the evening's featured books. The body of the show was then divided into two to four interviews, each lasting eight to fifteen minutes. Rounding out the program were light reviews of fiction, theater, or Parisian literary life (given between 1953 and 1959 by Nicole Vedrès, a novelist); interviews with "imaginary" guests from other epochs; and an "address to the reader" delivered in a static shot—often at some length—directly to the camera by the poet and critic Max-Pol Fouchet. In keeping with the tastes of the hosts, guests ran the gamut from literary celebrities (Umberto Eco, Italo Calvino, François Mauriac, Roland Barthes, Nathalie Sarraute, Vladimir Nabokov) to bright young talents (Françoise Sagan), to writers of popular fiction, to authors on current affairs, to pedestrian topics (pets, travel), and to such disciplines as philosophy, sociology, anthropology, and history (with Bachelard, Foucault, Aron, and Claude Lévi-Strauss, among others).[22] During the interviews the camera cut from long shots encompassing host and guest to alternating medium one-shots, to lingering close-ups. This gradual tightening of the frame mirrored the interview process, which sought through successive questions to expose the authentic private face hidden behind the public persona.[23]

The interviews began with a close-up of the volume under discussion. If at first publishers were neither mentioned in the prefatory

Publicity shot for *Lectures pour tous,* 1954: Pierre Dumayet and Pierre Desgraupes. (Reproduced by permission of the Institut national de l'audiovisuel.)

Opening shots for *Lectures pour tous;* co-host Nicole Vedrès.

monologues nor legible in the cover-shots that opened each sequence, it was nevertheless clear that the filmic choice was both descriptive and promotional.[24] It bears noting that *Lectures pour tous* was launched during a watershed in the French publishing industry. In 1953 Hachette pitched the *livres de poche*—mass-market, affordable paperbacks. Reeditions of the classics competed with new works, and sales (up to 200,000 copies per printing) shot off the charts. Within a decade the production of rival series (like *J'ai lu* [*I've read it*] and *Presses pocket*) signaled the arrival of *les trentes glorieuses,* thirty years of economic expansion in the literary world.[25] However, thanks to the impact of the television book show, the publishing market no longer responded solely to the careful assessments of literary critics in the pages of *Le monde, Le Figaro,* or *Les nouvelles littéraires.* The employment of a press secretary charged specifically with television relations at the Julliard publishing house indicates that under the influence of the small screen, selling books now meant selling writers. Indeed, René Julliard felt the new medium was so important that he actually equipped Monique Mayaud, his director of press relations, with a television set.[26] More than half the bestsellers published in 1958—including Simone de Beauvoir's *Memoirs of a Dutiful Daughter*—had benefited from exposure on *Lectures pour tous.*[27] The program made evident that, visually incarnate, the right book (and—more importantly—the right author) could charm a newly affluent public into loosening its purse strings and buying.

According to Dumayet, *Lectures pour tous* was conceived as a *chemin vers l'oeuvre,* a path to the work, and understood as an educational instrument for the diffusion of traditional culture.[28] Its explicit goals were twofold: to encourage the public to read, and to inform it about literary current affairs. Its implicit message was that there was something to be gained from the visible communion of author and text.

The attraction for the viewer lay in what the author would reveal, both verbally and physically, that the text could not. The potential results could be both intellectually hypnotic and commercially rewarding. To its creators, the visual element was vital: "We mustn't forget that television came from radio," Desgraupes remarked. "It was revolutionary to bring that 'something extra' that is the image, to an interview."[29] For the public, the identity of the author and the meaning of the work, the corporeal and the written, appeared symbiotic. To its fans, the notion of judging a work on the basis of its author was hardly new. It harked back to the salons of the eighteenth century. To its detractors (whose positions suggest emergent structuralist critiques), the results were blasphemous: the author was nothing more than a contaminant of the text. From this perspective, television, and particularly the television interview, threatened the sacred status of the text. *Lectures pour tous* scoffed at such criticism, asserting that the visual presence of the author opened up new possibilities for the textual encounter. These possibilities—even when politically hindered—applied particularly to the televising of philosophy.

### Existential Dilemmas and Subversive Strategies: Jean-Paul Sartre

Between 1945 and the early 1950s the philosophical movement known as existentialism put Paris back on the global cultural map. Famously reduced to the phrase "Existence precedes essence," and philosophically traceable to Søren Kierkegaard, existentialism insisted on the personal, subjective dimension of human existence. In its Sartrean incarnation, existentialism was inseparable from France's wartime experience, for it invoked the necessity of moral choice both under the German Occupation and after. In postwar Paris, existentialism led a double life: one philosophic, the other cultural. Despite resolute attempts to distance themselves from the latter, by the end of the 1940s, Sartre, Beauvoir, and—more peripherally—Camus were irreversibly linked in the public imagination to the cultish hordes of black-clad young people who be-bopped with feral abandon to the beat of American jazz in the smoky underground bars of Saint-Germain-des-Prés.[30]

While it had all the features of a surefire media sensation and drew attention in both the press and cinematic newsreels, existentialism received scant television coverage.[31] Famous for its purported transgression of gender norms, celebration of individual freedom, and avid promotion of new models of sexual morality, existentialism (especially in its cultural incarnation) tacitly critiqued the fragile state of the nation. Taking direction from the reinvention of conjugal morals devised in the late 1920s by Sartre and Beauvoir as a governing principle for their own legendary relationship, existentialists in general (and women in particular) were thought to embrace free love and reject marriage and family.[32] Consequently, for the television administration the topic was delicate. Yet as literary celebrities, existentialists were part of the cultural capital that the medium was eager to exploit. Camus was not the problem. Less politically strident than his colleagues, and a close friend of *Lectures pour tous*'s Fouchet, he was happy to appear before the cameras.[33] With Sartre and Beauvoir it was different. As chapter 1 illustrates, their support for revolutionary movements (particularly, by 1956, the cause of Algerian independence) and their anti-American, anti-imperialist beliefs increasingly brought them into conflict with the French government. Nervous about provoking government ire, through the 1950s and '60s TV news largely avoided the famous couple.[34] Meanwhile, Sartre and Beauvoir refused TV interviews, a fact that probably suited the state broadcaster, who was uncomfortably caught between political whims and the interests of both producers and the public. Both Dumayet and Desgraupes report wishing that Sartre had acceded to an interview on the show. While Desgraupes attributes the philosopher's reticence to his opposition to government politics, Dumayet recalls that the television administration "advised against" Sartre's presence on the broadcast. Regardless, since they were unable to entice Sartre to appear but eager to capitalize on his intellectual celebrity, the hosts of *Lectures pour tous* resorted to representing him indirectly.[35] The decision was a ratings coup and provided a prototype for covering controversial subjects in the years to come.

On 19 July 1955, Dumayet interviewed Francis Jeanson to discuss his recent study, *Sartre par lui-même*.[36] Sartre's face, captured in a photograph on the jacket of the book, opens the program. The still image—its serious bespectacled gaze, teeth clamped on a pipe, lips seemingly poised to utter profundities—introduces Sartre, as intellectual sobriety incarnate, to a public not yet entirely familiar with his features. The camera cuts to an over-the-shoulder two-shot, depicting Dumayet holding the book, angled across from Jeanson, who faces the camera. Dumayet's first question, "What is generally said about Sartre, and how does the book correct that opinion?" intimates the slant

Dumayet interviewing Francis Jeanson, author of *Sartre par lui-même*. From *Lectures pour tous*, 19 July 1955.

of the discussion that follows. This seemingly innocuous book review not only makes possible a conversation about the value of Sartre's work but also opens a public debate about Sartre's status in contemporary French society.

Jeanson quickly seizes the opportunity to champion his protagonist. Dismissing those who discount the philosopher's oeuvre because they find it excessively morbid, Jeanson argues that Sartre is interesting in part because "he performed his own psychoanalysis via his work." Leaning forward, body tense with the force of his convictions, he contends that it is Sartre's capacity for meticulous self-reflection that is the root of his philosophical brilliance. Jeanson acknowledges that Sartre is widely criticized for "being an absurdist" and for asserting "that life is necessarily failure." Sartre's detractors, he observes, were especially fond of quoting "that famous phrase from *No Exit*, 'Hell is other people,'" to illustrate the philosopher's pessimism. However (and here Jeanson draws heavily on his cigarette), the interpretation of Sartre as "a man who doesn't know what love is, and who always considers 'the other' an enemy, is wrong." Defending the Sartrean concept of "bad faith," Jeanson insists that Sartre's "denunciation of that which is inauthentic in interpersonal relations is born of his passion for what is true." It is this passion for the authentic, he claims, "that is properly the Sartrean passion." And if the philosopher's oeuvre is "a black literature and a literature of abjection," it is because "Sartre said that there was no point in pursuing fine principles on the moral level if we haven't shown man first that he is responsible for his own failure—and we can only show him that when he is at his most defeated." Yes, Jeanson concedes, "Sartre is generally reproached for creating a pessimist philosophy." However, he continues, one thumb pushing firmly into the other palm, "In his defense I would simply like to repeat something that he himself said to me one day, which to my mind covers his entire oeuvre: 'Men are only powerless when they declare themselves to be so.'" Given France's recent history of collaboration and occupation, this call for accountability rings strong. It also evokes Sartre's rather slow political awakening during the war years—an awakening that sometimes seems to undergird his philosophy like a whispered mea culpa.

Up to this point the clip remains uncharacteristically static, fixed on the two-shot described above. Not until seven full minutes have elapsed does the camera finally cut away.[37] During the final four minutes of the interview, the focus gradually tightens on Jeanson. When the frame changes, so too does the topic of conversation. Dumayet employs a favored technique, seizing a line from the text to pry open the subject at hand. "There is a word that you use a lot in your book, the word 'bastard,'" he remarks. Jeanson responds, intrigued: "This word unsettles you?" "No, no, not at all," Dumayet retorts, "but I was surprised at its frequent appearance." Jeanson explains that Sartre himself repeatedly used the term *mal-né* (literally "badly born") as a metaphor for marginality. All of Sartre's heroes (notwithstanding Jean Genet, who really *was* born out of wedlock), "live in slightly unbalanced situations" and, in so doing, "reflect in their double consciousness the contradictions of our time." Reminding Dumayet of his initial question, how Sartre is generally perceived, Jeanson observes, "There are more and more people who consider Sartre a good man, a generous man." Sartre's admirers, he continues, believe that the philosopher "dedicates his work, in instances that are evidently uncomfortable for him, to courageously defending the difficulties of our age." They understand that Sartre's aim is "to show the public [. . .] that we are all living in a contradictory epoch in a world that is heartrendingly divided against itself." What is essential, Jeanson concludes, his eyes troubled, is "the degree to which Sartre is forcing himself to live that contradiction, to *be* that contradiction, to assume it, while many among us feel that contradiction but seek rather to ignore it or to flee."

*Lectures pour tous* used Francis Jeanson to bring Sartre to the small screen. In a seemingly apolitical fashion, this second-degree incarnation—with the philosopher absent but discussed—created a platform for the defense of the man and his oeuvre, both tacitly banned from French television at that time. The program's spectacular dimension (presenting the author as an "embodied text") was necessarily deferred, since Sartre was not visibly present, but in this case Jeanson served as a physical conduit to the philosopher. Trust me, his earnest presence implied, you will like the guy. The biographical thrust of the discussion reflected the mounting fascination with philosophers as cultural celebrities. In a simple but effective way, this broadcast also demonstrates how television professionals had begun to understand that they could ignore both implicit government directives and authorial desires (in this case, to avoid TV) and fulfill their own agendas for programming content, thus exerting a modicum of control over the nature of public discourse.

### Death and Commemoration: Philosophy and the Television Obituary

Camus was killed in a car accident on 4 January 1960 while returning to Paris from Lourmarin, where he had retreated to write. He was forty-six. His death marked the postwar emergence of a new type of intellectual publicity: the television obituary. By the 1980s, the deaths of Sartre, Aron, Beauvoir, Foucault, and Vladimir Jankélévitch, among others, rendered television obituaries a sadly regular element in the televising of philosophy. In the grand tradition of the French *éloge funèbre*, TV obituaries perform a mythologizing function: noting the passing of great intellectuals underscores the magnificence of French cultural identity, glorifies French philosophers, and assists the collective visual creation of a culturally rich past. Commemorative broadcasts aired on the anniversaries of death further contribute to the power and longevity of this process.[38]

Most television obituaries appear on news programs. These spots provide an opportunity to re-use stock footage, emphasizing the self-referential nature of the television medium and reinforcing the ways in which TV selectively solidifies social memory. Camus's obituary, described in the *conducteur* for the 9 January 1960 evening news on *JT nuit* was typical.[39] The segment opens with a still image of Camus, visually identifying the writer/philosopher. It then cuts to a mangled car, the symbol of his tragic death, and to his coffin surrounded by crowds of mourners, whose numbers both reflect and produce his renown. Cut. The camera zooms in on members of the funeral cortège— the intimate image of their grief renders the personal, universal, and therefore accessible, identifiable, our own. Again Camus fills the screen—the photo mourns his embodied presence and marks his future absence. His books are displayed, linking the man to his work and offering perceptible evidence of his intellectual importance. A clip from the United Press follows, showing Camus—a French cultural treasure incarnate—accepting the Nobel Prize from the king of Sweden. The closing images are from the region of Tipasa, in Algeria, an area famous for its Roman ruins. Views of the countryside, fields of wheat, his mother holding Camus's photo in her wrinkled hands, then trees, gardens, columns, old stones, and the sea. Once again the sequence leads from personal to universal, from mortal to immortal. The rapid progression of cardinal images, intercut with brief interviews where prominent intellectuals memorialize the accomplishments of the deceased, established an enduring format for television news obituaries that remains familiar to French viewers today.

*Lectures pour tous* also aired eulogistic tributes. On 13 January 1960 and, two years later, on 17 October 1962, the program's contributing host Max-Pol Fouchet paid homage to Camus and Bachelard.[40] Like the obituaries on TV news, the tributes on *Lectures pour tous* perform symbolic work. Unlike the news spots, however, which have changed little over time, the obituaries broadcast on *Lectures pour tous* demonstrate a temporal and visual aesthetic worth analyzing because it is so foreign to television today.[41] While Camus's coverage opens and Bachelard's closes a broadcast, the eulogies are comparable in structure and content, except that Fouchet is visibly moved in the segment on Camus, who was a personal friend and whose accidental death shocked the intellectual community. Each time, Fouchet links biography to philosophical perspective. Evoking his memories of Camus, Fouchet describes the walks they took as youths along the cliffs that flank the bay of Algiers. Once, he remembers, they happened upon an Arab boy dying in his father's arms after being hit by a car. Fouchet wonders whether Camus's philosophy of the absurd, "born of that confrontation between humanity's plea and the world's unreasonable silence," was influenced by this incident, where, in Camus's words, "the sky said nothing" in response to the tragedy. Fouchet recounts how the Spanish Civil War gave Camus "very precise ideas about justice and injustice," discusses the relationship between Camus's adaptation of *Caligula* and his concept of revolt, and speaks of his friend's love of the theater. In conclusion, Fouchet calls Camus "a profoundly classic moralist" whose only rule, "to learn to live and to die, to be a man, and to refuse to be a god," was paradoxically, "in the end," a truly Promethean message.

In the Bachelard segment, Fouchet's commentary reveals that television had already changed the public imagination. "You may already know," he begins, "that Gaston Bachelard died yesterday at the age of seventy-eight. And without a doubt you have seen him on the television screen—and I am sure that you haven't forgotten his unforgettable face." Interweaving Bachelard's biography and intellectual philosophy, Fouchet portrays him as the "grandson of a family of shoemakers," an autodidact who "rolled his *r*'s," and pursued his studies because he had "married a teacher and wanted to be her equal." Fouchet clearly understands that Bachelard's humble beginnings were integral to his attraction. Indeed, the unusual path that led to Bachelard's scholarly renown is regularly outlined in studies of his work. Fouchet likewise recounts this trajectory before concluding that the philosopher was a sage whose twin passions for science and poetry produced an oeuvre of astonishing breadth and diversity.

Both tributes are remarkably long (Bachelard's lasts fifteen minutes), and structurally plain: for the duration, Fouchet is shown in close-up, solemnly speaking directly to the camera. No photographs illustrate the discourse. No cuts or camerawork embellish Fouchet's image. Forty years later, the static presentation of the delivery is haunting. From their brutally simple framing and sustained rhythms to the poetic elegance of their language, these obituaries speak to a radically different sensibility on the part of both television producers and their audiences. They illustrate a historically specific aesthetic of diffusion and reception that assumes a degree of concentration and patience on the part of television audiences that is unimaginable today. The *"zappeur"*—a disaffected couch potato slouching on the sofa with remote control in hand, rapidly flipping channels, is a figment of the future. The presumption that the public would watch an extended statically shot monologue was symptomatic of the period and—as we shall see—became crucial to the televised transmission of philosophy.

Co-host Max-Pol Fouchet on *Lectures pour tous,* eulogizing Albert Camus on 13 January 1960 (left) and Gaston Bachelard on 17 October 1972 (right).

## Gaston Bachelard: Philosophical Signifier

On 15 May 1957, five years before Fouchet's obituary of him, Bachelard appeared on *Lectures pour tous* in an interview with Dumayet and Gaston Berger.[42] The occasion was the publication of an encyclopedia of philosophy and religion compiled under Berger, himself a philosopher and the general director of higher education from 1953 to 1960.[43] Bachelard appeared as a representative of the sixty-one philosophers who had collaborated on the volume. The broadcast marked Bachelard's second television appearance[44] and also constituted the first discussion of philosophy ever broadcast on French TV. This particular show performed a variety of functions. Exemplifying the didactic aims of public service broadcasting, it used television as a democratic tool with which to educate the masses. It also trumpeted the importance of philosophy at a moment when the discipline (as we shall see in chapter 3) was coming under fire in the academy. Finally, (and ironically) even as the broadcast promoted philosophy as a textual discipline—urging viewers to read—the coverage asserted the new importance of the visual image.

Bachelard's life was the stuff of legends. As noted in his obituary, Bachelard was the grandson of a shoemaker. His father kept a *tabac,* a store in which he sold newspapers, tobacco, and cigarettes. Born on 27 June 1884 and raised in a working-class family in Bar-sur-Aube, Bachelard was a precocious child who did well in school. Upon finishing secondary school he passed the *baccalauréat* in philosophy, but financial hardship prevented him from pursuing further studies. He sought employment, working first as a teaching assistant in Sézanne, and then as a postal worker in Remiremont. Transferred to Paris in

1907, Bachelard enrolled in night classes at the Faculty of Sciences and obtained his *licence* (equivalent to a bachelor's degree) in mathematics in 1912. By 1913 he was granted a year's leave of absence from his job at the Postes, télégraphes et téléphones (PTT) to prepare for the telegraph engineering exam. After he married a young schoolteacher in 1914, his studies were interrupted by WWI. Bachelard volunteered and was mobilized immediately. He spent the years from 1914 to 1919 as a soldier—three of them in the trenches. Returning at the end of the war to his ailing wife (who probably suffered from tuberculosis) and to his native town of Bar-sur-Aube, Bachelard found employment as a physics and chemistry teacher at the local lycée. Shortly thereafter, he began making trips to the university library in Dijon, from which he famously returned with suitcases crammed with books. By the end of 1920, at the age of thirty-five (and after a year of solitary study), Bachelard passed the *licence* in philosophy. Widowed in the same year, he was left to raise his daughter, Suzanne, alone. He threw himself into his work. Teaching during the day, studying at night, in 1922 Bachelard—now thirty-eight—managed the remarkable feat of preparing alone for, and passing, the *agrégation* in philosophy. His thesis, "Essai sur la connaissance approchée" (Essay on Approximate Knowledge), which founded a new approach to epistemology, was completed in 1927 under Léon Brunschvicq and Abel Rey and awarded "honors with distinction." [45] In 1930, after three years as a lecturer in the Faculty of Letters at the University of Dijon, Bachelard was promoted to the post of professor in philosophy. His work began to garner positive attention. Ten years later he was offered the chair in the history and philosophy of science vacated by Rey at the Sorbonne. Bachelard took up residence in Paris on the rue de la Montagne in the Sainte-Geneviève quarter, just steps from his favorite market at Place Maubert. He taught at the Sorbonne from the age of fifty-six until his retirement at seventy in 1954. Eight years later, on 16 October 1962, Bachelard died, leaving a final manuscript—on poetry—unfinished.

Bachelard's early work theorizes the implications of radical developments in twentieth-century physics—from quantum mechanics to relativity theory—for the history and philosophy of science. Intrigued by the move from Newtonian to non-Newtonian mechanics, and from Euclidean to non-Euclidean geometry, Bachelard introduced the concept of cognitive discontinuities in order to explain how scientific breakthroughs are often premised on the rejection of precedent suppositions. [46] Although no direct influence is traceable, Bachelard's idea of the epistemological rupture anticipates the work of Karl Popper and of Thomas Kuhn, whose theory of paradigm shifts is better known among Anglo-American scholarly audiences. Bachelard's fascination with the epistemological rupture—or epistemic break, as it is sometimes called—later proved so fundamental to the work of Foucault that it is often attributed to him.[47]

The publication of *La psychanalyse du feu* (The Psychoanalysis of Fire) in 1938 marked a turning point in Bachelard's work.[48] In this study of eighteenth-century experiments with fire, Bachelard explores how symbolic understandings of fire—as dangerous, purifying, passionate, painful, and living—determined subsequent scientific discourse. The text confirmed his belief that "poetic knowledge of the world precedes, as it should, the reasonable knowledge of objects."[49] From this time forward, Bachelard's work is characterized by its methodological dualism. A prolific scholar, rooted in the traditions of contemporary science, Jungian psychoanalysis, and poetics, Bachelard produced more than ninety publications during his lifetime, including twenty-three books—twelve on the philosophy of science, two on time and consciousness, and nine on poetic imagination. Bachelard's subversive humanism refutes the Cartesian rational subject while simultaneously retaining the notion of the *cogito* and refusing its permanence. As such, his thought is precursor to the "humanist controversy" that later became so central to French philosophical debate. Bachelard's intellectual achievements were remarkable. Yet they alone are not enough to explain his media appeal. The power of his screen presence derived principally from two factors: his extraordinary personal magnetism and his astonishing physical resemblance to the iconic philosophers of old. Both are plainly evident in the interview that he gave with Berger and Dumayet on *Lectures pour tous*.

( · )

When Dumayet opens the program and introduces the evening's books, he deliberately hefts the encyclopedia towards the camera. Tonight's topics, he implies, are of weighty significance. After the classic jacket cover close-up, the camera cuts to a long shot of all three men seated in a semicircle in front of a triple-arched backdrop. Berger explains that the encyclopedia is intended as an overview of philosophy and an introduction to particular philosophers. Religion, also covered in the book, is virtually ignored during the discussion that follows. The

Pierre Dumayet interviewing Gaston Bachelard (with beard) and Gaston Berger. From *Lectures pour tous,* 15 May 1957.

ensuing conversation deals less with any specific text or philosophical system than with the importance of the discipline for the public at large. Thus, Berger acknowledges that he is "associating [the public] with a difficult enterprise," but he insists with evident delight that "philosophy is the business of each one of us." Like a sage adjusting his staff, Bachelard shifts his cane to one side, clasps his hands, and then gravely points out that "this type of book is not intended solely for readers who are purely and simply philosophers." Dumayet later concurs: "What hit me about this enormous volume is that it is *readable*." Leaning forward, his head tilted to one side, palms touching, Dumayet emanates deference. And whereas Berger is animated, punctuating his phrases with sweeping gestures, it is Bachelard who clearly holds the power. Settled heavily in his chair, he speaks only when spoken to, but when he does, his eyes are radiant, and his whole being seems to incarnate intelligence and an indulgent amusement regarding the circumstances in which he finds himself. Initially, the camera opposes medium shots of Berger and Bachelard against shots of Dumayet, but as the program progresses, the camera is repeatedly drawn to Bachelard alone. When it zooms in, it seems to fawn over the details of his face and hands.

Bachelard in close-up. From *Lectures pour tous*, 15 May 1957.

Because Bachelard is merely one of many philosophers involved in the production of the encyclopedia, his presence on *Lectures pour tous* is intrinsically interesting—especially since he is not questioned about his own contribution to the volume. With no public political affiliations, and no fictional, theatrical, or journalistic publications to his name (unlike Sartre, Camus, Aron, and Beauvoir), Bachelard was not well known to French audiences. Nonetheless, his physical presence performs a decisive function. He is the *embodiment of philosophy*— philosophy signified. His aged face, tufted beard, broad forehead, halo of white hair, mischievous eyes, and aura of wisdom—all so suggestive of the classical Greek image of the philosopher—confirm intellectuals' fears about the seductive visual powers of television. The camera adores him. Not one word of his work is read or even referred to, yet the results are captivating. Through his physical presence alone, Bachelard strengthens the message of the interview, visually linking contemporary discussions of philosophy to a revered classical past.[50] His televised image also serves his personal legacy and acts as a symbolic site for the national affirmation of an endangered cultural ideal.

Why endangered? We shall see in chapter 3 how the rapid pace of postwar transformation challenged French national identity and tested traditional values. Philosophers were flourishing outside the academy as journalists and cultural celebrities, but new economic opportunities in the worlds of business and science meant that in the rapidly expanding lycées and universities technical skills had begun trumping classical education. The nation's demand for young technocrats and the rise of the social sciences imperiled traditional disciplinary hierarchies. Bachelard, Berger, and Dumayet were involved in a process of cultural advocacy and democratization. The push to promote a generalized education in philosophy seen in the *Lectures pour tous* interview (and increasingly on television at large), must be understood as part of an effort to preserve traditional culture in the face of social change. The state broadcaster's didactic character supported this stance. At the same time, as Bachelard's majestic presence illustrates, in shifting the public's attention from text to visual technology, TV helped preserve traditional culture while launching itself as a new force in French intellectual life.

## Raymond Aron, Political Savant

Despite their dynamic presence in the press, philosophers rarely appeared on camera as either political commentators or activists during the early years of French TV. Indeed, between 1949 and 1969 there were only eighteen occasions (9% of total coverage) when a philosopher was shown on television in an overtly political capacity.[51] The philosopher, sociologist, and intellectual Raymond Aron was responsible for eight such occasions. These include six interviews on *Lectures pour tous,* all broadcast between 1959 and 1964 in the budding years of de Gaulle's political regime.[52] Since Aron was hardly the only philosopher producing politically committed work at this time, his presence as the lone intellectual on French TV speaking to political issues during the early Fifth Republic testifies both to his early political formation and to the politics governing broadcasting under de Gaulle's tenure.

Aron was born in 1905—the same year as Jean-Paul Sartre—into a bourgeois Jewish family, and like Sartre (his schoolmate and friend until a longstanding political quarrel almost severed their ties) he was an *agrégé* in philosophy and a graduate of the École normale supérieure.[53] After studies as a *normalien,* as students and graduates of that institution were informally called, and a brief stint in the military, Aron obtained a post under Léo Spitzer as a teaching assistant at the

University of Cologne. He attributes his political awakening to the three years between 1930 and 1933 that he spent in Germany. The following year he replaced Sartre at a lycée in Le Havre, when Sartre left for a year's study in Berlin. Aron's 1938 dissertation on the objective limits of historical understanding, published in English as *Introduction to the Philosophy of History,* reflects the political impact of his exposure as an intellectual, a philosopher, and a Jew to a Germany slowly succumbing to the menace of national socialism.[54] With the French defeat of 1940, Aron fled to London, where André Labarthe immediately engaged him as a writer for de Gaulle's political newspaper, *La France libre.* Following the liberation, Aron returned to Paris and began establishing a name for himself as a political journalist and commentator. He worked first for Camus and Pascal Pia at *Combat.* From 1947, Aron wrote for the more conservative paper *Le Figaro,* a post he abandoned in 1977 for *L'express,* to which he contributed regularly until his death. Aside from an early interest in socialism and a brief period between 1948 and 1952 when he was a militant member of the pro-Gaullist RPF, Aron refrained from associating definitively with any one political party. An intensely private man whose personal life was marred by tragedy (one daughter died at six of leukemia, another was born with Down's syndrome), Aron was described as reserved by his friends, cold and unfeeling by his adversaries. Elected to a chair in sociology at the Sorbonne, Aron returned to academia in 1955 after a long hiatus. By 1960 he had gone on to direct studies at the École pratique des hautes études, and from 1970 until his promotion to professor emeritus in 1981, Aron held the post of professor of the sociology of European civilization at the Collège de France.[55]

By the 1960s, Aron was a towering figure in intellectual circles worldwide. In addition to his prolific output as a journalist and academic (he authored forty books and thousands of articles), Aron made numerous television appearances between 1959 and his death in 1983.[56] Yet, despite widespread acclaim and substantial media exposure, for many years Aron was something of a pariah in his own country. His status as an outcast devolved from his politics, politics that often rendered him odious to the French intellectual left while at the same time ensuring the circumspect and sometimes troubled admiration of de Gaulle and the Gaullists. Michel Contat noted that Sartre and Aron constituted "the two poles between which the intellectual debate of the century has been stretched to the breaking point."[57] For if Sartre represented the dominant strain of postwar French intellectual left thought—revolutionary, anti-imperialist, and anti-American—Aron stood as a staunch Tocquevillian liberal in a Marxist age.[58]

On 30 January 1963, Aron made his fifth appearance on *Lectures pour tous* in an interview with Desgraupes in order to discuss his recently published *Dix-huit leçons sur la société industrielle* (Eighteen Lessons on Industrial Society).[59] Conceived at the time of Stalin's death and Khrushchev's speech to the Twentieth Party Congress, but prior to the Polish and Hungarian revolutions of 1956, the monograph (originally published in 1956 under another title)[60] was based on the first course that Aron had given at the Sorbonne in the winter of 1955–56. The book synthesizes his prewar research on the philosophy of history with his postwar interest in economic and social development. Aron's heuristic use of the concept of industrial society (which he describes alternately as "technical, scientific, or rationalized society") draws on the work of Saint-Simon and Auguste Comte, and the book includes sections on Tocqueville, Marx, and Montesquieu. Following Comte, Aron contrasts industrial society, organized around different economic systems of labor and production, with traditional society, whose organizing principles were military and religious. He maintains that Western and Marxist models of industrial society have far fewer rudimentary differences than the doctrine of Marxism would lead us believe. "Modern economies," he explains in his *Memoirs,* "despite the diversity of regimes and ideologies, contain common characteristics, particularly the potential for growth." The Soviet Union, with its "triumphant production of the rates of growth of gross national product," posed "a challenge to the West."[61] *Dix-huit leçons sur la société industrielle* is Aron's response to this challenge and his attempt to compare and evaluate Western capitalism and Soviet communism as optimal models for industrial society at the height of the cold war.

The *Lectures pour tous* interview opens with the requisite book cover shot, after which Desgraupes, in close-up, cautions the viewer "not to be frightened by this intellectual work," since it pertains to "a problem of burning relevance," the " 'match' between capitalist and Soviet socialist society." His prefatory comment again reveals an overriding concern among television professionals: accessibility. The camera pulls back to encompass both speakers.[62] Articulate and modulated, Aron projects calm erudition and the self-assurance characteristic of former *normaliens.* His delivery is rapid-fire. Opposite, Desgraupes is attentive, focused—and clearly at ease. It is evident that these men are not strangers. The interview summarizes the book in a straightforward

Pierre Desgraupes interviewing Raymond Aron. From *Lectures pour tous,* 30 January 1963.

fashion. Aron explains that the differences between industrial and traditional society are more important than differences internal to industrial society, that is, the differences between capitalism and communism. Nevertheless, as Desgraupes notes, the book "calls certain key ideas of Marxism into question," particularly the concept of surplus value. Smiling slightly, Aron agrees. Comparing capitalist and Marxist approaches to investment and production, Aron demonstrates the superiority of the capitalist model. "A few years of economic progress in a capitalist system," he asserts, "is better for the masses overall than socialism." Warming to his subject, Aron contrasts industrialized countries with those in the third world. The camera alternates from one man to the other, the shots continuously tightening until Aron's face fills the screen. Framed in tight profile, Aron discusses Marxism as ideology: "For my students," he concludes, "I try to teach them to read *Capital*. And for my readers, I try to get them to reflect on ideologies that are at once unreasonable and powerful." The interview culminates with a close-up of the book.

The Aron interview plainly carried out its aim: to inform the public about a book of sociology and political philosophy. In promoting a product, however, *Lectures pour tous* also communicated a pressing political argument about the importance of capitalism to industrial society and economic progress. The broadcast attacked the ideology of Marxism and endorsed consumption, so essential to the success of France's postwar economic recovery. From a Gaullist perspective, with the socialists and communists (previously divided over the Algerian war) beginning a tentative rapprochement in 1963, and the state alarmed at the possibility of a new union of the left, Aron's message was politically useful.[63] Television, with its penchant for extreme close-ups, strengthened and supported his argument. The implication was that the message was as honest and self-evident as the messenger.

As political messengers go, however, Aron was far from straight-forward. His stance vis-à-vis Gaullism was extremely complex. At times, he supported the Gaullist agenda (as when he had worked under de Gaulle in London on the production of *La France libre* and during his brief association with the RPF), but at other times his views differed.[64] He came out in favor of decolonization in 1956, years before de Gaulle himself. But his description of de Gaulle as "the best possible monarch in the least bad of possible governments" revealed the wavering of his allegiance.[65] In turn, Aron's personally "dubious" politics led de Gaulle himself to reportedly state, "He has never been a Gaullist."[66] Nevertheless, Aron respected the General, and the General (notwithstanding occasional appearances to the contrary) returned the sentiment.[67]

Aron embraced television, and it seems likely that his recurrent presence on the small screen during the late 1950s and early 1960s was due to a felicitous combination of political, administrative, and personal factors. (Decades later, in 1980, when asked if he would agree to film a three-part television documentary about his life, Aron responded, "Television amuses me, why not?".)[68] While Dumayet maintains that guest selection on *Lectures pour tous* was an entirely private (and surprisingly casual) affair, both professional and personal politics helped determine whether invitations were issued, and once issued whether they were accepted or (as with Sartre and a few others) denied.[69] Aron's professional involvement with Alain Peyrefitte, minister of information in charge of television from 1962 to 1966, and the support of his former colleague, avowed Gaullist and television programming director Albert Ollivier, was probably influential in this regard. In fact, almost immediately after Ollivier's death in 1964, Aron's television appearances declined. His decreased television presence over the next several years was also the result of his shifting politics. During the final years of de Gaulle's presidency, Aron notes, "political and media circles were aware of my 'anti-Gaullism,' and they attributed to the general a particular hostility toward me—with some exaggeration. Television producers hesitated to interview me, even on the subjects of my books."[70] Following a final broadcast appearance in February of 1965, Aron was absent from television until December of 1969.[71] It took the departure of a president to permit his return.

If, on the one hand, Aron's early television career reflected the political pulse of the times, on the other hand it introduced TV audiences to intellectuals as political actors. As de Gaulle (that master of television performance) so clearly understood, it also fostered a public response that equated the visual representation of intellectual charisma with political integrity. The fact that in this case the philosopher/sage—and not the politician—was seen as the font of this political knowledge reinforced the ethical power of the prose.

## Michel Foucault: Philosophy as Act

Gallimard's publication in April of 1966 of Foucault's *Les mots et les choses* (translated as *The Order of Things*) in Pierre Nora's new series *Bibliothèque des sciences humaines* was heralded as a major philosophical event.[72] From the lyrical opening discussion of Velázquez's *Las meninas* to the now famous closing paragraph cryptically announcing the death of man, this erudite and exceedingly complex book, a self-proclaimed "archeology of the human sciences," became the talk of the town, the coffee table must-have. Its first printing of three thousand copies sold out within days, before any reviews had appeared in the press.[73] By June, in the midst of the growing media whirlwind, Dumayet asked Foucault to appear on *Lectures pour tous*.[74] The invitation, as Foucault must have known, was a marketing coup, since by this time the potential commercial impact of such an appearance was well known. Two months later *Le nouvel observateur* reported that *Les mots et les choses* was still "selling like hotcakes," and by mid-August—along with an equally surprising text, Jacques Lacan's *Écrits*—it made *L'express*'s nonfiction bestseller list.[75] To his astonishment, Foucault had written one of the most popular books of the year.

When the success of *Les mots et les choses* thrust him into the cultural limelight in the spring of 1966, Foucault was hardly unknown among scholarly circles. Born on 15 October 1926 into a bourgeois family in Poitiers, Paul-Michel Foucault belonged to that generation of young people who came to maturity in the aftermath of WWII. Following the Liberation, Foucault was sent to Paris and enrolled at the Lycée Henri IV.[76] It was at this time that he came under the tutelage of the philosopher Jean Hyppolite, who, along with Georges Canguilhem, would exert an enduring influence over his intellectual development (and with whom he would appear in his earliest TV broadcasts). After an initial failed attempt, he successfully passed the entrance exam to the École normale supérieure, joining the ranks of *normaliens* in 1946 at the age of twenty. Foucault suffered serious bouts of depression during his years at the ENS (including a suicide attempt), and it is generally assumed that his homosexuality played a role in his psychic malaise. Foucault's later fascination with issues of transgression, delinquency, the limit experience, and the medical gaze can be traced to this formative period, as can his intellectual prowess and prodigious capacity for work.

Over the next several years Foucault obtained a *licence* in philosophy from the Sorbonne (1948) and both a *licence* in psychology (1949) and a *diplôme* in psychopathology (1952) from the Institut de psychologie de Paris. He interned as an informal clinician at the Hôpital Sainte Anne, where he attended the seminars of Jacques Lacan and worked under Georges and Jacqueline Verdeaux in both psychiatric wards and prisons. By the time that Foucault finally passed the *agrégation* in 1951 (once again on a second attempt), he had had considerable experience in the field. He had also been exposed to some of the most powerful minds then working in France. While still at the ENS, Foucault studied under Maurice Merleau-Ponty and formed a fast friendship with Althusser—then the philosophy tutor at the ENS and eight years his senior—whose position he would assume in 1953. It was also during this time that Foucault flirted with communism, joining the approximately 15% of his classmates who belonged to the French Communist Party.[77] Following a brief posting to the faculty of letters at the University of Lille, Foucault left France in 1955. He spent the next five years teaching abroad, first, on the recommendation of Georges Dumézil, in Uppsala, Sweden; then in Poland as the director of the French center at the University of Warsaw; and finally as director of the French institute in Hamburg, Germany. Foucault returned to France in 1960 to take up a position in psychology at the University of Clermont-Ferrand. It was here in 1962, just two years after the publication of his doctoral thesis *Folie et déraison: Histoire de la folie à l'âge classique* (later abridged in English as *Madness and Civilization*), that Foucault was promoted to professor of philosophy.

The 1960s are known as Foucault's "literary period." During these years he wrote extensively on the work of Bataille, Maurice Blanchot, Pierre Klossowski, and Raymond Roussel (about whom he published a book) and engaged with writers associated with the *nouveau roman* (new novel) and the budding literary review *Tel quel*. The middle and late sixties were also the era of Foucault's political awakening: his presence in Brazil when the military government was installed in 1965 as well as his involvement in the student revolts in Tunisia during his two years there (1966–68) were influential in this process. However, in the 1960s Foucault was still far from the politically committed public figure that he later became. And while *Folie et déraison* brought him recognition, admiration, and respect from his peers, he did not yet have the ear—or the eyes—of the general public. Foucault's first substantial engagement with the media nevertheless began at this time. In 1962 he inaugurated a series of radio programs on France Culture on the history of madness and literature. In 1963 he published *Naissance de la clinique* (*Birth of the Clinic*), exploring the concepts of death and disease through a history of Western medicine in the eighteenth and nineteenth centuries. The same year he joined the editing staff of *Critique* (a journal founded by Georges Bataille and edited by Jean Piel), a position he would retain until 1977. In 1965 he made his first television appearances: an interview on philosophy and psychology with Alain Badiou; and a conversation about philosophy and truth with Badiou, Hyppolite, Canguilhem, Paul Ricoeur, and Dina Dreyfus. Both programs were part of the educational series on philosophy (analyzed in the next chapter) produced by the educational wing of the French broadcasting service, Radio-télévision scolaire (RTS).[78] Throughout this time Foucault also widened his journalistic purview, writing for scholarly journals such as *La nouvelle revue française, L'arc, Tel quel* and *La quinzaine littéraire*—all in addition to *Critique,* mentioned above. With the publication of *Les mots et les choses* in 1966, Foucault found himself at the center of a highly publicized media debate over the methodological hotbed known as structuralism. It was only then that his work began to appear in newspapers, weekly magazines (*Le monde, L'express, Le nouvel observateur*) and television shows aimed at broader audiences.[79]

*Les mots et les choses* is widely conceded to be an extremely difficult read. What exactly is the project of the book? Simply put, its goal is to reveal what Foucault calls the *"positive unconscious* of knowledge," that is, the cultural codes implicitly imposing order on existence.[80] It was "a history of order" an exploration of "how a society reflects upon resemblances among things and how differences between things can be mastered, organized into networks" and "sketched out according to rational schemes."[81] Focusing on man as a speaking, working, and living being, Foucault constructs an "archeology of the human sciences" by investigating the Western construction of three discursive fields: language, labor, and life. He employs the term *epistēmē* to refer to the "historical a priori" that defines the conditions of possibility circumscribing what can be thought within specific fields of knowledge during specific historical periods. Setting aside questions of causality, Foucault seeks to describe the mutations between *epistēmē*s, mutations he explicitly recognizes, in the Bachelardian tradition, as arbitrary and discontinuous. The text focuses on "two great discontinuities in the *epistēmē* of Western culture": that between the Renaissance and the classical age (with the classical defined as mid-seventeenth to the end of the eighteenth century) and that which inaugurates the modern age at the beginning of the nineteenth century.[82] Foucault's analysis moves from general grammar, wealth, and natural history in the classical age to philology, political economy, and biology in the modern one.

As part of this larger project, Foucault develops an argument that "man is a recent invention," conceived at the beginning of the nineteenth century, contemporaneous with the production of the human sciences. By this, Foucault means quite simply that whereas in the classical *epistēmē* man was "absent" as the central focus of knowledge, at the beginning of the nineteenth century man was recognized in his factual and contingent existence as both subject and object of inquiry. The apotheosis of *Les mots et les choses* occurs when Foucault broaches a third epistemic rupture—visible in the discourses of psychoanalysis, linguistics, and ethnology—between the modern and the contemporary period, which he situates in the middle of the twentieth century. It is this rupture that heralds the key problematic that was to cause such controversy: the proclamation of the "death of man."[83]

Even reductive summations such as those proffered above invariably run aground on the work's conceptual complexities and perplexing prose. How could the "vulgarizing medium" of television address a philosophical work of this nature? One of my major contentions in the present book is that because of a confluence of factors—temperate pacing, dialogic interview structure, cultural and pedagogical imperatives, an intimate visual style, and altered audience expectations—early French television was particularly suited to the demands of philosophical thought. Another, already noted, is that philosophy's dual nature as both text and performative act made it uniquely suited to the demands of the medium, and particularly to the television book show. While other scholars appear on the small screen as writers, political actors, celebrities, or even cultural signifiers, philosophers are uniquely capable of using television to demonstrate a discipline in the act of its own becoming—philosophy as intellectual process. Foucault's appearance on *Lectures pour tous* on 15 June 1966 provides one of the first examples of this phenomenon. Because *Les mots et les choses* is such a dense and difficult text, the interview also presents an excellent opportunity to confront those prejudices that deem the marriage of philosophy and TV either impossible or blasphemous.

The interview is among the earliest instances of broadcast coverage of Foucault. When the segment begins, the cover of *Les mots et les choses* appears on the screen, followed by a medium close-up of Dumayet, directly facing the camera. Addressing Foucault, he begins, "You have written what you describe as a work of ethnology, an ethnology of our own culture. What can you tell us about it?" Dumayet is polite, but exhibits no deference. Foucault, who has yet to establish the formidable reputation he will later acquire, knows that he is being sized up and seems intent on making his mark. The camera cuts to an over-the-shoulder shot of Dumayet with Foucault in the background, facing us. Foucault clasps his hands energetically together, and begins to speak. He is animated, bubbling with excitement, rarely pausing for breath. With tremendous concentration, he carefully elaborates the principal concept he is interested in exploring: that knowledge is culturally and historically defined by a series of a priori categories that necessarily determine what it is possible to know. The problem so framed is both stunningly simple and extremely intricate. Foucault speaks at some length of his desire to "consider our own culture as something utterly foreign to us," as if "we were strangers to ourselves." This attempt to take "Western culture" as the object of study is inherently circuitous. "It requires," Foucault insists, "an utter contortion, a doubling back of our faculty of reason upon itself." Reason, he continues, "must move outside of itself; it must turn itself, like a glove, inside out—it is this effort, it is the beginning of this effort, that I am concerned with."

"And who," Dumayet inquires, "would be the ideal ethnologist for this work?" After slyly suggesting that Martians might do the job

well, Foucault avers that we ourselves are the ones best suited to the task. He explains that we alone exercise the singular option of knowing ourselves from the inside out, subjectively, while at the same time analyzing ourselves from the outside in, objectively—thus taking ourselves, "man," as at once object and subject of knowledge. Within the program's first few moments, in one staccato rush of language and enthusiasm Foucault has engaged both the question of the archeology of knowledge and the problem of man and his "empirico-transcendental doublet."[84] Throughout, Foucault's body is feral, coiled, leaning frequently forward, his energy propelled towards Dumayet. The camera focuses repeatedly on his hands as they dance to his argument, clenching, clasping, spreading, and emphatically marking each point.

Michel Foucault and Pierre Dumayet discussing *Les mots et les choses*. From *Lectures pour tous*, 15 June 1966.

Dumayet speaks little, intervening rarely, but his questions are incisive, "What idea of man do you have?" he asks. Foucault responds, "Well, I believe that man, if not a bad dream, if not a nightmare, is at the very least a very particular figure, very historically determined, situated at the interior of our culture." "Paradoxically," he asserts, "the development of the human sciences is conducting us now far more towards the disappearance of man than towards his apotheosis."

Foucault's dialogue with Dumayet is anything but facile, and the problems confronted are philosophically and epistemologically challenging. The Renaissance tradition of humanism is refuted: "It is a notion of recent date." The search for an archeology of knowledge is explained: "That which is lived by man is nothing but a sort of scintillating surface, with great formal systems of thought lying beneath it." The death of God is discussed: "This immense absence of the Supreme Being became the space of freedom." Philosophy itself, Foucault declares, "is disappearing," dissolving into "an age of pure thought, of thought in action" in which linguistics, logic, and literature ("since Joyce") will displace what was previously philosophy's domain. "Not," he specifies, "that they will take its place, but that they will in some sense themselves *be* the actual deployment" of philosophic thought. In conclusion, Foucault provocatively suggests that perhaps reason itself has an agenda far different from that of "prescribing to men what they should do." Foucault in action is a superb combination of philosophical brilliance and personal magnetism. The camera courts him, and Foucault, repeatedly captured in close-up and ever the consummate performer, complies. The spectacle is nothing short of dazzling.

The *Les mots et les choses* interview contradicts the assumption that television cannot provide a venue for complex philosophical discussion. In the space of fifteen minutes, Foucault poses an epistemological problem about the nature of man and attempts to demonstrate the radically contingent character of philosophical "truths." His vigorous delivery dictates the shape of the interview and masterfully embroiders its contents. Yet, if the responsibility for the success of this interview as a demonstration of philosophy in action lay first with the interviewee, a number of elements enabled the process. The interview structure mimicked a classical philosophical model: as in Socratic dialogue, one figure posed questions, the other responded—only here, as in Voltaire, the figures were reversed, with Dumayet playing Candide to Foucault's Pangloss. (In the Socratic tradition, it is the master who questions, and the student who responds). Temporal factors were certainly at play, with the uninterrupted broadcast supporting the development of sustained arguments. And, as with the obituary format discussed above, the program's audience, unaccustomed to "sound bites," split-second edits, and visual pyrotechnics, *watched* differently—with a degree of patience and constancy necessary for the consumption of intellectual programming. Technically, the camerawork enhanced Foucault's impact. The tight focus on his face, the close-ups of his hands, the studied framing of his dynamic—this deeply physical performance infused his language with movement, rhythm, and life. And, of course, the segment would never have aired at all without the French social imperative that demanded the televised transmission of traditional cultural forms.

Almost forty years later I asked Dumayet whether he believed that it was possible to learn philosophy from television. "I don't think so," he replied. "What we can do, however, is give demonstrations of this way of thinking. I think Foucault is an excellent example. Foucault was simple; [. . .] we watch him speak for ten minutes, we understand, we easily see that he doesn't speak like anyone else at all and that he has great form—like an athlete running." Dumayet softens, his voice lost in memory, "Foucault's conceptual form was superb." Nevertheless, he continues, "we cannot learn to do philosophy in fifty-two minutes or even in twice that. What we *can* do is touch people, if you will, or something akin to that. We can get you *interested* in philosophy." [85]

## "These are shows for cultivated folks"?

*Lectures pour tous* was produced in response to a national mission bent on exploiting television technology for the democratization of French education and culture. The show "embodied" the book and focused on the author, in hopes of personalizing high culture and rendering it both more attractive and more accessible to the nation's citizens. By 1964, Dumayet and Desgraupes (crowned "Terrorists of the Interview" by *Les nouvelles littéraires*) were hailed—over Sartre, Mauriac, Jean Cocteau, and Louis Aragon—as the new arbiters of intellectual power. "No one in France," the journal asserted, "has ever exerted so weighty an influence on the popularity of a book, the launching of a writer, or the demolition of a young career." [86] From this time forth, television personalities exercised unprecedented control over French intellectual life. For intellectuals, TV appearances became de rigueur. As we have seen, philosophers were well positioned to capitalize on this demand. Magnetic performances were symbolically resonant and commercially powerful, destabilizing the hierarchies that traditionally determined the attribution of intellectual value. Scheduled during primetime, and broadcast without interruption to viewers still awed by the new technology, *Lectures pour tous* set the standard for quality intellectual and cultural programming. Its influence on the publishing market (despite the show's professed disregard for publicity) was indisputable. (By the 1980s, Bernard Pivot's book show *Apostrophes* further underscored the importance of such television exposure.) But did the program really reach new audiences and achieve its stated agenda of spreading the influence of French high culture? Or did it merely preach to the converted?

( · )

The actual impact of *Lectures pour tous,* despite its brilliant reputation, remains ambiguous. In a series of interviews about popular attitudes towards television conducted by Janine Brillet for *Télé 7 jours* in 1962 and 1963, workers from the Renault factory, department store saleswomen, and coal miners all testified to their interest in the show.[87] But in a 1955 *télé-club* survey on the influence of television on the education of the working class, Joffre Dumazedier argued that among rural populations *Lectures pour tous* incited "almost completely negative reactions—in fact, *none* of the small farmers or laborers approved" of the show. "It seems that this type of programming," Dumazedier continued, "can address only a very restricted circle of French people, who have retained from *lycée* or high school the taste for literary studies or for games founded on intellectual allusions."[88] In a 1961 broadcast on the impact of TV on French society, an elderly farmer from Strasbourg (who chose to appear in full World War II military regalia) bashfully admitted, "We tune in—we tune in to the German broadcasts because in France there are mostly things that don't interest us so much, they seem bourgeois, so we're less interested, there are things that seem too difficult for us."[89] Producers André Harris and Alain Sedouy argued that television would never serve French society if it didn't stop forcing a dead nineteenth-century culture aimed at an elite down the throats of a public for whom this culture totally lacked pertinence or meaning.[90] Cultural shows, concurred the socialist critic Georges Hercet in 1969, "are made by the elite for the elite in an elite language; we're not going to bring about any meetings between elite culture and the masses here. [. . .] Most of the time, the workers and peasants aren't interested in these shows. They say humbly (and I don't blame them), that 'these are shows for cultivated folks' or 'reserved for certain people,' and they change the channel."[91]

With the war well over, the country on the road to economic recovery, and the education of the nation once again a central concern, throughout the 1960s the state ignored its critics and ceaselessly exhorted television professionals to harness the new technology as an elevating cultural force. In response, some television professionals dropped populist agendas altogether and came out in defense of elite broadcasts. Television should nurture heterogeneity, producer and host

Etienne Lalou staunchly maintained, the better to reflect a society that was less and less homogeneous. Calling *Lectures pour tous* "one of the best shows on television," Lalou acknowledged that it was "an intellectual program made by intellectuals, with intellectuals, for intellectuals." However, he continued, "We've reproached its authors enough under the pretext that *Lectures pour tous* [all] is really only addressed to a minority of spectators and better merits the title *Lectures pour quelques-uns* [a few]." In forty-five hours of programming, Lalou queried, "Can't television offer itself the luxury of a one-hour broadcast of the first order that *does not* address all of France? Where would we be if programs were authorized to run only if they captured 60% or 70% of the viewing public?" [92]

Lalou's perspective was persuasive to some, but the fact was that audience size was becoming increasingly pertinent to government officials. And there was no doubt that, as far as *Lectures pour tous* was concerned, over the term of its run audiences were estimated to have declined precipitously, from a high of 50% in 1958 to a low of 5% in 1967.[93] Granted, these figures are somewhat deceptive; as noted in my introduction, in gross numbers the size of the public was increasing while a greater number of viewing options—especially after the addition of Channel 2 in 1964—created competition and reduced the percentage of the public watching a particular show at any given time. But reports of popular disinterest in cultural programming were taken seriously. Adapting supply to demand was not an option.[94] As far as both the government and most television administrators were concerned, once quality programming existed, the only major problem on the table was getting the public to watch—and value—the shows.[95] If anything, resistance to cultural TV was interpreted as a justification for the continuation of the state monopoly. Education would render the masses both capable of appreciating and actually desirous of tuning in to cultural broadcasts.[96] Many believed that education in *philosophy* was an important part of this didactic agenda. But, as chapter 3 illustrates, philosophy's place in the new national order was far from secure. It was precisely at this moment that a committed group of educators turned to television to help justify philosophy's continued relevance for French society.

( · )

*Lectures pour tous* aired its final broadcast on 15 May 1968. The program was disrupted by the "May events." In support of the student uprising and in protest against government censorship and lack of television coverage of the conflict, members of the ORTF walked off the job from 13 May to 23 June. Desgraupes, Dumayet, and Fouchet (then president of the National Producer's Union) were among the strikers. *Lectures pour tous* was one of many programs canceled in the wave of governmental reprisals that followed the restoration of order.[97] Despite its untimely demise, it left a rich record of French cultural programming. Under its influence, the television book show became a staple programming genre, and the philosopher a familiar figure on French television.

# From Educational Television to Cultural Spectacle, 1964–1974

Descartes once said that "living without philosophy is like living with one's eyes closed and never attempting to open them." This quotation accompanied the opening credits of over forty programs on philosophy produced for national broadcast between 1964 and 1970 by the educational branch of the French public television administration, Radio-télévision scolaire (RTS).[1] Filmed in 16mm black and white and lasting approximately thirty minutes each, the series was directed primarily by Jean Fléchet and conceived by Dina Dreyfus, general inspector of philosophy for the Académie de Paris and—it is worth noting—the first wife of Claude Lévi-Strauss. Intended for viewing within the context of lycée classrooms under the guidance of an instructor, the shows were nevertheless open-circuit broadcasts available to the public at large. The program's objectives were threefold: to show students that "there is a city of philosophers" extending beyond the borders of the educational institution; to familiarize students with fundamental philosophical questions; and to show them, through example, philosophy in action. The broadcasts featured some of France's greatest living philosophers. Foucault, Aron, Jean Hyppolite, Georges Canguilhem, Michel Serres, Paul Ricoeur, and many others are all represented here.[2] Titled *L'enseignement de la philosophie* (The Teaching of Philosophy), the series also generated the first sustained intellectual inquiry into the problems posed by attempts to bring philosophy to television.

The same year that Dreyfus was busy preparing the opening season of *L'enseignement de la philosophie,* the newly developed research division of the ORTF known as the Service de la recherche began broadcasting a cultural magazine called *Un certain regard* (A Certain Perspective).[3] The program, which aired one Sunday per month from 1964 through 1974 and generally lasted between forty-five minutes and an hour, initially explored the aesthetics of the television medium (with programs on such topics as the camera, the image, and the interview).[4] By 1967 however, the program turned its attention to a new theme: major currents in twentieth-century thought.[5] Over the course of the next seven years, *Un certain regard* produced a number of important documentaries on major philosophers and other intellectuals.[6] Through specials on such figures as Bachelard, Aron, Emmanuel Mounier, Jacques Lacan, György Lukács, Georg Picht, Georges Dumézil, Hannah Arendt, Bertrand Russell, and Claude Lévi-Strauss, *Un certain regard* sought to create an audiovisual archive of the greatest thinkers of the contemporary age.[7] Despite the rapid spread of the TV documentary format, in no other country has television been used to capture the lives of philosophers in such a systematic fashion. Likewise, while educational television existed throughout the industrialized world by 1960, educational programs on philosophy are virtually unprecedented outside of France.[8] Why did this esoteric subject and its practitioners become an important part of both French educational programming and the national broadcasting agenda at this time? And what can an examination of these programs tell us, not only about the objectives of this investment, but also about broader transformations in the constitution of contemporary French society?

## Imperial Television: Colonizing the *Métropole*

The French defeat at Dien Bien Phu in 1954 signaled the beginning of the end of one of the world's most extensive colonial empires—second only to that of Britain. The ink was still wet on the Geneva Accords establishing the independence of Indochina when a series of terrorist bombs exploded in Algeria, marking the onset of the Algerian War. And Algeria was not alone in pursuing self-governance. Within two years, France had relinquished control over both Morocco and Tunisia. As its colonies clamored for independence, France was forced to confront a moral conundrum: How could a nation whose modern political heritage was premised on the exercise of universal rights practice colonial domination? When the bloodshed in Algeria escalated, the ideologically conflicted empire disintegrated. Political instability shattered the Fourth Republic and brought de Gaulle to power. Both the Organisation de l'armée secrète (OAS)—determined to keep Algeria French—and their opponents, the Front de libération nationale (FLN) propelled the violence home to the mainland. French police massacred over two hundred pro-FLN demonstrators in Paris in October of 1961. Eight months earlier, eight people had been killed at the Charonne metro station in an anti-OAS rally. Such incidents, combined with growing disagreement over both the country's reliance on French draftees to fight its colonial battles and the army's use of torture against the FLN and its supporters, ensured that problems in the colonies and the overseas departments were experienced as immediate, consequential, and viciously divisive within the *métropole,* or mother country. By the time de Gaulle held a national referendum on the question of Algerian self-determination in January 1961, the tide of public opinion had turned. With the signing of the Evian Accords in March 1962, France granted Algeria formal independence. Divested of its empire, France turned its gaze inward.

Empire is no longer viewed as a system in which change radiates inexorably outward from the *métropole* to the colonies. Indeed, a now substantial body of scholarship argues against this center-periphery model, claiming the importance of reciprocity, interdependence, and multidirectionality in colonial histories.[9] Colonial subjects are no longer viewed as the entirely passive victims of coercive force, and European nation-states are increasingly understood as malleable entities that were themselves shaped by the colonial projects they devised. For France, the messy course of decolonization redirected the energies of government administrators towards the interior. Authoritarian techniques for national assimilation originally intended to both instill republican values at home and "civilize" colonial subjects abroad were, I suggest, equally valuable to a modernizing nation whose diversifying population was rapidly multiplying. Intent on stamping out dissenting voices, enforcing unity, and rebuilding national dignity, the French educational project expanded. Educators, supported by Gaullist directives aimed at utilizing television as an instrument of national cohesion, quickly co-opted the emergent mass medium, and philosophical TV soon came into its own. However, as will be seen with the philosophy broadcasts examined below, educational agendas sometimes reinscribed the very differences they sought to efface.

One of the paradoxes of the Fourth Republic is that the tragic events of the wars of decolonization were played out against the beginnings of *les trentes glorieuses*—the most spectacular thirty-year period of economic prosperity that France had ever known. Postwar reconstruction and technological development transformed private life across the economic spectrum. The establishment of an extensive social welfare system created faith in lasting prosperity and saw the working classes purchasing big-ticket items—refrigerators, washing machines, cars, and television sets—on credit. Between 1946 and 1975 the French population grew by twelve million—as much as during the previous century and a half.[10] Demographic change brought problems that were both racial, a result of non-European immigration and the concomitant challenges of integration into the French republican model, and generational, in the wake of the baby boom and the subsequent radical expansion of the student population.[11] Modernization motivated conflicts in the social, intellectual, and academic spheres between tradition and technology, culture and science. Decolonization decisively challenged French national identity and tested traditional values. Moral redemption was vital. The philosophy programs produced on French television during the 1960s and early 1970s were a response to these challenges, and an analysis of their content and conditions of production should illuminate our understanding of the postwar world. But to perform this analysis, we first need to know more about both the history of philosophy within academia, and the history of educational television. Only then can these broadcasts support the exploration of a far more esoteric—and philosophical—problem: What does it mean to televise the mind?

## Philosophy, the Crowning Discipline

France is one of the very few countries where philosophy at the high-school level is required, taught by specially trained professors and evaluated by national, compulsory exams.[12] The discipline's unique status in the French school system is the product of a self-consciously produced and much vaunted correspondence between education and the modern state.[13] As discussed in chapter 1, classes in philosophy were first incorporated into the lycée curriculum under Napoleon I in 1809. Entry to the lycées (which were designed to produce the new bureaucratic elite and train the nation's teachers) was competitive, costly, and limited to males, thus falling far short of the democratic and inclusive ideals ostensibly espoused by the republican model. The philosophy taught in these institutions was informed by a profoundly political agenda: the establishment of ideological, linguistic, and moral unity in a country riven by two decades of violence and political chaos. It also tied together under state control two formerly independent operations: instruction, or the transmission of knowledge, and education, understood as the moral and social edification of the individual, previously under the dominion of the church.[14] A discipline-specific *agrégation* in philosophy was created in 1825. Shortly thereafter (in 1830), instruction in philosophy began to be conducted in French rather than in Latin.

Briefly suppressed with the founding of the Second Empire in 1852, both the *agrégation* and lycée instruction in philosophy were reestablished in 1863 under the direction of the minister of public instruction, Victor Duruy. The philosophy syllabus started to take on its characteristic form. Philosophy professors worked to ensure the supremacy of their discipline, steadfastly incorporating, assimilating, and subduing challenges from the social sciences, modern languages, and science—whose collective growth was supported by the founding, in 1868, of the École pratique des hautes études (EPHE), an experimental research institution divided into four branches: mathematics, physics and chemistry; natural history and physiology; history; and philology, to which a section for the scientific study of religion was added in 1886. The educational reform of 1874 established philosophy as the crowning discipline when the *classe terminale,* or final year of secondary studies, was given over to the subject. The Third Republic saw free, compulsory, secular primary schools founded throughout the nation in 1882 and lycées opened to girls (under the Camille Sée law). Two branches of the École normale supérieure, one at Fontaney and one at Saint-Cloud, were created to serve the higher educational needs of this new female public. Republicans waged a constant struggle against the church for control over the intellectual and moral formation of French youth.[15] With the passage, in 1905, of the law of the separation of church and state, they scored a major victory. For the next seven decades, philosophy's academic dominance remained free of serious challenges.[16]

Philosophy held virtually undisputed pride of place as the educational capstone through World War II. Despite the upheavals of defeat and occupation, the national educational system functioned without disruption, and the teaching of philosophy continued unabated. But in the decades after the war, the *classe de philo* came under attack.

In 1947 the EPHE established its Sixth Section, organized around the social (or human) sciences. While the Sixth Section offered new venues for philosophers (Jacques Derrida later held a post there),[17] its establishment reflected French academia's mounting fascination with a set of disciplines (including sociology, psychology, political science, and economics) that were soon vying with philosophy for students and resources. Lévi-Strauss and Bourdieu counted among those who abandoned formations in philosophy to pursue work in these fields. By the late 1950s, Marxism and structuralism had begun to exert a hegemonic hold over French intellectual life.[18] In 1957, Roland Barthes's *Mythologies* appeared. In 1958, Lévi-Strauss published *Structural Anthropology*. That same year saw the creation of a university degree in sociology. In his 1957 work *Pourquoi des philosophes?* (Why Philosophers?), Jean-François Revel pleaded for the modernization of philosophy with reference to these new domains of knowledge.[19] As discussed in chapter 1, outside the academy philosophers were increasingly recognized as literary celebrities (with Sartre, Beauvoir, the success of *Les temps modernes,* and the cultural phenomenon surrounding existentialism being the most obvious examples of philosophy's heightened popularity), but within the academy the discipline was soon in crisis. With the student population entering a period of unprecedented growth (between 1930 and 1965 the number of *baccalauréats* awarded in France multiplied sevenfold), and with the postcolonial influx of non-European immigrants (most of whom were functionally illiterate) straining the social fabric, this development was rather paradoxical.[20] Given its privileged role as a shaper of national values, dramatic demographic expansion would appear to reinforce, rather than challenge, philosophy's traditional dominance. How, then, could its changing fortunes be accounted for?

The philosopher Louis Althusser, a structuralist Marxist, believed the origin of the discipline's problems came "from the place given philosophy in education by the public powers."[21] The state, Althusser argued, had come to consider studies in philosophy a useless luxury. From a certain perspective, this appears to hold true. By the early years of the Fifth Republic, the French economy was growing at an astounding rate, averaging 5.8% per year between 1958 and 1970. The demands of a modernizing economy wrought havoc on the established hierarchies governing the pedagogical enterprise. The goals of a dirigiste state required bureaucratic expansion. Superpower geopolitics and cold war fears of Americanization propelled French desires for grandeur. Urbanization, industrialization, and technological developments—soon epitomized by de Gaulle's pursuit of a nuclear strike force—made new demands on the workforce. On a pragmatic level, concentrations in mathematics and the hard sciences offered more job opportunities than did the previously venerated domains of philosophy and literature.[22] As the journal *L'éducation nationale* observed, "Some have come to think that the concentration in philosophy is decidedly behind the times in a civilization where the only thing that counts is scientific knowledge."[23]

The quantitative expansion of student populations carried, as Michel de Certeau notes, a qualitative significance: it transformed the relation of culture to society.[24] In the past, restricted access to education had both produced and protected an elite culture. The democratization of education (fueled by the decision to make secondary education free and compulsory at the end of WWII) called the composition of that culture as well as the educational project itself into question.[25] By the 1960s, propelled by a modernizing market economy, education as intellectual and moral formation was pitted against education as vocational training.[26] Certainly, the economy increasingly required the latter, but to presume that the state had entirely jettisoned its previous commitment to philosophical education would also be misleading. Fearful of the threats that modernization and multiculturalism posed to national identity, advocates for philosophy within the Ministry of Education fought hard to promote their field. In her capacity as general inspector, Dina Dreyfus was among those who actively attempted to revitalize the discipline, in part by co-opting the fresh possibilities that television technology provided. Dreyfus's interest in the medium mirrored a broader cross-disciplinary excitement about television's educational potential. However, this excitement was not universally shared. Initially, many either rejected television wholesale or denied its educational promise. What were their claims? And how was television introduced, despite resistance, into the French educational system?

## Broadcasting French Education

"Academics," Henri Dieuzeide (director of both the Service de la Radio-télévision scolaire and its audiovisual laboratory) maintained in 1958, "see the television set as the Pandora's box of this century." They variously characterize television as an "infernal machine" that turns "children into assassins" or as a "terrifying spider" that "sucks the intellectual substance of the nation, destroys the life of the family, ruins civic awareness, [and] causes the loss of all national values."[27] Even American scientists, he noted, have argued that small children who spend too much time in front of the set are vulnerable to deformations of the lower jaw.[28] In France the newspaper *Le soir* alleged that the screen emitted "radio-active gamma rays."[29] Assertions about the medium's negative effects on reading practices were ubiquitous.[30] Meanwhile, "the argument most often advanced by school principals against the installation of television," Dieuzeide disparaged, "is that the antennae attract lightning." "Accept television as a new cultural element? Okay," admitted his fictive protestor. "But introduce the wolf into the sheep pen and television into the school? That's too much!" Where, Dieuzeide asked, does the truth lie in the midst of this maelstrom? He was quick to provide the answer: television is not a diabolical invention but merely a technology, a means of communication, an access to *all* cultural forms. And the French educational system Dieuzeide insisted, "must find its place in this *future balance* between the book and the image." "Education can no longer think of itself outside of television. For better or worse," he continued, "it has absorbed the book. Now it must integrate television."[31]

( · )

Ratifying the intellectual potential of the small screen, educational television was officially established in France on 4 July 1951 by a ministerial decree authorizing the Institut pédagogique national (IPN) the use of two hours of national airtime each week. Radio-télévision scolaire was born.[32] Under the enthusiastic direction of advocates like Dieuzeide, pedagogic programming was soon envisioned as a critical element in "the formation of the future citizen."[33] Twelve years later, in 1963, Christian Fouchet, then minister of national education, launched a plan for the massive exploitation and development of audiovisual resources.[34] In June of that year, Fouchet declared the programs of the RTS an "appreciable aid" to the French school system.[35] Educational programming jumped from five and one-half hours to fourteen hours and twenty minutes per week. Six thousand schools were equipped with television sets. Over one thousand possessed more than one set. By 1966, with fifteen out of a total of sixty hours of weekly airtime, educational television comprised *one-quarter* of all television broadcast nationally in France. At its apogee in 1971–72, the RTS was airing weekly for twenty-two hours and thirty-six minutes. For a time, television seemed to hold the key to the future of education in France.

Educational broadcasts were conceived with three publics in mind: students, as an addition to regular coursework; teachers, as a supplement to pedagogic preparation; and adults, as part of personal or career development. In some ways, the second of these was the IPN's dirty little secret. It was grimly acknowledged that the immense growth in the student population had led to the state's hurried hiring of an inordinate number of teachers who were grossly underprepared.[36] The programs produced for teachers were specifically intended to improve this situation. By the 1960s, a new project was added that aimed to deal with academic insufficiencies of another type. Called *Radio-télé-bac,* it was designed to assist students to prepare at home for the September *baccalauréat* exam. Most of the broadcasts were accompanied by documentation to be used either by the teacher in preparing the class or by the individual student as a study guide.[37] A survey conducted at the end of 1966 deemed the effort a resounding success, and plans were made to expand the project the following year.[38]

( · )

The production process shaping the development of *L'enseignement de la philosophie* followed the template established for educational programming at large. Its path was split between the Ministry of Education and the offices of national television, and it was laced with obstacles ranging from the hostility of academics, teachers, and psychologists, to bureaucratic red tape, insufficient funding, and limited technical resources.[39] The IPN determined program themes and contents. The production and direction were handled by the state television organization (until 1964 the RTF, and from 1964 to 1974 the ORTF). During the 1960s, a professor wanting to produce a program had first to pitch the project to Georges Gaudu, the head of the division of educational television and a filmmaker in his own right. He, in turn, presented it to a committee at the IPN consisting of twenty-two people, including directors, secretaries, eight professors, producers, and assistants. If the project got the green light, it entered preproduction. In addition to fulfilling regular academic duties, the professor (named *producteur libre,* or "freelance producer") was expected to script the show and develop its theoretical agenda. Three archivists provided documentary support, via film footage, still photographs, and books. Financial re-muneration was notoriously scant, provoking strikes in June of 1966. The combination of too much work (an average program required one hundred hours of preparation), too little pay, and insufficient guidance (professors functioned as both producers and actors with little or no formal instruction) resulted in another problem: after participating once, many were reluctant to repeat the experience. Consequently, the IPN was perpetually struggling to attract and train new "recruits"—a situation that made building a stable, experienced professorial body capable of guiding educational television an ongoing challenge. Thus, in terms of the history of the genre, both the longevity (six years) and productivity (over forty programs) exhibited by the philosophy broad-casts produced by Dreyfus and her team were highly unusual.

After a project was approved, it landed on the desk of Serge Grave, the man responsible for technical direction at the RTS who was charged with giving the shows a "telegenic" form. If the professor who had pitched the project did not want to act in it, another professor had to be found (usually from Paris or the surrounding area to reduce trans-portation costs). Grave then headed off in search of a director and an assistant director. Here too, problems frequently arose. TV profession-als considered educational television the dregs of the industry. Thus, although Grave did his best to hire from within the RTF (and later the ORTF), to the union's distress he frequently resorted to graduates of either the cinema school at IDHEC, or the photography school on Rue de Vaugirard.[40] Neophyte graduates from these schools (including the young filmmaker Eric Rohmer, who directed one of Dreyfus's shows) were less inclined to turn up their noses at his offers than were profes-sional directors. They also used the programs as a stepping-stone to the better-paid and more prestigious union jobs in cinema or at the RTF/ORTF.[41]

Once Grave managed to hire his director and a technical team, he had to chase down studios from which to broadcast. The responsibil-ity for providing space for educational television was divided between Paris and (after 1964) the provincial studios in Lille, Lyon, Marseille, and Bordeaux. In the early 1960s, programs produced in Paris were dis-tributed between the studios of the IPN (expected to provide locations for two hours of weekly airtime) and the RTF (which used studios at either Buttes-Chaumont or Cognac-Jay to meet its weekly three-and-one-half-hour quota). Problematically, the latter studios, which were the best equipped, were also in the highest demand since they were needed for the preparation of *all* the national broadcasts airing on Channel 1 (and after its addition in 1964, Channel 2). Costs normally prohibited taping educational programs to film, but occasional exceptions were made when the product was conceded to be of enduring value. Fortunately, several of Dreyfus's shows for *L'enseignement de la philosophie* were among them.[42]

Most programs aired live. With budgets tight and the clock ticking, preparations were minimal. A broadcast that aired between 2:00 p.m. and 2:30 p.m. had often been rehearsed only once, usually earlier that same morning. Finances allocated by the minister of education in 1963 helped to improve audiovisual resources. The relocation of the administrative branch of the RTS to the main buildings of the ORTF and of educational production to the maison de Radio-France, newly constructed on the Quai du Président-Kennedy in the sixteenth arrondissement, not only centralized pedagogical programming within the state television administration but also reflected the growing importance of the genre. However, as an analysis of the philosophy programs of the RTS will reveal, the state's commitment to extending higher education via the small screen was modified by a number of important caveats. It is to these programs and the messages that they contained that we now turn.

### New Publics, Old Masters: Fashioning "Frenchness" through Philosophy

The credit sequence that opens the 1964–65 season of *L'enseignement de la philosophie* captures the pedagogical objectives of the next six years of philosophical programming in France. It also encodes a set of national concerns regarding target audiences. "Philosophy has a life outside our classroom," the title voice-over begins; "A city of philosophers encompasses and nourishes us." The philosophy taught within the hallowed classrooms of the academy is portrayed within a wider world, a world of cafés, bookstores, parks, and city squares. The opening shots—feet walking along the pavement, men strolling deep in conversation, girls hurrying to class, a young man clutching a book as he crosses a busy intersection—situate us immediately. From the views of the Luxembourg gardens to the Place du Panthéon, it is clear that this is Paris. And not just Paris, but (as suggested by the street signs that flash in quick succession across the screen—rue Descartes, rue Pascal,

rue Platon) the city's fifth *arrondissement;* home of the Latin Quarter, an area crowded with France's most prestigious educational institutions, from the Lycée Henri IV and the École normale supérieure to the Collège de France. The very geography of the city seems to render homage to the mind. The subliminal message is that philosophy lives in the wider world, but also that this world is inimitably French.

A professor and a student step through the doors of an academy. White typescript appears on a black background. Title: *L'enseignement de la philosophie.* Cut. A teacher stands before the blackboard, addressing his class. Multiracial pupils—the camera zeros in on a North African girl—listen diligently, their faces depicted in extreme close-up.

Opening sequence for *L'enseignement de la philosophie,* 1965 spring season. (Reproduced by permission of the Centre national de documentation pédagogique.)

The choice informs us that in the postcolonial moment this material is particularly worthy of focus. Cut to a revolving rack outside a bookstore. A young woman chooses a book. Zoom to book jackets: Spinoza, Marx, Teilhard de Chardin. Jump to the bookstore interior. Students browsing. The frame tightens on an Asian boy reading. Works by Hegel, Epicurus, and Bachelard placed out on a table. Title: *An interview between M. Alain Badiou, professor at the lycée in Reims, and . . . .* Cut away to a bust of Plato, a drawing of Descartes, a photo of Marx. Traverse to a girl at a café, her finger brushing across her nose as she pours over her text. Zoom back to the photos. Freud. Bachelard. Sartre. Title: *Jean Hyppolite, professor at the Collège de France.* The clock chimes. Clang. A student enters through a heavy door. Clang. The Sorbonne encased in scaffolding. Clang. End credits. Professor Hyppolite—*normalien, agrégé* in philosophy, scholar of Hegel and Marx, professor at the Sorbonne and the Collège de France, director of the École normale supérieur—lights a cigarette, draws deeply on it, and leans forward towards Alain Badiou, his young interlocutor. The program begins.

What are we to make of this sequence? The opening lasts less than a minute and a half. In ninety seconds the camera has situated youthful fascination with philosophy within a venerable tradition. The individuals depicted are equally significant. They are old and young, male and female, white, black, Arab, and Asian. The mature figures—those shown speaking—are mostly white and male, a point to which I shall return. Since mixed-gender lycées were established in 1925, the images of young girls are unsurprising (all the more so given the feminization of the discipline following the exodus of boys into math and science).[43] However, the presence of racially diverse students raises questions. Throughout the 1970s, most broadcast coverage of non-European immigrants was focused on social problems: employment, housing, and racism.[44] The immigrant was presented as the *object of,* not a *subject in,* the discourse.[45] Families, children, and young people were all but absent. In the images shown here, the mingling of white and nonwhite students as self-possessed social actors underscores the importance of philosophy to multicultural student populations and, in so doing, betrays anxieties about national integration. It also gives a determined (and highly symbolic since almost illusory) nod towards equality of opportunity. And the carefully chosen locations emphasize, from the girl at the café—is it the Deux magots, favorite haunt of Sartre and his contemporaries?—to the façade of the Sorbonne, that if philosophy applies to everyone, regardless of race, gender, or generation, it also offers some sort of ineffable access to "Frenchness." The upshot of all this is an explicit example of the nation-building agenda inherent in the French philosophical project (egalitarian, democratic, republican) as shaped via an elite intellectual corps.

( · )

When Dreyfus first approached Dieuzeide with the idea of creating a series of programs on philosophy for Radio-télévision scolaire, she came eminently qualified for the job.[46] Of Russian extraction, Dreyfus spent her early childhood in Italy. An ardent socialist, committed to democracy and vigilantly antifascist, Dreyfus purportedly fought for the French Resistance during the Second World War under the name Denise Roche. Yet she rarely referred to this period in her life and hardly ever spoke of her association "with one of the major intellectual adventures of the twentieth century—structural anthropology." [47] This "association" had been both professional and deeply personal; while married to Claude Lévi-Strauss, she had collaborated on his studies of the Kaduveo and Bororo Indians in 1935 and 1936. In addition to working in anthropology and ethnography, Dreyfus was an *agrégée* in philosophy and had taught at every level of the French educational system before becoming general inspector in philosophy for the Académie de Paris.[48] Dreyfus was well connected in French intellectual circles. Badiou remembers her as possessed of a brilliant intellect and as an authoritarian, willful character. "She didn't work with people she didn't like," he notes. The philosophy programs of the RTS were shaped by Dreyfus's personal preferences. "And after all," Badiou says in her defense, "that's normal, isn't it? And so we ended up with a circle of philosophers whom she admired and with whom she had personal connections." Canguilhem, Foucault, and Hyppolite were her close friends. When Dreyfus decided to launch her project of televising philosophy, "she simply phoned them," Badiou recalls, "and said (in typically direct fashion), 'I want you to participate in this,' and they all complied." [49] Dreyfus believed that the ideal way to transmit the importance of the philosophical enterprise was to allow students to witness great philosophers in action. Significantly, her choices also served the state, since televising France's great intellectuals reinforced French national pride.

Dreyfus recruited Badiou, then teaching at a boys' lycée in Reims, to host the series. "At base," he told me, Dreyfus's idea was "inspired by the structure of Platonic dialogue. That is to say, a dialogue between an important, respected master and a young person who argues with him and ultimately serves as the mediator between the spectators and the master's discourse." [50] Badiou, twenty-five at the time and a recent graduate of the École normale supérieure, had placed first in the national philosophy *agrégation* and was recognized as a stellar junior scholar. He was a student of Hyppolite's (who knew him well), an acquaintance of Foucault's (whose work he admired), and had written his master's thesis under Canguilhem. Intrigued by the project, honored by the offer, and comfortable with the participants, Badiou agreed to sign on.

Needless to say, Dreyfus's desire to televise philosophy appeared singularly challenging to the RTS's technical staff. As head of educational programming, Georges Gaudu was impressed by the plan but doubted that what he perceived as Dreyfus's rather expansive ambitions could be fulfilled. How could the programs be rendered visually interesting without betraying their intellectual agenda? Would the content be too complex for students to follow? Convinced that the project required someone "with the perspective of a film director," Gaudu contacted the director Jean Fléchet and asked him to take on the project.[51] Trained in cinema at IDHEC, Fléchet had not yet worked in television. But when Dreyfus explained her ideas to him, he was immediately captivated by the challenge of filming thought.

*L'enseignement de la philosophie* was a product of the intellectual collaboration that emerged between Dreyfus and her newfound director. Dreyfus believed that there were two possible models for televising philosophy: the first merely used the medium as a way of documenting pedagogy; the second sought to express the cinematic dimension of the discipline.[52] (Interestingly, many of the directors associated with the film movement known as New Wave—including Jean-Luc Godard, Eric Rohmer, Claude Chabrol, and François Truffaut—were exploring philosophical themes in their work and in the pages of the *Cahiers du cinéma* during precisely the same period—sometimes explicitly so, as in Godard's 1966 *Masculin-féminine*.) While Dreyfus's aims were more aligned with film documentary than anything produced by the New Wave *auteurs*, she disdained the idea that her broadcasts were simply using television to transmit the typical classroom experience or to narrate philosophic texts. For in her eyes these shows didn't "*explain* philosophy"; they were "philosophic conversations."[53] Dreyfus understood the philosophical exchange as a way of existing in community and of bringing communities into existence. She argued, "The professor of philosophy doesn't 'practice dialogue' as an expedient for sparking the flagging attention of sleepy students; nor is he using it a concession to new methods of 'active pedagogy.'" Rather, "Dialogue belongs to the very essence of philosophy itself, because philosophy began and will always begin with the common life of the spirit, a life that is instituted by dialogue."[54] The challenge was to figure out how to "to film philosophers in the process of thinking [. . .], in the exchange of language, which seemed [. . .] to be the very origin of philosophy."[55]

In a twenty-six-page report written at the close of the first season, Dreyfus addressed this crucial problem: "Discourse speaks, it produces meaning; the image shows, it produces presence, contact. The real question, with respect to teaching philosophy [on television], is to know whether there is something to show, and how to show it." [56] Despite admitting that she was unclear about the response, Dreyfus insisted that "contrary to what certain people believe, television has a very special role to play" in this process. [57] Although never directly articulated, Dreyfus's commitment to this idea appears to derive from a belief that philosophy is, among other things, an embodied practice—for it is only when understood in this way that one can presume the discipline's visual dimension. Fléchet was likewise convinced that television was "effective and interesting" for philosophy because it could record thought in action, seizing the phenomenological manifestation of what he termed "the philosophical event" in the "act of its becoming." According to Fléchet, the director's task was to translate philosophy into cinematic performance by revealing it as at once an intellectual and a corporeal drama:

> We have tracked [this event] in the dialogue between two philosophers. It can also exist in monologue: we can imagine a philosopher constructing his thoughts out loud before an attentive camera, not only his words, but also that which is painted on his face, the fire that burns in his eyes. We can even imagine a philosopher expressing his ideas by writing, such that the characters [. . .], their inscription, the hand, the face, the forehead speak.

Determined to "analyze the instrument that is film, the varied possibilities that it offers, and to establish how its new powers might serve philosophic thought," Fléchet set to work. [58]

( · )

"Philosophy makes its entrance into educational television!" trumpeted the 1964 edition of the *Bulletin de la Radio-télévision scolaire*. [59] The goal for the inaugural season was to "put philosophy in the presence of what it is not, in hopes, through this comparison, of throwing a bright light on its actual function." [60] As mentioned earlier, under the influence of a new generation of thinkers the French intellectual climate was shifting. By the 1960s, existentialism, the dominant philosophy of the 1940s and '50s, was on the decline, and structuralism was fast becoming the new model for the explanation of social reality.

With philosophy struggling to ward off such intellectual challenges and to retain its supremacy over the newly powerful fields of mathematics and the social sciences, identifying qualities unique to the discipline was a vital task.[61] The result was the production of six programs that aired on Saturday mornings from ten to ten-thirty between 9 January and 4 June 1965.[62] The six themes were philosophy and history, with Hyppolite; philosophy and science, with Canguilhem; philosophy and sociology, with Aron; philosophy and psychology, with Foucault; philosophy and language, with Ricoeur; and philosophy and truth, with Dreyfus, Hyppolite, Canguilhem, Ricoeur, and Foucault.[63] A final broadcast, "The Teaching of Philosophy on Television: Conclusion and Synthesis," allowed the participants to engage in a philosophical and theoretical exploration of the aims of their TV project.[64] Badiou presided on all seven shows as host, interviewer, and mediator.

A self-reflexive approach is abundantly evident on the programs. Philosophy, the participants argue, is essential to a modernizing nation because it provides the framework through which all other fields of knowledge are produced, tested, and known. Thus, in "Philosophy and Science," Canguilhem asserts that science needs philosophy since it "does not contain within itself the interrogation of its own meaning." Similarly, in "Philosophy and Psychology," Foucault defends philosophy as "the most universal cultural form through which the Occident reflects upon itself." Philosophy alone applies to all other discourses because, as Ricoeur explains in "Philosophy and Language," "it is only in philosophical reflection and speculation that all the problems of signification and meaning within other disciplines reflect upon themselves." "In sum," Badiou concludes in the final program of the first season, "philosophy is a totalizing center for the experiences of an epoch."[65]

With slight variations, the shows produced for the 1964–65 season were all shot in a similar, straightforward fashion. Fléchet employed three cameras; one focused on each interlocutor and a third on the two participants together. His original goal was simply to capture the philosophic conversation as faithfully as possible. The faces of the philosophers were intended as the sole décor. Fléchet believed that television's "apparently contradictory powers," of "extreme intimacy" and "extreme disclosure" could be relied on to offer "a much more profound and true vision of the man filmed than simple, ordinary contact allows."[66] The set, consisting of two chairs, a table, and a black backdrop, was designed to be unobtrusive. In the first program the static positioning of the cameras demanded that the actors remain

Alain Badiou (top left); Badiou and Jean Hyppolite. From "La philosophie et son histoire," 9 January 1965. (Reproduced by permission of the Centre national de documentation pédagogique.)

virtually stationary. To curb the physical excesses of an exuberant Badiou, Fléchet actually resorted to tying a string to the young man's foot. Badiou recalls that each time he ventured out of frame, an emphatic tug would remind him to resume his proper position before the camera.[67]

Persuaded that "the movement of the body and the movement of thought often issue from the same dynamism," Fléchet came up with the idea of physically liberating his actors from the confined studio setting in order to inject greater energy and more activity into the shows. In the third program on philosophy and sociology, with Aron, Fléchet wanted to convey a sense of "sociology in society, architecture, movement, traffic and people," but the exigencies of the studio budget didn't allow it. By the fifth show, with Ricoeur, Fléchet attacked the problem of action head on, setting the cameras on tracks in order to offer his protagonists greater freedom of movement. Unfortunately, the device fell flat. "The interlocuters didn't move," he reported. "They didn't seem to feel any need to." Dissatisfied, but convinced that philosophy was not reducible to language alone, and armed with a bigger budget and more time (fifty rather than the usual thirty minutes), Fléchet entered production on the sixth show of the season.[68]

As regards its philosophical content, "Philosophy and Truth" represents the most challenging broadcast of the series thus far.[69] Not only is the central topic particularly abstract, but the show also features six rather than the usual two philosophers, and the interventions of these multiple participants (Hyppolite, Canguilhem, Ricoeur, Foucault, briefly, along with Dreyfus and Badiou) result in a less linear dialogue, requiring greater concentration on the part of the viewer. The program also illuminates a structural hierarchy that reinforces understandings of the *practice* of philosophy, if not its apprenticeship, as tacitly shaped by generation, gender, and (by omission) race.

"Philosophy and Truth" begins by elaborating two seemingly contradictory philosophical positions: Hyppolite's idea that "there is no error in philosophy," and Canguilhem's notion that "there is no philosophical truth." The broadcast asks a basic question about whether philosophical discourse can, or should be, judged according to the criteria of truth and falsehood. The opening image, a shot of a movie camera projecting a film over the heads of several students onto an unseen screen, establishes a sense of simultaneity. We watch them watch. Short excerpts from previous programs with Hyppolite and Canguilhem launch the opposing propositions. Hyppolite opens: "No, I would not employ the word 'error.' It appears to me—almost vulgar to speak of error within a philosophical system." Cut to another show. Badiou to Canguilhem: "Do you consider that there is no philosophical truth? You're going to shock us!" Canguilhem retorts: "Oh, I don't think that I will shock you personally. But I do say, 'There is no philosophical truth.' Philosophy is not a type of speculation whose value can be measured according to truth or falsehood." When the camera cuts abruptly to Hyppolite and Canguilhem inside a taxi, riding through the streets of Paris, the separate ideas are transformed into a conversation, and the philosophic dialogue is rooted in a recognizable environment. Conceding that there is no contradiction between the statements "There are no errors in philosophy" and "There is no philosophical truth," Canguilhem nevertheless insists that these propositions are not exactly the same. The light changes, and the cab stops. Nodding, Hyppolite asserts, "I am completely in agreement with what you have said about truth. There is none. There is no contradiction between what you said, that 'there is only scientific truth,' and what I said, that 'there is no error, alas, in philosophy.'" However, he contends, one must differentiate

Opening shot; Georges Canguilhem; Jean Hyppolite and Canguilhem in a taxi. From "Philosophie et vérité," 27 March 1965.

between truth and the "essence of truth," which is not of the same order as scientific truth. Canguilhem yields with a resounding "Yes!" The light changes again, and the cab lurches forward once more.

The picture shifts to a film projector casting its luminous image out of frame. Ricoeur fills the screen, caught in conversation with Badiou in the brief excerpt from "Philosophy and Language" in which he defines philosophy as a struggle for clarity and thus a privileged form of expression. The film ends, and the camera cuts to an interior hallway. Ricoeur, Foucault, and Dreyfus walk across a parquet floor and up some stairs, with Dreyfus silent as the men discuss Ricoeur's excerpt. In what follows she functions mainly as an *institutrice,* or schoolteacher, summarizing points or raising questions but rarely contributing to the development of the argument. Together, they enter a small library-cum-classroom. Badiou joins them. Meanwhile, Hyppolite and Canguilhem arrive at the same destination. As they exit the taxi, we catch a glimpse of the Panthéon. The visual cues suggest that we are at the École normale supérieure.[70] Crossing the threshold, the two men walk across a mosaic of the Owl of Minerva.[71] Moments later all six philosophers are ensconced in the second floor classroom. The heart of the discourse begins.

Paul Ricoeur; Foucault, Ricoeur, and Dreyfus; Foucault and Ricoeur. From "Philosophie et vérité," 27 March 1965.

Their dialogue can be schematized in the following manner. Canguilhem's assertion that "there is no philosophical truth" derives from his position that "truth" and "value" are not the same. Whereas "truth" is a scientific concept, philosophy, in contrast, is concerned with questions of "value." Though seemingly opposed, Hyppolite's position that "there is no error in philosophy" is actually quite similar: it refuses both "truth" and "falsehood" as criteria for the evaluation of philosophy. In the end, it is Ricoeur who represents an antithetical stance. Both Canguilhem and Hyppolite recognize "truth" as a term applicable only to specific forms of knowledge, such as the hard sciences. Ricoeur, in contrast, asserts that our relationship to the totality of knowledge is itself of the order of truth. At issue is whether truth is the central, normative value against which all other values are measured. The classic Kantian response, supported by Ricoeur, suggests that philosophy has access to truth, truth establishes the norm, and the norm is the rational legislator through which philosophy regulates all other values. The Nietzschean response proffered by Canguilhem (and seconded by Hyppolite), calls into question the hegemony of both truth and the normative, and demands a reevaluation of the philosophical relationship between truth and life.[72]

Hyppolite and Canguilhem; Owl of Minerva mosaic; left to right: Foucault, Canguilhem, Hyppolite (back to camera), Ricoeur, Dreyfus. From "Philosophie et vérité," 27 March 1965. (Reproduced by permission of the Centre national de documentation pédagogique.)

The broadcast came to no definitive conclusions, and no one position found unanimous support. This lack of closure was both characteristic of philosophical dialogue and—particularly when watched within the classroom—heuristically useful, since professors could employ opposing viewpoints to generate debate. But did the program actually capture philosophy as *act?* As we have seen, Dreyfus sought to demonstrate that philosophy was not an isolated intellectual discourse but rather a living practice, born in community and developed through dialogue.[73] To this end, Fléchet created a pastiche of images suggesting the omnipresence of philosophical discourse within the kind of pedestrian environments that viewers might encounter in their daily lives. The mundane details, from the shot of the taxi, its wheels spinning like the reel on the film projector, to the pan of Foucault, Ricoeur, and Dreyfus walking up the school stairs, to the delicate owl mosaic on the threshold, all conspire to infuse real spaces with the traces of philosophical dialogue. The images of Paris radiate the notion that philosophy is a constant conversation in France, and that philosophers are living, breathing people who smoke and take taxis, wear overcoats and engage in discussions, just like the rest of us. And in this sense, television's visual dimension was crucial. Interestingly, however, the show's

RTS production shot, 1965: Foucault, Ricoeur, and Dreyfus. (Photo Mark Pailoux–CNDP. Reproduced by permission of the Centre national de documentation pédagogique.)

didactic mission as educational programming ultimately undercut its ability to capture philosophy in vivo. The broadcast features France's most eminent philosophers self-consciously demonstrating a controlled form of classical philosophical debate that, through a combination of studied theatricality and careful intervention, is consistently readapted to the demands of the pedagogical enterprise. There is also an important disjuncture at play: with Badiou cast as novice, Dreyfus as teacher, and Ricoeur, Canguilhem, Hyppolite, and Foucault as masters, the program belies the invitation of the opening credits and, instead, represents philosophical thought as patriarchal, traditional, Western, and, in its universalizing evocation, fundamentally French. Dreyfus's gender and her status as a foreigner with experience in the non-Western world render her role in this project of philosophical embodiment all the more intriguing. Was she aware that the image of the "master thinker" captured on camera—white, French, almost exclusively male—may have shaped the message of the broadcasts as insistently as did the multiracial faces depicted in the opening credits?

### Evaluating *L'enseignement de la philosophie*

At the end of the first season, Dreyfus and her team solicited responses about the program from the professors charged with incorporating the broadcasts into their classrooms.[74] The questionnaires revealed a range of criticism. Most comments concerned the broadcasts' level of complexity. Given their brevity (averaging thirty minutes each), many thought the contents were too dense.[75] Perhaps the number of themes treated should be reduced and the rhythm slowed? Some deemed the philosophical vocabulary too sophisticated.[76] Others felt the overall plan required more structure. General classroom responses were equivocal: while some students were enraptured, others were bored silly. Discussions often concentrated on the image—Was it fuzzy or clear? What did famous people look like?—rather than on content.[77] Dreyfus was firm in her own defense. Philosophical television presented students with two tasks: first, to understand the philosophical discourse, and second, to analyze the image. As Marie-Hélène Lavallard, a member of the production team, commented, if the students sacrifice the discourse to the image, "that doesn't mean that we've failed, just that they are not yet trained in how to make use of television."[78] And while Dreyfus agreed that the role of television was, in part, to make accessible that which would not be accessible without it, she firmly reminded her viewers, "To make accessible does not necessarily mean to make easy."[79]

*L'enseignement de la philosophie* ran for a total of five years. Throughout this period the programs underwent a series of transformations. Although initially opposed to using philosophical television for textual exegesis, Dreyfus agreed in 1966 to experiment with this option. Several shows were developed in pairs, with the first structured as a philosophical dialogue and the second focused on a related text (such as Kant's *Critique of Practical Reason*).[80] In accordance with professors' requests, the theme selected for the 1965–66 season was "philosophy and morals."[81] The proximity of the student revolutions of May 1968 renders the choice noteworthy. In what Kristin Ross has termed "the flight from social determinations" that characterized the period, cultural and political hegemonies splintered, and the "domain of the expert" came under attack.[82] The program reflected these changes, offering a fleeting glimpse of philosophy reborn in democratic form. The May events interrupted the broadcasts when strikes at the ORTF brought television to a standstill. When the program resumed, the focus on the "master philosopher" had all but vanished, and students were televised working interactively on philosophical topics ranging from "will" and "love" to "science fiction."[83] Given the political context, the relevance of the theme—"the problem of liberty"— chosen for the 1969 spring season requires little explanation.

*L'enseignement de la philosophie* was discontinued after 1970. Badiou suggests that technological limitations justified the decision. Without the advantages of video, "the schedule for broadcasts had to be negotiated so that in all the lycées across France, all the philosophy professors could gather with their students at precisely the same moment" to watch the program.[84] "The shows themselves had tremendous success," Badiou recalls; "I watched them with my students at Reims. It was very primitive; there was one TV set in the basement, and you had to go down there with your whole class. Of course the kids were absolutely fascinated by it."[85] But scheduling was nothing short of a logistical nightmare. Further, since most broadcasts aired only once, the government found the costs prohibitive. To the very end, however, Dreyfus's commitment to televising philosophy never wavered.[86] In response to those who challenged her, she had included in the final show of the first season a small experiment: a passage from the interview "Philosophy and History" with Hyppolite was aired twice, first with the image and then without. Why televise philosophy? Dreyfus's answer was simple: "Listen, watch, and decide for yourselves."[87]

Dreyfus and her team were able to spend almost six years creatively experimenting with the question of how to televise philosophy effectively, largely because their series was developed as part of a broader pedagogical project dedicated to bringing television into French classrooms. As noted, the immediate motivation for producing these philosophy broadcasts was a disciplinary crisis within the academy. But the series was also sensitive to, and unwittingly reflective of, broader social anxieties provoked as much by the expanding economy of a modernizing nation as by the challenges a diversifying postcolonial public leveled at traditional perceptions of French cultural identity. The philosophy documentaries *Un certain regard* developed for the Service de la recherche between 1964 and 1974 display similar concerns about the importance of promoting and protecting a particular vision of France. However, unlike the philosophy shows of Radio-télévision scolaire, these documentaries were aimed at general audiences and were hence more vulnerable to commercial and political pressures, pressures that exacerbated considerably in the five years after *L'enseignement de la philosophie* went off the air. Indeed, by 1974 a number of changes had occurred within the television industry that, when coupled with economic and political developments, resulted in a complete overhaul of the state audiovisual administration, and ultimately reshaped the future of French cultural programming.

### The Service de la recherche and the Documentaries of *Un certain regard*

Created, like *L'enseignement de la philosophie,* in 1964, the cultural magazine *Un certain regard* was produced by the experimental division of the ORTF known as the Service de la recherche. The Service was established in 1960 under the direction of Pierre Schaeffer, whose intellectual rigor and passionate temperament guided the organization during its fifteen years of existence.[88] Deeply influenced by the mystical, spiritual teachings of Georges Gurdjieff, Schaeffer had conceived of the Service as a laboratory for the "parallel study of the means of expression and diffusion as well as the perfecting of possible correlations between radio, cinema, and television and, more broadly, between the arts and technology."[89] It was split into two sectors, each divided into five concentrations: research (information, sociology, criticism, technology, and "technical and economic studies for teaching") and production (magazines, experimental communication, "testing grounds," program development, and music research).[90] Physically and bureaucratically isolated from the ORTF in order to protect its creative independence, from the outset the Service was nevertheless considered the jewel in the crown of the French television administration. "All of

France basks in its glory," boasted the popular magazine *Télé 7 jours*. "No other television the world over," it continued, "even among those possessing multiple channels or color TV, has an equivalent organization."[91] In 1965, the more than one hundred employees "working for the TV of tomorrow" included "artists, technicians, electricians, and intellectuals recruited with advanced degrees in philosophy," all seeking to "reconcile artistic expression and technology" in the creation of original, socially stimulating television.[92] By 1970, the department was producing an average of one hundred hours of airtime annually.

*Un certain regard* was among the most important and longest running of the Service's programs.[93] Its in-depth studies of philosophers contributed to the creation of a new genre of television programming, the documentary biography, and honed a new category of television professional, the television documentary filmmaker.[94] In keeping with the ideals of cultural democratization, the program—like *L'enseignement de la philosophie*—sought to establish "the most direct form of communication between the mediators of knowledge and the viewing public," and in so doing to render its erudite protagonists and their works accessible to diverse audiences.[95] The intellectual elite depicted on *Un certain regard*'s broadcasts represented traditional patriarchal models, reinforcing a privileged status quo while supporting the state broadcaster's commitment to the diffusion of high cultural programming. In this sense, the philosophy broadcasts were characteristic of the ORTF's guiding ethos. However, as Raymond Kuhn notes, "the propensity of French television in the 1960s to transmit an output of peak-time programmes with a high cultural content should neither be exaggerated nor seen in isolation."[96] Indeed, throughout the 1960s, dissension within the ORTF over the proper purview of public programming was intensifying. Gaullist authorities retained firm control over political coverage, but proponents of cultural democracy began to gain ground, rejecting attempts at cultural democratization and insisting that the state broadcaster cater to a wider spectrum of popular tastes.[97]

By 1966, 51.7% of all French households possessed TV sets. As audiences grew, the ORTF struggled to expand its offerings and financial expenses spiraled upwards. Viewers subsidized rising costs through payment of the governmentally established license fee (the *redevance*) levied annually on set owners. Educational and high cultural programming remained national priorities, but growing financial troubles gradually began influencing administrative choices. Fiction, variety shows, game shows, and light entertainment increasingly vied with news, cultural magazines, and educational broadcasts for scheduling primacy. Technological advances led to the first color broadcasts on Channel 2 in 1967. Frustrated at their lack of financial independence (the Ministry of Finance set the ORTF's budget), pressure groups within the broadcasting administration began lobbying for the establishment of a commercial channel. Reluctant to relinquish its monopoly, the government grudgingly agreed to supplement the ORTF's income by opening its doors to commercial advertising in January of 1968. Strict rules applied; commercial breaks were limited to two minutes per day, and programs could be neither interrupted nor sponsored by advertisers.[98] Later that same year, the woefully inadequate television coverage of the May events called into question the legitimacy of the Gaullist regime and dealt a blow to public confidence in the state broadcasting system.[99] In an attempt to downplay the seriousness of the situation, and despite the fact that the press and radio covered little else, the Gaullist government had forbidden the ORTF to report on the May uprisings until almost a week after they had exploded onto the public scene. Journalists revolted, strikes immobilized the state broadcaster, and chaos reigned. As mentioned in chapter 2, when order was restored, the ORTF suffered massive reprisals, with hundreds of industry professionals fired, blacklisted, or transferred to the provinces. After de Gaulle's departure (following his failed bid for constitutional reform in the referendum of 1969), pressure to end the government monopoly multiplied, but fears of an increasingly united left among a fragmented right prevented the relaxation of state control. Indeed, in 1972, Georges Pompidou insisted that national television and radio must continue to represent "the official voice of France," and passed a statute reconfirming the state monopoly. Nineteen seventy-two saw the inauguration of a third channel, initially visualized as a regional complement to existing programming. By 1973, 79% of French homes contained television sets. Meanwhile, the ORTF was drowning in bureaucratic and financial difficulties.

The protests of May 1968 had undermined the cultural legitimacy of the "master thinkers" and challenged their social utility. During the 1970s, press reactions to biographical documentaries like those produced by the Service de la recherche testified to a sea change in attitudes towards the public role of intellectuals and indicated a growing rift between advocates of high cultural programming and supporters of a more entertainment-oriented, commercialized broadcasting model. An examination of two of *Un certain regard*'s most memorable programs, the first a special on Gaston Bachelard, the second a two-part presentation on Jacques Lacan, illustrates the controversy.

## "Bachelard among Us": The Philosopher as Everyman

Directed by Jean-Claude Bringuier, a master of early television documentary, "Bachelard parmi nous" aired on 2 October 1972.[100] The film was made to commemorate Bachelard's death ten years earlier and drew its substance from two hours of interview footage shot in 1961 with the philosopher in his Paris apartment by Bringuier and his then partner Hubert Knapp. Truncated to a brief twelve minutes for inclusion as a short in the celebrated newsmagazine *Cinq colonnes à la une,* the clip, which aired as "Portrait d'un philosophe," had been a disappointment to its directors. Rumor has it that shortly after the 1961 broadcast, the reels containing the original two hours of film disappeared. Whether mislaid or hidden, when the footage finally resurfaced in the early 1970s, Bringuier decided to take a second crack at the material. This time, however, he came intellectually armed. Not only did he "do his homework," reading extensively from Bachelard's work, but he brought philosophers Foucault, Canguilhem, and Jean-Toussaint Desanti, mathematician André Lichnerowicz, and theologian Father Dubarle on board, allowing their collective erudition to inform the program's overall assessment of Bachelard's life and work.[101]

From the perspective of the history of French television, "Bachelard parmi nous" represents a prime example of a new genre of television documentary. It also reflects Bringuier's emergence as a major player in the documentary field. Bringuier employs unorthodox choices regarding both tone and content to break with documentary conventions. For example, although the program uses a narrative voice, rather than mimicking the classical documentary style in which "the voice was the voice of God, falling objectively on people and things—'Toulouse is a city of 35,000 people, divided into industries,' etc.," Bringuier explains that here the tenor was intimate and personal, "like a nineteenth-century travel journal." Nor was this journalism understood in the traditional sense, obsessed with drama, violence, death, or events. For *Un certain regard* and for Bringuier in particular, the documentary format comprised "a much larger palette," one that sought not to "cover" something (or someone) but rather "to discover," and in so doing to reflect on life. In *cinéma vérité* style, Bringuier regularly shattered the suspension of disbelief that usually accompanies the nonfiction viewing experience: the Bachelard interview includes a sequence in which an interjection by the director is both audible to viewers ("No, no, continue filming, I just want us to redo this take as a close-up") and followed by an image of the slate used to mark the new take. The Service de la recherche encouraged such unorthodox techniques, granting its documentary filmmakers substantial creative leeway and procuring significant financial resources for their projects. All of the broadcasts on philosophers were allocated extensive time for preparation and production. Thus, whereas Bringuier's 1961 sequence for *Cinq colonnes à la une* was filmed on the afternoon of a single day with little forethought, "Bachelard parmi nous" involved over two months of research and was shot over a period of eight days.[102]

Since the biographies of *Un certain regard* attempted to present both a life and an oeuvre, they required distinctive directorial choices about the division and presentation of program content. As we shall see, disagreement over the broadcast's double agenda divided the viewing public, a fact that was indicative of shifts in the expectations and tastes of French television audiences and that ultimately had important consequences for the televising of philosophy.

( · )

"I was born in a country of streams and rivers," quotes the narrator, as the camera floats across the treetops to zoom in on a small town, nestled by a riverbank. Cut. A sign for "Bar-sur-Aube" swings suspended on an empty station platform. This town, where Bachelard once taught and where he is buried, is the site of our first encounter. In front of his house, on the street that now bears his name, we are introduced to three men, each of whom studied as boys under Bachelard's tutelage. Abruptly, the screen flashes to a block image of "1961" on a black background, and the voice-over introduces an excerpt from the earlier interview. While the narrator suggests that Bachelard incarnates childhood visions of the philosophers of old, the camera frames the master, seated heavily behind his desk in front of shelves laden with books. The sequence is shot almost entirely in close-up, with Bachelard responding to questions posed by Bringuier, who, after an establishing over-the-shoulder shot, remains off-screen. After tentatively inquiring how best to address the philosopher ("Shall I call you Master?"—to which Bachelard protests, "No, no, I'm just a man, everyone calls me Bachelard"), Bringuier observes that when they arrived earlier, Bachelard was listening to the radio. "Do current events preoccupy you?" he asks. The aging philosopher (who rarely leaves home) replies, "They seem essential to me. My daughter bought me a transistor, and I catch all the hourly news flashes from seven-thirty in the morning to nine at night. [. . .] It gives me the impression that the world around me is bringing me news of the universe." Bachelard quickly disabuses his young questioner of any illusions he might have about the sanctity of the philosophical life (pointing out that philosophers are not "immune to passions, unless they aren't fortunate enough to have any!") and assures him that he does know how to cook. When Bringuier (clearly awed) insists that Bachelard possesses "the art of living," the philosopher, amused, responds, "Well, one is obliged to find some art in life, or one is just a poor fool, right?"

Each question is answered, often at some length, with a sort of indulgent delight by the elderly Bachelard. When Bringuier asks, "Do you like this neighborhood?" the camera cuts from the interior interview footage to exterior shots of the market at the Place Maubert. We see Bachelard in his round hat and plaid scarf, chatting with the merchants, circulating among the stands, buying cheese. Meanwhile the voice-over continues a narration of the facts of his biography.

The film jumps back to the interview. "Tell us about the Champagne region, Monsieur Bachelard." "Were you happy in your profession?" As Bachelard reminisces about his life as a teacher, the camera cuts, and the narrative leaps a decade forward to a shot of his former students gathered inside a classroom around a bulky reel-to-reel tape recorder. They are listening to the audio from the interview that we have been watching, and are visibly moved. They ruminate over their memories of the philosopher. We cut back to the old interview footage. "You live in a little apartment in Paris?" "If you could return to the country, would you?" The final moments deal the most directly with Bachelard's oeuvre. The philosopher discusses his work on the poetics of reverie, and speaks, in an oblique reference to his then recently published study *The Poetics of Space,* about what he calls the "spaces of intimacy." At the interview's close, the camera pulls back from the intense close-up on the old man's face and frames his upper torso, hunched shoulders, and gnarled hands. "Alas," Bachelard observes, "You see how life changes? Sometimes it seems like months since I've left this room." "Is it sad to grow old, Monsieur Bachelard?" "Yes,

Bar-sur-Aube; the train station; Bache-lard's former students. From "Bachelard parmi nous," 2 October 1972.

yes, it's true that it is a little sad; one keeps thinking somehow that one shall get one's strength back; yes, it is a little sad—but you won't leave that in, will you?" The camera tightens on the magisterial image of the philosopher—long beard trembling, furrowed brow, flashing eyes. Part 1 concludes with images of Bachelard's beloved market at the Place Maubert in Paris, "where we haven't seen him for ten years," and with shots of the *bouquinistes,* the open-air book stalls that line the Seine, where Bachelard's works can frequently be found. The tone is intensely nostalgic. And, like the broadcasts of *L'enseignement de la philosophie,* the sequence promotes an understanding of Bachelard the philosopher as "Everyman," integrated at the most mundane levels into daily life in France.

In the words of its director, part 2 of "Bachelard parmi nous" attempts "to approach a different Bachelard from the one interviewed in our too simple interview ten years ago, a Bachelard entangled with some of the most important intellectual adventures of our time." At this point, the show changes key. Each of the experts is pictured and briefly introduced in voice-over before the successive interviews begin. The remainder of the broadcast dispenses with the photographs and illustrative sequences that embellished part 1. In the first segment,

Excerpt from "Portrait d'un Philosophe," 1961; Bachelard at home; Bachelard at Place Maubert. In "Bachelard
parmi nous," 2 October 1972.

Canguilhem, filmed at his desk, notes Bachelard's extraordinary ability to "do philosophy with the familiar things that he found all around
him," but immediately qualifies the statement so as to separate the philosopher from the quotidian. If, for example, Bachelard read "whatever came his way," that didn't mean, as Canguilhem clarifies, "mys-
teries" but rather "the literature of the eighteenth century—almanacs,
alchemy, and the like." In the next segment, Foucault takes up a similar theme, explaining that while Bachelard's work was informed by a
wide-ranging and unorthodox taste in books, their very range testified
to his genius: "Bachelard didn't hesitate to juxtapose Descartes against
a minor thinker of the eighteenth century, to counter a great poet with
a little poet that he'd come upon by chance in a bookstall." This vora-
cious approach, Foucault argues, permitted Bachelard to "trap culture
in its entirety," in its "interstices," in its "deviance," in the false notes
as well as the true.

    As the program progresses, the discussion becomes increasingly
erudite. The mathematician Lichnerowicz explores Bachelard as a
thinker of the "antisystem"; and Foucault, explaining Bachelard's interest in rupture and discontinuity, positions him in the history of science
"at that moment when Einstein grabbed the baton from Newton and

Georges Canguilhem; Michel Foucault; Jean-Toussaint Desanti. From "Bachelard parmi nous," 2 October 1972.

pushed physics into the modern age." Both Canguilhem and Desanti elaborate on Bachelard's concept of rupture, and on the transition from his work on science to his work on the philosophy of imagination and poetry. At heart, they explain, Bachelard believed that the very concepts that ground scientific thought are themselves born of reverie and metaphor. Thus, Desanti insists, Bachelard thought "it was not enough to show the mechanics of fluids." Instead, "we need to ask of water, how do we know it? What is the *image* of it"? What is the concept excluded from science? For Bachelard, Desanti explains, science was profoundly informed by something "extrascientific," something like the "flesh of the concept." Père Dubarle moves from this to a reflection on Bachelard's work on dreams. Bachelard, the program concludes, cannot be fully appreciated without attention to his two areas of interest: science and art. As a result of this double interest, "Bachelard is one of the most timely of all philosophers." "Any young person," Lichnerowicz concludes, "who would like to delve into the most evolved thought in the human sciences would do well to read Bachelard—and to read both Bachelards." Part 2 closes on a photo of the sage.

"Bachelard parmi nous" received considerable coverage in the local papers, all of which noted the distinction between the two halves.

Père Dubarle; André Lichnerowicz; Gaston Bachelard. From "Bachelard parmi nous," 2 October 1972.

Part 1 incorporates the footage from 1961 and captures the philosopher's life, painting a story in images—the town square, the classroom, the dusty study, the bustling marketplace. Part 2 returns to the "talking head" formula often associated with intellectual TV. Part 1 is colloquial in style, narrative in structure, and accessible, whereas part 2 is academic, abstract, and demanding. As demonstrated by the headline "Gaston Bachelard does his own cooking and shopping!" used to advertise the broadcast in *Télé 7 jours,* the popular presses were enthralled by the simplicity of the first half, which in truth was less a discussion of philosophy than a charmingly prosaic conversation with a philosophical old man.[103] But they disparaged the show's second half. "I'm not sure," wrote Janine Brillet at *Télé 7 jours,* "that all these witnesses added by Jean-Claude Bringuier were really necessary. The master alone is sufficient."[104] *France-soir* called it an "academic exercise."[105] *Hebdo TV* was more biting still: "All these academics who drag us through Bachelard's thought—especially Michel Foucault—are insufferable! Their specialist vocabularies, their sententious, complicated manners make deafeningly obvious what separates a Master from a professor."[106] In contrast, although everyone was enchanted by Bachelard's charm ("the presence of the old man with the long white beard, his simplicity, his wisdom, the sympathy that emanates from him are such that his portrait seduces us still"), the elite newspapers relentlessly mocked part 1.[107] Maurice Clavel, philosopher and television critic for *Le nouvel observateur,* scoffed at Bringuier's questions in the 1961 footage, calling them "silly" and "incapable of revealing anything." [108] *L'express* went further still, condemning the first half as "resembling an ABC of philosophy for ignoramuses," while praising the second as filled with "fruitful meditations." [109] Meanwhile *Figaro littéraire* was so enamored of the intellectual display in the second half that the paper actually published a special feature in which it printed transcripts—almost in their entirety—of the commentary of Canguilhem and company.[110]

The conflicting opinions expressed by the popular and highbrow presses about "Bachelard parmi nous" are not particularly surprising. Indeed, given longstanding divisions within the viewing publics, the predilection of the popular presses for narrative biography and of the elite presses for "high" intellectual content is predictable. It is this very predictability that renders critiques of *Un certain regard*'s two-part documentary on Jacques Lacan—that most inscrutable of all intellectuals—all the more extraordinary. Although Lacan was a psychoanalyst and not a philosopher, television coverage of the enigmatic intellectual bears analysis because he was a crucial contributor to postwar French theory, and his abstract and extremely challenging work presents problems comparable to those facing the televising of philosophy.[111] An examination of responses to the Lacan documentary further illustrates the transformation in popular attitudes towards intellectual television that is vital to our larger story.

### Jacques Lacan: Intellectual Theater or Theatrical Charlatanism?

By the early 1970s, Lacan ranked in the uppermost echelon of the French intellectual elite. The publication of his *Écrits* in 1966, which (as mentioned in chapter 2) topped the bestseller list the summer it appeared, was an intellectual victory for the controversial figure. He was the director of the École freudienne de Paris, and his weekly seminars regularly drew over five hundred adoring followers. Pierre Schaeffer was determined to include Lacan in the archives of *Un certain regard,* and he assigned a young filmmaker, Benoît Jacquot, the task of covering him. When approached by Jacquot, whom he found sincere and likable, Lacan agreed to the project on condition that he himself exercise total control over the format and that Jacques-Alain Miller (his son-in-law and a psychoanalyst in his own right) participate as interviewer.[112] The show made waves even before it aired. According to Miller, when the program was finished, the Service de la recherche didn't want it broadcast because they "thought it would be incomprehensible to the public at large." [113] According to *Paris match,* the problem was not content but timing; Lacan wanted the two-part show broadcast in February (when audiences tended to be slightly larger), rather than in March.[114] The Service refused. Angered when his demands were not met, Lacan published a written transcript of the program with Éditions du Seuil.[115] Eventually the two parties reconciled, and the show aired on two consecutive Saturday evenings, 9 and 16 March 1974.[116]

"Jacques Lacan: Psychanalyse I et II" broke from *Un certain regard's* now standard documentary biography format. In keeping with Lacan's demands, instead of blending biography and intellectual content, the film was conducted entirely as an interview, with all questions posed off-camera by Miller. Lacan's widely publicized intention was to hold forth in precisely the same fashion as he did in his lectures, for, in his words, "there's no difference between television and the public before whom I've spoken for a long time now, a public known as my seminar." However, this ostensibly populist claim was immediately qualified: "Do not," Lacan cautions, "get the idea that I'm addressing everyone at large. Rather, I am speaking to those who are savvy, to the non-idiots." In the discussion that follows, Lacan either sits or stands behind his desk. His monologue is punctuated by occasional questions from Miller, and his image is broken only by the use of captions expressing a word or theme—"Pleasure," "Repression," "The Unconscious," "Affect," "The Two Sexes," "Psychoanalysis and Psychotherapy," etc.—in white text on a black background.

"Viewers, buckle your seatbelts! *Un certain regard* with the psychoanalyst Jacques Lacan will be a bumpy ride!" announced *France soir.* As promised, Lacan refused all efforts to "vulgarize" or simplify his discursive style. On the unconscious, he states, "There are, insofar as the unconscious is implicated, two sides presented by the structure, by language [. . .] The side of meaning, the side we would identify as that of analysis [. . .]. It is striking that this meaning reduces to non-sense. [. . .] Whence the unconscious". On sex, families, society,

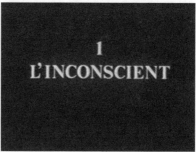

Jacques Lacan; "The Unconscious"; Lacan in action. From "Jacques Lacan: 1ère émission, Psychanalyse I," 9 March 1974.

and capitalism, he impishly suggests, "You *know* that I've got an answer for everything," adding, "Freud didn't say that repression *comes from* suppression: that (to paint a picture) castration is due to what Daddy brandished over his brat playing with his wee-wee: 'We'll cut if off, no kidding, if you do it again.' Naturally enough, however, it occurred to him, to Freud, to start with that for the experiment." On woman (more provocatively still) Lacan observes, "Let's state the axiom not that Man doesn't exist, which is the case for Woman, but that a woman forbids Him for herself, not because He would be the Other, but because 'there is no Other of the Other,' as I put it." Unabashedly self-promoting, Lacan declares, "Who doesn't know that it's with the analytic discourse that I've made it big? That makes me a *self-made man* [in English]. There have been others, but not in our lifetime." The final question, delivered at the end of the second hour of winding wordplay, concerns Lacan's "style." Unapologetic, he preens, "The interpretation must be prompt in order to meet the terms of the interloan—between that which perdures through pure dross and the hand that draws only from Dad to worse." [117]

Was this linguistically tortured charlatanism, or inspired brilliance? The jury was out. Neat divisions between popular and elite presses dissolved in a cacophony of spirited responses. *Le nouvel obser-vateur* christened Lacan "the most celebrated dandy of French psychia-try." [118] The more serious of the television journals, *Télérama,* advised its readers on the one hand that "you have better things to do than watch this show" but concluded in another article that it would never-theless be dangerous to banish Lacan from the screen on the premise that he speaks only to the few, since "the ORTF, as a public service, must speak of everything, including the most radical undertakings." [119] However, *Humanité dimanche* argued that the good doctor spoke "in the language of a specialist, helping *no one* to understand his theo-ries." [120] Not so, countered *L'express.* Lacan's lack of simplification was "an extraordinary mark of respect. [. . .] For once, this discourse has solicited *intelligence* from the viewing public." [121] The journal *Psy-chologie* agreed, insisting that if a psychoanalyst could speak "in the language of psychoanalysis," then that "gives the physician and the mathematician the right to speak to us of their sciences on our televi-sion screens." [122] But to what end? "Lacan speaks on TV on a Saturday night," reported *Combat.* "An event? Psychoanalysis for the people? Not at all. The master speaks only for himself." [123] "If you don't pos-sess the keys to his code," concurred *France-soir,* "you'll remain deaf and blind. The creator of the École freudienne de Paris will be per-forming no miracles tonight." In sum, *Le monde* spat, Lacan "reserves his texts for 'non-idiots.' We're flattered! Thanks." [124]

Despite the virulent debate, there was one point on which both the press and the public agreed: Jacques Lacan was *great* entertainment.[125] In the words of *France-soir,* "You don't really have to understand him to appreciate his satanic humor and to be fascinated by the insolent spectacle of this character standing, as if facing an amphitheater, ad-dressing the television audience as if they were the most enlightened of beings!" [126] Even that bastion of tradition, *Figaro,* conceded that "Lacan beats Jerry Lewis on his own ground." [127] "In my opinion," wrote in one viewer to *Télérama,* "the piece was in keeping with the best of Ionesco, and superbly interpreted by its actor. I've rarely laughed so hard!" [128] Another viewer insisted more sincerely, "We were literally fascinated by this extraordinary character; a phrase [of his], even deprived of meaning for us, revealed life in all its moving inten-sity. Personally, I've never been able to read more than three pages of Lacan. I think now that the situation will be very different." [129] Like no other intellectual before him, philosopher or otherwise, Lacan made clear on *Un certain regard* that no matter how obtuse, philosophical, opaque, or intensely intellectualized the content of his show, if the "actor gave good drama," the public would watch. Television professionals sat up and took notice.

( · )

Ten years after its creation, the unbridled admiration that the Service de la recherche had once generated was disintegrating. By 1970, *Télérama* wondered whether, "enclosed in an intellectual 'ghetto'" and programmed to air at later and later hours, the Service was actually just the "bad conscience" of the ORTF, a sort of "intellectual alibi" that allowed the television administration to churn out a steady diet of primetime mediocrity without much guilt. In the same article, Schaeffer defensively declared that if it was true that "nowhere in the world is there a research service such as ours," it was also true that nowhere in the world had such a resource been so abused.[130] By 1974 the romance was over. When the ORTF was dismantled under Valéry Giscard d'Estaing, the Service de la Recherche and all of its programs, including the documentary biographies of *Un certain regard,* became one more casualty in a sea of cancellations.

### Inform, Educate, *Entertain*—the Balance Shifts

*L'enseignement de la philosophie* and *Un certain regard* were among the first programs to grapple seriously with the question of how to film philosophy and philosophers for television—exploring TV's potential not only to expand public contact with the discipline but also attempting to do so in a way that remained true to the subject while trying to enlarge its discursive parameters. And yet, if the television programs fought to ascertain that philosophy is at heart an embodied practice (hence amenable to TV and available to all), they also revealed that its "performance" is not necessarily apprehended with ease. Because, even in the vernacular, philosophy speaks a language of its own—one that is no more accessible to the uninitiated than is a musical score to someone who reads no music, or an algorithm to someone not trained in mathematics. And while true that even philosophers themselves view the populist aspirations of higher education differently, this fundamental difficulty calls into question the real possibility of democratizing knowledge. Plainly put, despite philosophy's pretensions to universal enlightenment, not everyone can be Plato. Somebody has to build cars. Problematically, the system of meritocracy that purportedly justifies this division of labor is both highly prejudicial and failed to square easily with the Republic's egalitarian promises. On another note, however, the conflicting public reactions to the documentary biographies on *Un certain regard* suggested that not everyone aspired to the same intellectual ends.

The discordant elements evident in both *L'enseignement de la philosophie* and *Un certain regard*—their very mission of presenting abstract, philosophical discourse via television, the contrasting critical responses they evoked, and their paradoxical attempts to extend this elite form of knowledge to an increasingly heterogeneous national audience (visible in the opposition between the largely white male embodiment of the "master thinkers" and their multiracial and mixed-gender publics)—mirrored the forces fracturing the nation. For, what we see in France during the 1960s and early '70s are a set of competing demands: on the one hand for technological prowess, economic growth, military strength, modernization, and the satiation of consumer desire, and on the other for the legitimization of national grandeur on the basis of a cherished heritage of established cultural traditions. The fact that the Gaullist state, at once progressive and conservative, was desperate for scientists, engineers, administrators, and technicians while simultaneously promoting the humanistic discipline of philosophy on its tightly controlled broadcast media perfectly embodies these contradictions.

In 1968, the political and social crisis of the May movement nearly toppled the Fifth Republic. The collapse of the student revolutions and the end of the general strikes shattered utopian dreams for remaking civil society, but the experience had critical repercussions, challenging the domain of the expert and testing the forces of capitalism, American imperialism, and Gaullism. Following the failed referendum that precipitated de Gaulle's 1969 departure, Georges Pompidou took control of the French government, promising "openness within continuity" and capitalizing on the final years of the economic boom. Pompidou built monuments to French modernization (the Pompidou center, the skyscrapers at La Defense and Maine-Montparnasse, and the reconstructed Les Halles shopping center in Paris) and pushed French investment in nuclear power, technology, and telecommunications. Pompidou's untimely death (he was diagnosed with leukemia in 1972 and died two years later) occurred just months after the 1973 OPEC oil crisis. By January of 1974, the cost of oil had quadrupled. The centrist technocrat Giscard d'Estaing's presidential inauguration marked the end of *les trentes glorieuses;* his deflationist policies resulted in the worst recession to hit France since WWII. Convinced that a less state-oriented, more independent capitalist economy would revitalize the nation, Giscard committed his government to reform. Under the slogan "Change without risk," he halted some of Pompidou's less popular projects (an expressway on the Left Bank), legalized abortion, and integrated more women into the political structures of the French government. Along with his first prime minister, Jacques Chirac, Giscard also promoted a series of controversial educational reforms (some of which, as discussed in chapter 4, threatened the teaching of philosophy), and worked to reorganize radio and television, making media liberalization a symbol of the end of Gaullist domination.

Wary of antagonizing the right, Giscard didn't seek privatization for television and radio but rather a loosening of the political links binding those media to the government. He ultimately decided to maintain the state monopoly while encouraging regulated competition by breaking up the monolithic audiovisual administration. The dismantling of the ORTF in 1974 (a move that split the massive organization into seven autonomous companies) enabled French television to metamorphose into a full-fledged marketing tool representing (at least in theory) multiple political and popular perspectives.[131] By supporting audiovisual reform—even in a circumscribed way—Giscard opened a conversation for change. The French government had finally recognized that if a state-run television administration were to remain solvent while expanding its audiences, it needed to start acknowledging public opinion, liberalizing political coverage, and catering to popular taste. With respect to the televising of philosophy, one thing was clear: in the changed audiovisual environment, entertainment had to be the order of the day.

# The "New Philosophers" and Morality for the Masses, 1974–1986

Vladimir Jankélévitch appeared on Bernard Pivot's book program *Apostrophes* on 18 January 1980. Over the next few weeks, the seventy-six-year-old French philosopher, retired Sorbonne professor, and author of over twenty works on moral philosophy and half a dozen on music, sold more books than he had done during his entire career. He had been invited on the broadcast to discuss the revised edition of his 1957 work, *Le Je-ne-sais-quoi et le presque rien* (The I-Don't-Know-What and the Almost Nothing), and to participate in a debate, the theme of which was captured in the show's title, "A quoi servent les philosophes?" ("What Use Are Philosophers?").[1] Flanked by a former student, François George and by the political philosopher Blandine Kriegel, Jankélévitch was presented to the viewing public (like Gaston Bachelard before him) as a sage—a "philosophical signifier," at once the incarnation and the revealer of philosophical truth. Given his low profile outside of intellectual circles, the choice to cast him in this role, not to mention the astronomical sales that followed his appearance (when over thirty thousand copies of his book flew off the shelves) might seem curious.[2]

Jankélévitch's unexpected public appeal, his work's remarkable commercial success, and even the very question that prompted the *Apostrophes* broadcast bear witness to a series of changes taking place between the mid-1970s and the mid-1980s that definitively altered intellectual life, cultural practices, and the discipline of philosophy in contemporary France. In this chapter I explore these changes. First, I analyze two broadcasts selected from *Apostrophes,* on Michel

Foucault and on a group of young men—headed by Bernard-Henri Lévy and André Glucksmann—who came to be known as the New Philosophers. Second, I examine two series that took philosophy as their raison d'être (*Interrogations* and *Les idées et les hommes*) and an innovative political series known as *Tribune libre* (on Jean-François Lyotard). These shows function as a portal into a web of interrelated debates—over intellectuals, politics, publicity, and the social utility of philosophy—which were linked, either directly or peripherally, to the revival of interest in ethics that began sweeping France at this time.[3]

Classic ethical questions—questions of conscience, duty, the law, virtue, obligation and responsibility, right and wrong, and good and bad, which structure the reciprocal relationships between individuals, the community, institutions, the state, and universal humanity—persistently infuse the social universe. And yet there are times when ethics, understood as the rapport between what *is* (the ontic) and what *ought to be* (the normative, or what we may also call systematic morality), become particularly pressing. In France, the decades following 1968 were such a period. Disputes over abortion, immigration policy, gay rights, feminism, age of consent, the environment, medical and biological advances, the New Right, and reassessments of Vichy and the Holocaust brought ethical questions to the fore. To many, May 1968 represented the failure of revolution as a model for political, cultural, and social change. Ethical approaches to thought and action stepped into the vacuum created by the rejection of revolutionary discourse, a discourse that had obsessed French intellectuals since at least 1789. Ethics also appeared to offer options that Marxism—increasingly perceived as politically bankrupt and morally indefensible—had failed to deliver. Philosophy became a site, on multiple levels, of this articulation. Television played a vital part in its dissemination.

On and off the small screen, philosophers were both profoundly affected by, and instrumental in shaping, the ethical turn in contemporary French life. Some, as members of an intellectual left discredited for its allegiance to a totalitarian ideology that had resulted in the annihilation of millions, came under attack. Their detractors—mainly the New Philosophers but also, in very different ways, individuals like Foucault—attempted to refashion the role of the intellectual, either embracing specific interventionist agendas or assuming a new mantle of moral authority by renouncing party politics in favor of suprastatist perspectives on human rights. When they capitalized on the power of the mass media to perform such refashioning, their efforts often drew fire. Indeed, it has become commonplace to speculate that the rise of the "mass media intellectual" during the 1970s and early 1980s sounded the death knell for traditional intellectual culture in France while initiating a bastardization of French philosophical practice.[4] *Apostrophes,* with its unprecedented hold over the publishing market, and the New Philosophers, seen as intellectual shysters and masters of media manipulation, figure equally as the evil protagonists in this tale.

Rather than accepting this narrative of cultural decline, I argue that by demanding ethical and political accountability, the New Philosophers—regardless of the merits of their own work—actually advanced intellectual power and revalidated philosophy's public importance. They were not alone. As we shall see, while some broadcasts defended a now embattled national agenda aimed at bolstering access to philosophy, even those that called the relationship between intellectuals and the media into question could inadvertently support the very figures and discipline that they critiqued. Ultimately, neither the renaissance in political philosophy, nor the pervasive media presence of French intellectuals, nor the fascination with philosophy as a moral compass evident at the end of the twentieth century is explicable without reference to television's engagement with ethics in the 1970s and '80s. And while I am hardly suggesting that *Apostrophes* can be held single-handedly responsible for these subsequent developments, the series' influence was indisputable. I begin, then, with its history.

### *Apostrophes:* Culture as Mass Entertainment

First broadcast on 10 January 1975, *Apostrophes* became the most renowned cultural program in the history of French television. Sold to and broadcast in the majority of Francophone countries worldwide (and available in New York City on cable) during its fifteen years on the air, *Apostrophes* was a veritable emissary for French culture and language. Initially sandwiched between the popular *Au théâtre ce soir* on TF1 (formerly Channel 1) and the evening movie on FR3 (formerly Channel 3), the program quickly developed a loyal audience. Until *Apostrophes,* no other book show had succeeded in filling the void left by the demise of *Lectures pour tous* in 1968.[5] *Apostrophes* aired a total of 724 programs on Antenne 2 (formerly Channel 2), at nine-thirty on Friday evenings until June of 1990—summer vacations excepted. It averaged between two and four million viewers nightly in its first ten years, thus capturing between 12% and 20% of the French television public.[6] Philosophers either appeared or were discussed on ninety of *Apostrophes*' broadcasts. While some of these directly addressed the discipline of philosophy, the majority featured philosophers as public intellectuals.[7] As *Apostrophes* established its reputation as an important intellectual platform, access to its broadcasts became increasingly contentious. Its power over the publishing market was notorious: according to *Livres-hebdo*'s analysis of nonfiction sales between 1983 and 1986, 72% of the books that became bestsellers had benefited from television exposure on *Apostrophes*.[8] According to a publishing industry survey, 26% of *all* book purchases could be traced directly to the influence of the program.[9] Publishing houses presumed a 30% increase in sales for any book featured on one if its shows.[10] *Apostrophes,* was a marketer's dream: it both encouraged the consumption of books and was itself a marketable product.

*Apostrophes*' success was founded on its ability to attract the interest of the general public. Many factors have been cited as contributing to its pull: the topics chosen for the weekly broadcast, the relative unattractiveness of its competitors on other channels, the quality of the series that preceded it on the schedule, even the fact that "from Christmas to March, the chill in the air induced [audiences] to stay indoors."[11] I think the answer lies elsewhere. *Apostrophes* enthusiastically injected entertainment into the cultural mix. The broadcast was structured as a debate rather than as a conversation, presentation, discussion, or lecture.[12] Of course, as we have seen in the programs created by Dina Dreyfus for *Radio-télévision scolaire,* the debate format was not entirely new to philosophy broadcasts. For *Apostrophes,* however, debate was not simply a result of the dialogue; it was an end in itself—one supported by the presence of multiple participants deliberately chosen for their divergent points of view. *Apostrophes* intentionally aspired to build the tension inherent in verbal exchange. It produced entertainment by producing conflict. The fact that *Apostrophes* often aired live further heightened its dramatic potential. The other element critical to the series' allure lay in the personality of its charming and indomitable host, Bernard Pivot. Pivot regularly spiced up the broadcast by cultivating explosive situations. This was the case, for example, in a famous 1978 episode in which the American writer Charles Bukowski requested and was given the right to consume alcohol during the program. After downing two bottles of white wine,

Bukowski attempted to fondle his neighbor, the author Catherine Paysan. Pivot was obliged to escort the American off the set.[13]

"Everyone knows that the commercial success of a novel, or any book, come to that, pivots around Pivot and a few others," wrote Régis Debray in *Le Pouvoir intellectuel en France,* his 1979 attack on the deleterious effects of the audiovisual media (and especially of *Apostrophes*) on French intellectual production.[14] To Debray, Pivot's crime was that he was a country bumpkin—a hick, hopelessly underqualified to play such a powerful role in shaping French intellectual life. Satirizing himself, Pivot rebutted, "Who permitted you, little Pivot, to unleash the public battle of the New Philosophers," to expose the lofty intelligentsia "to the millions of people who, of course, are not all *normaliens,* are not all contributors to *Le monde,* are not all future academics, do not all belong to the elite?"[15] Yet despite Pivot's populist defense, Debray's critique should not be summarily dismissed. Like Dumayet and Desgraupes before him, only more so, Pivot used his media-derived power to bring certain authors into the spotlight and consign others to the shadows, thus calling into question the traditional structures controlling the attribution of intellectual value in France.[16] The general public embraced Pivot for the very reasons that he raised Debray's hackles: he was one of their own. Ironically, as Pivot later remarked, "The Debray affair did more for the reputation of *Apostrophes* than did any of the program's finest scoops."[17]

( · )

Born in Lyon on 5 May 1935, Pivot tried his hand at writing at an early age, and published an unremarkable novel, *L'amour en vogue,* when he was twenty-four. Disenchanted by the field of fiction, he turned to journalism. Studies at the Centre de formation des journalistes in Paris led to fifteen years of work as—in his own words—not a literary critic but "a columnist" for *Le Figaro littéraire.*[18] He wrote restaurant reviews (under the pseudonym Antoine Dulac) and covered literary and cultural events, including the festival celebrating the annual launch of Beaujolais nouveau. By 1971, Pivot had transferred to the daily *Figaro.* Although he continued to work there until 1974, he grew unhappy with the internal politicking at the newspaper and began looking for other options. From 1970 to 1973 he hosted a radio comedy program on Europe N°1, and between 1973 and 1974 made his first foray into television as producer and host of *Ouvrez les guillemets* (Open Quotation

Marks), a book program airing on the ORTF's Channel 1. In 1974, a potential promotion at *Figaro* stood to make Pivot director of all non-political aspects of the paper (literature, sports, entertainment, arts, travel, etc.). When the post was offered on the condition that he abandon television work, Pivot quit the paper instead.

On being approached in January 1975 by Marcel Julian, the president of Antenne 2, Pivot agreed to drop *Ouvrez les guillemets*, and jump ship to the newly reconstituted second channel to host a book series to be called *Apostrophes*. Pivot served as producer and host, Anne-Marie Bourgnon was hired to handle relations with publishing houses, and Monique Wendling (later replaced by Renée Bernard) dealt with press reviews and functioned as liaison to the directors and technical team.[19] The small production staff kept costs low, as did the collapsible set, reconstructed weekly for filming. The show was broadcast live, first from Studio 4 at Cognac-Jay and later from Studio 40, a large hangar at Antenne 2's new location at 26 rue Jean-Goujon. Rather than reproducing the program that he'd hosted on the competing channel, in which he presented successive unrelated book reviews (a format that dominated the book show genre), Pivot developed *Apostrophes* around a weekly theme. Subjects included politics, history, sexuality, science, feminism, literature, medicine, language, and philosophy. He had a particular fondness for nonfiction. Pivot reasoned that nonfiction, being less subjective, lent itself more readily to debate. He chose the themes for each Friday's show after working his way through the cartons of review copies delivered daily by book publishers. When not thematic, broadcasts featured single publications that Pivot deemed newsworthy for cultural or political reasons, or dealt with an individual author, living or dead, from the world of politics, the humanities, science, or religion.

Most weeks, Pivot assembled four to six guests around a large table elevated on a raised circular platform. A silent audience was seated in the shadows behind the principal participants, evoking the phantom presence of the television public in the privacy of their living rooms. Director Claude Barma equated the set to a literary salon transformed into a boxing ring, a sort of stadium conceived for intellectual jousting.[20] Three mobile cameras, directed at eye level, captured the action and relayed it to the director, who edited live by selecting the feeds that were to go to air. Careful staging heightened the tension. Pivot intentionally seated potential adversaries either opposite one another or (preferably), side-by-side, anticipating that uncomfortable physical

Bernard Pivot, from *Apostrophes,*
27 May 1977; opening shot, and Vladimir Jankélévitch, from "A quoi servent
les philosophes?" 18 January 1980.

proximity would provoke theatrical performances. As the narrator of
a 1990 television retrospective about the French book show genre observed, "A lot of audiovisual evolution occurred between the serene
tranquillity of Desgraupes and Dumayet" and "the crazy, candid approach of the sports fan known as Bernard Pivot."[21] Often described
as a *bonhomme du peuple,* a man of the people, Pivot was a regular
guy who loved his Beaujolais, his football, and his food. Given that
he had "neither the formation, nor the language, nor the allure of an
intellectual," where did Pivot's talent lie?[22] Like his precursors at *Lectures pour tous,* Pivot had a flair for "making a spectacle of inert objects." "A book doesn't move," he wryly stated, "so I use the author to
give the spectacular dimension required."[23] However, by stoking the
dramatic potential inherent in the multiple-participant debate, Pivot
increased the theatrical possibilities fivefold. At the same time, he
rescued high culture from the ivory tower and made it approachable,
visceral, gossipy, amusing, nasty, sexy, garrulous, and, above all, eminently entertaining. His brash style was an unalloyed success. When
*Apostrophes* married culture to spectacle, it fulfilled both high and
popular cultural aspirations, cornering the book show market.
    By the time *Apostrophes* debuted in 1975, the television debate
was a regular fixture on the small screen. From *Les dossiers de l'écran*

to *L'avenir du futur,* from *À armes égales* to *Cartes sur table,* during the 1970s at least twelve new debate shows found their way to the viewing public. But these programs were, almost without exception, political magazines.[24] The parameters conventionally governing political debate—aggressive, disruptive, and temporally delimited—were ideally suited to the demands of the medium. But television debates, even those not subject to the theatrical machinations of enthusiastic hosts, pose particular problems for philosophy.

Characterized by the participation of two or more guests and incorporating the presence of an *animateur,* or host, television debates are governed by strict protocols.[25] The host presents the guests, regulates exchanges, poses questions, confers the right to speak, and—if dramatically motivated—responds to the resulting dialogue with expressions of naïveté, provocation, astonishment, interest, or outrage. The guest's role is to reply in turn: to explain, evaluate, or defend his or her position. The challenge for the interviewee is to successfully state that which he or she desires to communicate without submitting to the host's agenda or allowing the questions and comments of fellow participants to lead the argument astray. Ever since *Apostrophes* first appeared, intellectuals have critiqued the structure of television debate as hostile to considered intellectual and philosophical exchange. This format, they argue, lacks intellectual flexibility, censoring thoughtful discussion and accelerating dialogue. Pierre Bourdieu, in his brief polemic against television, seizes on the negative connection between speed and philosophical thought. He maintains, "It's an old philosophical topic—take the opposition that Plato makes between the philosopher, who has time, and people in the *agora,* in public space, who are in a hurry and under pressure. What [Plato] says, more or less, is that you can't think when you're in a hurry." Television thrives on the immediate ingestion of "received ideas," of "commonplaces," whereas at "the opposite end of the spectrum, thought, by definition, is subversive." And the logical process, Bourdieu concludes, of "*thinking* thought, of thought in the process of being thought, is intrinsically dependent on time."[26] Media sociologist Noël Nel concurs that analysis on TV "must be rapid, executed in common, and acceptable as a substitute for truth."[27] Television debates foster urgency, offering a platform to speak and then constantly admonishing guests to respond *faster.* Consequently (as will be apparent when we turn to Michel Foucault's 1976 appearance on the show), when substantive philosophical dialogue *did* occur on *Apostrophes,* it was often because the demands of debate were being held in abeyance.

While *Apostrophes'* theatrical version of the debate model was particularly challenging for philosophy, the broadcast nevertheless performed a critical cultural service: it brought both philosophers and their ideas—however reductively presented—into the public eye. More controversially, *Apostrophes* managed not only to reflect current intellectual and philosophical trends but also to create them. Themes inviting ethical debate (on such issues as "intellectual life under the Occupation," "romantic love," "crime and punishment," "the Jews in question," and "birth"—a broadcast on abortion) were common.[28] Discussions begun during a show were often continued the following day in the major journals and periodicals, meaning that the press could amplify the effects of a single appearance, rendering programs that might otherwise have passed unnoticed far more important. Foucault, Aron, Barthes, Bourdieu, Catherine Clément, Maurice Clavel, and many others all wrote such commentaries.[29] Pivot was also able to enter the fray, since from October of 1975 until 1993 he was the editor-in-chief of the literary magazine *Lire,* a position he used quite unapologetically to publicize *Apostrophes* during its run.[30] Few topics addressed on the broadcasts excited more press than the brouhaha that erupted in the mid-1970s around the apparent moral failure of the French intellectual left to identify (and reject) the ideology of Soviet socialist totalitarianism.[31] The proximate motivation for this ruckus was the 1973 publication of Alexander Solzhenitsyn's *The Gulag Archipelago,* but, as we shall see, the "Gulag effect" quickly became the vehicle for the expression of a much wider range of philosophical, ethical, and political concerns.[32]

### Not the *History of Sexuality:* Michel Foucault Returns

On 17 December 1976, Michel Foucault appeared on *Apostrophes* in order to discuss his recently published work, *La volonté de savoir* (*The History of Sexuality,* volume 1). The theme for the broadcast was "Quel avenir pour l'homme?" ("What is the future of man?").[33] Given the post-'68 disenchantment with revolutionary dreams, and the disillusioned retrenchment that characterized the current social climate (typified by a retreat into the presentist pleasures of consumerism and civic conformism), the program's topic—a probing reflection on the future—was provocative. In an unusual move, the show aired live from a specially installed set in the Sumerian room at the Louvre. Live music

(Rachmaninoff) played by a chamber group enhanced the introductory credits. French cultural supremacy (amusingly dramatized here as sub-suming all great cultural achievements, from ancient art to Russian music) is both demonstrated and ostensibly democratized. "French" culture, the Louvre setting implies, belongs to *you*, the French public. Situated in an apparently apolitical realm dominated by art, science, and culture, the show appears poised to tie speculative assessments of the future to the celebration of a rich and glorious past, while simul-taneously performing its customary task of reifying the intellectual dominance of the book. However, Foucault's presence soon ensured that this was one production that would not unroll as planned.

Pivot opens the broadcast in his customary fashion, moving pro-gressively around his little circle, engaging with each author individ-ually before opening the debate to general participation. He queries his first three guests—the professor of medicine Jean Hamburger, the astronomer Albert Ducrocq, and the political journalist André Fontaine—about their recent books on genetics, globalization and life on Mars. The discussion shifts from Hamburger on evolution and genetic patterning (implying the need to look back in order to move into the future), to Fontaine on globalization, commodification, and the rise of the two great powers (implying the need to examine the present in order to move into the future), to Ducrocq on advances in space exploration and the possibility of life on Mars (implying that we are actually living in the future). If ethical questions were not yet at the center of public discourse, there is no denying that the evening's themes invited such consideration. The formal environment seems to have had a sobering influence on the group, rendering the ambiance less convivial and the debate less confrontational than was typically the case. Each interviewee maintains a respectful silence until his turn to speak arrives. Pivot then turns to Foucault.

"I don't want to discuss *The History of Sexuality*," Foucault de-clares, "I want to talk about something else." Startled, Pivot peers over his glasses at the unruly speaker. Foucault continues, "You write things partly because you think them, but also so as not to have to think about them any more." "Ah, we can see that here we have a philosopher," Pivot interjects with acerbity. Persistent, Foucault re-sumes, "You write when you are in love with a subject, a book, but once you're not fascinated by it anymore, you finish it, you stop writ-ing it." Foucault's body language is dynamic, centered, and consum-mately articulate. Shoulders up, legs crossed, he hunches forward in his tan suit. "I want," he continues, "to talk about another book, a book that doesn't have an author and so has no one to defend it." It quickly emerges that Foucault's preferred agenda is the problem of Soviet dissidents and the Gulag as embodied by *l'affaire Stern*. The Stern affair concerned the KGB's prosecution of a doctor for sexual misconduct, perversion, and fraud in May of 1974. Tape-recorded transcripts of the trial had been smuggled out of Russia and published in French as *Un procès ordinaire en URSS* [An Ordinary Trial in the USSR]. Dr. Mikhail Stern, a member of the Communist Party and a Jew, had been denounced for refusing to dissuade his two sons from trying to immigrate to Israel. For this "failure" he was arrested on a series of trumped-up charges. At the trial, his patients (peasants whose "written depositions"—though many were illiterate—were purportedly contained in an incriminating dossier compiled against him) refused to cooperate with the state, claiming that their testimonies were delivered under duress and insisting upon the doctor's innocence. Stern was nevertheless condemned to eight years of hard labor. At the time of the *Apostrophes* broadcast, he was serving the third year of his sentence in a prison camp in Kharkov. Meanwhile, his sons, who had made the clandestine tape of the courtroom proceedings, fought for his release.

The Stern affair figured in the debate over Soviet oppression that had raged in the French media since the appearance of Solzhenitsyn's book on the Gulag. Now, by the1970s, French intellectuals could hardly plead ignorance to the horrors of Stalinist repression (the writer and militant politician David Rousset had exposed these almost thirty years prior in the wake of the Kravchenko affair; Trotsky's and Victor Serge's testimonies were available; and none could deny the impact of Khrushchev's 1956 report to the Communist Twentieth Party Congress).[34] Most had long since repudiated Soviet socialism as a viable political model. This being so, what was the furor about? During the 1970s, French debates over totalitarianism fulfilled at least two crucial functions. On the one hand, Solzhenitsyn's text and the critiques it inspired provided politically efficacious tools for those on both the right and the noncommunist left who were interested in condemning an important alliance—established in 1972 and known as the Union of the Left—between the Parti socialiste (PS) and the Parti communiste français (PCF). Many French intellectuals feared that if the Union's "common program" (which advocated a state-centered socialism) should bring the left to power, the PCF, despite having less electoral influence, would become ideologically dominant within the new government.

Antitotalitarian critiques of communist regimes sought to undermine the PCF's credibility and inhibit this possibility.[35] On the other hand, as Michael Scott Christofferson contends, identification with the "prophetic figure" of Solzhenitsyn allowed antitotalitarians—and here he is referring specifically to individuals like Glucksmann, Claude Lefort, Jean Daniel (then editor of *Le nouvel observateur*) and Bernard-Henri Lévy—"to disguise the origins of their positions in the mundane realities of French politics and make the claim that what they said was also universal in significance."[36] Within a few short years, the New Philosophers used this move to valorize the ethical over the political, reinterpreting May '68's failed revolution as the founding moment of an individualistic, almost spiritual rebirth, in which the intellectual was once again endowed with the authority to speak on behalf of a suffering world.

What was Foucault's stake in this controversy? In his discussion of the broadcast, Foucault biographer David Macy argues that Foucault "felt that he had enjoyed enough media exposure, and was therefore prepared to use his media appearances to bring something 'useful and unknown' to the attention of his viewers. In the circumstances, Stern's book was more interesting than his own."[37] I would argue that Foucault's motivations were less straightforward. For one, Foucault was stridently anticommunist and intensely critical of the Union of the Left. Supporting Soviet dissidence was his way of combating the PCF. Second, since the 1960s Foucault had made sophisticated use of the media to increase his intellectual renown. He was acutely aware that politics affected the reception of scholarship.[38] Dissatisfied that *The History of Sexuality* had not attracted more critical attention, and equally irritated by the PCF's failure to publish his essay on Stern's trial in the pages of *La nouvelle critique,* Foucault determined to take matters into his own hands.[39] Finally (and despite his undoubted political interest in the injustices of the Soviet regime and humanitarian concern for the particulars of Stern's oppression), I submit that Foucault's attention to the Stern affair was fueled by its extraordinary utility as a theoretical frame.

The philosophical problem that Foucault wanted to discuss in 1976—a problem that had dominated his intellectual explorations throughout the early 1970s and that both informed and exceeded his work in *The History of Sexuality*—was the power/knowledge nexus. Foucault's goal was to ascertain "the possibility of constituting a new politics of truth" by "detaching the power of truth from the forms of

The Sumerian Room; the Stern affair;
Foucault in action. From "Quel avenir
pour l'homme," 17 December 1976.

hegemony (social, economic and cultural) within which it operates at
the present time."[40] The Stern affair provides, he declares, his index
finger jabbing the air, "a remarkable example of how state-controlled
power" can "intervene and infiltrate into the most elementary of
human relations, that which exists between a doctor and a patient."
Demonstrating through his actions the very dynamic he sought to
illustrate with his words, Foucault subverted the power of the media
and deployed it to his own ends. Ignoring the unspoken rules governing the host/guest interaction, Foucault overrode convention, diverting
the focus and directing both guests and the television audience towards the issues (both political and philosophical), that he deemed
important.

Just as Foucault used his "repressive hypothesis" in the *History
of Sexuality* to reveal how the confessional practices of the church,
science, and medicine produced the "truth" of sexuality, in the *Apostrophes* broadcast he explains how the Soviet courtroom invoked these
practices to produce the "truth" about Stern. Because "the sexual" was
often considered morally reprehensible, the police extracted testimonies that painted Stern as sexually perverse. An endocrinologist, Stern
documented his patient's deformities with photographs (often nude).

These were found when his files were searched. From this "evidence" the KGB concluded that he was collecting pornography. The argument for sexual perversion, Foucault reports, was further substantiated when a woman attempting to testify on Stern's behalf admitted that yes, the doctor had examined her adolescent son naked and that yes, she was present during the exam. The prosecution inferred the abuse of a minor and deduced sexual misconduct. The confessional practices of the medical and the judicial fields collided in the courtroom, creating a twisted version of truth. If the purpose of *The History of Sexuality* was, as Foucault states in his book, "to show how deployments of power are directly connected to the body," the Stern affair presented an opportunity to observe philosophy in practice.[41]

Foucault's hijacking of Pivot's program needs to be understood as a double move. His actions on the broadcast implied not a rejection of the media but rather an explicit embrace of its demands. Indeed, Foucault appropriated both the medium (television) and the message (the Gulag), choosing a major media event in order to drive his ideas home. Ironically (and, I suggest, intentionally), Foucault's discussion of the Stern affair articulated not only the principal themes of *The History of Sexuality* but also the major tenets of his overarching philosophical project, from its fascination with medical, penal, and sexual discourses to the power/knowledge nexus and the production of truth. With its investigation of the relationship between the state and sexual morality, the Stern affair also provides a concrete expression of the theoretical turn to ethics that marks Foucault's later work.

For Foucault, the task of philosophy was to "undertake the diagnostic of that which we are today."[42] The Stern affair let him perform that diagnostic. Foucault's analysis of the affair also permitted him to demonstrate his philosophical concerns while achieving a political objective. It is worth noting that his televised intervention on *Apostrophes* was effective in directing public attention to the case. When the International Committee for the Liberation of Dr. Mikhail Stern brought Stern's situation before the Helsinki Conference, the increased publicity generated by Foucault's gesture helped ensure that the doctor was freed and eventually able to make his way to Paris. At the same time, by engaging an issue that was truly *au courant,* Foucault took maximum advantage of the media's ability to provide the broadest possible audience for his own philosophical ends.

Significantly, in embracing the media, in annexing the topic of discussion, and in shifting the terms of debate from a book to the

discursive production of knowledge, Foucault challenged contemporaneous arguments about the growing power of television—and especially of *Apostrophes*—to dictate the contents of the intellectual field.
The elements of philosophical activity, defined as "the theoretical analysis of the principles underlying conduct, thought, knowledge, and the
nature of the universe," were all present.[43] In this show, speed—the enemy of philosophic exchange—was kept in check. Despite the fact that
the debate format was intentionally structured to provoke conflict, Pivot's comparative silence, coupled with the unusually polite manners of
his other guests, ensured that Foucault dominated the discussion and
shaped it to his desires. Of course, despite the merits of its instigator,
the successful redirection of "Quel avenir pour l'homme?" would not
have been achieved without the collaboration of all the program's participants, and particularly of the show's host. Why did Bernard Pivot,
the man controversially nicknamed "the dictator of letters," submit
so readily to Foucault's agenda?[44] Because he knew that controversy
makes good drama, and good drama makes good television.

By all accounts, Foucault was a man possessed of remarkable personal charisma. In a 1995 broadcast that aired almost a decade after
Foucault's death, Gilles Deleuze recalled that when Foucault entered a
room, "it was as if, truly as if the air changed. As if there were a special current of air, and things changed. It was truly atmospheric. Believe me, there was something there, a radiance."[45] There is no doubt
that the man who once claimed that "one writes so as not to have a
face" was blessed with an unusually photogenic talent for transmitting
his ideas via the small screen.[46] And if few critics concur with Bernard-
Henri Lévy's claim that the television camera "cannot lie," or that we
"read an open book in the faces we see," Foucault's television performances nevertheless demonstrate that audiovisual acumen results in
real cultural capital.[47] This is not to say that he always emerged triumphant from his skirmishes with TV. In 1972, Foucault attempted
(along with Sartre, Beauvoir, Cixous, and Deleuze, among others) to
voice the opinions of the Groupe d'information sur les prisons (GIP)
by phoning into a live discussion on prison reform during a broadcast
of the series *Les dossiers de l'écran*. None of these phoned comments
was broadcast. Such failures emphasize that reigning media paradigms
cannot be subverted unless there is access to the rostrum.[48] It is also
true that despite his media-savvy strategies, Foucault never pursued
publicity, on television or elsewhere, as aggressively as the young philosophers he inspired. And to some, this made all the difference.

## From the "New Philosophers" to the New Mediocracy

The media celebrity of the New Philosophers was consecrated on 27 May 1977, when Bernard Pivot devoted a broadcast on *Apostrophes* to the confusing spin that surrounded their work.[49] Introducing, as was his custom, the evening's theme prior to the opening credits, he raised questions about "the New Philosophy":

> Is this just the Parisian effervescence of a few gifted spirits, or is it a genuine philosophical movement? Is it a marketing strategy or a spontaneous cultural revolution? Is it so much stardust in the eyes, or is it an intelligent approach to the truth? And are these philosophers on the left or the right? A tentative response in this one hundred and third edition of *Apostrophes*![50]

According to Antenne 2, the episode, which (echoing Pivot) was titled "Les nouveaux philosophes, sont-ils de droite ou de gauche?" garnered a mediocre audience of six to seven million viewers.[51] It nonetheless became a signal reference in the history of French intellectuals. Indeed, *Apostrophes'* coverage of the New Philosophers is repeatedly employed both to discredit the possibility of truly intellectual (not to mention philosophical) dialogue on the small screen, and to illustrate what many consider to be an irreversible historical tipping point: the moment when French intellectuals lost their souls to a devil named television. It may well be that *Apostrophes'* coverage of the New Philosophers signaled the arrival of the *intellectuel médiatique,* with all the negatives it entailed. But I would argue that the broadcast was also propitious. For with their intensely polemical conversations about ethics, politics, and the "rights of man," the New Philosophers brought the scholarly concerns of a renascent moral philosophy into the center of French public discourse. They also contributed—perhaps more than anyone before or since—to establishing a market for popular philosophy in France. These two feats shaped the future of the field. Who were the New Philosophers? What did they stand for? And what happened on that fateful broadcast?

By most accounts, the collective identity of the New Philosophers was established by Bernard-Henri Lévy in an article unambiguously titled "Les Nouveaux Philosophes," published in *Les nouvelles littéraires* on 10 June 1976. One of those young scholars who circumvented the overburdened university system in the 1970s and established their intellectual bona fides outside the academy, Lévy helped to break as Rémy Rieffel observes, "the enchanted circle of consecration behind closed doors" that had long legitimized the intellectual field.[52] Framing the dossier with discrete texts by such luminaries as Lévi-Strauss and Barthes, and peppering it with references to Nietzsche, Heidegger, Marx, Lacan, and Foucault, Lévy sought—disingenuously?—to legitimize the group through a kind of associative prestige. Lévy had graduated from the École normale supérieure and studied under Derrida and Althusser, was an *agrégé* in philosophy and the author (at age twenty-five) of a book on nationalism and revolution in Bangladesh. As an ambitious young editor at Éditions Grasset, he wrote the article to promote the amorphous philosophical projects expressed in two of the book series ("Théoriciens" and "Figures") published under his direction.[53] Although his most significant prior publishing experience was the launching of *L'imprévu*, a left-wing Parisian daily that folded after eleven issues, Lévy had charmed Françoise Verny, one of Grasset's directors, into offering him a job. When Verny immediately gave him carte blanche to launch a new series aimed at a younger, hipper readership, Lévy quickly solicited book proposals from among his former classmates. He received twenty within two weeks. To accommodate their intellectual diversity, the projected series was split in three (*Énjeux* and the two mentioned above). Many of the books that resulted formed the New Philosophy's core. But although most of the New Philosophers (including Guy Lardreau, Christian Jambet, Jean-Paul Dollé, Philip Nemo, and André Glucksmann) were friends of Lévy's or had their works published by Grasset, neither factor was requisite. Some who worked with Lévy, like Catherine Clément and Michel Serres, were not considered part of the phenomenon, while others who published elsewhere, like Guy Hocquenghem, Jean Baudrillard, and Nikos Poulantzas, were so regarded.[54] The group did share certain biographical traits: with few exceptions, they were male, born between 1940 and 1950, *normaliens,* and *agrégés* in philosophy.[55] Most were also former militants with political roots in Maoism, "third-worldism," and the Gauche prolétarienne (GP, Proletarian Left).[56]

The New Philosophers believed that the revolution had backfired. Politics, they argued, was a dead end. Disillusioned with political theories of renewal and deeply pessimistic after 1968 about the perfectibility of the social order, they sought solace in a domain of ethical theory that sometimes verged on the religious.[57] While their theoretical consistency is both elusive and contested (not least by the New Philosophers themselves), the thinkers held at least five slogans in common: "Marxism is barbarism, everything is only discourse, one must escape the political conception of the world, socialists are imposters, and one must wager." [58] Equating Marxism with an oppressive and monolithic totalitarianism, the New Philosophers endeavored to come to terms with the failure of May, and identified ethics as the preferred realm for philosophical action and reflection. [59] Drawing on the discourses of human rights and liberal individualism, they attempted to establish forms of intellectual dissidence that functioned outside the state and party politics. In their hands, antitotalitarianism (arriving twenty years too late, according to those who point to the Soviet invasion of Hungary in 1956 as the proper moment for revelation) extended from a cold war analytic encompassing East and West to one that took in the entire third world. Their return to metaphysics and their rejection of both structuralism and Deleuzian "philosophies of desire" marked a generational shift in sensibilities. [60]

It is often suggested that the New Philosophy was the result of a marketing blitz. Certainly, a dense, even nepotistic web connecting its authors to publishing houses, to the press (especially at the influential new weekly, Le nouvel observateur, at Le magazine littéraire, and at Le monde), to philosophical colloquia (at the Centre Beaubourg and Théâtre oblique), to radio (on the programs of France Culture), and to television (Apostrophes, but also other programs, including Tribune libre, and the nightly news) propelled the group into the public eye. [61] They reviewed one another's books, collaborated in public engagements, and generally practiced forms of mutual promotion. This activity, while hardly new to the Parisian intellectual scene, was so prolific (and successful), that it raised eyebrows. The problem, according to Gilles Deleuze (one of the New Philosophers' harshest critics—a fact that led to his falling out with Foucault, who supported them), was that the effort they put into marketing implied "an activity exclusive of philosophy, or at least excluded from it." [62] But it was the New Philosophers' timely involvement with French antitotalitarianism (and its political repercussions), not their promotional skills, that confirmed their stratospheric rise to media celebrity. And it was this association that led Bernard-Henri Lévy and André Glucksmann to be identified as the New Philosophy's ringleaders—an appellation that each man simultaneously profited from and contested. [63]

Lévy and Glucksmann were French Jews—and their Judaism affected their theoretical trajectories in ways that are connected to the future of both philosophy and intellectual life in France.[64] Eleven years Lévy's senior, Glucksmann was born in 1937 to Ashkenazic Jews of Austrian origin who had immigrated to France in 1936 via Palestine and Germany. His father was killed during World War II. His mother and sister were active in the Resistance; the family narrowly escaped deportation to the camps. Jonathan Judaken remarks that Glucksmann's "antitotalitarian assault was, in part, a compensatory displacement" for the ways in which he personally experienced "the Final Solution to 'the Jewish Question.'"[65] Certainly the formative role that the Holocaust played in Glucksmann's life helps explain his passionate attachment to a vision of the state as the ultimate source of barbarism. As for Lévy, he was born in Algeria in 1948 into a family of Sephardic Jews. Although his father fought with the Free French, Lévy was too young to have experienced the Nazi horrors. Nor is he, as is Alain Finkielkraut (discussed in chapter 5), the son of survivors. Nevertheless (and this is explicit in both his 1979 *Le testament de Dieu* and his 1981 *L'idéologie française*), both Judaism and the problem of anti-Semitism are central to his thought. Like the turn to moral philosophy per se, these concerns were acutely connected to the rekindling of interest in the Holocaust and the resurgence of anti-Semitism (both discussed in chapter 5) that formed the background to the French antitotalitarian debates of the1970s and early 1980s. It is no small irony, however, that it was "popular" philosophers like Lévy and Glucksmann, who, in their diverse responses to totalitarianism as inflected through the "Jewish question," replaced the "specific intellectual" articulated by Foucault and Deleuze in the early 1970s with the revivified figure of the "universal intellectual" as moralist.[66] In order to explore how they did this, let's examine the *Apostrophes* broadcast.

( · )

"Les nouveaux philosophes, sont-ils de droite ou de gauche?" provides a glimpse of the kind of moralizing repartee (and hyperbolic theatrics) that came to characterize media appearances by the New Philosophers and their antagonists. The lineup, poised for confrontation, was classic Pivot. Indeed, as the show progressed, tempers escalated so ferociously that by the end the participants could barely control themselves. This was verbal jousting at its nastiest—and, some might conclude, its most entertaining. The program pitted Lévy, Glucksmann, and Maurice Clavel against François Aubral and Xavier Delcourt, the young authors of *Contre la nouvelle philosophie*—a scathing indictment of the "movement." After introducing his guests, Pivot cautions that before "throwing gasoline on the fire" and launching into the arguments, each guest in turn should explain his position to the audience. Perhaps out of deference to his age (or perhaps because he was the television critic at *Le nouvel observateur*—a post he held from 1966 to 1979), Pivot began with Clavel and his book, *Nous l'avons tous tué, ou ce Juif de Socrate* (We Have All Killed Him, or The Jew Socrates).[67]

From an older generation than that of the other guests, but like them a *normalien* and an *agregé* in philosophy (1942), Clavel was frequently referred to as the *tonton* (uncle) or, less generously, the godfather of the New Philosophers because of his active interest in, influence on, and promotion of their work.[68] Although he was famous for his participation in the Resistance and the 1944 liberation of Chartres, Clavel's politics were complicated; active on the right following the war, he grew progressively more sympathetic to the left. He supported de Gaulle until the Ben Barka affair.[69] By the time of the *Apostrophes* broadcast, Clavel had experienced a "particularly unquiet Christian conversion,"[70] was teaching philosophy in a lycée, and had become a powerful advocate of young, ex–Gauche prolétarienne Maoists, including Glucksmann, Lardreau, and Jambet. While he had no great affection for Lévy (whose integrity as an ex-militant '68er he—like many—questioned, and whose publishing house, Grasset, had rejected his book on Socrates), he found common cause with the younger philosopher's antitotalitarianism. Clavel's reputation as an icon of the noncommunist left was secured in a 1971 live television broadcast when (after observing that the producers had cut crucial scenes from his film about May '68) he famously stormed off the set of the political magazine *À armes égales,* proclaiming, "Messieurs les Censeurs, bonsoir!" Clavel's 1975 *Ce que je crois* (What I Believe) sold over 100,000 copies within months of its release, and Éditions du Seuil had high hopes for his latest book.

A self-described "transcendental journalist," Clavel aimed to draw ethical or religious lessons from everyday events. *Ce Juif de Socrates,* Clavel explains, his large, meaty hands working the air, was an attempt to come to terms with the disillusionment that followed the "divine experience" of May '68. While May left us frustrated by the inefficacy of political activism and wary of the dangers entrenched in ideology, Clavel argues that, despite its failure, it also heralded a religious and cultural transformation of the highest order. (To this end, Clavel in 1976 had formed the *Cercle socratique,* a group of ex-GP activists, including Glucksmann, Lardreau, Jambet, Benny Lévy, Pierre Victor, and François Ewald, dedicated to examining the theme of revolution. Interestingly, their first meeting featured a presentation of a text on Emmanuel Levinas, an early example of their interest in ethics.[71] Rarely pausing (and railroading Pivot's attempts to intervene), Clavel equates Socrates' murder by the *polis* with the twentieth-century "assassination of the self-transcendence of man" accomplished under the political state. In Socrates' statement, "I know only one thing, that I know nothing," Clavel discerns humanity's dependence on a transcendent other, namely, God. For Clavel, Socrates represents—referencing Glucksmann—the "antimaster thinker" par excellence, the one capable of "liberating liberty" and engendering a new world. As Clavel states elsewhere, "I believe in despair, and I don't cease to believe—and this is a classic theme in mysticism and poetry—that real hope only emerges through [an encounter with] hopelessness."[72] It is because he feels, Clavel posits, spitting the words through his teeth, that just such an "existential experience" was at "the origin of their critiques and their metaphysics" that he has placed his faith in the New Philosophers. In his near-fanatical enthusiasm we get the distinct sense that the lumbering, near-sighted Clavel is a man possessed who, given the chance, would happily dominate the entire evening. But Pivot finally manages to put him in check, remarking, "If you continue, we won't have to read your book!" and then laughingly suggests that we move on to Glucksmann.

André Glucksmann first attracted popular attention in 1975, when his *La cuisinière et le mangeur d'hommes* (The Cook and the Cannibal)—a comparison of Nazism and communism in which he lauded Russian dissidents for helping intellectuals in the West "to know ourselves better," and condemned the left for failing to reject Marxism—became a bestseller.[73] The book amplified the vitriolic intellectual debates sparked by Solzhenhitsyn's work and brought them to a wider audience. It also brought Glucksmann to television: in 1974 Bernard Pivot interviewed the philosopher in a special on Solzhenitsyn on the short-lived *Ouvrez les guillemets.*[74] But it was the publication of Glucksmann's *Les maîtres penseurs* (The Master Thinkers) in the spring of 1977, an analysis of German philosophy's contribution to totalitarianism, that established him as a major media presence and a spokesperson for the antitotalitarian left. The book sold 30,000 copies in less than a month.[75]

On the *Apostrophes* broadcast, Glucksmann, his whole body vibrating with the force of his convictions, argues that ideas matter. The

problem he focuses on (a recurrent concern in his television appearances) is that of intellectual responsibility. He reads "the grand final
solutions of the twentieth century" as the natural product of the four
"master thinkers"—Marx, Hegel, Fichte, and Nietzsche—of the "German nineteenth century." "But how," ask Pivot, "is an intellectual
climate responsible for the Gulag?" These men, Glucksmann asserts,
echoing the argument of his book, "put into orbit a certain number
of values and beliefs that everyone in the Western intellectual world
holds true." And these beliefs—in science, in Marxism, in the Cult of
Revolution, in the death of God and the dream of a rational society—
blind us to, and substantiate, abuses of power by the modern state.
But, Glucksmann insists, political revolt against the state apparatus
is not the answer, since such revolt reifies (and is open to recuperation
by) the absolute power of the object it attacks. Instead, Les maîtres
penseurs situates revolt in a figure—conceived as Rabelais's Panurge,
as Socrates, or as "the Jew" (the perennial wanderer)—who is eter-
nally external and resistant to power. Positively incarnated, this "anti-
barbaric" dissenter practices a pessimistic ethics to refute the unspeak-
able horrors performed in the name of modern power politics. And
Glucksmann clearly casts himself in this role. Indeed, Glucksmann is
forever championing the sufferings of the silent "plebs" (a term he uses
to designate the politically disenfranchised masses whose hopeless resistance renders them almost sacred in his eyes).[76] When he decries the
fate of "forty million dead deportees in the camps in Siberia" at the
beginning of the show, his words perform a symbolic act, legitimizing
him as one identified with, and authorized to speak for, these voiceless
hordes.[77] Thus, Glucksmann's position as a "rehabilitated" militant allows him (and philosophers like him) to resurrect the intellectual as
moralist, a role repudiated in May of 1968 and now deployed in support not of political parties but of the individual and of ethical themes
such as "human rights" and "democracy."

When it's his turn to speak, Lévy expands upon these matters,
outlining the main tenets of the New Philosophy ("the only successful
revolutions have been totalitarian," and "socialism is a form of barbarism") and describing the generational, anti-Marxist, and Lacanian
influences common to this group of thinkers. Asked whether his new
book, La barbarie à visage humaine (Barbarism with a Human Face—
also a runaway bestseller, selling 37,000 copies in its first two weeks
on the market),[78] expresses a "philosophy of pessimism," Lévy says yes.
"I try to show," he states, crooning at the camera, "that the historical
optimism that I attack in my book is always founded on some idea

of a golden age, before power, before the masters, and that we need to try to rediscover this." And he adds, "The revolutionaries and the socialists are all obsessed with this idea and believe they can achieve it through revolution, but that's a false perspective." Consequently, as he states in *La barbarie à visage humaine*, "We no longer have politics, a language, or a recourse. There remain only ethics and moral duty." [79] Inspired by the work of Camus, Levinas, and Jankélévitch, Lévy would further develop this position (in his 1979 *Le testament de Dieu*) into a vision of "political morality" practiced by a "free subject" whose ethics were "a product not of the atheistic, secular and scientific age of Enlightenment, but of the antipagan, monotheistic tradition in which humans were created in the image of God." [80]

Only after Pivot turns from Lévy to Aubral and Delcourt does the offensive begin in earnest. Both men quickly condemn the New Philosophy's content: its pessimism, its suspicion of history, and its rejection of progressive models. Lévy's work is dismissed as trivial, derivative, and incompetent. Quoting from *Contre la nouvelle philosophie*, Pivot reads: "This book was born of that feeling of disgust aroused in us by these sham philosophers who wallow in a swamp of nonsense." [81] Aubral and Delcourt launch into an extended harangue in which they accuse "these guys" of being "hardline Stalinists who, since they failed at revolution, are now saying that politics doesn't exist"—a perspective that gives rise to a philosophy that is "useless," "derisory," and "utterly pessimistic." Glucksmann bristles visibly at this string of invectives. Building momentum, Aubral quotes triumphantly from Lévy: "'the real doesn't exist' (page 56); 'nature doesn't exist' (page 57); 'history doesn't exist' (page 61); 'the past doesn't exist' (page 64); 'the individual doesn't exist' (page 79); 'the proletariat doesn't exist' (page 100)." He then cries, "It's sheer fantasy!"

When Pivot asks, "Why is this dangerous? For philosophy? Politics? France?" Delcourt explains that his and Aubral's critique of the New Philosophers functions on two levels: one political, the other philosophical. [82] Addressing Lévy, Delcourt suggests that when the New Philosophy seeks to eradicate party politics, it is practically in bed with the New Right. For when we adopt a philosophy "that would forbid all political thought," one that claims that "if we think politically we are perverts" and attacks "any political concept" by yelling "Gulag," then we actually advance conservative political agendas. And the powers that be understand this. Indeed, Delcourt remarks, no less a force than President Giscard d'Estaing professed interest in Lévy's *La barbarie à visage humaine* precisely because he believed it would "serve to fight in the intellectual milieu against the Common Program of the Left." [83] Given the national political context in 1977, the parties of the right needed all the help they could get.

Following the closest electoral victory of the Fifth Republic, in 1974 (when Mitterrand's socialists lost with 49.2% of the vote), Giscard attempted to implement a new vision of French liberal society. But, in the wake of the OPEC crisis, the nation floundered under the impact of the worldwide economic downturn. The left profited from the country's problems, and after a sweeping success in the 1977 municipal elections it expected victory in the important legislative elections the following year. In anticipation of this outcome, the Parti communiste français sought to radicalize the Common Program. The resulting debates threw the left into disarray and dominated the media through the spring and summer of 1977. The PCF lost domestic support as anti-Stalinism slid towards anti-Marxism in an international political context shaken by events as varied as the genocidal massacres committed under Pol Pot in Cambodia, the revelations (following Mao's death in 1976) of oppression during the Chinese Cultural Revolution, the plight of the boat people fleeing communist Vietnam, and escalating acts of terrorism in Germany and Italy. In this fragile political landscape, arguments about the New Philosophers were quite simply arguments about the political future, not only of the left, but also of the French nation. Yet if media coverage enjoyed by the New Philosophers resulted in part from their political utility, as Delcourt is quick to point out, it also permitted them to dominate discussions of philosophy, to the detriment of other—some would argue more serious—work. Consequently, as the broadcast continues, it is the New Philosophy's compelling *aspect publicitaire* that becomes the target of attack.

Holding up with evident disgust a copy of *Playboy* in which Lévy had published an article, Aubral disdainfully quotes: "I live in a contained space, extremely limited, in a tiny village within Saint-Germain-des-Prés." "*This*" (implying both the insular Parisian community and the bourgeois fantasy rag), Aubral snorts, snapping shut the offending magazine, "is *not* where philosophy happens." Philosophy, he continues, happens in the academy, in the journals, in periodicals like (Jacques Rancière's) *Revoltes logiques,* or (Pierre Bourdieu's) *Actes de la recherche en sciences sociales,* without celebrities and certainly without *Playboy.* Glucksmann immediately rushes to Lévy's defense. But although he protests that one can indeed "philosophize" in the cafés of Saint-Germain-des-Prés just as genuinely as in a journal, it is glaringly evident that Glucksmann would prefer to disassociate himself from the whole business. Thus, when Pivot asks, "André Glucksmann, do you consider yourself a New Philosopher?" Glucksmann's response is an unequivocal, "Absolutely not!" Lévy is not far behind. But when he likewise denies having anything to do with the group or its genesis, Lévy's intractable opponents thrust the incriminating evidence—the cover of his 1976 article "Les Nouveaux Philosophes," mentioned earlier—before *Apostrophes'* cameras.

In the face of this onslaught, Lévy's cool demeanor dissolves. "Maybe you aren't the Gulag police but you sure act like them! Digging up all these old articles!" he hisses. The aggression is palpable. The debate escalates, and with it the volume. Throughout the broadcast, Pivot keeps attempting, with scant success, to restore order, alternately shushing and barking "Non! Non! Non!" at those talking out of turn. When the group briefly settles, Pivot asks, "Why is it so important to denounce Bernard-Henri Lévy's book?" "Because," Aubral responds, "everywhere in the media we find nothing, we talk about nothing, but the New Philosophy! It has a power that is eclipsing all other forms of philosophy. [. . .] We are asking for room to breathe." Clavel quips, "Well then, everything is working out fine, because now we're talking about *you!*" Later, Aubral dubs Lévy a "publicity genius," to which Lévy replies, "Well, if publicity is about getting my ideas to the maximum number of readers possible—I'm all for it!"

As luck would have it, if the notoriety of the New Philosophers can be separated neither from the crisis on the political left nor from their marketing strategies, their legacy is symbolized almost exclusively by the very television exposure that they were receiving at that very moment. And it is the visual component of this performance (especially in the case of Lévy) that is considered intellectually damning, largely because during the 1970s it became the most important part of what Régis Debray calls "the imperiously and naively extra-cultural [. . .] criteria that direct the demand for cultural goods." Debray's distaste for this process is telling. Mimicking conversations rampant at the time, he quips, " 'That [is] my idea of a philosopher.'—'You were convinced by his arguments?'—'No, by his looks.' "[84]

( · )

*Apostrophes'* footage of Bernard-Henri Lévy created the stereotype that has defined him ever since. Fingers curved gracefully around a cigarette, with his boyish good looks, dark tousled hair, white shirt dramatically open at the collar, and elegant demeanor, Lévy comes off like a cross between a Baudelairean poet and a nineteenth-century *flâneur*. This was perhaps not the first time that a French intellectual generated sex appeal, but never before had one embraced the camera so directly. Some twenty years later, the press was still referencing the "look" established on this broadcast. In a 3 March 1997 article titled "BHL drops his shirt," the magazine *Elle* chided,

> Is there life after the white shirt cunningly unbuttoned on a svelte torso? This existential question stirring all Paris for some time may finally be settled. There is not a television show, not a public appearance without our philosopher rigged out in a grayish tee shirt without a collar! This is a change that hasn't escaped the "Minister of Info"!

Lévy's 1993 wedding to the French actress Arielle Dombasle further cemented his celebrity status. Following the publication of his twenty-ninth book, a bestselling investigation of the murder of the *Wall Street Journal* reporter Daniel Pearl, *The Observer* (15 June 2003) introduced Lévy as a "philosopher, political campaigner, pundit and luscious-locked superstud," describing him as "an unfathomably French combination of Melvyn Bragg, J. K. Rowling and David Beckham," and noted that

> his clothes (open-necked white shirts and designer suits), his friends (Yves Saint Laurent, Alain Delon, Salman Rushdie), his homes (the flat in Saint Germain, a hideaway in the South of France, an eighteenth-century palace in Marrakech that used to belong to John Paul Getty) are endlessly commented on.

It's hard to imagine that Lévy would have endured as a media darling if not for the close attention he paid to physical presentation. Articulate, animated, and disarmingly self-assured, Lévy is a casting agent's dream. Consequently, he consistently receives broadcast coverage despite often biting criticism of his work. His television exposure rivals Sartre's.[85] But whereas Sartre, Bachelard, and Foucault were recognized as philosophers prior to their television appearances, Lévy was arguably *produced* as a philosopher by the media, and particularly by television. Controversially, he often orchestrated the production himself.

Glucksmann was another case entirely. Brooding, intense, and re-lentlessly serious, his dour face framed by a perennial pageboy, Glucks-mann's indignant demeanor made him less visually appealing than Lévy. On the other hand, his bullish obstinacy enlivens the debates in which he takes part (a fact that made him an interesting guest from Piv-ot's perspective). Despite his ready use of television (the *Apostrophes* broadcast marked his fourth appearance on the small screen), Glucks-mann feigned rejection of Lévy's media strategies.[86] He insisted that he used television not to promote his own work but only when he thought his presence could be employed against society's crimes. Given that exposure always equals publicity, the honesty of this sentiment is dif-ficult to gauge. It is true, however, that Glucksmann's numerous televi-sion interventions over the next ten years—supporting the "boat peo-ple," Soviet dissidents (notably Andrei Sakharov), the Holocaust, and the Polish Solidarity movement, and protesting the proliferation of nu-clear arms—were uniquely connected to struggles for human rights.[87] This was not the case for Lévy, who was no less likely to appear on French TV as the judge of a contest for the most beautiful legs than he was as a champion of human rights in Chile, Cambodia, Argentina, and later, Ethiopia, Bosnia, Afghanistan, and Iraq, or as an enemy of

Bernard-Henri Lévy. From "Les nouveaux philosophes, sont-ils de droite ou de gauche?" 27 May 1977.

anti-Semitism or racism in France.[88] Scholarly assessments aside, it is not surprising that Glucksmann attracts less censure from the French intellectual community than does the self-promoting "BHL."

An important result of the media hype surrounding the New Philosophers was that a link was made between their fast and loose philosophizing and the perception of television as necessarily superficial. Certainly, judged in light of the *Apostrophes* episode (with its premium on entertainment and its overwrought theatricality), the small screen appears ill suited to meaningful engagement with ideas. Intellectual television, the New Philosophers "proved," equals surface without depth or substance; this view continues to dominate discussions of the medium. Yet it fails to account either for the successful production of philosophy on TV or for the fact that television became the vehicle that enabled these self-appointed guardians of international human rights and censurers of totalitarianism to reenergize the public presence of philosophy and reaffirm the importance of intellectual engagement in the public sphere.

By retreating from the political to the ethical domain, Lévy, Glucksmann, and the New Philosophers resuscitated interest in metaphysics and recuperated the "classic" intellectual as the universal

André Glucksmann. From "Les nouveaux philosophes, sont-ils de droite ou
de gauche?" 27 May 1977.

moral voice. This newer incarnation circumvented the older Sartrean
model by claiming a sort of spiritual brotherhood with the oppressed,
effacing the ways in which bourgeois class affiliation divided intellectuals from "the people."[89] This move was made possible by the New
Philosophers' recourse to ethics (especially apparent in the work of
Lévy, Lardreau, Jambet, and Nemo), identified by Patrick Pharo as
"defense of the Rights of Man, critique of the political and of its statist
realization, rehabilitation of the individual and the intellectual, [and]
affirmation of the moral as foundation for historical action."[90] As
Kristin Ross explains, having once "united with the people in revolt,"
the New Philosophers claimed to have reconciled contradictions and
joined "the popular masses" in "a world now riven into stark ethical polarities: power and resistance, the state and civil society, good
and evil."[91] The New Philosophers' desertion of the political in favor
of the ethical marked a stunning rejection of the positions (both political and ideological) held by a majority of French intellectuals since the
late nineteenth century. But their use of what Deleuze calls "gross conceptual stereotypes" ("THE law, Power, Master, THE world, THE revolution, Faith, etc.") and "gross dualisms," ("THE law *and* THE rebel,
Power *and* Angels") has been attacked as intellectually simplistic and

dangerously reactionary.[92] Likewise, although they identified with the noncommunist left, many of their positions were actually drawn from the repertoire of the right, a fact that opened the gates to right-wing renewal. Equally important, by extending (as did Foucault), the concept of power to all social relations, the ethical discourse that the New Philosophers popularized emptied the political of significance, effectively eradicating the possibility of revolutionary change.[93] Its hazards should not be underestimated.

But if the New Philosophy was ultimately dismissed for its lack of intellectual rigor, and if its ethical theses were less than effective, its broader cultural impact cannot be ignored. Television thrust the basic ethical questions raised by the New Philosophers—about the quality and meaning of life, about human rights, about the role of the state and the intellectual, and even about "the Jewish question"—into the public sphere. Within a decade, Levinas, Jankélévitch, and Ricoeur, not to mention a whole new generation of "popular philosophers" including Luc Ferry, André Comte-Sponville, Alain Finkielkraut, and Michel Onfray, would start to reap the profits.

### Philosophy for Everyone: *Interrogations* and *Les idées et les hommes*

Although *Apostrophes* and the New Philosophers monopolized much of the attention paid to philosophy on television in the 1970s and early 1980s, other broadcasts also treated philosophical themes at this time. In 1975, concurrent with the start of *Apostrophes*, another philosophy program was initiated. Like the programs of the Radio-télévision scolaire discussed in chapter 3, *Interrogations* (1975–76) was organized around philosophical themes and displayed an avowedly didactic agenda. The brainchild of Denis Huisman, *Interrogations* was the first philosophy series produced specifically for a national (as opposed to a school-age) audience. After it was discontinued, Huisman went on to produce a series called *Les idées et les hommes* (1976–83).[94] It too had an unacknowledged predecessor: its format strongly resembled that of the biographical documentaries produced for *Un certain regard* in the late 1960s and early 1970s. However, while *Les Idées et les hommes* was similarly conceived as a series of specials on the lives of important philosophers, writers, and intellectuals, it differed from *Un certain regard* by including pre-twentieth-century figures. In keeping with its title, all of its subjects were male. Among the philosophers Huisman focused on were Alain, Camus, Pascal, Kierkegaard, Bergson, Comte, Spinoza, Tielhard de Chardin, Descartes and Plato.

Born in 1929 into a solidly bourgeois upper-middle-class family, Denis Huisman did not hold the *agrégation* in philosophy but had obtained a joint *licence* in philosophy and psychology. He went on to gain a doctorate in letters at the Sorbonne. At nineteen, Huisman began teaching philosophy in a number of Parisian lycées.[95] In 1950 he was taken on as an assistant by the aesthetician Étienne Souriau at the Sorbonne (a position he was to hold for ten years), and in 1953 he was granted a research post at the Centre national de la recherche scientifique (CNRS). The early 1950s also saw Huisman's first experience with the media: between 1952 and 1955 he hosted the radio show *Heure de culture française* for the RTF. He served in Edgar Faure's Ministry of Finance in 1958, and in the same year became involved in the publishing industry.[96] In 1961 he founded the École française des attachés de presse, which aimed to train journalists in multiple media formats. (By the end of the 1980s, he had established similar schools in the United States and Africa, as well as elsewhere in France and Europe.) Throughout the 1960s Huisman continued to teach in various capacities. He also began a prodigious career as an author, becoming particularly well known for his work as one of the preeminent editors of introductory philosophy texbooks for students.[97] "In France," he recalls, "philosophy profs hate textbooks. [. . .] I don't hate them myself [. . .], but then I don't take much interest in the excellent students—they don't need a professor—they read the authors in the original on their own."[98] Huisman's extended involvement in and commitment to the "vulgarization" of the discipline gave him a special perspective on bringing philosophy to mass audiences via television.

*Interrogations* was not Huisman's first foray into television. Between 1972 and 1973 he had produced a series on psychology titled *Les grands problèmes de la psychologie* for the ORTF's Channel 2. Fascinated by the medium, he was eager to repeat the experience. When Jean Cazeneuve (who had previously participated on one of the psychology shows) took over the presidency of TF1 in 1975, Huisman saw his chance. Cazeneuve, a sociologist and former *agrégé* in philosophy, was both a strong proponent of cultural television and eager to develop a style that would "satisfy the tastes of the viewers, while also enriching them."[99] His goals were in keeping with TF1's commitment to establishing itself as the channel of tradition, stability, and continuity. Knowing that Cazeneuve had enjoyed his program, Huisman pitched the concept of a series on philosophy directly to the new president. Cazeneuve seized on the idea with such vigor that he actually volunteered to introduce the series to the viewing public in the first broadcast. Cazeneuve's opening address, with its convivial but somewhat patronizing attitude, set the tone for the broadcasts and bears quoting at length:

> Ladies and gentlemen, good evening. The program that you are about to see, the first of a monthly series, is an entirely new television initiative. For the first time we are addressing frankly, openly, directly, and in a straightforward fashion the major and eternal human questions:[100] Does God exist? Are we free? Are we the masters of our acts and thoughts? Is life more than matter? Do we have a soul? What is the beautiful? The true? The good? What are we doing here? These are questions that we cannot exclude from our thoughts, much less from our existence, without considering them. But why, you ask, should we address these questions on television? Because for centuries (indeed, since we have been on earth), man has asked himself these questions, and he has never found definitive answers. But why translate them into sound and image? Well, above all because these questions are no longer formulated in the same terms that they used to be, so that we no longer have the right to ignore the place of philosophy in our modern world. Therefore we simply want to help *you* to ask these questions, and to justify your responses by presenting to you, as objectively as possible, the arguments that can be invoked either for or against them. Finally, you will clearly see on these shows that *you* are always in question, *you* are being questioned, along with us.[101]

The major themes for the programs followed Cazeneuve's lead and bore titles such as "Does God exist?" "Liberty and Determinism," "The Self and the Other," "Responsibility," "Justice," "Truth," "Art, the Beautiful, and the Useful," "Happiness," "Death," and "Love."[102]

*Interrogations* was taped at very little cost on site at the studios at Buttes-Chaumont. It aired on the third Wednesday of the month, beginning between nine-thirty and ten-fifteen in the evening.[103] The set, with its Greek phi suspended behind the plateau, was designed for the program by TF1. The show was shot with a fixed video camera immediately prior to broadcast ("semi-live") during a session lasting an hour and a half, requiring the director Janine Guyon to cut thirty-five to

Jean Cazeneuve (president of TF1) introduces *Interrogations* in 1975; the set; producer and host Denis Huisman.

forty minutes (minus the added length of any short film inserts) for the final fifty-two-minute product. To Huisman's dismay—and the show's detriment—Cazeneuve held sway over the choice of participants.[104] Guests were not paid, and Huisman indicates that since "Cazeneuve had many friends that he wanted to please," invitations often reflected personal favor as much as scholarly interest. Huisman believed that the principal drawback of the show, the one element that "finally killed it," was the participation of a "dusty" group made up of "members of the Académie française, of the Institut," people "of a certain age and a certain social position," none of whom was "young, dynamic, or aggressive enough" to wake the program out of its hyperacademic stupor.[105] As Huisman acknowledged, his own exceedingly wooden presentation added nothing to the proceedings. "I was often reproached for not being natural as a host," he recalls. He was "freaked out" by being seen and heard by people he considered his intellectual superiors.[106] Additionally, the fact that some guests insisted on reading prepared responses, as well as Huisman's use of notes and general reticence to engage his guests (often responding merely with "Uh-hum," or "Yes," to their ideas, and then turning away to pose some completely unrelated question to another person), stilted the program's rhythm and inhibited the development of any real dialogue, philosophic or otherwise. Structurally, however, *Interrogations* presented significant innovations in the televising of philosophy. Although the basic format—consisting of a roundtable with the interlocutors seated in a horseshoe responding to questions prepared in advance—was fairly staid, Huisman attempted to enliven the broadcast by including filmed sequences to illustrate the evening's theme. And if quite unable to conduct a debate, Huisman remained convinced of the importance of both embodying philosophical dialogue and translating central philosophical questions into sound and image.[107] Consequently, two or sometimes three film clips were incorporated during the course of a show.

Each broadcast opened with Huisman introducing the evening's theme and his guests. The standard format was to proceed directly to a short film, its scenario written especially for the program dramatizing the philosophical topic under discussion. The series' limited budget meant that these sequences were produced quickly—usually in less than a week. According to Marie-Agnès Malfray (Huisman's first wife and constant collaborator), these opening sequences were intended to render abstract philosophical problems concrete and to place them in dialogue with daily life.[108] Pedagogically, these films situated the topic within the history of philosophy, quoting from or summarizing arguments by major philosophers in order to support the theme under discussion. Malfray wrote the scenarios and narrated; an archivist located stills; and the show's director, Janine Guyon, shot the clips. These little films were the most creative aspect of the show.

Once the first sequence aired, Huisman typically asked his guests to debate the issue that it raised. Later in the show, other film excerpts were often used to illustrate other aspects of the philosophical question at hand. These subsequent clips were either taken from well-known films (by directors as diverse as Jean Renoir, Roberto Rossellini, Ingmar Bergman, and Charlie Chaplin) or consisted of brief interviews conducted off-site. Unfortunately, Huisman and his participants rarely engaged in any substantive fashion with either the material or each other, and the programs proceeded in fits and starts from one grandiloquent monologue to the next. Bernard Pivot had nothing to fear here.

Following the break-up of the ORTF in 1974 and the dissolution of the Service de la recherche in the same year, Pierre Schaeffer had been charged to preside over a "quality commission" that, though lacking executive powers, was authorized to send off its advice to the different

"Le moi et les autres," 24 September 1975.

"'I advance masked,' stated Descartes. Are not people constituted by an infinite series of masks?"

"Is compassion the best form of penetration of the other? Doesn't love (which, according to Pascal, is the best form of knowing) render us more blind to another's reality?"

"Or must we think, with Jean-Paul Sartre and contemporary existentialism, that hate, more clearly than love, permits us to know ourselves in others, and others in ourselves?"

channels at the end of each month. According to Huisman, Schaeffer and Cazeneuve were "sworn enemies": "Everything that Cazeneuve did, Schaeffer criticized, and in turn Cazeneuve thought Schaeffer was a fool." In any event, one morning Huisman was called into Cazeneuve's office and informed that after its thirteenth show *Interrogations* was to be taken off the air "on account of its poor quality." The series was deemed "too elementary to interest specialists, and too specialized to interest the general public." Determined to keep his hand in the pot, Huisman responded, "But sir, it's a question of means. [. . .] We are working with a stationary camera, and it's very boring for the public to simply watch a bunch of people talk. What if, instead of taking themes, we took philosophers—for example, Plato, Descartes, Kierkegaard, or Spinoza—and made real films about them?"[109] Although *Apostrophes*' success (on a competing channel) suggested that it was indeed possible to get "the public to simply watch a bunch of people talk," Cazeneuve acquiesced. Generously multiplying Huisman's budget (from 40,000 to 800,000 francs per broadcast hour), TF1 gave him carte blanche to produce a new program, to be called *Les idées et les hommes.*[110]

The broadcasts of *Les idées et les hommes* were conceived as documentary portraits. The majority of these focus on great philosophers.[111] Given a 7:1 shooting ratio (seven hours shot for every hour aired), production values were considerably higher than they had been for *Interrogations.* With the increased funds and greater freedom, not only could Huisman take cameras and crew on location—to Athens for the special on Plato; to Vésinet, where Alain had made his home; to Amsterdam for the show on Spinoza; to Copenhagen for Kierkegaard—but he could also coax stronger casts to participate. This time, almost all of the interviewees were themselves philosophers, among them Emmanuel Levinas, who shared his thoughts on Kierkegaard (as did a young Sylviane Agacinski), and Raymond Aron, who discussed Alain. Guests were no longer expected to dialogue with one another. Instead, they spoke directly to the camera, providing philosophical insights and personal anecdotes aimed at making both the ideas and the individual under examination accessible to the television audience. To the general benefit of the programs, Huisman's time on-camera was considerably reduced. Malfray (once again co-producing and more gifted dramatically than Huisman) often participated on screen or taped the narration. The two of them split production responsibilities, with Huisman choosing subjects and Malfray writing scripts and biographical commentary. He handled the shoots and contacted the guests; she oversaw the editing and organized the directors and their crews.[112] Stylistically, the programs owed much to Malfray's experimental sequences for the opening of *Interrogations,* since like these they often incorporated a mélange of still photographs, landscapes, and "philosophically evocative" imagery. Many of Huisman's former critics (including Claude Sarraute, the television reviewer at *Le monde* who had raked *Interrogations* over the coals) conceded that most of the films produced for *Les idées et les hommes* were informative, fairly interesting, and—perhaps more important, given the television climate—somewhat entertaining.[113] To its detriment, the series was produced and broadcast

Denis Huisman: "Once upon a time there was a great philosopher from a small country, Denmark, named Søren Kierkegaard." From "Søren Kierkegaard," 11 November 1977.

sporadically, which meant that it had difficulty developing a faithful audience. *Les idées et les hommes* hung on intermittently through the end of the 1970s and disappeared after 1983, having aired just eighteen programs over its seven years of existence.

The two philosophy series that Huisman produced for French television have been long forgotten. Neither *Interrogations* nor *Les idées et les hommes* has been analyzed or documented in any of the many histories of French television that exist to date. Certainly this had much to do with their mediocre quality. Technicians and not artists filmed the shows, and the results showed as much. And whereas both intellectuals and TV professionals considered the philosophy programs produced for Radio-télévision scolaire and the philosophical biographies filmed for *Un certain regard* to be pedagogical and artistic successes, responses to Huisman's work were ambivalent at best. Nor did either of his series achieve the kind of entertainment quotient or influence over the cultural market that *Apostrophes* was asserting on Antenne 2.

Like the creators of *Apostrophes*, however, Huisman and Malfray were instrumental in developing a different kind of cultural audience from that previously imagined in France. And it is above all in this respect that their programs remain historically significant. Huisman maintains that he "always tried, insofar as it was possible"—though without adequate help from the president of the channel or the department head—"to communicate a message in the absolute simplest of forms, to make [philosophical ideas] accessible to a large and diverse public." In the end, he believed that he "succeeded, more or less, at different times." [114] Malfray agrees: "We succeeded in reaching a certain number of people who were neither philosophy students, nor apprentice philosophers, nor actual philosophers. Otherwise stated, I believe we succeeded in touching the *real* audience." [115] These goals betray the emergence of a new attitude towards the French public. For if *L'enseignement de la philosophie* and *Un certain regard* carried the Gaullist stamp, dedicated to raising the culture of a people seen as inherently and limitlessly educable, both *Interrogations* and *Les idées et les hommes* (like *Apostrophes*), had more modest ambitions. Like the television stylings of the New Philosophers, they were resolutely aimed at a broad general public that was not now, and never would be, part of the elite of *la civilisation française*. By the 1990s, it was this humbler and perhaps more realistic vision of the nation that came to dominate both cultural television and the televising of philosophy in France.

### The Media Philosopher Challenged: Jean-François Lyotard and *Tribune libre*

By the end of the 1970s the media blitz surrounding the New Philosophers had constructed a climate in which the combined package of intellectual authority and television were disparaged as the worst of partners. Paradoxically, it was a 1978 television program provocatively aimed at confirming this perception that also provides one of the most creative examples of philosophical television ever broadcast in France. Jean-Claude Courdy produced the brief show, which featured Jean-François Lyotard, as part of a series called *Tribune libre* (1975–81).[116] Airing Monday through Friday at approximately 7:00 p.m. on the regional channel FR3 (France Régions 3), *Tribune libre* offered a fifteen-minute open forum to various interest groups, from associations, political parties, and unions, to intellectuals, scholars, and other individuals who wanted to bring their messages to the French public via television.[117] During the year in which Lyotard appeared on the program, groups as diverse as the Ligue nationale contre la vivisection, the far right Front national, the green organization SOS Environnement, the Fédération des aveugles (Federation for the Blind), Alcooliques anonymes, the Conféderation française de travailleurs chrétiens (French Confederation of Christian Workers), the Rassemblement pour la République (Union for the Republic), and the Armenian Church all appeared on the broadcast. As this list illustrates, ethical themes were prominent. Over the life of the series, other philosophers featured on the show included Jankélévitch, Glucksmann, Beauvoir, Julia Kristeva, and Michel Serres (twice).[118] Both *Tribune libre* and a similar series, *Libre expression* (airing on Antenne 2), were intended to demonstrate that the new government, under the banner of Giscard's "advanced liberal society," was willing to relinquish control over the television administration.[119] Although not as free in practice as in theory (Glucksmann's program, in which he interviewed three Russian dissidents was delayed for political reasons when Leonid Brezhnev's visit to Paris coincided with the broadcast), *Tribune libre* nevertheless offered an unusual degree of liberty in terms of both form and content to its producers and participants.[120] The broadcast on Jean-François Lyotard provides a prime example of the kind of creative license that the program allowed.

In March 1978, Lyotard had yet to write either *La condition post-moderne* (1979), the book that would make him famous in humanities departments of universities throughout the Anglo-American world, or *Le différend* (1983), which is considered by many to be his most important work of philosophy. Born in 1924, Lyotard had completed his philosophical studies and passed the *agrégation* by the age of twenty-six. He then taught for over ten years in the lycée system (the first two of these in Algeria) before becoming a university professor. Over the course of his career he held academic posts at the Sorbonne, Nanterre, the CNRS, and Vincennes (where he was teaching at the time of the *Tribune libre* broadcast) as well as at the University of California (Irvine) and Emory University in Atlanta. He was also a founding member (with Jacques Derrida), of the Collège international de philosophie. Lyotard's work is heavily influenced by the phenomenology of Maurice Merleau-Ponty. Resistant to structuralism because he felt that it did not address the gap between experience and the language used to express that experience, Lyotard was so fascinated with "language-games" and the structures that legitimize knowledge that he wound up rejecting the grand metanarratives of Western thought (Kantian, Hegelian, Marxist, religious, etc.), which he saw as dangerously contaminated by discourses of power. Politicized during the Algerian war—he protested French involvement—Lyotard later participated in the events of May '68. Although he devoted twelve years to Lefort and Castoriadis's group Socialisme ou barbarie, by the late 1970s his philosophical positions led him to join other former *gauchistes* in rejecting Marxism. Lyotard's "postmodern politics" argues that metanarrative schemas, far from delivering on their promises of truth and justice, actually operate according to their own immanent criteria. Given that such universal references cannot hold, Lyotard wanted to discover how human beings should determine criteria for judgment. Many of these concerns are visible in the program he taped for *Tribune libre*.

*Tribune libre*'s producer, Jean-Claude Courdy, shown in close-up against a black screen, introduces the broadcast.[121] He starts: "Good evening. As usual on Mondays, here is our intellectual, Jean-François Lyotard. Jean-François Lyotard is professor of philosophy at the University of Vincennes, but a rather unusual philosopher." After providing a brief biographical sketch, Courdy continues, "Tonight, Jean-François Lyotard has been brought before you to critique his own discourse and to ask himself questions concerning his presence among us on television this evening." The screen cuts to black. Another voice (Lyotard's) begins to speak. "You are going to see him; you are going to hear him. You don't know who he is. [. . .] He's an intellectual, he has written several books [the camera begins a pan of his books] that are attempts to philosophize." The pan sweeps from left to right: "You have seen them, you see them now, you don't recognize them. [. . .] You didn't ask him to speak this evening. You think that he must have friends at FR3; if he has any, they are unknown to him. The truth is even simpler than that. The producer of *Tribune libre* thought he should give intellectuals some space on this program. This intellectual's turn has come."

Lyotard goes on to address the utility of philosophy and philosophers. Since philosophy (unlike the work performed by a doctor, a train driver, or a toolmaker) has no obvious social use, he asks, how does one know when philosophy "works"? He begins to interrogate society's criteria for assessing knowledge. *As the program continues, Lyotard's voice remains out of sync with the images projected on the screen.* Philosophers, Lyotard suggests, ask themselves all sorts of "utterly mundane questions"—the same kinds of questions that most people do, "about their work, about their neighborhood, about their family, about their love life." This being so, he reflects rhetorically,

Jean-François Lyotard, speaking of himself in the third person.
From "Jean-François Lyotard," 27 March 1978.

"The questions you should ask Lyotard and the others, the questions that he perhaps asks himself are these: Why is he allowed to speak in these conditions? What is expected of him?"

"If he were famous, his appearance would obviously be of benefit to the program [. . .] But he isn't famous."

"Does someone want to do him a favor by giving him a chance to become well known? Certainly, and he thanks the program's producer for it. Yet, can he make something known by speaking for a quarter of an hour one evening in front of a camera?"

"Maybe his face, take a good look."

"Maybe also his name, but that's less likely."

Name disappears.

"What is least likely is that he will make known what he believes he has to say, since that has already taken him one or two thousand written pages and several years (he is not so young), so it should be impossible for him to say all that in fifteen minutes."

"I bet he won't tell you anything about what he does."

"He doesn't just write books, he's a professor of philosophy at the University of Vincennes; so he does philosophy. No one has ever been quite sure what that consists of."

Quick turn to face the camera.

"Has Lyotard *really* been put on the air for a quarter of an hour just to ask these questions? You don't really need to be a philosopher to ask them". Lyotard's response is that the issue at hand is that the philosopher is expected to *answer* these questions. And in the case of this broadcast, the "authority function" assigned to the philosopher engages the dynamics of television. Fade to black. *Lyotard's voice is synchronized to the visual track in the next sequence.* Television viewers, he informs us, believe they can distinguish between "simple opinion and true expertise." Yet, just as we are not competent to judge a surgeon's skill, nor can we judge the skill of our philosopher: "*We* can't tell whether he knows what he is talking about." *Voice once again out of sync for the remainder of the show.* However, Lyotard insists, we are meant to assume that since he has been asked to appear on television, "he is expected to be an authority on these matters [. . .] because if he's authorized to speak freely for a quarter of an hour to hundreds of thousands of his fellow citizens, it's because he has the authority to do so." It's because Lyotard realizes that "there is no true and certain competence and authority in these domains" that he refuses "to appear before your eyes and ears as an authority." He claims that he has chosen to do this by using "this little mechanism of transmission by which you don't see the person who is speaking and you don't hear the person you are looking at." "The big question," Lyotard asserts, "is the need to believe in authority; authority's need to be believed." "For a long time in the West," he concludes, "philosophers have been exposed to the temptation of the role of the intellectual, they have been tempted to turn themselves into the representatives of an authority. And there are not many, since Plato, over the past twenty-five hundred years, who haven't succumbed to that temptation. It seems to me that Lyotard would like to belong to that minority; that's what he told me to tell you." Cut to black. Credits.

The program is a fifteen-minute tour de force that sequentially attacks the problem of media access, the subject of marketing, the impediments posed by time limits to substantive philosophical communication, the difficulty of verbal presentation for written disciplines, the issue of authorial identity as inherently validating, both the social utility and the definition of philosophy, and, finally, the intellectual's right to speak to, or on behalf of, the public.[122] Further, it does all this, by way of its fractured audio and visual format, while challenging the "reality effect" induced by the visual representation of the embodied philosopher. At the same time, as an oeuvre, the broadcast of "Jean-François Lyotard" refutes all claims about the necessary anti-intellectualism of the television medium, taking the demonstrative model of philosophical programming one step farther: the broadcast actually engages philosophically with television as both a technology and a cultural form. The camera work engages philosophically with the dialogue; the soundtrack engages philosophically with the image; the dialogue engages philosophically with the question of what it means to be on television and with the illusion of authority that television necessarily bestows on everything that passes across its screen. Thus, the program accomplishes what Dina Dreyfus and Jean Fléchet had tried so hard to achieve in their broadcasts for Radio-télévision scolaire: it renders the television medium absolutely integral to the philosophical argument being conveyed. Interestingly, the contents of the program call into question the effects of the form while simultaneously reinforcing these effects. For, even as Lyotard uses the broadcast to question the role of the intellectual, his very presence on the screen accentuates his special status.

## Intellectual Transformations, Philosophical Mutations, and the Evolving Public

The years between 1974–86 witnessed the transformation of the French audiovisual landscape. The eradication of the ORTF in 1974, the elimination of the government monopoly in 1982, and the establishment of private channels after 1984 (all discussed in chapter 5) contributed to the emergence of an increasingly competitive climate in which the race for audiences was key. As never before, the entertainment value of television programming was at a premium. The extension of the debate format to television book shows and the meteoric success of *Apostrophes* illustrated not only that culture (and even the discipline of philosophy) could be entertaining; it also influenced the development of a media-savvy intelligentsia, capable of playing to the camera while delivering their opinions in sound bites. As the spectacular commercial response to Jankélévitch's 1980 *Apostrophes* appearance demonstrated, philosophers who mastered these skills benefited from television exposure, since successful broadcasts meant good publicity, and good publicity sold books. However, functioning as it did outside of traditional intellectual channels, television's newfound ability to control the distribution of cultural capital was highly suspect, and the new "mediocracy" quickly became a bitter target of intellectual opprobrium.

Regardless, Jean-Claude Guillebaud observes that under the persuasive self-promoting influence of figures like the New Philosophers, "the entire Left Bank changed course like a school of dolphins."[123] The left intellectual orthodoxy of the postwar era was turned on its head, abandoning Marxism and calling into question progressivism and rationalist universalism. The fact that the embryonic New Right was capitalizing on a similar antiprogressive, antirationalist platform only complicated matters. By the early 1980s this sea change in intellectual sentiment appeared as a double crisis: on the one hand, as the "silence of the intellectuals" announced with fervor in 1983 by Max Gallo, *sécretaire d'État* and spokesperson for Mitterrand (amusingly, he first met the future president on a 1976 episode of *Apostrophes*), and, on the other, as a more generalized crisis in French intellectual identity.[124] As Lyotard has pointed out, while the role of the philosopher as philosopher and that of the philosopher as "intellectual" (whose demise he announced) are not identical, the tremors crossing the intellectual field had multiple repercussions for the future of philosophy.[125] Not the least of these, as we have seen, was the renewal of interest in human rights and ethics.

Despite their rhetorical shortcomings, the New Philosophers reintroduced these concerns into the public domain and cast themselves in the role of—in Alain Peyrefitte's words— *l'intellectuel non-dupe du pouvoir,* an intellectual who refuses to be fooled by power. However, following Mitterrand's triumph in the 1981 presidential elections (which brought a socialist government to power for the first time in almost fifty years), maintaining such positions of "moral exteriority" presented new challenges. In resuscitating what Peyrefitte calls "the classic figure" of the "apolitical intellectual," the New Philosophers, for one, appeared to defend the perspective that power is only legitimate "if it *opposes* another power—considered by definition as oppressive. Starting with the idea that all power is might, one arrives at the conclusion that counterpowers alone are morally good." This purportedly novel stance, Peyrefitte concludes, is merely "a brilliant, deep, and seemingly new appearance of the old refusal of Antigone when faced with Creon."[126] Written in 1978, Peyrefitte's comment was prescient. As we shall see in chapter 5, within a decade a celebrated television debate on Antigone's story served as a potent vehicle for working through the ethical dimensions of philosophical, intellectual, and personal responsibility in the face of the state.

The denunciation of the "silence of the intellectual left" was actually a plea from the newly installed socialist government for support from the nation's intellectual elite. The debate over their supposed silence (after the historic 1981 socialist victory) provoked reams of scholarship.[127] It occupied the pages of *Le monde* and other newspapers from July 1983 to January of the following year, rekindling older disputes over the role of the intellectual in modern France. A slew of academic studies on French intellectuals appeared, continuing the lines of argument opened in the early 1970s by Pierre Bourdieu in his sociological attempts to unmask intellectual prerogative.[128] Meanwhile, the voices of two generations of "master thinkers" were vanishing from the horizon. The years 1980–84 saw the deaths of Sartre (1980), Lacan (1981), Aron (1983), Beauvoir (1984), and Foucault (1984, from AIDS). Barthes was struck by a car and killed in 1980. In the same year, Althusser murdered his wife in a psychotic fit and was removed from the intellectual scene until his death a decade later. Television was careful to mark these disappearances, and, in a tradition established in the 1950s (discussed in chapter 2), used obituaries to mythologize French philosophical greatness. While established philosophers like Lyotard were struggling to walk the fine line between what Jeremy Jennings has called "media-treason" and silence, the recently vacated limelight was quickly taken over by a new generation.[129] If the history of this era has been dominated by rancor over the dominant media presence of this younger and (for the most part) less intellectually gifted group, such rancor may well have been born, at least in part, of loss.

While controversies erupted over definitions of intellectual responsibility and the attribution of intellectual power, the discipline of philosophy was wrestling with problems of its own. As discussed in chapter 3, by the 1960s the pressures of an expanding economy meant that philosophy was fighting an uphill battle within the academy against mounting interest in mathematics and the social sciences. There is little doubt that the École normale supérieure, long the bastion of French intellectual glory, was losing ground to the École nationale de l'administration and its technocratic elites. This shift reflected a new pragmatism in government attitudes towards the education of the French public; education as information and career training was gaining ground over education as intellectual and personal growth. Oriented entirely towards the reproduction of a national teaching corps, the ENS suffered from this change. As Lyotard summarizes, "Today no one expects teaching, which is discredited everywhere, to train more enlightened citizens—only professionals who perform better."[130] Disputes over the place of philosophy within universities reveal that the fundamental nature of the French citizen was newly open to debate.

Nothing illustrates competing attitudes towards the relationship between philosophy and the French public quite so compellingly as the 1974 Haby reform. Taking its name from René Haby, minister of education from 1974 to 1978, this educational initiative threatened to eradicate the generalized teaching of philosophy in the *classe terminale*. Philosophy was to be demoted from its privileged obligatory position within the curriculum and relegated to optional status. As such, it would, in Olivier Godechot's words, "lose, de facto, a very large part of its public." [131] Although defeated in 1979, the proposition was a visible manifestation of national anxieties (discussed in chapter 3) about the failure of the French educational system to produce an adequate supply of scientists, economists, and engineers. Since philosophy potentially enticed students away from these pursuits, it was officially recognized as an obstacle to French modernization. Given that overall student enrollments were rising, while enrollments in the humanities were dropping dramatically, this perspective was more imagined than real. More to the point, I suggest, after May 1968, philosophy—with its emphasis on the teaching of critical thinking, argument, and logic—was unofficially understood in some quarters as a breeding ground for revolt. The Haby reform sought to quell this possibility by arguing that not every member of the nation was either suited for, or capable of profiting from, philosophical education.

Philosophers banded together in protest. Their responses included a rally of more than twelve hundred people gathered in the grand amphitheater at the Sorbonne, the formation (under the partial direction of Jacques Derrida), of GREPH, the Groupe de recherche sur l'enseignement philosophique, and the call for a reunion of the États généraux de la philosophie in June of 1979. Significantly, the ensuing debates generated intense interest in, and attracted public attention to, both philosophy and philosophical pedagogy. In combating the Haby reform, GREPH defended philosophy's privileged role in the educational process and fought not just to preserve but also to expand training in the discipline throughout the academic curriculum. GREPH further argued that the practice of philosophy should be decentralized beyond institutional boundaries and made available to everyone, everywhere.[132] The production of television programs like Denis Huisman's *Interrogations* and *Les idées et les hommes* can be seen as part of this conversation. But Huisman's perspective on the general public diverged sharply from that put forth by his academic colleagues. For whereas their defense of philosophy was vested in a model that saw philosophy as a human right culminating in the fullest attainment of individual enlightenment (Derrida's book on the matter was actually titled *Du droit à la philosophie* (The Right to Philosophy), Huisman's aims were much more modest. Although less politically motivated, Huisman can be seen as embracing the vision of the public and the practical approach to education that the Haby reforms espoused. He agreed that not everyone had inherent academic potential, and believed that education needed to adapt in order to better address this reality. Yet Huisman was also convinced that a modicum of familiarity with the discipline of philosophy was a positive thing, and his programs sought to provide this introductory service. The fact that they ultimately failed as television was beside the point.

The rise of the media intellectual, the emergence of a new public market for philosophy, and the turn to ethics cannot be separated from these arguments over philosophy, education, and the French public. The government's changing academic priorities produced concrete effects. After 1968, posts in philosophy were drastically reduced: whereas in 1968 some 90 secondary school jobs were available to successful *agrégés*, by 1979 only 20 were listed. The situation was even worse at the university level, where 68 jobs in 1970 fell to 9 in 1975. Although the abandonment of the Haby reform and the democratization of educational access meant that these statistics eventually reversed (in 1994, *agrégés* competed for 87 lycée posts), during the mid and late 1970s, with academic jobs scarce, a generation of young philosophers were drawn to seek employment elsewhere, often in the domains of publishing, administration, politics, or the media.[133] In the light of this lamentable academic context, Olivier Godechot remarks, "the development of a 'pessimistic' philosophy, the renunciation of both radicalism and—in order to reach a larger public—of a certain philosophical intellectualism, become much more understandable."[134] By the late 1980s, the recuperation of French intellectual culture launched by *Apostrophes* and epitomized by the New Philosophers revitalized popular interest in philosophy. The New Philosophers' insistence on intellectual accountability joined forces with the liberalization of the airwaves to promote the presence of philosophy on the small screen. Interestingly (and despite the New Philosophy's ostensible rejection of politics), throughout the next decade philosophers were most prominent on the television news, where their appearances pertained almost exclusively to political and ethical themes. Whenever television covered significant debates—over the Polish government's harsh repression of democratic reforms, over the electoral successes of the far right Front national, over reassessments of French involvement in the Holocaust, and, eventually, over the rise of Islamic fundamentalism and conflicts in the Balkans—philosophers were there.

The *Apostrophes* broadcast featuring Foucault and the *Tribune libre* special with Lyotard discussed here are but two examples countering the prevailing assumptions about the necessary anti-intellectualism of the television medium. There are many others. Like the programs of the Radio-télévision scolaire and the Service de la recherche before them, these shows make it clear that television has tremendous powers not only to transform philosophers into media icons but also to create, in limited but nonetheless important ways, new forums for philosophical expression and avenues for political and ethical change. They further illustrate that while philosophically sophisticated programming was possible, by the late 1970s and early 1980s it was produced in opposition to both industry standards that prioritized marketing and entertainment over cultural content and educational prerogatives that privileged outcome over process. By the mid-1980s, the privatization of television promised to up the ante. And despite the best efforts of its champions, for the televising of philosophy the outlook appeared bleak.

# Bucking the Ratings
## *Antigone,* Abraham, Heidegger, and the Holocaust, 1987–1992

The electoral victory that brought the Socialists to power in 1981 led—ironically, given their political mandate—to audiovisual privatization and instigated a decade of rapid, destabilizing change in French broadcasting. Since the transition from public, state-controlled TV to private, commercial channels is often mirrored by a shift from cultural to entertainment programming, one might have expected dire consequences for the televising of philosophy. Interestingly however, it was just at the moment that public television was floundering that a series titled *Océaniques* was created, which presented some of the most sophisticated, compelling, and now best-known philosophical television ever produced.[1] Over the course of its run, 1987–92, *Océaniques* included programs on Emmanuel Levinas, Simone Weil, Louis Althusser, Michel Foucault, Jacques Lacan, Roland Barthes, Mircea Eliade, Salman Rushdie, Umberto Eco, and Carl Jung and featured subjects like "postmodernity," "the exile and the absolute" and "the figure of the angel." Four shows—on the myth of *Antigone,* the biblical story of Abraham's sacrifice of Isaac, and a two-part documentary about Heidegger's affiliation with Nazism—left particularly strong impressions on the French public. What was it that caused these broadcasts to burn themselves into the annals of French intellectual life? More generally, how do we account for the creation of a series like *Océaniques* at this decidedly inopportune time for cultural television?

I want to begin by exploring the distinctive circumstances surrounding the privatization of television in France. I argue that it took the threat of the commercial market to rejuvenate belief in the small screen's potential as an instrument for cultural good. However short-lived, *Océaniques* was among the most vigorous results of this revival. But if its producers viewed the series as a testament to TV's civilizing capacities, both the press and the public responded strongly to specific programs because the material presented was at once fascinating and topically relevant to the debates—about ethics, genocide, anti-Semitism, the rise of the New Right, and the memory of Vichy—then percolating through French society. The enthusiastic reactions to the four shows that launched *Océaniques* in the fall and winter of 1987—on *Antigone*, Abraham, and the two on Heidegger—cannot be understood apart from the contested processes of historical excavation and sociopolitical recovery that had mesmerized the nation throughout the preceding spring and summer. That philosophy served as a vehicle for exploring these debates (as well as an object of their contestation) simultaneously reinforced its national significance and revealed new cleavages in the French intellectual field.

### Shaping a Commercial Market: The Privatization of French TV

When the socialists took control of the government in 1981, they were handed three public television channels and a state monopoly that had endured for almost forty years. A mere five years later, France not only had seven terrestrial channels—four of which were private—but also was pursuing both cable and satellite alternatives. Ostensibly committed to greater competition in programming, yet afraid to trust market self-regulation, the government sought to control the process of audiovisual privatization via a combination of political and legal interventions. With the passage of the Fillioud law on 29 July 1982, the state abolished its longstanding media monopoly. The Fillioud law established the nation's first independent audiovisual regulatory body, the Haute autorité de la communication audiovisuelle, sanctioned the existence of private radio stations, and deemed that public TV networks could be commissioned to private companies.[2] A patent rejection of the right's repressive legacy of media censorship, the law was the first in a spate of government initiatives aimed at liberalizing the audiovisual sector. Over the next four years, President François Mitterrand authorized the creation of Europe's first encrypted pay television network, Canal Plus (1984), as well as of two commercial channels, La Cinq (1985) and TV6 (1986)—the latter being a music channel modeled after the immensely successful American MTV and Canadian Much-Music. Opponents claimed that political interests rather than moral principles were driving these developments, arguing, for example, that La Cinq and TV6 were conceived in an anxious bid to win public support prior to the 1986 parliamentary elections.[3] As if to underscore the truth in such charges, when the right joined the left in power in 1986, Prime Minister Jacques Chirac promptly replaced the Haute autorité by a new administrative body, the Commission nationale de la communication et des libertés (CNCL), whose directorial board better reflected his government's more conservative political distribution.[4] He then annulled franchise rights over La Cinq and TV6 (renamed M6), reassigned their licenses to his political allies,[5] and—in a move that was unique in European television history and critical for the future of French TV—endorsed the privatization of the main public-sector channel, TF1.[6] Thus, unlike Great Britain, where privatization was carefully regulated to guarantee both pluralism and competition, or Italy, in which the market drove commercial development (a scenario that came to be known as "Wild West television"), France experienced a privatization that was politically partisan, legally controlled, nationally interventionist, and disarmingly speedy.[7]

The results were devastating for the public channels that remained, largely because politics, not market potential, pushed French privatization. Simply put, the fiscal policies underpinning the public system were ill equipped to handle this change. When Mitterrand abolished the audiovisual monopoly in 1982, all three of the state networks, TF1, Antenne 2, and FR3 were heavily dependent on a combination of license revenue and commercial advertising and not (as is often the case with public channels elsewhere), primarily reliant on government grants or other forms of national funding. On the eve of privatization, the public channels had already been pursuing both advertising and audiences for some time. Competition among networks, however, was kept under control, for common cultural and educational imperatives at the start of the 1980s meant that the division of the advertising field—and hence of financing—among the public channels was relatively stable. The sale in 1987 of the principal state-owned channel, TF1—which captured 40% of the audience and more than half of all advertising revenue—into private hands upset this balance. When TF1 found itself "in a hegemonic position in terms of audience share" and hence able to "indirectly [determine] the advertising rates of its competitors," the public channels were bound to suffer.[8]

Though long associated with high cultural programming (from *Cinq colonnes à la une* and *Lectures pour tous,* to *Gros plan* and *Un certain regard*), TF1 quickly jettisoned the state's cherished agenda. Francis Bouygues, TF1's new owner, argued, "We are private. We are commercial. There are things that we do not wish to do, such as broadcasting cultural, political, or educational programs."[9] The remaining public channels were forced to compete for advertising in a field newly flooded either by the variety shows, game shows, and—despite quotas—American imports airing on the private networks, or by the feature films and uninterrupted sports programming broadcast on Canal Plus. Financial exigencies demanded that television professionals at Antenne 2 and FR3 produce shows capable of attracting mass audiences. In most cases, cultural programming was pushed off of the public channels' prime-time schedules and subjected to *la dictature de l'audimat* (the dictatorship of the audience ratings).[10] Antenne 2 was afflicted by bruised egos, a vicious struggle for viewers, and the specter of losing its media stars (Bernard Pivot, Michel Drucker, Jacques Chancel) to the lure of TF1's higher salaries.[11] Whereas the privatization of France's oldest and most successful public channel was couched in the language of continuity (and publicized under the slogan "There is only ONE, and it is the ONE [TF1]"), the effects of this move on public programming were both disruptive and demoralizing.[12] The proponents of an American-style industry catering to audience desire seemed to be carrying the day. Yet in September of the same year, Yves Jaigu, the newly appointed director of FR3, in conjunction with the fledgling public channel La Sept (which was headed by historian Georges Duby and was the first French channel ever financed entirely by public funds), created one of the most ambitious cultural programs—and some of the most erudite philosophical shows—ever broadcast in France. What was Jaigu's agenda, and how did it fare in the midst of this volatile media landscape?

## Public Television Revivified: Creating *Océaniques*

At the moment that Yves Jaigu became the director of programming at FR3 in 1986, he had already dedicated two decades of his life to promoting culture in the French media. He was born in 1924 into a bourgeois family in the city of Rennes, in Brittany. The son of a lawyer, he was educated locally before being sent to Paris to the prestigious

Lycée Henri IV. He studied law, obtained a degree in philosophy and a certificate in mineralogy, and worked first as cultural attaché to the French Institute in Edinburgh (1951–53) and then as director of external relations for the nuclear power plant at Marcoule (1957–58). Stints as director of information for the Atomic Energy Commission (1958–63) and as the head of the Delegation for Territorial Management and Regional Action in Datar (1963–70) followed. It was during this later period that Jaigu married and found his way into the employ of the state broadcasting system, where he was responsible for international coproductions from 1967 to 1972, prior to being made director of programming on Channel 1 (1972–74). His early efforts at the ORTF included the production of a series dramatizing the founding texts of Western civilization, including the *Aeneid* and the *Acts of the Apostles* (the latter directed by Roberto Rossellini). Jaigu became fervently committed to high cultural programming. Of his first encounter with the small screen he recalls, "I simply understood that in this extraordinary instrument of universal diffusion there was something truly passionate, something that was almost a new form of philosophical engagement." The thrill associated with this discovery never waned.[13]

While working at the ORTF, Jaigu met Jacqueline Baudrier, a journalist and dedicated Gaullist who became the director of news at Channel 2 following President Pompidou's reorganization of the administration in 1969. When Baudrier was appointed head of Radio France in 1974, she asked Jaigu to follow her. Although initially hesitant because, as he recalls, "Television interested me too much!" Jaigu was quickly persuaded. He spent almost ten years as president of France's premier cultural radio network, France Culture (1975–84). In addition to overseeing regular programming, Jaigu's projects included such creative experiments as fifteen continuous hours of radio debate on the future of democracy in Athens. These experiences convinced him of the importance of time. "On television, as well as on the radio," he says, "we keep trying to diminish the time necessary for production and direction. But it's easy to see that in many TV shows [. . .] the camera doesn't have enough time to meditate. [. . .] And the camera does meditate, you know!" Once Jaigu returned to television (he became director of programming at FR3 in 1986), this consciousness of the value of the temporal became critical to his approach to the medium.[14]

*Océaniques* was conceived as "a vast ocean of ideas, like the vast ocean of the soul," a program with the potential to "open onto an infinity of subjects" and to be "a sort of immense public conversation at a very high level [. . .] produced with great suppleness, great familiarity, and great simplicity." Discouraged by the network from his original plan of "taking over prime time" on a nightly basis, Jaigu nevertheless succeeded in obtaining his bottom line: the show aired for an hour three times weekly, on Monday, Wednesday, and Thursday nights, usually starting between ten and ten-thirty.[15] Given the unstable audiovisual climate and the concurrent privatization of TF1, this was no small victory. Since the program's contents were envisaged as intentionally diverse, focusing successively on ideas, men, and works, three elements were essential to establishing loyalty among the viewing public: a unifying title, a common credit sequence, and the repetitive thrice-weekly time slot. In the opening moments of each show, a gannet soars (to the music of Sibelius) over crashing waves in a vast expanse of ocean. For Jaigu, the segment with the bird was vital, for its movements represented the act of thought itself. "In the wildest storms," he maintains, these birds are "calm; they play with the wind, they glide overhead, they brush the waves that can sink boats while they alone remain. [. . .] They are symbols of the kind of thought that analyzes, digests, and sublimates events; [. . .] they are the calm in the storm."[16]

Most broadcasts were built around a combination of new and old footage, not infrequently incorporating rare or previously unused documentary materials procured from other networks—including foreign ones, as was the case for shows on Heidegger, Althusser, and Foucault, for which the archival footage hailed from Germany, Italy, and Belgium.[17] These archival elements were deemed crucial, and their availability often influenced the choice of subject matter. Shot with five cameras and one director on a modest budget, the new portions of the show resembled live broadcasts, in that they were edited simultaneously in the control room.[18] Although some were filmed on location (a conversation between Marguerite Duras and Jean-Luc Godard took place in the writer's home), the philosophy broadcasts were mostly shot in a TV studio in the north of Paris. The meticulously designed set resembled an amphitheater, with the guests seated around a central table, and the audience forming a semicircle behind. To produce and host the shows and to choose and develop program themes, Jaigu selected a friend and associate from his television days, Pierre-André Boutang, and a former colleague from France Culture, Michel Cazenave.

Both men were well-educated members of the Parisian bourgeoisie. Though not formally trained in philosophy, Boutang came, in his words, "from a family of *intellos*" and "had practically bathed in" the discipline.[19] His maternal grandmother was the first woman in France to earn an *agrégation* in philosophy and was friends with Leon Blum and the philosopher Leon Brunschvicg. Boutang's parents both graduated from the École normale supérieure. But whereas Pierre-André's mother, like her mother before her, was an *agrégée* in philosophy and a leftist (as well as the translator of a version of *Antigone*), his father, the virulently right-wing philosopher Pierre Boutang, was a former member of the ultranationalist, royalist Action française.[20] Pierre-André's half-brother Yann Moulier Boutang published a bestselling biography of Louis Althusser. Pierre-André's father and half-brother both appeared as guests on now classic shows of *Océaniques* (the former, as we shall see, in the shows on *Antigone* and Abraham, the latter in those on Althusser).[21] To his parents' distress, the young Pierre-André failed to follow in the family footsteps, forsaking the ENS for the Institut d'études politiques and then abandoning the program in the late 1950s to break into the film industry. Disappointed by a few false starts, a frustrated Boutang entered the ORTF and became, at the age of twenty-five, responsible for selecting all the feature films broadcast on French television—a job he held from 1962 to 1967 and one that he remembers with immense delight. "I flew to Hollywood and bought all the Marx Brothers' films, and Gary Cooper's, Dietrich's, and Cecil B. De Mille's. [. . .] I got to eat in the MCA mess with Hitchcock and Cary Grant—oh it was fabulous!" he recalls, laughing. The breezy informality of it all ("And when I had an Italian girlfriend for a while—well, let's just say there was a renaissance in Italian film on French TV") betrays the casual, shoot-from-the-hip atmosphere that reigned in those parts of the industry dissociated from Gaullist politics.[22]

During the early 1960s, in addition to selecting feature films, Boutang began working as a television producer and assistant director. From 1967 to 1986 he added work in cinema (most notably producing Alexandre Astruc and Michel Contat's 1972 feature-length biographical documentary *Sartre par lui-même*) to a heavy television schedule. Once employed at FR3 (in 1987) under Yves Jaigu, Boutang produced and directed *Océaniques* for the duration of its run—in the process winning two prestigious 7 *d'Or* awards for his fine portraits of philosophers. Following the demise of the collection, he joined La Sept-ARTE as director of programs. It was there, during the 1990s, that he produced the cultural magazine *Métropolis,* on which he broadcast *L'abécédaire de Gilles Deleuze,* a series of informal interviews between the philosopher and Claire Parnet, which Boutang had shot in 1988–89.

Like Pierre-André Boutang, Michel Cazenave was also engaged as producer, director, and host of *Océaniques.* Born in 1942 into a family of bourgeois French Jews, Cazenave and his kin narrowly escaped death in the concentration camps—a fact that, judging from his participation in the broadcasts examined here, profoundly shaped his development. Repatriated with his family to Paris after the war, the young, withdrawn, and somewhat recalcitrant boy seemed destined for an academic career. He was sent to the Lycée Louis-le-Grand and entered the ENS where he began preparing for the *agrégation* in philosophy. However, thanks to what he describes as his "horribly cynical character" and his membership—despite his staunchly Gaullist beliefs—in "the revolutionary generation of 1968," Cazenave refused to take exams and quit the program in protest. An activist during the late 1960s (he was the national president of the Young Gaullists and secretary general of the Union démocratique du travail from 1967 to 1971), he lost faith in politics following the deaths of de Gaulle and Malraux. "Once they were gone," he confided to me, "I told myself that politics was over, and I determined to return to my roots, in culture."[23] It was around this time that he found work in radio at France Culture and began to write prodigiously (he has since published over forty works of theater, poetry, history, fiction, and biography—including studies of de Gaulle, Malraux, and Jung). In Yves Jaigu, his director at France Culture, Cazenave found a mentor and kindred spirit, a fellow intellectual equally committed to the exploration and extension of high cultural programming. During Jaigu's tenure (and long after his departure), Cazenave produced and hosted numerous radio shows on philosophy. Thus, when Jaigu dreamed up *Océaniques* for FR3, he immediately contacted Cazenave and asked him to climb on board. Self-effacing, reserved and deeply reflective, Cazenave balanced the more ebullient Boutang, lending an important ballast to the broadcasts.

Not unlike the ORTF's *Un Certain regard* (discussed in chapter 3), *Océaniques* was predominantly intended as an exploration of the Western heritage and an enduring record of the most significant intellectual and cultural developments of the time. "Our desire," reflects Boutang, "was to film for as long as possible, with the most qualified interviewers we could find, on the most durable stock available (that is, 16mm film), everyone who really has something to say. You could call it a sort of voluntary archive." "Maybe I'm naive" he adds, "but I find it completely bizarre—especially now that we have the means to do it, with digital cameras and all—that in all the countries of the world there aren't people out filming the great minds, getting them to speak!"[24] Jaigu, Boutang, and Cazenave were equally convinced that philosophers were central to their project. Their attempts to broadcast philosophy generated passionate responses from the press.[25] However, if *Océaniques* and its philosophy shows became, according to the up-scale TV guide *Télérama,* the "must-see TV of the Parisian late-night crowd," it was not simply because their archival value and cultural erudition piqued media interest, but also because they addressed pressing national debates and framed fundamental ethical and ontological questions in socially relevant ways.[26] These broadcasts also propelled a reexamination of the issues that perpetually trouble the genre of philosophical television: the place of the image and the body in thought; the knotty relationship between linguistic complexity and temporal limitations; mass access and cultural democracy.

### "The Myth of *Antigone*," and "Abraham's Sacrifice"

Shoulders hunched, brows beaded with sweat, hands gesticulating, bodies angled sharply forward as if drawn together by the force of an invisible magnet, two men face off across a table. Improbable friends divided by an immense ideological abyss. The one, Pierre Boutang, aged seventy-one, ardent Catholic philosopher, Parisian, white-haired, with rosy sagging flesh and small bright eyes, professor emeritus at the Sorbonne whose right-wing anti-Semitic history rouses the ire of the intellectual left; and the other, the writer George Steiner, aged fifty-eight, bespectacled, pipe-smoking, Jewish, polyglot, cosmopolitan (born in Paris into a Viennese-Czechoslovakian family, exiled to America, educated at Yale, Chicago, Harvard, and Oxford, resident of Geneva, professor at Cambridge), a seemingly placid man who was nevertheless described by the press as "capable of terrible anger, inhabited by the suffering of the world."[27] The two broadcasts were shot back to back on a long September morning in 1987 and aired one week apart. What was at issue? A Greek tragedy and a story from the Old Testament probed in a debate, asserted *Le nouvel observateur,* the likes of which had not been seen on television "since before the

The gannet soars; detail from a Grecian urn; Michel Cazenave, Pierre Boutang, and George Steiner. From "Le mythe d'*Antigone*," 21 September 1987.

Deluge" (i.e., privatization). [28] In the hands of Steiner and Boutang, the broadcasts provided an opportunity at once for the careful exegesis of ancient texts, the investigation of fundamental ethical questions, and a visceral confrontation over the claims shaping recent historical memory.

( · )

Part 1 aired on 21 September 1987.[29] The opening credits are followed by the title shot, "Le mythe d'Antigone" superimposed on flat figures dancing in profile across a Grecian urn. The frozen image emphasizes a point addressed in the broadcast: the significance of the temporal distance separating us from the work under discussion. Michel Cazenave acts as host. Seated at the end of the table between his two guests, he begins, "There was a tradition in antiquity that instead of working in classrooms, philosophers would dialogue while walking along the river." While admitting that we are not in such picturesque surroundings today, he continues, "We are going to try to imagine that we are in a garden, at the very least in the garden of ideas. [. . .] We know that Plato's *Symposium* begins with great joy and ends with great philosophy—and we will try to do this too!" After requesting that his interlocutors present themselves to the audience, Cazenave withdraws from the conversation. He remains almost completely—and unusually, given the examples set by hosts like Pivot, Michel Polac, and others— silent for the duration of the broadcast. This stance reveals his belief that true philosophical dialogue only flourishes when the interjections (and non sequiturs) of presenters— "three-quarters of whom are quite incapable of conducting informed philosophical debate" and "most of whom are more interested in vaunting their own authority than discussing the issues at hand"—are held at bay.[30] It becomes apparent by the second show that Cazenave's technique makes the moments when he *does* intervene in the dialogue all the more powerful.

Sophocles' *Antigone* recounts the struggle between a young woman, Antigone, and her uncle, King Creon, over the treatment accorded the corpse of her brother, Polyneices, killed while battling to gain control of the kingdom. In retribution for his treason, Creon decrees that Polyneices should be denied burial and his body exposed to the elements. When Antigone defies the king's edict and covers her brother's corpse with earth, Creon orders that she be buried alive. In pitting the written laws of the state and the ruler against the unwritten laws of the gods, the family, and the individual, *Antigone* raises ethical questions of enduring import. Who has the right to determine law? Should the common good prevail over individual interests? Is political authority inviolable? When should we follow the dictates of conscience? What is the role of forgiveness? Are there actions so grave as to demand defiance of earthly rules? Such questions were clearly relevant to contemporary French experience, from collaboration and resistance during the Nazi occupation of France, to the wars of decolonization, to the revolutions of May 1968, to then current struggles over immigration, communism, and the third world.[31]

Fittingly, the body of the broadcast begins with the dilemma posed by *Antigone*'s apparent modernity. This is a seemingly universal myth, whose basic storyline recurs, Steiner assures us, "in both Christian and non-Christian cultures." But what's important, Boutang retorts, is that *Antigone* "is also unique." Agreeing, Steiner cautions viewers that though its "words burn before us," we must nevertheless be careful, for there are "conceptions here that are archaic, remote." Can we remain aware of the antiquity of this myth, of its historical specificity, when the issues it raises are "knocking so insistently at our door"? It is precisely because the participants manage to maintain a "double consciousness" and to shift the discussion of *Antigone* from a concern with origins to its repercussions in history and to its resurgence in contemporary politics that the program proves so fascinating.

From questions of temporality, the dialogue turns to death. "We are in a culture," Steiner reminds us," that doesn't like to speak of death, that doesn't like to see it—it's one of the taboos of our culture." He continues, "Two and a half thousand years ago, it was thrown in our faces that not to bury someone was an insult to Being, to the sun, even to the universe." By keeping the dead above ground and entombing the living, Creon reversed the divine order. Ruminating on this decision, Steiner suggests, "Perhaps we could try to elucidate what this fascination [. . .] with burial, and with burying alive, is all about?" Boutang agrees, and by way of illustration points to the controversy over the burial accorded the head of the Vichy government, Marshal Philippe Pétain. "Here we have an old leader," he avows, "buried who knows where?—well, we do know where—but we wanted to prevent his dust from being close to that of his soldiers." As Boutang knows, the reference is politically loaded. Pétain was buried on the Ile d'Yeu, the site of his final imprisonment, and not as his supporters felt he deserved, in the WWI cemetery at Douaumont. Although later recovered, Pétain's coffin was actually stolen from the Ile d'Yeu by right-wing militants in February of 1973.[32] The campaign to transfer his ashes to Douaumont continues to be couched by the right as a gesture of national reconciliation.[33] Media references to Pétain, especially to his burial, historically generated huge viewer response. Thus, the reference likely had a divisive effect on the TV audience. At the same time, the symbolic value attributed to the location of *every* burial is also embedded here (in the unspoken question, "Why does it matter where the body is laid to rest?"), as is the notion that the corporeal shell—Hamlet's "quintessence of dust"—remains, for the modern world, imbued with meaning.[34]

Waxing more personal, Boutang moves from the example of Pétain to the death of his own father (killed in 1940), "who would've been one hundred years old next July 9." What does it mean, he asks, to visit his father's grave, a ritual he performs with some regularity? The presence at the gravesite, Boutang submits, "is an affective presence of something that's not he. And I know very well that it's not he. The Greeks knew that too." Funeral rites are of consequence, he proposes (adding that "Christianity has this in common with Greek religion") because "the services rendered to the dust are that which permit the unshackling of the soul." Implicitly shifting the emphasis from Polyneices to

Antigone, Steiner points to the recent "historic experience in Cambodia, in Pol Pot's vast massacres, where we buried people *alive*. We buried hundreds, thousands, some say hundreds of thousands of men and women alive."[35] Calling this "the ultimate obscenity," Steiner submits that a tragedy like *Antigone* is there to warn us: "Wake up! Human progress, or the human spirit, is a very fragile thing and has no moorings." This comment turns us towards the moral center of the dialogue and to the notion that *humanity itself* is mortal.

Like moths to a flame, the cameras gravitate towards whoever speaks, framing first one, and then the other of the protagonists, alternating smoothly between over-the-shoulder two-shots, upper torso shots, and full-frame close-ups. Although a live audience is watching, the tight focus creates an illusion of intimacy. All the elements of scholarly discourse are present. The pace is restrained but intense, the dialogue nuanced, punctuated throughout, as in a seminar, by recourse to carefully annotated books, meticulously stacked at the elbows of each participant. The infatuation with language is palpable: "There is *anti*" in Antigone, Boutang notes, "which doesn't mean 'against' like the Latin *contra*, but 'in the place of.'" And Steiner later comments, "One must always practice philology modestly, because it means 'to love truth,' the Logos." A clock ticks on the table. Both trained professors, these men are conscious that their exchange has a predetermined length.

The energy builds as the dialogue deepens. "*Voilà!*" cries Steiner, "a play written 440 years before Jesus Christ that reminds us constantly of ourselves. But how do we read it today?" In a roundabout, rather pessimistic response, Boutang recites a long passage by Charles Maurras to demonstrate that winners since antiquity have had a propensity to "completely destroy vanquished peoples." So how is it, asks Steiner, that after thousands of years we are unable to learn from history, from "the world of Antigone and Creon"? While their responses—voiced in various terms throughout the broadcast—have an evident philosophical importance, they also articulate the ways in which an ancient text like *Antigone* matters. And, as for any program, getting the audience to understand how they are implicated in the topic at hand is crucial to getting them to connect to the show. In the *Océaniques* broadcast, two aspects of the exchange between Steiner and Boutang facilitate this bond. The first consists in an appeal to conscience, in arousing compassion—and outrage—in the face of the atrocities perpetuated by humankind. The second consists in an investigation of the forces that

George Steiner (wearing glasses) and Pierre Boutang. From "Le mythe d'*Antigone*," 21 September 1987.

inspire action in response to such tragedies. We see the former at work when Steiner tells us that he is haunted "by a childish dream." This dream, he muses, "is that when we first became aware of the genocide in Cambodia," when "modern television introduced the apocalypse into our homes," the countries of the world would have united and said:

> We don't know the exact economic or tribal circumstances of this atro-
> cious conflict, but after the world of the Holocaust, of the Shoah, after
> the great massacres, we have had enough. We are diminished as men
> and women by a phenomenon of massacres, living burials, genocides

on the scale of Pol Pot. And so we shall intervene, we shall stop this, in order to remain men [. . .], not to find a political solution, we won't find one, or to perform some sort of abstract justice, which is far too complicated and distant a notion, but as Antigone says, because I am me, because I am, in the sight of God, a human being, and I will not live with this news, which is the oldest news on earth.

Steiner's observation subtly positions both him and the spectator (tacitly invited to identify with him), on the moral high ground: *we* would not be passive in the face of such news. Or would we? For alas, Steiner concludes, faced with this tragedy, the countries of the world "didn't say a word." Steiner's despair over the failure of the state, and his privileging of the ethical over the political, also echoes stances held by the New Philosophers (discussed in chapter 4). Here too, recognition of the world's unfathomable silence is troubling, and clearly meant to unsettle. In this case, however, it also leads to the second investigation— What motivates action?—which starts with an exploration of the responsibilities of governance.

Boutang begins by contending that, insofar as the Cambodian genocide and other humanitarian disasters are concerned, democratic entities (in this case the United Nations) have no authority to intervene if the nation's people have themselves placed their leader in power. So when, Steiner asks, is rebellion or revolution justifiable? Gliding from Antigone, to Joan of Arc and to Simone Weil, the men examine what it means to defy the state when—as they claim was true for these women—one is unwilling to hold power oneself. Despite such an "abdication," Antigone's determination to act and, in so doing to repudiate the written law in favor of sacred edicts elicits their respect. Earlier, Boutang had insisted, "Antigone is in action. She is in action each time there's a threat." In this regard, she sets an example. But "what obsesses me," ponders Steiner, "is that [. . .] as we know very well, one can read *Antigone* in the morning and be a torturer in the afternoon." This being so, "what's the good of reading it?" "I will tell you," answers Boutang triumphantly, holding out the promise of hopeful resolution, *Antigone* must be read *well*, and "to read well is to read with such intensity that we can find the means to act."

The remainder of the broadcast turns on the relationship between one's ability to act and one's faith. Does the defiance of earthly power require recourse to a kind of "transcendent force"? As Steiner points out, Hegel posits that the dialectic that pits the individual against the state necessarily ends in a draw. Is Antigone's strength then born of grace? Does such a concept even exist (and Boutang claims it does) in the pre-Christian Greek world? This line of questioning leads to an exegesis of the famous lines 450–55, the "key to the play," in which Antigone justifies her defiance of Creon's orders.[36] The scene is dramatized with a brief excerpt from Stellio Lorenzi's film version of *Antigone*—the only break in the broadcast from the tight focus on the two men (and the only moment that reads now, at the space of almost twenty years, as strangely dated). When the excerpt ends, Boutang quotes from *Antigone* in Greek: "The words we are thinking of are *Ou gar ti moi Zeus ēn o kēruxas tade*. We will seek their meaning." Boutang translates the Greek as, "It wasn't Zeus who gave me those commands," and then goes on to add, "but surely she said something more ironic, more violent." And he reaches for "page 30 of the original edition" of Henri Estienne's sixteenth-century *Traité de la conformité du language françois avec le grec* to elucidate the exact meaning of that *moï*, that "me."

In their excitement, Jaigu recalls, these two learned men, "agitated by a tornado of thought" leaning intently towards one another, each of their bodies straining "like a bow trying to launch an arrow," lose all awareness of the cameras, of the audience, of everything except an ardent search for meaning.[37] Steiner and Boutang are utterly inhabited by the force of their ideas. And so, Jaigu declares, "You can see what it means to *do* philosophy on television, rather than to speak about philosophy." "There they are, the two of them," he enthuses, "so tightly connected to one another that it's just as if we were watching a boat in a fierce wind, its sails billowing. And they are philosophizing physically." "I remember very well," he asserts elsewhere, "that *Océaniques* exploded in the press and in intellectual circles with these two shows [on Antigone and Abraham] because, all of a sudden, the folks who watched them [. . .] saw that with thinkers of that level, in effect, *everything* is mobilized. It isn't a theoretical debate, in the negative sense of the term" but rather "an extraordinary performance." "Yes," he states with great satisfaction, "On television, you can show this."[38]

Jaigu was convinced that it was the spectacle of "intelligence *in vivo*" that totally differentiated the broadcasts on *Océaniques* from "an ordinary debate, the kind you see a hundred times, where the guy who interviews wouldn't know his own questions if they weren't on an index card."[39] Still, while the embodied nature of the intellectual pyrotechnics captured in these programs was certainly gripping, it was the combination of this performance and the contemporary pertinence of the philosophical questions examined that made the broadcasts uniquely compelling. The second show demonstrates this even more clearly.

Like part 1, "Abraham's Sacrifice" links the historical to the contemporary.[40] But it also ventures onto ground that is even more urgent socially and more sensitive personally. When the show aired (on FR3), it followed a debate on La Cinq between the Front national's Jean-Marie Le Pen and the communist André Lajoinie. According to one reviewer, the contrast could not "have been more striking" between the earlier show, in which "ontological baseness battled with degraded morals," and the intellectual heights displayed on "Abraham's Sacrifice."[41] And the pertinence of a conversation on the intellectual values of the Judeo-Christian tradition to a nation being courted by a populist, anti-immigrant party of the extreme right could not have been more apparent. The story from Genesis moves the conversation away from *Antigone*'s more abstract ethical discussion of divine versus earthly justice to a direct confrontation with religious doctrine—and it is immediately evident that when it comes to both religion and scriptural exegesis, the opinions of the Catholic Boutang and the Jewish Steiner diverge radically. Further, when Cazenave, breaking his self-imposed silence, heatedly kicks off the show with a pointed and accusatory intervention, he propels the discussion into territory that had been dominating intellectual debate for months. How, asks Cazenave, could Steiner and Boutang's analysis of *Antigone* have blatantly referenced Pol Pot's crimes in Cambodia while making only the briefest of allusions to the Holocaust and thus "largely gliding over Nazi barbarism?" Of the little said here, he continues, he found Boutang's comments about Pétain "atrocious, maybe because I'm part of a family who were denounced by the people of Vichy to the Gestapo, and who escaped the camps by a miracle."

Cazenave's hard-hitting accusations are not entirely accurate—the Shoah was regularly mentioned during the previous program, even if Nazism was not directly engaged—but they ratchet up the stakes and set the tone for what follows.[42] Boutang immediately springs to his own defense, arguing that he is a supporter of Maurras, who was decisively against "the Nazi barbarism." Steiner too, is rattled. "Everything I write," he asserts, "everything I teach, my whole thinking [. . .] revolves around the catastrophe of Auschwitz." As if to substantiate these claims, the show's ostensible subject—the test of faith contained

in the story of Abraham's three-day journey to Mount Moriah to sacrifice his only son, Isaac, in accordance with God's commandment—is
explored via the Holocaust, Vichy, anti-Semitism and Nazism. As in
*Antigone* we are once again dealing with judgment and justice, but in
this case the justice is primarily divine, not earthly, and its substance
calls the very nature of its legislator into question. In so doing, the
story tackles faith, and particularly the question, How do we maintain
belief in God's law when confronted by the incomprehensible, by suffering, by evil?

Steiner opens with an extended reflection on the kind of deep self-
knowledge that can only be gained when one has been tested by ex-
tremes, as was Abraham when ordered to sacrifice his only son. "Come
on, let's take some risks," he insists. "Let's talk about things that we
rarely say on television. [. . .] I ask myself how I would have acted if
they'd come to my door, the murderers, [. . .] the *milice,* the Camelots
du roi, and the Croix de feu.⁴³ Would I have screamed, 'Have pity on
me'? Would I have betrayed everyone?" Steiner admits that he cannot say, and he considers this lack of knowledge a fatal flaw. Solemnly
confessing ("It horrifies me to divulge this before the spectators, but
let's be honest") that he knows that both he and Boutang, like Wag-
ner, Nietzsche, and Hitler before them, often feel more love for ani-
mals than for men ("because we know too well what men do to one
another"), Steiner admits that if the puppy he adores were beaten in
front of his eyes, he would "crack in fifteen seconds." Nevertheless, he
contends, "I don't know how I would have handled myself before the
Boutang of the other side." "Not you, necessarily," he adds, nodding
across the table, "but the Boutang of the Action française." The comment, though tempered, is personal and intensely provocative, even in-
flammatory. Backpedaling, Steiner concedes that Boutang knows how
he would act under such conditions, and then further concedes that
such knowledge, which is only gained through experience, merits a
certain respect, whatever its outcome. Why? In part, he implies, because it gives those who possess it insight into the actions of those (like
Abraham) who have survived ordeals.

Steiner's observations lead to a discussion of Abraham's silence
during his three-day journey, in so doing moving us from a consideration of human action to a meditation on God's intentions and the
question of faith. "Why did he keep silent?" asks Boutang. A good
question, concurs Steiner, given that "God did not order him to." Was
it, Boutang speculates, because language would only serve to justify

God's ways, and God cannot be judged right or wrong? Steiner, evoking "that archetypal scene between the parent and the youth" before the gas chambers, wonders whether the instinct to verbally reassure is "a modern instinct." Documents from the Holocaust tell us that some of those faced with the horror of death by gas "attempted to prepare their children" for the end, while others disguised it; "both reactions are possible." In contrast, he marvels, Abraham "said *absolutely nothing.*" Of course, Boutang replies, because Abraham "is not the bearer of a message." Man's role is not to justify, but to hope, to believe.

The biblical facts of Abraham's story are quickly transposed into material through which to reflect on different conceptions of evil in the Jewish and Catholic religions. The two men skirmish over anti-Semitism, Boutang arguing that "everyone knows that the kings and the popes and the church protected the Jews [. . .] against the others. [. . .] Criminal anti-Semitism is something that arises from 'the rabble,'" and Steiner scoffing, "You can't take us in with this, Boutang. [. . .] It isn't an accident, this abyss between us." They debate the connections between the "refusal of Judaism," the idea of sacrifice, and the crucifixion. For Steiner, the parallels that Boutang employs between Abraham's sacrifice, the genocide of the Jews, and the death of Christ are inadmissible. How is it possible, asks Steiner, if Christ truly *was* the messiah, that two thousand years after his crucifixion "the world continues to drown in blood, barbarism, torture, and the worst forms of filth?" Where is the transfiguration in the quality of human behavior that, according to the Jewish religion, the messiah's arrival should announce? Rejecting Steiner's position, Boutang affirms the existence of grace ("there is Antigone, there is Joan of Arc, there is [. . .] the regard of a child"), and he asserts that we must not seek to understand God's ways—indeed, it is our willingness to trust without questioning that is the very essence of belief. Steiner's reply, given in due course, is somber, "For a Jew, even a very religious one, and certainly for a Jew like myself, [. . .] the world of the death camps calls into question [. . .] the very possibility (and not only the eventual arrival) of a messiah." Surely, Steiner continues, "For a survivor (and we all are survivors today) the question of what is the God of Judaism, of what is God, is posed as never before. How, for a Catholic like yourself, does the world of the death camps not call your faith into question? I don't understand." Ultimately, Steiner charges: "the death camps were a test [. . .] that God posed to the Christian world, and you scored zero." Denying Steiner's accusation, contending that there were

"Christians who responded" and who were "gassed for their efforts," Boutang argues that if "the church is an old whore," she is also "the *Mater dolorosa*" who carries the unhappiness of the world upon her shoulders. And Steiner should know, Boutang goes on, "that she has not said her last word."

As the program wraps up, Steiner proclaims that the chasm that separates him from Boutang can be encapsulated in two citations. He explains, "Kant says that if there is a voice that tells a father to sacrifice his only son, by definition, it is the voice of the devil, it cannot be the voice of God." Kierkegaard, Steiner continues, had a more troubling and contrary idea: "Kierkegaard said, 'If a voice dares to tell you: "You must sacrifice your only son," then that *proves* that it is the voice of God.'" As far as Steiner is concerned, the world of the Holocaust has confirmed that Kierkegaard was right, for God did ask, and did not save the child. "For Boutang," he murmurs, "If I understand correctly, it's the devil" who is asking, for according to Kant, if "God knows in advance that he will save the child, he will not demand such a thing of a father." (Interestingly, Steiner does not conclude that Nietzsche was right—and that the world of the Holocaust proves that God is dead.) When Boutang objects to Steiner's equating the sacrifice of Isaac—or, in his view, the sacrifice of Christ—with the deaths of children gassed in the camps, it becomes evident that the program will end in stalemate. Reluctant to "do what they do all too often in talk shows on television," that is, "to produce false agreement," Steiner declares himself pleased with this outcome. Where they do agree, he notes, is that "for the last two hours, we have spoken seriously of texts and of the question, Can we read [important works] without speaking of the existence of God or of God's role?" This question is especially pertinent given Steiner's interest (apparent in the next broadcast examined here) in Heidegger, whose "theory of intersubjectivity," as Samuel Moyn explains, "demanded a secular philosophy that cast doubt on the familiar basis of ethics."[44] Thus, when Steiner and Boutang debate "God's role" in broadcasts on Antigone and Abraham, they are also implicitly discussing a debate over the secularization of philosophy that was, in the wake of Heidegger's argument for the end of metaphysics, a growing concern—also visible in the work of Levinas, Derrida, and Ricoeur, among others—in postwar French thought. Finally, Steiner summarizes, it is their respect for "the Word," for "the Logos," and for the idea that "without theology there can be no poetry" that sets them apart from a world in which youth can declare (as did one student during a conference that Steiner attended in Frankfurt in 1968) "Here, Mr. Steiner, we don't quote." "'Here we don't quote,'" Steiner reflects in closing, "is the end of Western culture as we have known it."

( · )

When the reviews began to role in, the verdict was unanimous: the show was a smashing success. *Libération* held nothing back: "In this strange and impressive program known as *Océaniques,* the very concept of debate has been rehabilitated in this confrontation between two brilliant minds." "We love them," it declared.[45] And the memory endured. Almost without exception, press and television reviews of the careers of *Océanique's* producers, as well as interviews with them, refer either to the broadcasts with Steiner and Boutang or to the two-part special on Heidegger, discussed below. While all four programs were effective demonstrations of intellectual programming, numerous other shows in the collection—on Althusser, Foucault, and Levinas, for example—were of similar quality. Given that they were neither the first nor the last programs produced (a factor often worthy of note), how can we account for the deep impressions that these particular shows made? I have suggested that, whereas these broadcasts were acclaimed as rarified cultural products in an increasingly privatized media landscape, their abiding impact also derived from the ways in which they intervened in a set of emotionally charged issues—ethics, genocide, anti-Semitism, the rise of the New Right, and the memory of Vichy—being thrashed out with unusual vigor in the French mass media since the previous year. What was the catalyst for these debates, and how did television help to nurture them?

## France on Trial: The "Butcher of Lyon" and Justice (Not) Televised

From 11 May, the day on which it began, until 4 July 1987, the day on which the Nazi war criminal Klaus Barbie was convicted of crimes against humanity and sentenced to life in prison (and for many months before and after), the trial and prosecution of the famous "butcher of Lyon" was a central obsession of French social debate.[46] Barbie had been an object of media attention since 1983, when he was extradited—thanks in part to the tireless efforts of the famed Nazi hunters Serge and Beate Klarsfeld—to France from Bolivia, where he had established nefarious connections with military rulers in La Paz and was living under the assumed name of Klaus Altman. A German, Barbie had been an SS captain and head of the Fourth Section of the Lyon security police from 1942 to 1944. The first person ever brought to trail for crimes against humanity in France, Barbie stood accused—among other acts—of the arrest and deportation of eighty-four people (mostly Jews) in a 1943 raid in Lyon, and of forty-four Jewish children and seven adults in a 1944 "action" in Izieu.[47] He was also alleged to have deported or tortured to death numerous members of the Resistance, most notably the celebrated hero and Resistance leader Jean Moulin.

After the war, Barbie dropped out of sight. With the assistance of the American army's Counter-Intelligence Corps (then recruiting former Nazis to spy against the communists), he was spirited out of Europe through an escape route organized under the auspices of the Catholic Church. Although Barbie was sentenced to death in absentia by a Lyon court in the 1950s, by the time of his 1983 capture the twenty-year statute of limitations on war crimes had expired, and he could only be tried for persecuting civilians—again, mostly Jews. When it became clear that his offenses against non-Jewish Resistance fighters (whose members had fought to be recognized as soldiers, not as civilians) would not be prosecuted, a French criminal court of appeals took a historic decision in 1985 to expand its interpretation of crimes against humanity such that certain acts against the *maquis* could be included in the indictment. Since, as Alain Finkielkraut has observed, "France rebuilt its national identity around the Gaullist epic of underground soldiers fallen for their country, that is to say, in judicial terms, by supplanting crimes against humanity with war crimes," the move, while perhaps understandable, was also paradoxical and resulted in a "competition of memories" between those victims persecuted for *who they were* (the Jews) and those punished for *what they did* (political resistors).[48] In the ensuing trial, Barbie's defense lawyer, Jacques Vergès, attempted to defame members of the French Resistance and contended that the French state lacked the moral integrity to try his client given its own inhumane conduct in the colonies—specifically its use of torture during the Algerian War. When the thirty-nine lawyers for the prosecution argued over whose suffering—that of the Jews or the Resistance—deserved precedence, the proceedings became even more of a media circus.[49] Debates about Vichy and the Holocaust were not new to the French public. So what made this case so momentous?

The 1970s had seen a sea change in France's thinking about the Occupation, a change that by the end of that decade was reflected, produced, and amplified by the television media. National debates challenging the Gaullist myth of wartime France as a "nation of resistors" had been opened by Marcel Ophuls's controversial 1971 TV documentary about occupied France, *Le chagrin et la pitié* (*The Sorrow and the Pity,* initially shown in theaters when banned from state television for its critical portrayals of French collaboration and anti-Semitism); by the 1973 French translation of Robert Paxton's book *Vichy France* (in which he challenges Pétainist claims that the Vichy government served as a "protective shield" against Germany); by Louis Malle's 1973 film *Lacombe Lucien* (in which a young boy recruited by the *milice* falls in love with a Jewish girl); and by an ongoing scandal over the presidential pardon granted by Georges Pompidou to Paul Touvier (a leader of the *milice* in the region of Lyon, who had been condemned to death in absentia for war crimes and resurfaced decades later—after the expiration of his sentence—to request the abrogation of penalties against his estate).[50] Once the Mitterrand government came to power in 1981, *Le chagrin et la pitié* was finally shown on French TV as part of Mitterrand's attempt to honor campaign promises of audiovisual reform.[51] In the same year, Bernard-Henri Lévy's *L'idéologie française*—a virulent if crudely argued denunciation of French fascism as the very core of French political culture—drew substantial media attention and was discussed on every TV channel in the months following its publication.[52] Concerns over antifascism and anticommunism, framed by the polarization of the cold war and decolonization, eclipsed the topic of France's participation in the genocide of the Jews until the late 1970s.[53] It was not until the winter of 1979 that the broadcasting of the American miniseries *Holocaust* on Antenne 2 made the tragedy—and questions about France's contribution to it—a matter of public concern.[54] The 1985 cinematic release of Claude Lanzmann's *Shoah* (a marathon nine-plus hours of footage on the deportation of Polish Jews, which aired in four parts, and without commercial interruptions, on TF1 during the Barbie trial) furthered this end, as did Louis Malle's 1987 film *Au revoir les enfants*—whose story contained striking echoes of the children's deportation from Izieu that figured so prominently among Barbie's crimes.[55]

Unfortunately, as Henry Rousso notes in *The Vichy Syndrome*—his analysis of France's attempts to grapple with its memories of the "dark years" of 1940–44 (published, not incidentally, the same year as the Barbie trial)—the largely positive process of historical recovery outlined above had a sinister underside. The postwar decades saw a resurgence of anti-Semitism, from the French government's growing support for Arab claims against Israel (exemplified by de Gaulle's reference to the Jews as "an elite people, sure of themselves and domineering" in a press conference he gave not long after the 1967 Six-Day War), to the Holocaust negationism of Darquier de Pellepoix, Robert Faurisson, and Henri Roques, to the rebirth of the extreme right, as seen in the waves of anti-Semitic attacks that marked the early eighties and the electoral successes of Le Pen's Front national.[56] All of these issues attracted the attention of television cameras.[57] But while this litany demonstrates that by the time of Barbie's trial, conversations about Vichy, collaboration, anti-Semitism, and genocide had proliferated for almost two decades in French society as well as on French television, the trial was certainly, in Rousso's words, far more than just another "eddy in the turbulent currents of postwar memory."[58]

Like the historian Emmanuel Le Roy Ladurie, who predicted in 1983 that the Barbie trial would be "an enormous national psychodrama," Alice Kaplan equates the case with "an abreaction in psychoanalysis, a single relived piece of trauma that brings the other buried pieces back to life."[59] Certainly it served as a powerful crucible, in which social, intellectual, political, and economic forces converged in a cathartic—if not necessarily purifying—act of historical regurgitation, and which, perhaps for the first time, emphasized the global ramifications of the issues at hand. For one thing, as Finkielkraut asserts in his brilliant polemical essay on the affair, *Remembering in Vain,* Barbie's defense cast the imperialistic West as the forebear of Nazi brutality. Barbie's lawyers, consisting (significantly, given their client's incontestable racism) of the French-Vietnamese Vergès, the Algerian Nabil Bouaïta, and the Congolese Jean-Martin M'Bemba, achieved this by "treating the *victims* of Hitler's racism as *symptoms* of Western racism and imperialism" and contending that "the extermination of the Jews was a crime of local interest, a drop of European blood in the ocean of human suffering, and thus offended only the consciousness of white people." These rhetorically obfuscating strategies not only rendered the third world the herald of progress; they also blew open (albeit in twisted ways) the moral ground under examination. By making the genocide of the Jews irrelevant to the sufferings of the third world, Barbie's defense attacked the idea that the Holocaust was a crime against humanity. In so doing, his lawyers were in effect seeking to nullify "the official finding established by the international community following the victory over the Nazis—that humanity *itself* is mortal" as well as the claim (integral to the very notion of "crimes against humanity") that "it was society as a whole that had suffered an irreparable wrong." This argument and the way in which it threatened "humanity's mortality" can be recognized as among the most potent of the dilemmas addressed in the *Océaniques* programs on *Antigone* and Abraham examined above.[60]

The role of the media, and television in particular, in shaping national perceptions of the trial was sharply debated. Newspapers, magazines, and journals gave the event massive coverage: during the eight weeks the court was in session; at least one hundred and thirteen articles were published in *Le monde* alone.[61] *Libération* ran dispatches on an almost daily basis.[62] In the weeks preceding the trial, *Le nouvel observateur* featured pithy biographies of noted collaborators, from Robert Brasillach to Henri Beraud, Louis Ferdinand Céline, and Drieu La Rochelle. Many saw the event as an enormous pedagogical opportunity (it is reported that schoolchildren were given special lessons on the deportations during the trial).[63] Minister of Communication Georges Fillioud urged that the trial be broadcast live on TV. Finkielkraut disagreed violently, arguing that "there are things that are not yet televisable" and insisting that the exercise of justice was one of them. He acknowledged that such an "anti-Nazi lesson" might have benefited everyone. and might even have prevented "four million French voters" from giving their support to a Holocaust negationist (Le Pen) in the following year's elections. Nevertheless, Finkielkraut—using a particularly potent image of the viewer flopping down to "munch an apple" while watching events in the courtroom develop—maintained that television is incapable of protecting "the sacred" and that "the drone of daily life has to be suspended so that the judicial ceremony can unfold."[64] Finkielkraut's opposition to televising the trial (an event that would have necessarily included the horrific testimonials of survivors) derides the apparent banality of the medium, but it also indirectly raises the fraught question of the "representability" of the Holocaust and, perhaps by extension, of any genocide. Is the normalizing closure so easily generated by narrative, and narrative imagery, necessarily obscene in the face of an event that lacks all coherence, that is beyond the scope of comprehension?[65] And, if so, how do we approach, discuss, commemorate, or publicize not only its history but also the ethical problems it raises? For those like Jaigu, Boutang, and

Cazenave, who have faith in TV as an instrument for public enlightenment, philosophical discussions of the type broached on *Océaniques*
offered a potential way in.

Ultimately, the Barbie trial was not televised. Robert Badinter,
Mitterrand's minister of justice from 1981 to 1986, a man instrumental
in arranging for Barbie's extradition to France (and whose father, arrested in one of Barbie's raids, had perished at Auschwitz), initially
supported the idea, but settled for a compromise solution in which the
proceedings became the first in France to be filmed to tape, on condition that they not be shown for thirty years.[66] Throughout 1987, however, more than 384 television broadcasts either discussed or referred
to the trial, many of them after its conclusion.[67] This enormous out-
pouring of media interest may have been partly voyeuristic, but it also
suggests that the Barbie affair kindled a desire to grapple publicly with
the complicated issues it addressed. The success of the dialogues between Steiner and Boutang broadcast on *Océaniques* cannot be understood outside this context. As we shall see, the shows on Heidegger
take up a connected intellectual crisis, while bringing even more firmly
to the fore the topics of the Holocaust, anti-Semitism, and Nazism and
the critical rapport between philosophy and practice, or thought and
action. Let us now look more closely at this second set of broadcasts.

### The Heidegger Controversy

"Dream a little," coaxed the review; "One day, on television, people
will sit around a table and talk seriously about serious things."[68] That
day came, according to television and cinema critic Serge Daney, on
the night of 7 December 1987, when *Océaniques* aired the first in a
two-part special entitled: "Martin Heidegger: La parole et le silence"
(Martin Heidegger: Speech and Silence).[69] With Boutang hosting, the
show featured Glucksmann, Steiner (by satellite from Geneva), Jean-
Pierre Faye (translator and scholar of Heidegger), François Fédier (a
disciple of Jean Beaufret, who was the addressee of Heidegger's "Letter on Humanism" and is generally recognized as his French interlocutor), and Cazenave (this time as a participant). According to Boutang,
the proximate inspiration for the broadcast was the discovery several
weeks earlier of the sole interview footage ever shot of Heidegger
(filmed for German TV in the late 1960s when the philosopher was
almost eighty).[70] More accurately, I suggest that the tape and the still

photos chosen to accompany it allowed *Océaniques* to weigh in on the
ethical questions at the heart of the Barbie trial while making a crucial visual contribution to a polemic that had detonated in the French
press the previous October following the publication of Victor Farias's
controversial monograph, *Heidegger et le nazisme*.[71] A Chilean who
had studied with Heidegger and had gone on to teach at the Institute
for Latin American Studies at the Free University in Berlin, Farias had
written his text in Spanish. Submitted to and then rejected by a German publishing house, the book was first published in French translation in the fall of 1987. It quickly triggered what became known as the
Farias affair and sparked a vicious debate over the relationship between
Heidegger's philosophy and his politics, specifically his adherence to
national socialism. Within months of the book's appearance, every
major intellectual of note, from Jean Baudrillard, Maurice Blanchot,
Pierre Bourdieu, Jacques Derrida and Luc Ferry to Alain Finkielkraut,
Philippe Lacoue-Labarthe, Emmanuel Levinas, and Alain Renaut had
taken a stand on the issues it raised.[72]

Victor Farias's book argues that Heidegger was an unrepentant
Nazi and that his politics rendered his philosophical work not merely
suspect but dangerous. However, when the Farias affair broke, the
German philosopher's political inclinations were hardly unknown.
Sartre addressed Heidegger's association with Nazism in 1944.[73] Between 1945 and 1948, these connections were further examined in
the pages of *Les temps modernes,* but the discussion remained largely
abstract, barely touching on Heidegger's ignominious activities while
rector of Freiburg University (1933–34) and focusing instead on more
formal questions about how the philosopher's ideas might be associated with the rise of Nazism.[74] Things took a more personal turn in
1961, when the publication of Jean-Pierre Faye's translations of some
of Heidegger's proclamations from the period of the rectorate clarified
the extent of his support for the nascent Nazi Party.[75] A new debate
erupted in *Critique* following the 1966 publication of François Fédier's passionate defense of Heidegger in a review essay attacking three
German books (including one by Adorno) critical of the philosopher.[76]
But even after Faye and Fédier sparred over whether Heidegger's
*post*rectorate politics were also faithful to national socialist doctrine,
the overall conversation was all but restricted to a circle of committed "Heideggarians."[77] Given that by the 1980s, as Derrida observed
at the time, Heidegger's Nazism was common knowledge among the
scholarly community, why did Farias's book provoke such violent

reactions?[78] And what part, if any, did *Océaniques* play in shaping the debate? Before addressing these questions, let us take a look at the contents of the two-part broadcast.

( · )

In the opening moments of the first part, Boutang, heard in voice-over, introduces the debate "on the relationship between Heidegger and the Nazi regime" to footage of the philosopher strolling down a country road. He then calls attention to the recent media polemic through a photomontage of the Farias's book, followed by shots of press coverage (with *Libération's* full-page article "Heil Heidegger!" figuring prominently).[79] When the camera cuts to the specially designed set, Heidegger's image is superimposed onto the low wall that separates the speakers from the audience. On its opposite side, an image of Socrates looms large.

After identifying his guests, Boutang asks Steiner (who had published *Martin Heidegger* in 1978) to speak to Heidegger's significance as "perhaps the most important philosopher of our century, in any case, one of the greatest in the entire history of Western thought." After demurring that the task is quite impossible, Steiner claims that "Heidegger did nothing less than rethink Western philosophy and metaphysics by posing and reposing a single question [. . .], 'What is 'Being?' That is to say, how do we think, how do we speak, 'Being'?" "Without Heidegger," Steiner observes, "few things would be the same in the contemporary climate of French thought." Yet he knows "of no other case where there is so much division over a thinker's ideas." As if to illustrate this discord, Cazenave situates himself firmly in the anti-Heidegger camp, declaring that he refused to host this show (a role that presumably would have required his objectivity) after being "blown away" by Farias's demonstration of the "organic unity between [Heidegger's] thought and the phenomenon of Nazism." Glucksmann soon echoes Steiner's idea about Heidegger's importance in France, noting that Alexandre Kojève's influential lectures on Hegel—given between 1933 and 1939 at the École pratique des hautes études and marking an entire intellectual generation from "Sartre and Beauvoir to Bataille, Lacan, Merleau-Ponty, and Raymond Queneau"—were themselves distinctly shaped by a seminar delivered previously by Heidegger in the winters of 1930–31.[80] Since "we now know," Glucksmann gravely concludes with his characteristic theatrical intensity,

*Libération* headline; The *Océaniques* set; Fédier and Glucksmann; Heidegger; Glucksmann. From "Martin Heidegger: La parole et le silence: 1ère partie," *Océaniques*, 12 December 1987.

that the Heideggerian-inflected Hegel of Kojève "led French thinkers to become Marxist, or at least fellow travelers, as well as existentialist and structuralist," it is no surprise that the Farias book provoked such "dramatic" reactions across the French intellectual field.[81]

Glucksmann's insight still fails to account for the magnitude of the current response. However, as Derrida mordantly remarks in an article published the previous month in *Le nouvel observateur,* the unspoken and, he suggests, reductive assumption to be drawn from this line of reasoning is that if Heidegger's thought should prove inextricably fascist, the entire (and constantly growing) edifice of postwar French philosophy that draws upon it might be contaminated too.[82] In Derrida's words, "There are persons who seize upon the pretext of their recent discovery [of Heidegger's Nazism] to cry (1) *'To read Heidegger is a disgrace!'*; (2) *'Let's draw the following conclusion and balance: everything, especially in France, which refers to Heidegger in one way or another, even if it is called "deconstruction" is Heideggerianism.'"* [83] Thus, when Faye, during the broadcast, articulates the problem at the nucleus of this debate: "Is it possible to separate Heidegger the Nazi from Heidegger the philosopher?" adding, "I believe that if the greatest philosopher of the century was a Nazi, it follows that he wasn't the greatest philosopher of the century," it is implied that the consequences are as important for the future of French thought as they are for the philosophical fortunes of the gentleman in question.

In explaining the case against Heidegger, Faye tells viewers that in the years following the 1927 publication of *Being and Time,* Heidegger's ultraconservative, militant German nationalism led him to sympathize with the emergent Nazi program. Elected rector of Freiburg University in 1933, just months after Hitler came to power, Heidegger joined the Nazi Party. During his ten-month tenure, Heidegger quickly revealed his dedication to the principles of national socialism in numerous speeches and public proclamations. By way of example, Faye loosely quotes a political address in which Heidegger describes the Führer as "the truth of Germany and its law." Heidegger had long justified his acceptance of the post at Freiburg as an attempt to protect the autonomy of the university and ward off political extremism. Part of the importance of the Farias book, which drew heavily on the research of Hugo Ott, a German scholar whose work had not yet been translated into French at the time of the 1987 broadcast, was that it gave the lie to this claim.[84] Determined to demonstrate to the viewing public the gravity of Heidegger's political leanings, the increasingly excited Faye launches into German. Boutang swiftly intervenes, reminding him to translate for the audience. Faye stops short, his expression suggesting that he is caught between the desire to express the philosophical core of Heidegger's politics and the realization that attempting to communicate anything but the most rudimentary understanding of that philosophy in a format such as this is patently absurd.

The program changes tenor when a member of the audience comes to Heidegger's defense, suggesting that Nazism in 1933 was not necessarily the same as the Nazism that produced Auschwitz. His comment is clearly intended to render Heidegger's politics less indecent, since it implicitly refers to the fact (unannounced to the spectators thus far) that the philosopher quit the rectorate in 1934, at which point he claims to have disassociated himself from the Nazi Party and its ideals. The speaker, Gérard Guest (who unbeknownst to the TV audience is himself a philosopher and Heidegger scholar) insists that while Heidegger's support for the Nazi Party must be viewed as an error, it becomes understandable when placed in the context of the philosopher's defense of the university and his attempt to "interpret the situation of modern times" via "an interpretation of the tradition of reason." Guest's comments provide the bridge to the next shot, an image of the Parthenon, followed by one of Heidegger seated in what appears to be an Athenian market square—an *agora*. Boutang elucidates Heidegger's belief that "the Greeks put into motion" the "ultimate transformation of our world into a world of technology" and adds, "His journey to Greece allowed him to verify this premise." The next cut takes us to a close-up of Heidegger, interviewed in a subtitled excerpt from the 1960s footage shot for German TV.

The sequence addresses three central issues: the way in which Heidegger understands the relationship between "Being" and the human condition, the thorny puzzle of his perspective on science and technology, and his contention that philosophy is "at an end." Each of these problems holds a central place in Heidegger's oeuvre. The first relates, of course, to the interest in "being-in-the-world" that was the ontological obsession of his life's work or, as he states here, "the fundamental notion of my thought." The second hones in on Heidegger's concern for technical nihilism (a theme that, while visible in earlier texts, finds particular expression in the four lectures delivered in 1949 that formed the basis of *The Question Concerning Technology*).[85] Although it is now commonly thought that Heidegger originally viewed Nazism as a "political antidote to nihilism" and saw the Nazis as the "heroic 'new pagans' who would save the West from a seemingly irreversible process of Spenglerian decline," not surprisingly he makes no reference to this idea in the footage shown here.[86] Instead, in this interview as elsewhere, he takes pains to approach technology without judgment, specifically stating, "I am not opposed to technology." Heidegger nevertheless reveals his belief that in its modern manifestation, technology is a looming, if vaguely defined system, a form of "enframing" (*Gestell*), whose essence infiltrates human existence and thus poses a danger to human freedom.[87] The final topic covered in the excerpt from the German interview, in which Heidegger explains that he "differentiates between philosophy, that is to say, metaphysics, and thought, in the sense that I understand it," addresses the famous "turn" that characterized his later work, especially following the war—visible, for example, in the 1946 "Letter on Humanism" with its rejection of the metaphysics of subjectivity, its attack on humanism, and its attempt to elucidate "the thinking that is to come." [88]

There is nothing in this excerpt that is particularly damning with respect to the relationship between Heidegger's philosophy and his political beliefs. Yet the *Océaniques* show promotes an explicitly litigious ideological agenda. The careful use of still photographs alone suggests that *Océaniques*' audience was being encouraged to interpret Heidegger's answers through the political history of the Third Reich. When Heidegger's unseen interviewer asks, "Those of your critics who maintain that Heidegger is so concerned by Being that he has forgotten the human condition—are they right?" there is no doubt that the question's subtext is the legacy of genocide. Brow furrowed, Heidegger replies that this "is a serious misinterpretation! For the question of Being and of its deployment presupposes precisely an interpretation of *Dasein*, that is to say, of the essence of man," adding, "How can we question Being without questioning man?" Here one feels compelled to wonder whether his response is a philosophical smokescreen. (As Arnold I. Davidson observes, speaking of Heidegger's silence on the Final Solution, "Humanism aside, what has become of the human?") [89] So too, when Heidegger claims that "the phrase 'science does not think' is not a criticism: it is simply a statement of fact," or contends (although he is "not against technology") that technology represents "a peril greater than that of the atomic bomb" because its essence reveals "the fact that human beings are in the grip of a power that challenges them, and in reference to which they are not free," each of these statements can easily be understood as apologetic justifications for the excesses of technological modernity, of which Nazism represents a culmination. [90] Throughout, Heidegger's body language is deliberate and somber, his facial expressions serious but inscrutable. Interestingly, given the agenda that directs the *Océaniques* broadcast, the questions posed in the German footage seem designed to provoke responses that would ground Heidegger's philosophical beliefs in actual historical events. Yet Heidegger's abstract theoretical answers illustrate not only that such an agenda is inherently problematic (since there is no reason why he should reply in this fashion) but also that any attempt to judge his responses without a broader philosophical knowledge of his work will necessarily fall very short indeed.

When the excerpt ends, the program cuts back to a projection of Steiner, joining the broadcast once again by satellite from Geneva. As if to fill the lacuna in our understanding, Steiner assures viewers unfamiliar with Heidegger's work that in 1927, the year *Being and Time* was published, there was obviously "no Nazism" in his philosophy. For those familiar with Steiner's work, the statement is an alarming about-face, since a decade earlier he had argued that the evidence was "incontrovertible: there *were* instrumental connections between the language and vision of *Sein und Zeit* [Being and Time], especially the later sections, and those of Nazism. Those who would deny this are blind or mendacious."[91] On this occasion, however, Steiner proposes that the question that really needs to be asked is not "What did Heidegger find in Nazism" but rather "What did Nazism find in Heidegger's earthy, ontological thought?" Faye, reluctant to watch Steiner let the philosopher off the hook so easily, breaks in and begins quoting—with devastating results—from Heidegger's 11 November 1933 "Declaration of Support for Adolf Hitler and the National Socialist State."[92] From Heidegger's belief that the Führer has awakened the "will in the entire people and has welded it into one single resolve," to his closing "Heil Hitler," Faye's intervention leaves no question as to where the philosopher's political sympathies lay—at least at the start of Hitler's regime. It is on the heels of this indictment that François Fédier, whom Boutang earlier dubbed "the guardian of the Heideggarian temple," finally takes the floor.

Like Gérard Guest, the audience member who intervened earlier, Fédier is intent on pointing out the dangers of retrospective judgment. "If we look at Heidegger's use of the term 'national socialism,' in 1933," Fédier asserts, "it doesn't take a lot of brains to determine the difference between what he meant and what we mean by it today."[93] To illustrate, Fédier draws our attention to the images that have been circulating in the press. The first frame shows Heidegger at a Nazi Party rally in Leipzig on 11 November 1933, seated at a table surrounded by flags bearing the Nazi swastika; the second is a portrait of Heidegger wearing the Nazi party pin. While a picture may be worth a thousand words, however, and while Heidegger obviously wrote texts in which he supported national socialism, as Farias's book proves, Fédier's aim is to demonstrate that the movement didn't mean the same thing then that it does now. Perhaps. But when the cameras linger intently on the incriminating photos as a voice-over begins reciting excerpts from Heidegger's 1933 discourse on "the self-assertion

Nazi Party rally in Leipzig, 11 November 1933 (Heidegger fourth from left in front row, seated); close-up of Heidegger; portrait of Heidegger wearing the Nazi Party pin, taken while he was rector, University of Freiburg, 1933–34.

of the German university" (also known as the rectorship address) in which the philosopher calls for German students to bind themselves, through "labor service, military service, and knowledge service" to "the destiny of the state," the effect, predictably, is to reinforce rather than discredit Heidegger's problematic politics.[94]

When the cameras finally cut away and revert to Steiner, he raises an "anguished question" that "hardly comes up in Farias's book at all": that of Heidegger's enduring silence "regarding Auschwitz, regarding the camps" in the years following the war.[95] The remainder of the broadcast converges on this final point: How could "a man who expressed in the years after the war, in profoundly lucid terms," his thoughts on issues of "capital importance" such as the dangers posed by "American and Soviet technology and technocracy for our planet"—a man who "didn't hesitate to think and rethink the politics of postwar Europe"—have remained silent on the Final Solution? As Levinas would observe barely six weeks later in the pages of *Le nouvel observateur*, "Does not this silence, even in peacetime, about the gas chambers and the death camps—something beyond the realm of all 'poor excuses'—attest to a soul that is in its depths impervious to compassion [*sensibilité*], is it not a tacit approval of the horrifying?"[96] The stakes are huge, since both the man, and the oeuvre are at issue.

Steiner's question has clearly touched a nerve. Fédier sheepishly suggests, "If there was silence, it was because [Heidegger] realized that he wasn't capable of pronouncing anything worthy of the level of horror that was attained." Straining at the bit, Glucksmann responds that their audience should distinguish between appraisals of the card-carrying Nazi philosopher of 1933–45 ("who was not Barbie, and whom we cannot reproach" on the same grounds) and the "much more important question" of the Heidegger who, between 1946 and 1975, manages to speak "of technology and modernity, but who doesn't find the words to speak of Auschwitz." When Steiner remarks, "As far as I know, not one of those poor Nazi dogs understood a single word of [*Being and Time*]," Glucksmann angrily retorts, "Well, maybe Heidegger didn't understand Hitler's reality, either," but, he tartly adds, that doesn't absolve him from the subsequent responsibility of addressing the Final Solution. In the face of Glucksmann's rejoinder, Fédier admits that "Heidegger is no hero" but contends that we must forgive the philosopher for his "human failings" ("I just try to put myself in his place, when you have sons, and a wife"). Although Glucksmann concedes that "we can't ask philosophers to be heroes," the problem that Fédier ignores is not that Heidegger made an extremely bad mistake but that he never acknowledged it. Drawing a negative comparison with Solzhenitsyn's willingness to reevaluate his own Stalinism, Glucksmann argues that Heidegger's failure to produce an equivalent mea culpa obliterates his status as a reputable thinker in the postwar period. In closing, the camera zooms in on the photograph of Heidegger at the party rally, his face adorned by the manicured mustache he preferred (a mustache that can only be described as alarmingly Hitleresque). The broadcast ends with a final quote from Heidegger's 1933 speech to German students: "The Führer himself, and he alone, is the reality of Germany today, and tomorrow is his law. [. . .] Heil Hitler!"[97] There is little doubt as to where the producers' sympathies lie.

The second part of the Heidegger broadcast was shot immediately after the first and aired one week later, on 14 December 1987, with the same guests in attendance.[98] Opening with another excerpt from the 1960s Heidegger footage, in which the philosopher speaks once more about the importance of "the question of Being," part 2 then picks up where the last show left off. Beyond a few specifics, it mostly revisits issues addressed previously and settles on the meaning of these issues when it comes to reading the philosopher's work. The gravity of the problem is reemphasized when an agitated Glucksmann (after insisting that he's "not a book burner" but admitting that "we can't cut people in two") quotes one of the most damning of all of Heidegger's post-war pronouncements: "Agriculture today," the German philosopher affirmed in 1949, "is a motorized food industry, in essence the same as the manufacture of corpses in gas chambers and extermination camps, the same as the blockade and starvation of countries, the same as the making of atomic bombs." [99] Despite the fact that these comparisons reveal a sort of "systemic thought" that philosopher Philippe Lacoue-Labarthe has termed both "absolutely just" and "scandalously insufficient," they leave the viewer staggered by Heidegger's insensitivity towards the fragile fate of real human beings. [100] Overcome by the weight of the evidence, Steiner ponders, "Are we speaking of a great philosopher, or have we all been taken in?" Where, one might ask, is the concern for "Being" now?

As the broadcast continues, it is increasingly evident that the issue is not whether Heidegger was a Nazi—something no longer in doubt—but rather the question of what this fact implies for the history of twentieth-century philosophy. "Reading Heidegger, that is the great difficulty today," asserts Steiner; "reading him seriously, understanding what he wanted to say." And "I don't think," he adds, "that the great silence after 1945" relieves us of this task. "The more interesting question to me," submits Guest, intervening yet again, is whether we can "condemn the Heidegger of 1933–34 on the basis of his own thought?" Steiner offers that from Socrates to Hegel to Hobbes we can find "a certain kind of despotism," a "terribly profound, dangerous flirtation with the absolute" in the thought of great philosophers. But this doesn't mean we should avoid their works. Glucksmann agrees, owning that it is because he shares Steiner's pleasure in reading Heidegger that the whole issue is so complicated. Here Cazenave interjects: "What I want to ask is, 'Is there a relationship, yes or no, between Heidegger and the position that he holds?' and if yes, 'What does that mean?' because it poses a true philosophical problem." Could Heidegger have been fundamentally in error? Would we do better to forget him? "Heidegger cannot," objects Fédier, "be at once the height of intelligence and the lowest of the low." Fédier, pace Glucksmann, suggests that we have to listen to Heidegger "with two ears"—one for the philosopher who commented so brilliantly on Sophocles, the other for the man of 1933–34. The broadcast lets Heidegger himself have the last word—appropriately mystifying, given his reputation as the modern founder of "a complete atheistic philosophy." "No man," Heidegger concludes, "can survive without religion: otherwise expressed,

each man, in a certain sense, overflows himself." Or, as he states elsewhere, "Only a God can save us."[101]

( · )

Both prior and subsequent to the *Océaniques* double broadcast, the
book at its center, *Heidegger et le nazisme,* was roundly criticized;
even Farias's champions admit that his scholarship is "occasionally
lacking in the proper methodological rigor."[102] The text is demonstra-
bly less persuasive in handling Heidegger's philosophy than in collat-
ing disparaging details about his admittedly scurrilous political biography, and it contains numerous errors of fact and interpretation. The
most frequently cited of these include the faulty analysis of Heidegger's
references to the seventeenth-century monk Abraham a Sancta Clara
(1644–1709) and the tenuous association of Heidegger with Ernst
Roehm, leader of the Sturmabteilung (SA).[103] But despite the book's
widely acknowledged flaws, it has generally been applauded for making previously unavailable sources accessible while providing persuasive documentation regarding Heidegger's enduring ties to national
socialism. The book confirms that Heidegger was a convinced supporter of the Nazi party who refused even after the war to condemn
Nazi policies, address the Holocaust, or recant his earlier politics. As
we have seen, the TV broadcast did its best to visually reinforce these
conclusions. However, as Serge Daney observes in a review published
in *Libération,* viewers accustomed to programs that degenerate into
venomous "wrestling matches" with clearly defined winners and losers
might have been bewildered by the investigation that was conducted
during the show.[104] For, even after the second broadcast, the participants remain equivocal about the core question of whether Heidegger's
philosophical works are, or are not, intimately linked to his political
beliefs. Yet this very equivocation is a strength, for it speaks to a willingness to forego closure and honor complexity. And, of course, as
Daney remarks, "the 'scoop' in 1987 was less 'Heidegger the Nazi'"
than the way in which Farias compelled "the Heideggerians (and the
others)" to confront the philosopher's "obstinate silence." A silence,
Daney continues, "that drives them to speak out on television" and
elsewhere.[105] Daney fails to note, however, that "Heidegger's silence"
would not have proved so provocative in France if the book that proclaimed it had not opportunely intersected with specific issues in a variety of critical domains—social, philosophical and *médiatique.*

It should now be quite apparent that the timing of Farias's book, which was published on the heels of the Barbie trial, and its engagement with a related set of political and historical concerns was particularly propitious. But unlike the Barbie case, in which the defendant was being prosecuted for a series of heinous *acts*, the Heidegger affair emphasized that *ideas*, too, must be held morally accountable—a point that held considerable purchase in France. Indeed, as discussed in chapter 1, it was this long-standing notion of intellectual responsibility—expressed in postwar debates over the public accountability of the writer—that contributed to the growing power of French intellectuals in the aftermath of the Second World War. Using arguments about anti-totalitarianism and human rights to legitimize their claims, Glucksmann, Lévy, and their epigones had just revived the connection between ideas and ethics via the figure of the intellectual as moralist. Indeed, Christian Jambet (one of the New Philosophers) observes in his introduction to the French edition of the Farias book that Heidegger's case was deemed particularly odious because it flew in the face of the sacred link between philosophy and virtue, thus defying the idea of the social relevance of reason so dear to the French philosophical tradition. In addition, recent studies had clarified that in France, ideological complicity was by far the most pervasive form of collaboration during Vichy—a fact that almost certainly wasn't lost on the television public and likely made it all the more difficult (particularly in this period of extended critical reappraisal of both the Occupation and the wars of decolonization) to keep Heidegger's personal politics at a comfortable remove. Recurrent bursts of conservative nationalism (typified by the electoral victories of the Front national, Holocaust revisionism, and the anti-Semitic violence mentioned earlier), as well as a resurgent interest in human rights, reinforced the value of ideological vigilance in the current social climate.

Philosophically, the attack on Heidegger occurred just after the philosopher's substantial influence in the French intellectual world had come under fire. In their important 1985 essay *French Philosophy of the Sixties,* the young scholars Luc Ferry and Alain Renaut called to task their intellectual elders (Foucault, Derrida, Bourdieu, and Lacan—all of whom draw on Heidegger's work in crucial ways) for abandoning the promises of modern democratic humanism and rejecting the metaphysics of the subject.[106] They later argued that after the collapse of Marxism, a "politically purified" Heidegger had offered even more seductive foundations for a radical critique of "both the totalitarianism of the East and the bureaucratic, repressive, disciplinary, and consumer-oriented society of the West." [107] Farias's book provided a means first to expose and then to morally condemn this move, thus delivering powerful ammunition to the neohumanist camp while challenging the work of the large number of French intellectuals whose philosophical stances were indebted to the German thinker. In the wake of its publication, the French intellectual community split, with the traditional Heideggerians (Beaufret and Fédier most prominently) mounting an extreme, unconditional defense, followed by Derrida, Lacoue-Labarthe, and Lyotard (who, put simplistically, distinguish between an objectionable "Heidegger I" identified as pro-Nazi, a humanist, and metaphysician, and a redeemable, largely postwar "Heidegger II" understood as a politically benign antihumanist), all opposed by Ferry and Renaut, among others. While the specifics of these arguments are beyond the scope of the present study, Hugo Ott's comment that "in France a sky has fallen—the sky of the philosophers" aptly captures the spirit of the times. [108]

Stylistically slick, variously characterized as "yellow journalism" and "crime writing," Farias's prose made Heidegger's story uniquely accessible and set the emotionally loaded tone for the debate that followed. [109] All sides blasted their opponents with accusations of intellectual incompetence. In his assessment of the Farias affair, Pierre Bourdieu contends that "the debate began very badly" since from the beginning the "parties [were] only concerned with 'judging' and taking sides," which meant that everyone could "participate without knowledge of the texts and their contents." In Bourdieu's opinion, the worst part of this is that "the constant reference to the Holocaust, which via the philosopheme of 'absolute evil' is rapidly made into a *topos*," leads to "the *dehistoricization* of thought and the thinker." [110] While the charge was not without substance (particularly when it came to the ways in which the case manifested in the media), *Océaniques* indicates that restraint could have been exercised. And although Michel Cazenave admitted, "To tell you the truth, I wasn't very happy" with the two shows, because "we could've treated the material far more profoundly"—especially if Glucksmann hadn't been "playing the showman" and Fédier hadn't "intentionally avoided dealing with the texts"—he disputed the notion that the players were ill informed. "After all," Cazenave concluded, "at least we opened a space for discussion." [111] And on this there seemed unanimous agreement. *Océaniques* made it possible, for the first time in twenty years and for the first time ever in France, to view rare footage of a controversial but tremendously important intellectual figure. While stopping short of a clear verdict on Heidegger's philosophy, the show condemned his politics, deploying visual and aural evidence—from iconic symbols like swastikas and party pins to more subtle (and problematic) "cues" derived from appearance, body language, and even the simple fact that Heidegger spoke German—the language of the enemy—in the interview, to great rhetorical effect. More importantly, from the perspective of its producers, the broadcast not only amplified media interest in an intense philosophical debate but also exposed Heidegger's saga to a wider audience, thus encouraging a disparate public to think about the broader intellectual and moral ramifications of the issues his story raised.

( · )

Interestingly, the question of Heidegger's politics resurfaced recently in French intellectual debate. The latest and most volatile installment in the tale occurred in the spring of 2005, when Emmanuel Faye (whose father, Jean-Pierre, was featured on the *Océaniques* shows) published a book in which from an analysis of new sources (including the texts of two seminars from 1933–35) he deduced that Heidegger's entire intellectual project was ideologically and politically inextricable from Nazism.[112] This time there was no Barbie trial to drum up popular interest, but the still bitter memory of Jean-Marie Le Pen's electoral victory in the first round of the 2002 presidential elections (when he finished second to Chirac, to the shame of much of the nation) indicates that the broader questions at its core were once again of widespread concern. Emmanuel Faye's *Heidegger: L'introduction du nazisme dans la philosophie* went so far as to suggest that Heidegger was the inspiration behind many of Hitler's own speeches. Both the press and television immediately took note, and France 2 covered the book in two separate broadcasts.[113] Meanwhile, spearheaded by the writer Stéphane Zagdanski, Heidegger's French supporters mounted a massive Internet campaign, flooding the websites of over three thousand philosophy departments, as well as hundreds of other cultural websites with a manifesto in thirteen languages, condemning Faye's "delirious" attack against the master philosopher.[114] Within weeks, numerous philosophers (Jacques Bouveresse, Jacques Brunschwig), historians (Pascal Ory, Pierre Vidal-Naquet, Paul Veyne), Germanists

(Jean Bollack, Georges-Arthur Goldschimdt), activists (such as Serge Klarsfeld), and other intellectuals issued their own manifesto in Faye's defense.[115] With the support of the European University for Research, a one-day conference, "Le nazisme de Heidegger, son langage et sa reception en France," was organized between Faye and the American Heidegger scholar Richard Wolin on 26 May. In the midst of these intellectual fireworks, the minister of education decided to add three of Heidegger's works—*Being and Time, Introduction to Phenomenological Research,* and *The Fundamental Concepts of Metaphysics*—to the 2006 curriculum for that highest test of philosophical knowledge in the nation, the *agrégation.* In reporting on the phenomenon, *Télérama* commented that "the ministerial decision has a strong chance of restarting [an old] polemic, since certain malcontents, overjoyed to call into question that extremely French exception which is the teaching of philosophy in the *classe terminale,* will undoubtedly bark in chorus, demanding the suppression of this useless, jargon-filled, if not downright dangerous discipline." [116] It is too early to tell what, if anything, television may make of this paradox.

## Public Television Attacked: Assessing *Océaniques*

In the 1980s, the privatization of French television exacerbated the race for ratings and threatened to eradicate the conditions that the production of high cultural programming requires. But as we have seen, under the impassioned protection of one man, Yves Jaigu, a program emerged that managed for a time to buck the pressures of the new media environment and to produce, among other broadcasts, a series of shows on philosophy that left an enduring imprint on French cultural memory. Indeed, in the vast wash of broadcasts that have flooded the small screen over the past fifty years, the programs on *Antigone,* Abraham, and Heidegger have—like the documentary on Bachelard, Foucault's appearance on *Lectures pour tous,* or the numerous references to *Apostrophes* that pepper the scholarship—become touchstones, unavoidable references in the history of French television. In the admittedly unscientific sample of French archivists, television professionals, philosophers, colleagues, and friends that I have talked to over the years—including the merchant at my local wine store on the rue Mouffetard in Paris who declared the shows with Boutang and Steiner "absolutely sublime"—almost all report some memory of these shows. As I have argued in this chapter, the reputation acquired by *Océaniques* obtains both from the unique contents of its broadcasts and from their particular relationship to a number of highly significant historical and cultural transformations. That said, the two sets of broadcasts function quite differently. For whereas the those on *Antigone* and Abraham stand as examples of philosophy in action, those on Heidegger operate as a forum, providing an opportunity to think about philosophical issues via the framework of a debate over the ethical substance of a specific biographical narrative.

Intent on proving that "culture is not a synonym for boredom," Jaigu envisaged *Océaniques* as no-holds-barred cultural immersion, a means to render accessible to the widest possible audience—in the best tradition of French public programming—the vast riches in philosophy, literature, science, and the arts that might otherwise be unavailable to them.[117] *Télérama* compared Jaigu to Victor Hugo, arguing that through *Océaniques* Jaigu had fulfilled the mission that Hugo had assigned to public instruction, putting "the genius of France in communication with the heart of the people."[118] Boutang described the program as "an exercise in curiosity, a sort of encyclopedic megalomania, [. . .] an insatiable urge to return to all of the sources that carry meaning for people today."[119] As rousing as it sounded, their agenda echoed the conservative aims of Malraux's cultural policy initiatives in the early Fifth Republic and incubated similar tensions. When it came right down to it, whereas *Océaniques* was hailed as an unqualified success by the print media, its ratings—on average the program drew between half a million and two million viewers, or approximately 2% to 3% of the TV audience—were considered less then spectacular by certain industry professionals.[120] Boutang felt these to be respectable results and claimed that since "we cry 'triumph' if a book manages to sell 100,000 copies" the fact that their shows regularly more than quintupled these numbers was nothing to scoff at.[121] Interestingly, in his examination of films on Vichy, Henry Rousso reports that in the 1980s "a really successful movie in the Paris region [was] normally seen by 800,000 to a million people in the first *year* [emphasis mine] after release."[122] While Rousso acknowledges that it is difficult to gauge what the public actually thought about what it viewed—a sentiment that applies equally here—the contrast in audience numbers is nevertheless striking. For his part, Jaigu "knew very well that the audience [numbers] wouldn't be at a maximum for a program like *Océaniques*," but as director of programming at FR3 he believed that he could "accept a drop in audience if the quality of the contents and the form of what we were broadcasting was topnotch." [123] Clearly, however, in the newly privatized and increasingly cutthroat audiovisual climate, the demands of audience polls had to be suspended for the series to survive.[124]

*Océaniques'* producers thumbed their noses at commercial TV's marketing objectives. "Don't come tell me that at the same hour *Supersexy* had better ratings," Boutang snorted in a 1991 interview; "I didn't give a damn." [125] Almost a decade later he reiterated, "I thought [*Océaniques*] was good, and [Jaigu] thought it was good, and the press thought it was *amazing,* so we lived on our reputation. [. . .] We were concerned with quality, not ratings." [126] The problem with the new audiovisual environment, Jaigu remarked, was that too many television professionals "confused the multiplication of channels with variety in programming." It is "totally false," he explained, that "the more channels" that exist, "the more choices people will have," for in fact, "the more channels there are, the less money there is to be divided" among them. The ensuing financial competition leads not to "a heterogeneity of programs but to homogeneity and hence absence of choice." [127] This absence "creates a false mental consensus" about the public, who are all assumed to want to watch the same things.[128] And the unfortunate result, as Boutang scathingly observed, is that "now, whether you turn on France 2 or TF1, you have the same type of programs: big talk shows on pressing social problems such as 'What can you do if you are a homosexual dwarf who was raped by your father at the age of three?'" [129]

Jaigu and his producers coupled their commitment to high cultural programming and disregard for ratings with a solicitous concern for their viewing public, whom they conceptualized as socioeconomically, intellectually, and culturally diverse. Thus, while they understood that their broadcasts "required effort" and were not "an easy exercise" for spectators, they still insisted that *Océaniques* was far from elitist.[130] "True mediation," Jaigu told me, "consists in knowing how on national airwaves you can combine the possibilities of general access and an authentic improvement in the [public's] understanding" of something as complex as Heidegger's *Dasein*. "This" he assured me, "is the role of the media: to be that absolutely unique space of immense liberty where the things that didn't seem accessible suddenly are." [131] The sentiment is beautiful but betrays an almost naïve faith in what Jeremy Ahearne calls "the direct amorous encounter between individuals and the enduring moments of high culture," a faith that harked back to Malraux's flagship cultural policy of "aesthetic shock." In Malraux's view, the human capacity to experience beauty functioned as an abrupt mediator between reason and instinct, allowing people direct access to high cultural productions.[132] But Pierre Bourdieu has argued at some length that without access to the proper codes (an access enabled solely by education or immersion in the requisite socio-familial "habitus"), this kind of unmediated "direct experience" can result in only the most superficial of encounters.[133] Jaigu and his crew were aware that some viewers were disadvantaged in this regard, yet they remained fervent advocates of the small screen's emancipating potential. "Just let Boutang tell you," recounted one journalist in 1988, "about how his Arab grocer loved the show on Heidegger, or how some other shopkeeper from his neighborhood adored the debate on the myth of *Antigone*." [134] More than ten years later, Boutang repeated these anecdotes to me virtually verbatim, adding, "Even if there is only one Arab grocer who watches and who understands something of these TV shows on philosophy, well, for me that constitutes a success." [135] Whether Arab grocers could be consistently counted amongst *Océaniques* viewers is perhaps less important that what the oft-repeated sentiment betrays (and here we have echoes of Dina Dreyfus's programs for Radio-télévision scolaire) about an underlying conviction in the value of transmitting the Western tradition—through the televising of philosophy—to an increasingly multicultural nation.

"Television, in general, symbolizes the ephemeral," observed Boutang. "We broadcast it once, and then it's over, forgotten. It's true that *Océaniques* was of another dimension. We had, modestly, pretensions to longevity." [136] Unfortunately, noble intentions were not sufficient to ensure *Océaniques*' future. Repeatedly pressured to heed the demands of commercial advertisers and rethink programming with an eye to wider audiences, unable to freely produce material of the caliber he was committed to, and carped at by bosses in the upper echelons, Yves Jaigu resigned his post as FR3's director of programming on 17 October 1989 after only three years on the job. On hearing the news, a colleague purportedly cried, "Erich Honecker[137] and Yves Jaigu are leaving. It's the end of the world!" Ironically, Jaigu quit on the very day that the Bibliothèque publique d'information at the Pompidou Center opened a special homage to the broadcast—making over 150 videos from the series available to view.[138] Assessing the new order that he left behind, Jaigu minced no words: "Technocracies that submit to the reign of quantity replace intelligence by consensus. In running too fast after viewers, we wind up forgetting what we have to say." "True," he admitted to a journalist from *Télérama* on his final day, "you are not wrong to call into question a few 'excessively brainy' shows that might better have been broadcast on an educational network modeled after the BBC's *Open University*," but overall, he insisted, "*Océaniques* was a triumph" without equal.[139] Although the program limped on after Jaigu's departure, Boutang recalls that "once Jaigu was gone, everything went downhill and dissolved into stupidities." [140]

Jaigu believed that the people in charge of directing a "great national public television network" have "an obligation to look around at the state of the world" and to let their programs speak to the realities that they find. When in the 1980s he had "looked around" and seen "the fading of religious belief" and "the disappearance of ideologies," he became convinced that in this "intellectually stormy era" it was more important than ever to televise philosophy, "as *Océaniques* had fought to demonstrate." Why? Because he believed that this is an age in which "it is necessary—and this is magnificent" to produce new concepts. "And radio and television have a role to play in this production. For heaven's sake, they *must* participate in, encourage, and support this process." To do otherwise would be irresponsible, since "every idea that is replaced by a sensation, or even by a feeling, and that isn't conceptualized, that isn't made symbolic, that doesn't reflect upon itself, is dangerous, because it tends to make all subjectivity into an absolute—a being in itself." Philosophy, Jaigu claims, makes it possible to exit from this subjectivity, from this " 'totalitarian state' that is translated by those terrible phrases: 'I like this, I don't like that' 'I think he is an ass' 'I feel like this, I feel like that.' " Philosophy, and philosophy alone, makes it possible to "leave that confusion behind [. . .] and through confrontation with other ideas to attempt to approach the truth or, rather, to approach a certain clarity that is, in fact, the very bedrock of social harmony." [141]

### "The most beautiful landscape on TV is an intelligent face"

France's reexamination of the war years during the 1980s was symptomatic of the larger crisis over national identity that we have been tracing throughout this book. The public arguments over the legacies of World War II (arguments that intensified in the 1990s with the trials of Paul Touvier and Maurice Papon and the murder of René Bousquet)[142] provided ways of understanding a variety of social pressures—visible in everything from immigrant demands for "the right to difference," to rising race-related violence, to the growing power of the Front national, to the controversy over *laïcité* that erupted in the 1989 *affaire du foulard* (headscarf affair")—that were challenging French society in new ways.[143] Postwar generations drew on debates about Vichy and the Holocaust to promote their own political and social agendas. The collapse of communism simultaneously presaged the "end of ideologies" that Jaigu had remarked on, the resurgence of liberal politics, and the onset of globalization. Philosophy provided a space to explore the moral implications of these changes. The rejection of Heideggerianism in favor of a renewed interest in ethics (apparent in the revival of interest in Jewish thought and the work of Emmanuel Levinas; in the philosophy of the neo-Kantians Luc Ferry, Alain Renaut, and André Comte-Sponville; and in the essays of Alain Finkielkraut) testifies to the ways in which social anxieties were mirrored by a philosophical crisis of faith that sought solace in a return to the rationalist promises of Western modernity.[144] And despite the obstacles posed by privatization, television made the ensuing philosophical explorations available to a broader and more ethnically diverse public than had previously been possible. *Océaniques* reflected these concerns, prefiguring the interests in ethics and politics that dominated the televising of philosophy in the years to come.

Entrusted with a mission of national cohesion, the televising of philosophy in France was inseparable from the aims of the French state, even after TV began to undergo partial privatization. Protected for decades from the competition of the private market by government monopoly, French television had long been assured a public. Less pressured to visually seduce its audiences and uninterrupted by advertising, French programs possessed a level of temporal continuity, unimaginable in North America, that supported the kind of sustained argument necessary to the televising of philosophy. *Océaniques,* with its thrice-weekly, fifty-minute broadcasts and two-part programming formats thrived on these advantages. True, filmed as they were on a circular platform adorned with images of Descartes and Socrates set off against a background of a luminous starry blue, the philosophy shows in particular were structurally conservative; despite the regular introduction of archival footage, their basic format remained that of the "talking heads" that had long dominated the genre. But as Serge Daney asks, "How, in fact, should one 'dress' the naked discourse of a broadcast on 'philo'? How should one furnish this theater, in which the actors are men, but also concepts?"[145] From the perspective of Boutang, at least, the answer was simple. For although he conceded that "it's very hard to illustrate concepts," he nevertheless maintained that "the most beautiful landscape on TV is an intelligent face."[146]

Televising philosophy and philosophers seemed understandable in the 1950s, '60s, and '70s, when located inside of a national dialogue on culture that sought "to make accessible humanity's greatest masterpieces, and especially those of France, to the greatest possible number of French people; to reach the largest possible audience with our cultural heritage, and to promote the creation of works of art and of the intellect which will further enrich it."[147] But what happened when this dialogue waned? Privatization is often assumed to presage the death of cultural programming.[148] The history of philosophical television complicates the seamlessness of this assumption, and in so doing calls into question traditional interpretations of television history. Thus, while true that the emergence of a commercial market delivered a body blow to public TV, *Océaniques* demonstrates that even after privatization there were important exceptions to the field's generalized decline. And in the 1990s, long after the demise of the public service monopoly, long after the cultural paradigm—driven off by the ubiquitous audience poll—lost ground to the advocates of entertainment, long after the elements that purportedly not only supported but also justified the presence of philosophy on the small screen had all but disappeared, philosophical television not only survived but experienced a remarkable revival. The reasons for this renaissance, as well as the diverse responses to it, are the subject of the conclusion of this book.

# Philosophical TV in the 1990s

Between 1994 and 1997, eight new television series on philosophy were created for national broadcast in France.[1] By the late 1990s it seemed that you couldn't turn on a French TV set without laying eyes on a philosopher. And television was not alone in its predilection for the discipline. Philosophy was, literally and visually, everywhere. Across the nation, a new phenomenon called the *café philo*—organized philosophy discussions held weekly in local cafés—became the rage.[2] *Philo-cabinets,* in which, in lieu of a psychoanalyst, one could consult a philosopher for "philosophical counseling," promised more personalized forms of enlightenment.[3] In 1993, almost thirty years after their genesis, five of the philosophy programs produced by Dina Dreyfus for *Radio-télévision scolaire* in the 1960s were reissued on videocassette for general consumption.[4] The city of Lille and the regional counsel of Nord-Pas-de-Calais inaugurated *citéphilo,* an annual month-long philosophy festival featuring seminars, roundtables, book expositions, theater, and music. The city of Montpellier soon followed suit.[5] News-magazines lauded philosophy as "the new passion."[6] André Comte-Sponville's *Le petit traité des grandes vertus* (1995) aimed to tell us "what we should do, who we should be, and how we should live," and rapidly sold 150,000 copies.[7] The French translation of Jostein Gaarder's *Sophie's World* (a semifictionalized introduction to great philosophy) became even more of a publishing sensation, sweeping to the top of the bestseller list within weeks of its appearance in 1995 and selling 800,000 copies in France alone by the end of the year.[8] By 1997 the radio station France Culture was celebrating philosophy's astonishing cultural prominence with a week of special broadcasts.[9] Television broadcasts of *L'abécédaire de Gilles Deleuze* and *Cogito,* proved so successful that they were immediately released on video. Meanwhile, philosophy was also featured on less specialized TV programs, from cultural magazines to news.[10]

The French penchant for philosophy soon attracted international attention. In a 1997 article subtitled, "A nation of Sartres ponders life's meaning," the *New York Times* marveled at the Gallic capacity to "dispense pithy aphorisms on every topic from reptiles to social mobility."[11] In the same year, the British *Economist* declared, "Descartes did it by a stove. Diderot did it in the garden of the Palais Royal. But there really is nowhere like a Paris café to think about the world."[12] By 2002, versions of the *café-philo* could be found in more than twenty-four countries, including Sweden, Finland, Scotland, the Netherlands, Belgium, Germany, Switzerland, Italy, Canada, Mexico, Brazil, Peru, Israel, Japan, China, and Australia. Popular interest in the discipline caught on especially quickly in the United States.[13] But despite a few discrete productions—such as the Swiss pop-philosopher Alain de Botton's six-part series *Philosophy: A Guide to Happiness* (based on his book *The Consolations of Philosophy* and produced for Britain's Channel 4 in April–May 2000), or Ken Knisely's *No Dogs or Philosophers Allowed,* which aired in various incarnations on cable television in the USA between 1993 and 2004—no nation besides France became similarly enamored of philosophy on TV.

From an Anglo-American perspective, the wealth of broadcasts about philosophy and philosophers on French television during the 1990s is staggering. In 1994, at least 208 television shows dealt with philosophy or its practitioners—more than twice as many as in any of the three previous years. By 1995, the number had risen to over 460. The trend peaked in 1997, when French TV aired more than 500 broadcasts on the topic.[14] Since philosophy was also present on private networks like TF1 and the encrypted Canal Plus, even the creation of the public Franco-German cultural channel ARTE (which took over the airwaves used by a defunct La Cinq, and began airing in the evening in 1992) and the public educational channel La Cinquième (which shared the same frequency as ARTE, and began airing during daytime hours in 1994) fails to fully account for this upsurge.[15] Television's role in promoting the discipline was widely noted in the press: "Philosophy erupts everywhere, overruns everything," announced *Le monde de l'éducation,* "from bookstore window displays [. . .] to primetime

TV programs." [16] In "La philo dans la lucarne" (Philosophy on the Small Screen"), Jean-Marie Cavada, president of La Cinquième, marvels, "Television has been taken over by philosophy." [17] "Philosophy," proclaimed the journal *Les écrits de l'image,* "is in fashion. [. . .] On television, it enters by every door." [18]

France's seemingly newfound fascination for philosophy during the 1990s has generally been explained in one of two ways. Either the phenomenon is described in the language used above as simply a fad—one produced by and promoted through the media—or it is understood (as maintained in chapter 5) as an important response to a world in crisis. In this view, philosophy provides a sort of panacea for rapid social change, characterized in the 1990s by the end of ideologies, the fall of communism, the tragedy of genocide in the Balkans, the scourge of AIDS, the threat of terrorism, the forces of globalization, and the overwhelming challenges that a multiethnic, religiously diversified population was delivering to the French republican tradition. Philosophers themselves were quick to speculate on the motivations pushing this effulgent resurrection of their field. Asked, "Can we speak, at the present time, of a need for philosophy? Where does it come from?" Jean-François Lyotard agreed that there has been an intensification in the demand for the discipline, and reflected, "Obviously, we are in a civilization that doesn't know how to respond to humanity's most difficult and simplest questions: To what end are we living? And in the name of what do we die?" He perceived the demand for philosophy as "a result of this lack, of this doubt, of this anxiety, within a questioning that has no response." [19] In *Le cercle de minuit*'s 1996 special "Philosophie" (which features excerpts from Foucault's 1966 appearance on *Lectures pour tous*), Foucault scholar François Ewald suggests that the French renaissance in moral and political philosophy is explicitly linked to this same lack. "Maybe," he wonders, "we are asking philosophers today to [. . .] offer us those values that we need in order to make choices." [20] These sentiments are echoed repeatedly, whether in Luc Ferry's notion of the "disenchantment of the world," in which "politics have become desacralized and religion is in retreat," or in André Comte-Sponville's observation that "there is a certain anxiety among people who have the feeling that society has lost its reference points." [21]

As these responses make apparent, explanations for the resurgent interest in philosophy in France in the 1990s tend to stem from assessments of the immediate historical moment—in essence, from the experience of the present. While these perspectives each contain elements of truth, such narratives fail to account either for the ways in which France's fascination with philosophy during the 1990s manifested itself—quite explicitly—*on television,* or for the meanings that should be derived from its presence there. They also fail to account for the ways in which this presence is the product of a particular historical trajectory, inseparable first from the evolution of the field of French philosophy per se, and second from the role that philosophy has played in the constitution of contemporary French national identity.

Philosophy is traditionally understood as a self-contained activity, one driven by an internal logic that produces its discourse freely and universally, in which ideas beget ideas through some sort of unstoppable dialectical process. Television is likewise a medium that erases its own genealogy in the immediacy of its delivery. The televising of philosophy has recurrently produced a distinctive group of ahistorical assertions regarding the rapport between form and content, idea and image, the abstract and the embodied, the complex and the comprehensible. In this book I have aimed to write against this set of transcendent claims. Let's look again at one of the most significant of these: the contention that television is inherently anti-intellectual and thus necessarily debases any philosophy it seeks to represent. Advocates of cultural television ardently attack this stance. Pierre-André Boutang insists:

> We only vulgarize when we ask vulgar people to speak. [. . .] What is said by Deleuze, or Sartre, or Levinas, or Glucksmann, for example, in a debate on Heidegger [. . .] doesn't vulgarize at all; it isn't the *Reader's Digest* for God's sake. It isn't "I'm going to tell you in two minutes about the concept I've worked on all my life," [. . .] but of course if we put a philosopher on the television news and tell him, "Look, Deleuze just died; you have two minutes to explain Gilles Deleuze's philosophy," that's idiotic![22]

In an earlier interview, Yves Jaigu replies more precisely still. "This is the choice," he reflects: "you must discipline yourself never to go below a certain line of vulgarization. That line has one very simple criterion: the moment you go below it, with the pretext of simplifying, you begin to lie. You begin to say what isn't so."[23]

My sources support what Boutang and Jaigu maintain. When the requisite parameters are observed, ambitious philosophical programming is indeed possible—not least because, as a dialogic, performative, and embodied practice, philosophy is uniquely equipped to capitalize on the televisual form. However, historical circumstances determine both the nature and the outcome of this process. This history of the televising of philosophy shows—not surprisingly—that the pressures militating against such shows have been myriad and changeable and have increased with the privatization of the industry. At the same time, one of the overlooked aspects of the philosophy craze in France in the 1990s was that, as a result of the long courtship between the discipline and television, both philosophers and media professionals trained in philosophy were increasingly active within the television industry.[24] With respect to televising philosophy, this growing presence (though perhaps insufficient to ensure the creation of quality broadcasts) not only was an outcome of the historical processes that have persistently brought philosophers to the French small screen but was bound to affect the nature of the material produced.

Bernard-Henri Lévy formalized his relationship with television in 1993, when he became the chairman of the program advisory committee of La Sept-ARTE, a post he held until 2000. Two years earlier, Lévy had produced a four-part documentary on intellectuals for French television entitled Les aventures de la liberté, in which he himself figured prominently.[25] In 1997–98, the philosopher Alain Etchegoyen—professor at Lycée Louis-le-Grand, director of research at the Centre national de recherche scientifique (CNRS), and a self-described "moralist," "essayist" and "businessman"—produced Grain de Philo for France 3.[26] Philosophers Luc Ferry and Sylviane Agacinski (wife of former French prime minister Lionel Jospin) were regular participants. Ferry was also among those responsible for conceptualizing Philosophies, a half-hour series on La Cinquième that was intended as "an example of philosophy in action."[27] Its first broadcast featured Ferry with Jean-François Lyotard in a dialogue interrogating the notion of progress.[28] Ferry, Etchegoyen, Ricoeur, and Comte-Sponville each filmed one-week sequences on ethical themes (love, responsibility, morals, justice, religion, secularism, humanity) for Inventer demain, a four-minute daily spot on La Cinquième's Les écrans du savoir. Michel Field, an agrégé and professor of philosophy turned novelist and radio journalist (at France Culture), regularly assembled philosophers on the cultural magazine Le cercle de minuit, which he developed and then hosted from 1992 to 1994 on France 2 (formerly Antenne 2). His successor, Laure Adler (1994–97), continued this tradition. Field, along with fellow *agrégée* Claire Parnet (who interviewed her former professor, Gilles Deleuze, in *L'abécédaire*, mentioned above), working as principal writer, also produced *L'hebdo,* a cultural magazine and debate show on the cable network Canal Plus. Field went on to produce and host *Pas si vite!* (Not So Fast!) a four-minute "express" dialogue on a philosophical theme, word, or idea that aired from 1995 to 1999 on the same channel. The philosopher of science Michel Serres became a frequent guest on Jean-Marie Cavada's *La marche du siècle,* a prime-time weekly debate show that aired from 1987 to 1991 on Antenne 2, and until 1999 on FR3 (later renamed France 3). The philosopher's first appearance on the program produced "the Serres effect"and left 3.5 million spectators in thrall to his charms.[29] In 1994, Serres became the president of La Cinquième's Conseil scientifique, a body made up of specialists responsible for guiding the network's fields of interest. By the time he created, wrote, hosted, and occasionally directed the series *La légende des sciences* on La Sept, 1997–99, Serres had become a popular philosophical reference for French television audiences. Ironically, even Pierre Bourdieu—whom Luc Ferry calls the "antimedia media-monger par excellence, the prof antiprof who criticizes the academic system and, in so doing, finds himself at its summit," the man whose *On Television* was considered a quintessential intellectual critique of the medium—played a supporting role: a 1985 report encouraging the use of new media technologies that he had drafted for the Collège de France became a principal impetus for the creation of La Sept.[30]

Bourdieu has denounced the cadre of "imposter" philosophers who engage with television as a sort of second-tier company of charlatans. According to him, the work of these "philosopher-journalists" who "illegally sport the philosopher's uniform" and vaunt their wares on the small screen ("You see them every day") never quite measures up to that of their more strictly academic cohorts.[31] Bourdieu's comment epitomizes the way philosophers who interact regularly with television are often summarily dismissed as intellectual lightweights, despite Foucault's observation that one should "never be convinced that a book is bad just because it has been on television."[32] However, it bears repeating that the issue here is not the caliber of what is produced but rather the potential of the product for the evolution of French philosophy, for histories of philosophy and television, and for a certain discourse of national identity in late twentieth-century France.

The presence of philosophers within the television industry in the 1990s was a result of the historical liaison between the technology and the intellectual discipline. Program contents must also be situated within this larger legacy. For the topical reasons described earlier, didactic broadcasts on ethical questions motivated by current events were particularly popular at this time. This is evident in shows like *Grain de Philo*'s "La notion de responsabilité," which linked the ongoing AIDS crisis to what was known as the "contaminated blood affair," and "Procréation ou reproduction," which debated the philosophical issues raised by the first successful cloning of a mammal (the sheep Dolly).[33] And, as the coverage of Heidegger examined in chapter 5 demonstrates, by the early 1990s television was also subjecting philosophers themselves to ethical interrogation. Foucault's sexuality came under scrutiny on television and was used, after his death, to reconfigure his public persona. Between 1988 and 1994 (and despite Foucault's repudiation of identity politics), at least seven broadcasts tied his memory to the AIDS cause.[34] In a tribute aired on *Le cercle de minuit* commemorating the tenth anniversary of Foucault's death, Didier Eribon asserted that memorializing Foucault involves both fighting against AIDS and for homosexual rights before the law. Significantly, these are issues on which Foucault had remained largely silent in France.[35] Such politically motivated recasting reminds us of television's power to shape public knowledge about the intellectual world. It also demonstrates how, by the 1990s, the turn to ethics heralded in the late '70s by the New Philosophers (a return amplified by the renewal of scholarly interest in Levinas and Jankélévitch during the 1980s) had come to dominate discussions of philosophy on the small screen. There is no doubt that philosophy on television in France is continuing to exhibit an increasingly prescriptive ethical dimension in the twenty-first century.

( · )

Early in 2004, Roger-Pol Droit declared in *Le monde* that interest in philosophy "is a phenomenon both enduring and visibly globalizing." Droit was referring to an "avalanche of books" aimed at popularizing the discipline that had appeared in the first two months of that year alone. Referencing both the French and German Enlightenments, and harking back to Greek and Roman antiquity, Droit suggests that every age has sought "to break with elitism" and to "open wide the doors of reflection." In his brief essay, however, Droit points only to the publishing world to explain the popularity of philosophy in France.[36] Yet,

as Olivier Godechot observes, the emergence of "a parallel commercial sector of 'mediatic' philosophy"—in other words, the televising
of philosophy and its attendant publicity—had dramatic effects on
the publishing field.[37] The likes of *Lectures pour tous, Apostrophes,*
and *Cercle de minuit* had done their work well. In the 1990s, the editorial market in philosophy books split between traditional, narrow
projects aimed at long-term, small-volume sales, and a new, heavily
commercialized sector aimed at short-term, large-volume sales. Television helped to create the new reading public responsible for this shift.
With the success of its "Collège de philosophie" series, Éditions Grasset (the publishing house that launched the New Philosophers in the
1970s) has continued to capitalize on this audience.[38] Michel Onfray,
philosophy professor and the founder (in 2002) of the tuition-free Université populaire, is a Grasset author and one of popular philosophy's
most recent success stories.[39] He is also a vivid example of the ways in
which televising philosophy has influenced philosophy in France. He
recalls:

> I'm from a modest milieu, with a farmer for a father and a housewife
> for a mother. We lived in a two-room apartment [. . .] with a living
> room on the first floor and a bedroom above it. When everyone was
> sleeping upstairs, I would watch Pivot and his show. I saw philoso-
> phers speaking in flesh and blood. [. . .] The idea that philosophy could
> be alive, incarnated by real, photogenic people, was first a shock and
> then a veritable joy. I was sixteen or seventeen years old.[40]

By the age of forty-six, now a radical libertarian socialist and self-
described "Nietzschean of the left," Onfray had published over thirty
books. To some, this massive record is enough to discredit the work,
since it speaks of a speed that is seemingly incompatible with serious scholarly production. And although Doug Ireland maintains that
Onfray "has deliberately rejected the incestuous and corrupt Parisian
mediatic-politico-academic microcosm," [41] in favor of life in the small
Normandy town of Argentan, the philosopher's frequent appearances
on French television have certainly helped make Onfray one of the
better-known names in contemporary French philosophy. Within
weeks of its publication, Onfray's 2005 *Traité d'athéologie,* a polemic
against religious dogma of all stripes, was debated on French TV
among a panel of Catholic theologians. Soon afterward it became the
bestselling nonfiction book in France.

Alain Badiou has argued that "what took place in late 20th-century France was ultimately a moment of philosophical adventure [. . .], which, *toute proportion gardée* [relatively speaking], bears comparison to the examples of classical Greece and enlightenment Germany." He bases this audacious claim on the ways in which postwar French philosophy developed a new "relation between the philosophical concept and the external environment." According to Badiou, this relation sought to insert philosophy into daily life, in part by abandoning the "Kantian division between theoretical and practical reason," by making philosophy not just a "reflection upon politics, but a real political intervention," and by reinventing, "the 18th-century figure of the philosopher-writer." Collectively, these postulates contributed to the philosophical embodiment of what Badiou calls "one essential desire":

> to turn philosophy into an active form of writing that would be the medium for the new subject. And by the same token, to banish the meditative or professorial image of the philosopher; to make the philosopher something other than a sage, and so other than a rival to the priest. Rather the philosopher aspired to become a writer-combatant, an artist of the subject, a lover of invention, a philosophical militant— these are the names for the desire that runs through this period: the desire that philosophy should act in its own name.[42]

While even Badiou's activist stance remains emphatically textual, it is but a small step to see how television offered a contemporary response to this "one essential desire"—inserting philosophers into the life of the city and providing political platforms for "philosophical militancy," while exploring philosophy as "an active form of writing" that was not textual but dialogic and visual. These processes ultimately gave rise to a novel and resolutely populist genre of philosophy.

France presents philosophy and philosophers as the apogee of its rich, culturally sophisticated patrimony. Television promoted this status, while creating new forms of philosophical identity and new branches of philosophical production. It has also cultivated a broad public, which associates a knowledge of philosophy with national literacy and believes that the discipline carries a certain cultural cachet. To some extent, the surge of interest in philosophy visible in the 1990s was a product of this understanding. Likewise it was a function of the way the French public, diverse and with a level of education higher than at any previous time in history, had come to see philosophy as an answer to the dilemmas of contemporary life. According to the French press, even television succumbed to this perspective. When *Téléscope* asks, "Why philosophy? Is it not the miracle solution to resolve all problems, including that of the redemption of TF1?" or *La Croix* observes, "At a time when the networks are 'on a quest for meaning,' philosophy is appearing on the small screen," it becomes evident that philosophy is presumed to provide a propitious type of social legitimacy.[43] Clearly, philosophy signifies a set of attributes—intelligence, sophistication, gravity, wisdom, depth, and tradition—that have been culturally coded to capture and convey a certain idea of what it means to be French. As I hope I have shown, this popular understanding is inextricable from the ways in which French television has publicized philosophy as a national right (the Derridean "right to philosophy), as a cultural asset, and as a moral guide. This tripartite function is particularly potent, given the challenges to French national identity currently posed by the forces of globalization, technological change, and postcolonial minorities.

( · )

Throughout the postwar period, France has been concerned with maintaining the sanctity of its national identity and preserving its capacity for cultural radiance. As expressed in everything from the Blum-Byrnes negotiation in 1946, to the panic over Coca-colonization in the 1950s, to the cold war promotion of a Gaullist "third way" in the 1960s, to distress over the "Disneyfication" of Europe in the 1980s, to the defeat of the Multilateral Agreement on Investment in 1998, to the media fanfare over sheep farmer José Bové's attempt to tear down a McDonald's restaurant in 1999, France has historically situated itself squarely in the antiglobalization camp. As Sophie Meunier remarks, "criticizing globalization 'sells' in France." Yet for the past three decades the French have also employed a practice that Meunier terms "globalization by stealth," in order to adapt to the demands of a world economy.[44]

Globalization challenges France's *dirigiste,* protectionist, state-oriented political and economic traditions and menaces the country's international stature as a beacon of universalism and a force for global democracy. Meunier and Philip Gordon observe that globalization "breaks down both the *natural* barriers to external cultural influences via technology . . . and the *artificial* barriers (such as trade and investment restrictions) via increasingly open trade that extends deeper and deeper into the national economy and society."[45] Importantly, given the global dominance of the United States, the result of this bipartite erasure of boundaries is that globalization is often interpreted in France as a code word for Americanization. And modernization and technological change are frequently equated in the French mind with the loss not merely of political, economic, or ideological autonomy but with the eradication of the very notion of France itself. By the 1990s, many industry professionals believed that televising philosophy provided one way to combat this danger. On practical grounds, since globalization has actually improved general living conditions, increased prosperity, and created jobs in France, the battle against its extension has been paradoxical. Politicians from both the right and the left therefore center their arguments against globalization on policies of "cultural exceptionalism" that seek to protect national identity in the cultural domain. Much of the argument concerns protecting the French entertainment sector from international and, especially, American influence. Television and cinema have been a major focus of these efforts. Consequently, since the late 1980s (when they pushed the European Union's passage of a broadcasting directive ironically known as Television without Frontiers, establishing minimum national content quotas), the French have legislated a series of protectionist initiatives aimed at preserving the national production of audiovisual goods. In the 1990s, France played a key role in exempting such products from the regulations on free trade during the international negotiations of first the General Agreement on Tariffs and Trade and then the World Trade Organization.

Advances in communications technology, particularly those (like digitalization) that render the public increasingly participatory and selective in the media arena, have tested the French state's vision of itself as the manager of cultural sovereignty. The globalization of communication networks, often described as "synonymous with a monopoly of Anglo-Saxon language and culture," has also contributed to a conceptual shift; today, the defense of French identity and culture is often promoted on the basis not of "cultural exceptionalism" but rather of "cultural diversity."[46] In this view, the preservation of French national identity is seen as consonant with the preservation of pluralism, political democracy, and cultural diversity on a global scale. For the French, television, arguably because it reaches a mass public, and the Internet, due to the linguistic dominance of English, have been particular targets of concern. Premonitions of the global impact of television technology were already apparent in the 1980s: the Gaullist vision of French television as an organ of national self-representation and the "voice of France"[47] was replaced by Mitterrand's outward-looking desire to broadcast "the cultural radiance of France" to the wider world.[48] The international broadcasting of the French-language channel TV5 (established in 1984 and now called TV5Monde) sought to defend French culture through a kind of audiovisual diplomacy. This initiative has only strengthened with time. Thus, on 6 December 2006, Jacques Chirac announced that France was joining "the global battle of the images" and unveiled France's first international news channel, France 24. Intended as a French alternative to CNN and BBC World, France 24 was launched on the Internet, with plans to broadcast later.[49] These global ambitions, however, presume a unified vision of French national identity and an affinity for elite cultural policies, both of which are belied by the greater control that France's increasingly heterogeneous public exerts over the production and consumption of cultural goods through new technologies.

Philippe Douste-Blazy, French minister of culture from 1995 to 1997, argues that France's continued cultural influence over the global market will depend upon its mastery of multimedia. And certainly, in recent years, great strides have been made towards increasing online access to various aspects of the French cultural heritage. INA made television history in May of 2006 when it made thousands of hours of radio and television archives freely available on the Internet. Footage of French philosophers is included among these holdings. This is just the latest in a long list of such campaigns (including the establishment of *Joconde,* an art and museum database; the development of a CD-ROM database at the Panthéon; and the digitization of the catalogues at the Bibliothèque nationale de France). But despite their reliance on new technologies, as Louise Strode points out, these projects all reflect "an elite conception of French identity" that supports a "monolithic, universal, and static" vision of French culture. This perspective denies the ways in which the individualized, unregulated sociocultural practices that the Internet promotes are antithetical to "traditional French cultural policy aims, which may wish to unify citizens around a narrow and anachronistic conception of identity."[50] While disagreement over the pace of change exists, the multiplication of channels, digitization of communications, and merging of broadcasting with telecommunications and computing technologies poses related problems by further fragmenting the viewing audience. These evolutions have transformed "the citizen-viewer" into a "consumer of audiovisual products and services that can be bought on demand."[51] In so doing, they have called into question what has long been a unidirectional relationship between broadcasting and French national culture. For the televising of philosophy, which, despite claims otherwise, has been primarily produced as a national project directed at inculcating a specific set of ethical values into an increasingly heterogeneous public, such changes raise special challenges. Whether the advent of the Internet will alter the parameters of this project remains to be seen.[52]

( · )

Philosophy seeks a portal into the fundamental nature of human existence. By providing a framework for interrogating the nature of being-in-the-world, ethics, aesthetics, logic, and epistemology, it promises the kind of conceptual emancipation that goes hand in hand with political democracy. But as cultural signifier, as political tool, as celebrity iconography, and as demonstrative lure, philosophy remains part of a conservative project that seeks to consolidate and protect national identity through the democratic construction of a common cultural imaginary and an epistemological frame. Whether or how philosophy will change to accommodate French diversity is an important question.

A confluence of systemic factors supported the transmission of complex philosophic thought in France during the 1950s, '60s and early '70s. During these years, broadcast coverage of philosophy reveals that television not only affirmed the importance of the philosophical tradition; it also served as a site for the creation of national cultural icons and emphasized the emergent power of the image within the intellectual field. Under the influence of the New Philosophers, television contributed to a revival of popular interest in philosophy, anchoring the discipline within the quotidian practices of French life. The retreat of the public television model inspired fears about the inevitable disappearance of high cultural programming. But expectations that the demise of the state broadcaster would signal the end of cultural—or philosophical—television have proved unsound. By the 1980s, innovative philosophical programming negated claims that the medium necessarily vulgarizes intellectual discourse and promoted philosophy's status as an integral component of French national identity. By the

1990s, the televising of philosophy had revolutionized publishing and effectively challenged the dominance of the academy. To this day—despite the multiplication of channels, the fragmentation of consumption practices, the rise of the Internet, and other changes in the audiovisual environment that have weighed on the form, the content, and above all the scheduling of programs—French television persistently attempts to indoctrinate (or "discipline" in the Foucauldian sense) an increasingly diverse public into recognizing philosophy and those who practice it as valuable cultural commodities. The conflicts over education, integration, tradition, and technology that have permeated the postwar period have all orbited around one central question: What does it mean in a modern, multicultural world, to be French? The persistent presence of philosophy on television in France makes clear that this question has yet to be resolved.

## Introduction

1. I compiled this corpus using the television databases at Inathèque de France, the research division of the Institut national de l'audiovisuel, or INA, the French television archives. The first televised mention of Sartre, discussed in chapter 1, occurred on 22 November 1951; see chap. 1, "From Stage to (Small) Screen."

2. On elite culture and the mass media as diametrically opposed, see Adorno and Horkheimer, *The Dialectic of Enlightenment*. For French scholars see especially, Bourdieu, *On Television*, and Debray, *Teachers, Writers, Celebrities*.

3. Debord, *La société du spectacle*.

4. It is worth noting that the triptych "educate, inform, entertain" was also integral to successive versions of the British Broadcasting Company (BBC) charter.

5. Ferry and Renaut, *Philosopher à 18 ans*, 17–20.

6. Although not referring to television, Alan D. Schrift also makes this argument in his *Twentieth-Century French Philosophy*.

7. This omission is especially interesting since TV challenges the importance of literacy—which is often considered crucial to the development of national consciousness. See Anderson, *Imagined Communities*; Hobsbawm, *Nations and Nationalism*; Greenfeld, *Nationalism*; Weber, *Peasants into Frenchmen*; and Hall, *Civilising Subjects*.

8. For example, both Michel Winock's *Le siècle des intellectuels*, and Jean-François Sirinelli's *Intellectuels et passions françaises* address the impact of television on French intellectual life without examining specific broadcasts.

9. See Comte-Sponville and Ferry, *La sagesse des Modernes*; Derrida and Stiegler, *Echographies of Television*; and Deleuze, "Letter to Serge Daney"and "Mediators" in *Negotiations, 1972–1990*, 68–80, 121–34. See also Baudrillard's essay on the TV mini-series, *Holocaust* in *Simulacra and Simulation*, 49–51, and Bourdieu, *On Television*. Jean-François Lyotard's 1978 Channel 3 broadcast on *Tribune Libre* proves the exception to this rule, since the show was itself a philosophical exploration of the medium. A transcript of this broadcast is published as Lyotard, "A Podium without a Podium." I discuss this program in chapter 4.

10. Jean-Noël Jeanneney's *L'écho du siècle* is among the most comprehensive treatments of the history of French television. See also Jeanneney, *Une histoire des médias;* Brochand, *Histoire générale de la radio et de la télévision en France;* and Michel, *La télévision en France et dans le monde.* In English, see Kuhn, *The Media in France;* and Rigby and Hewitt, eds., *France and the Mass Media.* Political treatments can be found in: Bourdon, *Histoire de la télévision sous de Gaulle;* Bourdon, *Haute fidelité;* Chalaby, *The de Gaulle Presidency and the Media;* and Esquenazi, *Télévision et démocratie.*

11. This situation is currently improving. In April of 2006, INA revolutionized access to its sources, making over 10,000 hours of short clips available for download. A few pertain to philosophy. See: http://www.ina.fr/archivespourtous. On the problems associated with the archival preservation of television sources, see Macha Séry, "Les archives de l'INA menacés de mort naturelle," *Le monde,* 4 April 2003.

12. Isabelle Veyrat-Masson's *Quand la télévision explore le temps* on the history of the televising of history, and Sophie de Closets's *Quand la télévision aimait les écrivains,* on the history of the book show, are among the few historical monographs that concentrate on programming. However, the former draws almost entirely from print sources, and the latter deals exclusively with one series.

13. Catherine Clément's 2002 report for Jean-Jacques Aillagon, minister of culture and communication in the Raffarin government, assesses the plethora of studies debating the merits of cultural programming. See Clément, *La nuit et l'été.* Jacques Rigaud, Pascal Ory, Jean-Pierre Roux and Jean-François Sirinelli, Marc Fumaroli, Alain Finkielkraut, and Claude Patriat have all written important work in this field. In English, see Lebovics, *Mona Lisa's Escort.* Jeremy Ahearne's edited volume, *French Cultural Policy Debates* is a useful collection of excerpted texts in English translation. For a brief assessment of French cultural television, see Monia Lecomte, "La mission culturelle de la télévision française."

14. Martin Jay's *Downcast Eyes: The Denigration of Vision in Twentieth-Century French Thought* demonstrates the split between high and popular culture that characterizes much scholarship. An otherwise fascinating, encyclopedic study, Jay's text completely ignores the presence of television (arguably key in vision's modern demise) in both intellectual discourse and material life.

15. Competitive entry to the ENS follows the acquisition of a high school diploma (referred to as the *baccaleauréat,* or "bac") and two years of specialized study, called *hypokhâgne* and *khâgne* (often at the Lycée Henri IV or the Lycée Louis-le-Grand in Paris). The ENS is part of the system of Grandes écoles that, along with institutions like the Collège de France and the Sorbonne, form the privileged branch of France's higher educational system. Those who continue studies and do not enter the Grandes écoles enroll in French universities. The first two years of undergraduate studies generally lead to the Diplôme d'études universitaires générales or DEUG. A *licence* is awarded following the third year of undergraduate study. Unlike the American system, a fourth year of undergraduate work concludes with the *maîtrise,* or master's degree. Completion of the first year of graduate study results in a Diplôme d'études approfondies, or DEA. The *doctorat,* or doctorate, used to come in various forms of difficulty and prestige. As of 1984 these variations were unified as a *doctorat du troisième cycle,* which is roughly the equivalent of an American Ph.D. and requisite for employment as a university professor. It requires additional years of graduate work and the completion of a lengthy dissertation. Graduates of the ENS obtain their degrees through the French university system, and often complete the *doctorat du troisième cycle.*

16. Alain Finkielkraut and Albert Camus are two such examples (Finkielkraut's *agrégation* is in literature; Camus has a university degree in philosophy, but never sat the *agrégation*).

17. For example, in the recuperation of political philosophy that has character-ized recent scholarship, Raymond Aron, long considered a sociologist and political theorist (but a graduate of the ENS and an *agrégé* in philosophy), is increasingly included in the philosophers' camp. Long reviled by the left, his 1979 reconcilia-tion with Sartre (a consequence of both men's activism on behalf of the persecuted Vietnamese "boat people"), along with the discrediting of Stalin and the subse-quent decline of French Marxism, also contributed to the startling reversal that Aron's intellectual reputation has undergone in France during the quarter century since his death. And while Albert Camus is chiefly known as a writer, no less a tome than the *Oxford Companion to Philosophy* describes him as an "Algerian French philosopher who is best known for his concept of 'the absurd.'" (118).

18. Bourdieu, "Le fonctionnement du champ intellectuel."

19. On the reasons for this absence, see Drake, *Intellectuals and Politics in Post-War France*, 7–8.

20. Although I have been unable to discover why, Irigaray is completely absent from the small screen. Prior to 2000, Le Doeuff appeared only once, on "Droits d'auteurs," 14 February 1999.

21. Williams, *Communications*, 19.

22. Gans, *Popular Culture and High Culture*.

23. For an overview of this evolution, see Kelly, *The Cultural and Intellectual Rebuilding of France*, 23–32. See also Nora, ed., *Lieux de mémoire*, vol. 2, and Rioux and Sirinelli, eds., *Histoire culturelle de la France*.

24. Many of the individuals involved in these initiatives were instrumental in shaping postwar policy in both the cultural and audiovisual arenas. As discussed in chapter 1, Ollivier later served on the editorial board of Sartre's *Les temps mod-ernes* and then became director of television programming from 1959 to 1964. Joffre Dumazadier was the founder in 1945 of the association Peuple et culture (People and Culture) and later a leader in the *télé-club* movement discussed in chapter 1.

25. The decree of 24 July 1959 is quoted in Poujol, "The Creation of a Ministry of Culture in France," 256. Excerpts from the decree can also be found on the web-site for the French Ministry of Culture and Communication, http://www.culture.gouv.fr/culture/historique/index.htm.

26. See, for example, Finkielkraut, *La défaite de la pensée* and Fumaroli, *L'état culturel*.

27. "Spécial: Philosophie," 6 December 1994.

28. Bourdieu, *On Television*, 28.

29. Ibid., 29.

30. This belief, that older equals longer equals better for philosophy, issued forth like a mantra from the people I spoke with in France about this project. Philoso-phers (Luc Ferry, André Comte-Sponville, Alain Badiou), historians (Marc Ferro, Jean-Noël Jeanneney, Isabelle Veyrat-Masson) television producers (Yves Jaigu, Pierre-André Boutang), and television hosts (Laure Adler, Michel Cazenave, Pierre Dumayet, Paula Jacques) all shared this perspective.

31. "Pourquoi la philosophie est-elle si populaire?" 20 December 1996.

32. On the history of philosophy in French education, see Poucet, *Enseigner la philosophie*.

33. Sponville, "Pourquoi la philosophie est-elle si populaire?"

34. Deleuze and Guattari, *What is Philosophy?* 5.

35. Luc Ferry, interview with the author, 23 November 1999.

36. Yves Jaigu, interview with the author, 25 November 1999; Jean-Noël Jeanneney, interview with the author, 11 October 1999.

37. Alain Badiou, interview with the author, 24 May 2000.

38. In his famous 1898 tract "J'accuse," Émile Zola attacked the highest echelons of the French state when he defended a Jewish army officer falsely accused of treason against the charges of a corrupt, anti-Semitic military. The conservative press responded by pejoratively labeling Zola an *intellectuel,* marking the first use of the noun in the French language. Winock and Julliard, eds., *Dictionnaire des intellectuels français.*

39. Stoekl, *Agonies of the Intellectual,* 2–3. See also Judt, *Past Imperfect,* 249.

40. Régis Debray was among the first to make this observation, in *Le pouvoir intellectuel en France.* See also Rieffel, *La tribu des clercs.*

41. Those so bold as to court its dominion (dubbed the "mediocracy") were subject to derision. Dominique Lecourt popularized this expression in his *The Mediocracy.*

42. Figures from the website of the Institut nationale de l'audiovisuel, http://www.ina.fr/actualite/dossiers/2002/Juin2002.en.html.

43. Rebroadcasts occurred in 1962 (twice), 1963, 1968, 1972, 1978, 1980, 1981, 1982, 1983, 1984, 1986, 1991, 1995 (thrice), 1996 (thrice), 1997, and 1998. The original broadcast was "Portrait d'un philosophe," 1 December 1961. The segment's director, Jean-Claude Bringuier, later incorporated the original footage into a full-length biographical narrative, "Bachelard parmi nous," which first aired on Channel 1 on 2 October 1972. The latter documentary was so popular that it was reissued on video in 1993 as "Bachelard parmi nous," directed by Jean-Claude Bringuier and Hubert Knapp, in the series *Voir et lire,* INA 1993. Both the 1972 program and the series it appeared in are analyzed in chapter 3.

44. As early as 1965, Director of Television Claude Contamine collected daily estimates of audience size based on telephone surveys. Such surveys were systematized in the 1970s, and it is now routine to record statistical data about the percentage of market shares garnered by particular programs. However, this information fails to translate into reception studies, since numbers alone cannot explain how broadcasts were understood and received.

## Chapter One

1. On this phenomenon see especially the fascinating 1955 UNESCO study by Dumazedier and others, *Télévision et éducation populaire.* For a historical analysis see Marie-Françoise Lévy, "La création des télé-clubs."

2. Quoted in ibid., 110. After the war, the Direction des mouvements de jeunesse et d'éducation populaire was established under the auspices of the Ministry of Education in order to implement this goal.

3. Other associations such as the Fédération des foyers ruraux (Federation of Rural Households) and the Fédération départementale des oeuvres laïques post et périscolaire (Departmental Federation of Secular Post- and Extracurricular Works) also participated in the national project.

4. UNESCO was founded in 1945. For a recent statement of its mission regarding philosophy, see Vermeren, *La philosophie saisie par l'UNESCO.* See also Klibansky

and Pears, *La philosophie en Europe;* and Droit, *Philosophie et démocratie dans le monde.* Both works were a follow-up to UNESCO's *L'enseignement de la philosophie* (1953).

5. On the *télé-club* survey see, Dumazedier, *Télévision et éducation populaire,* 105. Roger Louis shepherded two of these series to air.

6. Benoist, "La télévision et le télé-club en milieu rural," 212.

7. On the lack of clarity surrounding French television's early educational and cultural aims, see Bourdon, "Old and New Ghosts."

8. Klibansky and Pears's *La philosophie en Europe* provides a comparative overview of the status of philosophy in modern Europe. They argue for the importance of culture, tradition, language, experience, and educational history in explaining the diverse development exhibited by differing national philosophical traditions.

9. Alan D. Schrift provides a trenchant examination of this question. While I don't entirely agree with his conclusions—as will be apparent in chapter 5, I think the French give more emphasis to Heidegger's influence than he allows—Schrift articulates a number of often overlooked reasons for what I call "French philosophical specificity." See both Schrift, "Is There Such a Thing as 'French Philosophy'?" and Schrift, *Twentieth Century French Philosophy.*

10. Like the American series *No Dogs or Philosophers Allowed,* in spring 2000 Britain's Channel 4 aired a six-part series, *Philosophy: A Guide to Happiness,* hosted by Alain de Botton. The show was based on Botton's book *The Consolations of Philosophy.* While it is not my intention to suggest that philosophy and philosophers have never been televised outside France, both the quantity of programs produced and the historical persistence of the genre are unique to that country.

11. Delbos, *La philosophie française,* preface.

12. Huisman offers a recent incarnation of this argument in his aptly titled *Histoire de la philosophie française.* See also, Serres, *Éloge de la philosophie.*

13. Descombes, *Modern French Philosophy,* 1.

14. Lévy-Bruhl, *History of Modern Philosophy in France,* 474.

15. Diderot, quoted in Mah, "The Epistemology of the Sentence," 64. Mah remarks that according to Diderot, "the so-called 'direct order' of the French sentence, its linear syntax standardized in the seventeenth century, [was] equivalent to the linearity of reasoning itself"(64). He observes, however, that in opposing civilization and barbarism such claims rely "on the *telos* of a civilizing process to legitimate the superiority of French"(68).

16. Ibid., 67.

17. Taine, *Les philosophes classiques du XIXe siècle en France,* x.

18. Comte-Sponville, interview with the author, 9 November 1999.

19. Roger-Pol Droit comments that the attempt to bring *philo* to the people has a long history; it was also apparent in Ancient Greece, Rome, and Enlightenment Germany. However, the vulgarization of the discipline has remained important in France in a way no longer true elsewhere. On this latter point, see Droit's review of the eight books on popular philosophy published in France in the first two months of 2004, "Philosophie populaire, avantages, inconvénients," *Le monde,* 27 February 2004.

20. On the spread of literacy and the progressive adoption of standardized French, see Weber, *Peasants into Frenchmen.*

21. Bergson quoted in Droit, "Philosophie populaire."

22. Christian Delacompagne, in "Bilan d'un siècle de philosophie," 27–28, argues, "Intervening in a public space always exposes him who does so to the risk of oversimplifying his thought when attempting to clarify it. But simplistic is not necessarily clear; these are two rigorously antagonistic notions. [. . .] I have nothing against vulgarization, *au contraire*: but it is difficult to do it well."

23. Comte-Sponville, interview.

24. Descartes, *Discourse on Method and Meditations*, 5.

25. These debates are discussed in chapter 5.

26. Debray, in *Teachers, Writers, Celebrities,* points to the media's appetite for personality, sensationalism, and singularity as the source of the degradation of the "intellectual function."

27. Ferry, interview with the author, 23 November 1999.

28. Virtue was so vital to Rousseau's thought that it produced a model for revolutionary discourse. See Blum, *Rousseau and the Republic of Virtue.*

29. Diderot and d'Alembert, *Encyclopédie, ou Dictionnaire raisonné des sciences,* 509.

30. Simply put, moral philosophy is understood specifically as that branch of philosophy that seeks to formulate codes and principles of moral behavior and to discern the nature of the good and the just and of right and wrong action.

31. On the history of ethical inquiry in France, see Bourg, "Forbidden to Forbid," 8–30.

32. Comte-Sponville's *A Small Treatise on the Great Virtues,* is a good example of the contemporary work to which I am referring.

33. For television's role in this process, see chapter 4. As an example of the revival of interest in Levinas, see Gutting, *French Philosophy in the Twentieth Century.* Indeed, by closing with a chapter on Levinas, Gutting both reflects and produces this trend.

34. For Descartes, reason's domain was limited; religion and the customs of the country fell outside its horizon. In the eighteenth-century public sphere, private reason aspired to flourish unfettered: *all* areas, including the religious and the political, were considered fit subjects for judgment and critique. On this point see, Cassirer, "The Mind of the Enlightenment."

35. While Dan Gordon suggests that the emancipation of reason was not inconsistent with the absolutist model of the ancien régime, it is nevertheless true that France, unlike England, proved incapable of institutionalizing its critical impulses. What Jürgen Habermas calls the "critical reasoning of private persons on political issues" led to challenges against state authority and, ultimately, to revolution. Gordon, *Citizens without Sovereignty;* and Habermas, *The Structural Transformation of the Public Sphere,* 29.

36. Rogers Brubaker states, "As a bourgeois revolution, [the French Revolution] created a general membership status based on equality before the law. As a democratic revolution, it revived the classical conception of active political citizenship but it transformed it from a special into what was, in principal if not yet in practice, a general status." See Brubaker, *Citizenship and Nationhood in France and Germany,* 49. Citizenship based on civil equality is a progressive model that has its roots in absolutism. Citizenship based on political rights has its roots in the Aristotelian conception of the civic body of the city and is conservative and inegalitarian.

37. Alain de Botton, citing the Socratic argument challenging democracy, during a radio discussion of the philosophical implications of the stalemate in the

2000 presidential elections in the United States. The comment was in reference to the efficacy of hand re-counts of ballots rejected by machine. Interview with host Scott Simon, "Philosophical Implications" (2 December 2000).

38. See Joseph Lakanal's report *Rapport fait au Conseil des cinq-cents,* arguing for general education in philosophy and the founding of the ENS, presented to the Convention on 25 February 1795. On the significance of this event for the future of philosophy, see Droit, *Philosophie et démocratie,* 24–25. Paul Ricoeur, Gilles Deleuze, and Jean-François Lyotard are among the few important twentieth-century French philosophers who did *not* study at the École normale.

39. Napoleon, quoted by Taviollot, "L'invention de la classe de philosophie," 157.

40. See especially Baker, "On the Problem of the Ideological Origins of the French Revolution"; and Chartier, *The Cultural Origins of the French Revolution.* Since few *philosophes* advocated political equality, recent scholarship often challenges arguments that have cast them as direct theorists of Revolution (Gordon, *Citizens without Sovereignty,* 3). Even Rousseau, whom Rogers Brubaker calls "the great revolutionary of a revolutionary age," was a proponent of only limited political enfranchisement (Brubaker, *Citizenship and Nationhood,* 42).

41. The expression is from Descombes, *Modern French Philosophy,* 3.

42. Figures from Aguhlon, *The French Republic,* 326. These figures are disputed. Gordon Wright (*France in Modern Times,* 407) sets the number of official death sentences lower, at 2000, but agrees that approximately 800 executions were carried out. Tony Judt (*Past Imperfect* 59) rounds off to 7000 death sentences, with 3900 *in absentia* and fewer than 800 executed.

43. On the purging of the intellectuals, see Assouline, *L'épuration des intellectuels;* Ory and Sirinelli, *Les intellectuels en France,* 143–54; Sapiro, *La guerre des écrivains;* and Winock, *Le siècle des intellectuels,* 80–88. In English, see Drake, *Intellectuals and Politics,* 9–33; and Judt, *Past Imperfect,* 45–74.

44. On the significance of Brasillach's execution for French intellectual history, see Alice Kaplan's exemplary work *The Collaborator.*

45. Beauvoir, *Force of Circumstance,* 30.

46. The Comité national des écrivains (CNE) was a broad-front organization of intellectuals that unofficially controlled access to publishing and the press. Although it was established by the PCF during World War II, its power peaked immediately after the Liberation, at which time its members agreed to boycott reviews and newspapers that accepted material from ex-collaborators.

47. The MRP later migrated slightly towards the right and ended up more centrist than leftist in its political allegiances.

48. Benda was not against political engagement per se. Rather, he advocated political practice informed by dispassionate rational reflection. His book *La trahison des clercs* was primarily an attack against the growing threat posed by the nationalist movements sweeping across Europe in the wake of World War I.

49. Beauvoir, *Force of Circumstance,* 46. Sartre scholar Michel Contat goes even further, claiming that "Existentialism [was] France's only intellectual export in the postwar years." Quoted in Ewald, "Une philosophie pour notre temps," 18.

50. Jean d'Ormesson, quoted in Eribon, *Michel Foucault,* 17. As will be discussed in chapter 3, philosophy's newly gained prominence was challenged in the battle for disciplinary hegemony that took place between it, the social sciences, and literary studies in the 1960s and '70s.

51. For an overview of French intellectual reviews in the latter half of the twentieth century, see Rieffel's *La tribu des clercs,* vol. 2. With few exceptions, French intellectual reviews and newspapers exhibit a degree of political partisanship unfamiliar to Anglo-Americans.

52. Mounier, quoted in Boschetti, *The Intellectual Enterprise,* 156.

53. Jean-Paul Sartre, "Situation of the Writer in 1947," 216–18.

54. Scriven, *Sartre and the Media,* bibliographic citation, 143.

55. "Conference de Jean-Paul Sartre sur la liberté et la responsabilité de l'écrivain," broadcast 1 November 1946, cited in the bibliography of Scriven's *Sartre and the Media,* 143.

56. To be sure, this enthusiasm was tempered by his belief that in the hands of the state or conservative corporations the media tend towards mediocrity, profit, and propaganda. Sartre ("Situation," 216–18) nevertheless recognized that if intellectuals failed to make use of the media, they must "resign [themselves] to be forever writing for nobody but the bourgeoisie."

57. On television under de Gaulle, see especially Bourdon, *Histoire de la télévision.* In English, see Chalaby, *The de Gaulle Presidency;* and Kuhn, *The Media in France.*

58. Pierre Dumayet, interview with the author, 17 November 1999. Dumayet, who was the producer and host of *Lectures pour tous* (discussed in chapter 2), told me, for example, that he had tried to interview Sartre during the 1950s, but he admitted rather obliquely that "it hadn't worked out" for political reasons.

59. Censorship was evident across the audiovisual spectrum. Sartre experienced it firsthand when the final three of nine radio broadcasts produced as "La tribune des *Temps modernes*" in October and November of 1947 (on themes ranging from party politics to socialist ideology, democracy, and the cold war), were prevented from airing by the Schuman government. See Scriven, *Sartre and the Media,* 72–86, for analysis of these shows.

60. On France's slow adoption of television, see Kuhn, *The Media in France,* 109–12.

61. See Rigby, *Popular Culture in Modern France.* On French intellectuals and America see Mathy, *Extrême Occident.* On postwar French-American relations more generally, see Kuisel, *Seducing the French.*

62. Thierry Kubler and Emmanuel Lemieux's book *Cognac-Jay 1940* recounts this early history. See also Lalou, *Regards neufs sur la télévision;* and Jeanneney, *Une histoire des médias,* 267–68.

63. For more on Hinzmann's remarkable story, see Kubler and Lemieux, *Cognac-Jay 1940.*

64. Les Buttes Chaumont was formerly the site of the Gaumont-Franco-Film-Auber cinema studios. These were adapted for TV in 1957 following a disastrous fire three years earlier. The studios at Cognac-Jay continued to broadcast into the 1990s. For wonderful footage of these two locations as well as interviews and excerpts from early shows produced there, see Pierre Tchernia's six-part series, *Notre télévision,* especially "À vous Cognac Jay," 15 July 1993; and "Les Buttes," 19 August 1993.

65. Bourdon, *Haute fidelité,* 21.

66. Marc Martin, "La télévision," 418–25.

67. Although allocated a budget, the RTF remained under the financial control of the state and was without legal status. Not until the decree of 4 February 1959 was it legally identified as a public establishment of an industrial and commercial nature, and given autonomous control of its state-determined operating budget.

68. The high-resolution analog broadcast signal of 819 lines made the quality of French television images superior to those broadcast at lower resolutions. In 1952 a process was discovered that enabled electronic conversion from the foreign (405 or 625 lines) to the French (819 lines) signal. This invention facilitated the use of foreign content in French productions and opened the way to global exchange. France later converted to the European-wide 625 standard.

69. See, Bourdon, "Les techniques," 22.

70. Pierre Tchernia, quoted in "Inventer la télévision," in Bourdon and others, *La grande aventure du petit écran,* 20.

71. Lalou, *Regards neufs sur la télévision,* 10.

72. It is worth noting that both of d'Arcy's predecessors (1949–1951), Jean Arnaud and Jean Luc, were *agrégés* in philosophy. Cazenave, *Jean d'Arcy parle,* 61–62.

73. France was not an anomaly in this respect. While 33% of British households had television sets in 1958, only 6% of West German homes, and 5.5% of Italian ones did. Beaulieu, *La télévision des réalisateurs,* 145.

74. On television directors, see Beaulieu, ibid.; and Bosséno, *200 téléastes français.*

75. Television news programs were first broadcast between 29 June 1949 and 24 July 1949, dates of the celebrated *Tour de France* bicycle race. However, regular news broadcasting did not officially begin until October of that year. See Lustière, "Le journal télévisé," 43–64; and B. Miege and others, *Le J.T. mise en scène de l'actualité à la télévision.*

76. Quoted in Bourdon, *Haute fidélité,* 35.

77. On the history of the cinematic press, see Huret, *Ciné actualités.*

78. The earliest extant *conducteur* dates from December 23, 1949. The kinescope was invented in 1956.

79. Pierre Sabbagh is a legend in French television history. Originally a press journalist, he conceived the idea for TV news in 1948. For more on Sabbagh, see his autobiography, *Encore vous, Sabbagh.*

80. This is not to say—given the paucity of television sets in France at the time—that it necessarily reached the largest audience. Initially the news aired thrice weekly, then nightly at 8:00 p.m., followed by an abridged version of the same the following day at 12:30 p.m. By 1958, three different programs were airing daily: at 8:00 p.m., again at 11:00 p.m., and the following day at 1:15 p.m.

81. The legislative elections of 2 January 1956 heralded the first televised political campaign. Each side was granted five minutes airtime to promote its platform.

82. The relationship between French television and politics has generated considerable scholarship. See especially Bourdon, *Histoire de la télévision* and *Haute fidélité;* and Esquenazi, *Télévision et démocratie.* Also on French television and democracy, see Patrick Lecomte, *Communication, télévision et démocratie,* and Mermet, *Démocrature.* Note too the excellent analysis by Missika and Wolton, *La folle du logis.* On politics and television news, see Asline, *La bataille de 20 heures;* and Mercier, *Le journal télévisé.* On the relationship between democracy and television more generally, see Kellner, *Television and the Crisis of Democracy;* Popper and Condry, *La télévision: Un danger pour la démocratie;* and Wolton, *Éloge du grand public.*

83. See Lustière, "Le Journal Télévisé," 47.

84. With few exceptions, the philosopher and not philosophy served as the relevant focus. Philosophy per se was not addressed on the news until 1974, when the questions set for the annual *baccalauréat* examination (known as the *bac*) in

philosophy began to be broadcast. (The *bac* is written at the end of secondary studies and is the preliminary requirement for entrance into the university system and the *grandes écoles*).

85. "Diplôme *Honoris Causa* en Belgique" (15 December 1956). The title of this document seems to be in error since the program was produced in London and refers to the presence of Queen Elizabeth. Although I have been unable to confirm this, since in 1956 Queen Elizabeth the Queen Mother was chancellor of the University of London, it seems likely that the latter institution conferred the degree.

86. "Attribution du Prix Paul Pelliot," 25 February 1960.

87. "Prix des ambassadeurs," 17 October 1962.

88. "Prix Hachette et Larousse," 19 October 1963.

89. The footage was originally shot for a newsreel that received cinematic distribution. It first aired on television as part of Camus's obituary and was used repeatedly in subsequent specials. "Retrospective et obsèques d'Albert Camus, Le Prix Nobel," 9 January 1960.

90. "Interview de M. Albert Camus, Prix Nobel," 23 October 1957. This clip was also shot by *Les actualités françaises*.

91. "Monsieur Jean-Paul Sartre Prix Nobel," 22 October 1964.

92. "Le refus de Sartre," 23 October 1964; and "Sartre et le Nobel," 23 October 1964.

93. "Albert Camus," 7 November 1963.

94. "Rétrospective Albert Camus," 4 January 1965; and "Rétrospective Nobel," 17 June 1965.

95. "Ce jour-là: Camus Prix Nobel," 17 October 1968.

96. Parinaud, *Bachelard*, 492.

97. "Prix Goncourt et Renaudot," 6 December 1954.

98. Beauvoir, *Force of Circumstance*, 327–28.

99. Jérôme Bourdon also makes this argument in "Les programmes: Sous le signe du service public," in Bourdon and others, *La grande aventure du petit écran*, 108.

100. Dumazadier, *Télévision et éducation populaire*, 90.

101. "Inventer la télévision," interview with Pierre Tchernia, Claude Santelli, and Michèle Cotta, in Bourdon and others, *La grande aventure du petit écran*, 16–21: 20.

102. By my estimate (and thanks largely to Sartre and Camus), during the first ten years of the Fifth Republic fully 15 per cent of all TV coverage of philosophers concerned theatrical productions. Between 1969 and 1989 that percentage dropped by half.

103. "100ème de 'Le Diable et le bon dieu' de Jean-Paul Sartre fêtée au Claridge" (22 November 1951).

104. For a detailed analysis of Sartre's relations with Stalinism, see Birchall, *Sartre against Stalinism*.

105. The exceptions were Pierre Viallet's 1952 televised adaptation of Sartre's cinematic screenplay *Les faux nez*, and Pierre Dumayet's 1955 review of Francis Jeanson's book *Sartre par lui-même* on *Lectures pour tous*, examined in the next chapter. Unfortunately, all traces of Viallet's version of *Les faux nez* have been lost. However, the program is mentioned in Bosséno, *200 téléastes français*, 208.

106. The interview with Reggiani occurred on "Discorama: Émission du 22 mai 1959," 22 May 1959. The 1963 program was "Les séquestrés d'Altona de Jean-Paul Sartre," 26 November 1963.

107. According to *Les lettres françaises,* out of 170 subjects treated on TV news between 24 May and 26 June 1954, only 10% dealt with national or international politics. The rest of the coverage was divided between sports, festivals, ceremonies, anniversaries, expositions, other special events, and cultural news. "Bilan du journal télévisé" *Les lettres françaises,* July 1954.

108. Pierre Desgraupes points out that when a program compliantly serves the politics in power, "the pressure consists above all in appointing as news directors men who are complicit with the government. Sometimes they even surpass the hopes of the ministers!" Desgraupes, *Hors antenne,* 120. Following de Gaulle's departure, Jacques Chaban-Delmas publicly repudiated this practice by appointing Desgraupes (a socialist) as news director on Channel 1 in 1969 in order to counterbalance his appointment of the Gaullist Jacqueline Baudrier as news director on Channel 2.

109. Chalaby analyzes this perception in his book *The de Gaulle Presidency and the Media.*

110. For an overview of French radio and television coverage of Algerian decolonization, see Bussière and others, *Radio et télévision au temps des "Événements d'Algérie."*

111. According to Jean-Pierre Esquanazi (*Télévision et démocratie,* 39), the effect was "to precisely localize television broadcasts: we knew that we were speaking from the 'studios at Cognac-Jay,' which were themselves closely connected to the minister of information, and hence to the Elysée."

112. Jeanneney, *Une histoire des médias,* 284.

113. Quote from *Le monde,* January 6, 1960, cited in Ulmann-Maurait, "Le critique de télévision," 167.

114. Sartre's politics have been well covered by other scholars. See, for example, Bertholet, *Sartre;* Birchall, *Sartre against Stalinism;* Cohen-Solal, *Sartre;* Drake, *Intellectuals and Politics;* Hayman, *Sartre: A Life.*

115. Sartre definitively broke with the PCF following Khrushchev's denunciation of Stalin at the communists' Twentieth Party Congress and the invasion of Hungary by Soviet troops in 1956. On this point, see especially Sartre, *The Communists and Peace;* and Winock, *Le siècle des intellectuels,* 491–500.

116. In 1958 Sartre also reviewed *La question,* Henri Alleg's firsthand account of torture at the hands of the French, in *L'express.* Alleg's book was seized (as was *L'express*), and when Sartre's review was published separately it was immediately confiscated. The text of the review is reprinted in volume 5 of Jean-Paul Sartre, *Situations.* Sartre's position on the Algerian conflict was far more radical than that espoused by the PCF. Whereas the PCF enjoyed considerable support amongst the French-Algerian petite bourgeoisie, Sartre openly supported the FLN and the cause of Algerian independence.

117. Charles de Gaulle quoted by Joël Roman, "Sartre," in Julliard and Winock, *Dictionnaire des intellectuels français,* 1029.

118. Hayman, *Sartre,* 380.

119. See "Plastic chez Jean-Paul Sartre," 8 January 1962.

120. Coverage of the Prague opening of Sartre's *The Condemned of Altona* depicts Sartre and Beauvoir arriving at the Prague airport. In the footage, Beauvoir receives flowers. "Jean-Paul Sartre à Prague," 18 November 1963. De Sica's film was reviewed on the news. "Les séquestrés d'Altona de Jean-Paul Sartre," 26 November 1963. See also the 1965 reviews of Paris productions of both *The Condemned of Altona* and *No Exit.* "Extrait Les séquestrés d'Altona," 9 September

1965; and "Théâtre: 'Gigi' et 'Huis-Clos,'" 27 June 1965. The former includes an interview with director François Perier and clips from the play featuring Serge Reggiani and Claude Dauphin. The latter depicts the billboard of the theater façade, and shows excerpts of the play (with Danièle Lebrun and Michel Vitold). This is followed by a montage of still photographs of Sartre's face, accompanied by a voice-over in which the philosopher explains the nature of human interaction.

121. *Huis Clos,* 12 October 1965.

122. "Cinéma: Émission du 28 Septembre 1967," 28 September 1967.

123. The archival reference for this program lists both Sartre and Beauvoir as participants, but gives no further information. The reference to Roi Gustave VI of Sweden in the title implies that it dealt with Asturias as a Nobel Prize winner. "Miguel Angel Asturias: Un Maya à la cour du Roi Gustave," 6 October 1968.

124. "Spectacles de la semaine du 17 novembre 1968," 17 November 1968; and "Extrait de 'Le Diable et le Bon Dieu,'" 30 November 1968.

125. Title not translated in English.

126. "Lectures pour tous: Émission du 23 octobre, 1957," 23 October 1957.

127. "Albert Camus présente 'Les possédés,'" 24 January 1959.

128. "Lectures pour tous: Émission du 28 janvier 1959," 28 January 1959.

129. "Albert Camus," 12 May 1959.

130. Cardinal, *Realités,* 99–100.

131. This is the first of the several comments sprinkled throughout the monologue that deal with Camus's struggle to reconcile his artistic and political impulses.

132. Camus, *The Outsider* (an alternate title for *The Stranger*), 117.

133. In his defense he said, "One side thinks I am not [. . .] patriotic enough and the other thinks that I'm too patriotic. I don't love Algeria in the same way a soldier or a colonist does, but can I love it other than as a Frenchman?" Quoted in Todd, *Albert Camus,* 394.

134. Camus, quoted in Judt, *The Burden of Responsibility,* 92.

135. Thus, while it has been claimed that in the decade after his death Camus was trivialized and his brand of staunch *moralisme* either rejected or ignored, television sources suggest that such assessments disregard both the general public's enduring fondness for the man and the degree to which his memory was persistently deployed by the French state on the small screen.

136. Peyrefitte, quoted in Guérin, *Camus et la politique,* 22.

137. Judt makes this claim in *The Burden of Responsibility,* 107.

138. Since his death, there have been numerous televised retrospectives of Camus's life. In 1961 the program *L'art et les hommes* aired the first in a series of tributes augmented by old newscast footage of Camus; the initial broadcast was entitled "À la recherche de: Albert Camus: Documents sur la guerre d'Espagne," 21 February 1961. *La dévotion à la croix,* Camus's 1953 adaptation of the Spanish author Calderon de la Barca's play *Devoción de la cruz,* was included in its entirety in the broadcast. *La dévotion à la croix,* 21 February 1961. *L'art et les hommes* aired a second retrospective on Camus in January of 1964. "Varese; Lipchitz; J. Villon; Camus," 1 January 1964. In the same year, excerpts from Camus's dramatic exploration of contemporary nihilism, *Caligula,* which was being presented at the Avignon festival, were broadcast. Michel Vitold, who played the lead, reassured TV audiences that "the piece has not aged, its concerns are as pressing now as ever." "Extraits de 'Caligula' et de 'Le Journal d'un fou,'" 14 June 1964. The years 1967 and 1968 saw two more full-length television documentaries on Camus and his work. Interest was motivated in part by the release of Luchino Visconti's film version of *The Stranger,* starring Marchello Mastroianni. The first

show, which was produced for the program *Panorama,* was a forty-minute special, "Un souvenir de Camus," 24 February 1967. The show examines Camus's life and work and includes excerpts from the Visconti movie. The 1968 special—this time a two-part documentary, "À propos d'un crime" and "À propos de *L'étranger* d'Albert Camus," 23 February 1964—took Camus and his work as its subject, once again debating at length his novel *The Stranger* (as well as the Visconti film based on it) and Camus's philosophy of the absurd.

139. According to the program rundown, none of Sartre's views are expressed in the accompanying commentary. "Débat sur le Viêt Nam," 11 November 1966.

140. See "L'affaire de Song My: Jean-Paul Sartre," 11 December 1969. The program is discussed at length by Scriven in "Sartre and the Audiovisual Media." While the film *Sartre par lui-même* (Sartre by Himself), produced in 1976 and broadcast on national television on 21 and 22 April 1980, also contained significant interview footage with the philosopher, it was initially intended only for cinematic release.

141. Scriven ("Sartre and the audiovisual media," 220) argues that Sartre's absence from the small screen during the Gaullist years was an active boycott of the period, and that his 1969 presence on *Panorama,* for example, was in direct response to "a marked improvement in the free transmission of information." While I agree with Scriven's general conclusions, given Sartre's self-avowed desire to conquer the new technology, I am inclined to posit a more contested relationship, in which Sartre's "boycott" may have actually been a face-saving response to his inability to gain free access to, much less master, a platform he believed crucial. On this question, see also "Les impossibles chemins de la liberté: L'affaire Sartre," chapter 4 of Veyrat-Masson's *Quand la télévision explore le temps,* 281–94; Veyrat-Masson offers a detailed account of the aborted television series, tentatively titled "75 ans d'histoire par ceux qui l'ont faite," that Sartre negotiated to produce for Marcel Julien on Antenne 2 in 1975.

142. The third broadcast was Gaston Bachelard's appearance on *Écouter, voir,* 10 June 1955.

143. Figures from Jeanneney, *L'écho du siècle,* 574.

144. Contrary to popular rumor, however, few of the individuals working in the creative end of French television at the time were actually avowed communists.

145. Kant, "What is Enlightenment?" 298.

146. The public could also, of course, reject the cultural opportunities that the small screen afforded, exposing conflicts between the producers and consumers of cultural goods that plague television programmers to this day. For a summary of *télé-club* audience attitudes toward TV, see the results from the 1955 UNESCO study in Dumazedier, *Télévision et éducation populaire,* 101.

## Chapter Two

1. Sullerot, "Télévision et culture traditionnelle," 34.

2. For a list of the 106 *émissions littéraires* that aired in France between 1954 and 1989, see Barbier-Bouver and others, "Catalogue des collections littéraires," 221–31.

3. Book shows that regularly featured philosophers include *Lectures pour tous* (1953–56), *Italiques* (1971–77), *Apostrophes* (1975–89), *Boîte aux lettres* (1983–87), *Droit de réponse* (1981–87), and *Un siècle d'écrivains* (1995–).

4. During the occupation, Fernsehender Paris briefly aired a book show called *Le salon de Paris.* However, *Lectures pour tous* is generally recognized as the

first book show of French origin ever broadcast in France. The series' title was originally *Avez-vous vu? ou Lectures pour tous* (Have you seen it? Or, Readings for All). The double title remained on the show's credits until 1959.

5. Philosophy or philosophers were featured on 11% of the 280 broadcasts of *Lectures pour tous.*

6. On television as a form of "mediatic legitimation" that produces "experts," see Chevalier, *L' "expert" à la télévision.*

7. *Lectures pour tous* was initially broadcast on a Tuesday, a Wednesday, a Thursday, or a Friday. After 1956 it acquired a fixed spot on the Wednesday night schedule. Channel 2 began airing regularly on 18 April 1964. Channel 3 joined the line-up on 1 January 1973. Although all three channels were reconfigured following the break-up of the ORTF (and renamed TF1, Antenne 2, and FR3 [France régions 3], respectively), it was not until the addition of Canal plus in November of 1984 (and after the abolition of the government monopoly in 1982) that more channels became available to the French public.

8. This changed by the 1960s, when the show often aired at 10:00 p.m. or later. The fact that working-class audiences complained that *Lectures pour tous* was broadcast too late testifies to the varied composition of its viewing public. See Brillet, "La TV ne pense pas à ceux qui doivent se lever tôt."

9. *La semaine radiophonique,* 2 June 1953.

10. Bourdon, "Pour une histoire des programmes."

11. These figures are from a 1962 report by Joffre Dumazedier cited in "Les émissions littéraires amènent-elles les spectateurs à lire davantage," *Le monde,* 30 November 1967. Audience percentages diminished in the late sixties, in part because of increased competition from the second channel after 1964.

12. Cazenave, *Jean d'Arcy parle,* 61–62.

13. Yannick Dehée ("Les magazines littéraires," 417–18) asserts that as early as the 1920s, radio also "defended a classical culture founded on the book."

14. Starting in 1924 French national radio offered book shows to the public (including by the 1950s Étienne Lalou's *Goût des livres* and Michel Polac's *Le masque et la plume*), first as a rubric on the news and then as a genre in its own right. However, perhaps because radio had less impact on book sales, the genre failed to motivate the kind of vociferous debate that erupted over the relationship between television and the book.

15. Desgraupes, *Hors antenne,* 64.

16. Dumayet, interview with the author, 17 November 1999; and Desgraupes, *Hors antenne,* 69.

17. The quote is from Desgraupes, *Hors antenne,* 135. Dumayet reiterated this perspective in our interview.

18. Kubler and Lemieux's *Cognac-Jay 1940* describes the early history of this location.

19. "Avant-propos de Pierre Dumayet," September 1992.

20. Jean-Pierre Colas, *Télé 7 jours* 441 (5 April 1953): 6. For a brief biography of Prat, see Bosséno, "Jean Prat: Un créateur en péril," in Bosséno's *200 téléastes français,* 46–50. Beaulieu's *La télévision des réalisateurs,* provides filmographies of Prat and others (153–78).

21. Mourgeon, "Comment apprendre à lire," 8.

22. Closets' *Quand la télévision aimait les écrivains* provides an excellent analysis of quantitative data concerning *Lectures pour tous.* Over fifteen years the show averaged 59% fiction and 41% nonfiction works (136–38).

23. See Desgraupes, in Brusini and James, *Voir la vérité*, 97.

24. Despite the ban (until 1968) on television advertising, by the mid-1960s publishers were systematically cited on the show, implicitly acknowledging the function that the broadcasts exerted on book sales.

25. On postwar developments in French publishing, see Assouline, *Gaston Gallimard;* Autrand and others, *La littérature en France de 1945 à 1968;* Fouche, *L'édition française depuis 1945;* Lamy, *René Julliard;* and Simonin, *Les éditions de minuit.* On the relationship between editors, sales, and *Lectures pour tous,* see also Closets, *Quand la télévision aimait les écrivains,* 115–19.

26. Closets, *Quand la télévision aimait les écrivains,* 117.

27. Ibid., 86.

28. Brunswic, "Pierre Dumayet et Robert Bober," 8–9.

29. Desgraupes, *Hors antenne,* 112.

30. Sartre, for example, insisted, "Those young people have nothing to do with me, and I have nothing to do with them." Quoted in Cohen-Solal, *Sartre,* 266.

31. The first *televised* mention of existentialism did not occur until the book *L'âge d'or de Saint-Germain-des-Prés* was reviewed: "L'âge d'or de Saint-Germain-des-Prés," 4 December 1965. A film newsreel entitled *L'existentialisme à Saint Germain-des-Prés,* produced for cinematic release in September 1951 and featuring images of Sartre, Beauvoir, and Juliette Greco, provides the sole audiovisual record from the period. Excerpts from the clip became stock footage in intellectual retrospectives produced for TV during the 1980s and '90s.

32. See Cohen-Solal, *Sartre,* 261.

33. For Camus's appearance on the program, see "Lectures pour tous: Émission du 28 Janvier 1959," 28 January 1959. See also "Albert Camus," 12 May 1959.

34. As noted in chapter 1, the only interview footage of Sartre shot specifically for television aired after de Gaulle's resignation. See "L'affaire de Song My: Jean-Paul Sartre," 11 December 1969.

35. Desgraupes, *Hors antenne* 111–12. See also Desgraupes, quoted in Broglie, "'Hors antenne' avec Pierre Desgraupes," 14; and Dumayet, interview with the author, 17 November 1999. Michael Scriven supports Desgraupes' recollection of the incident in *Sartre and the Media,* 94. Sartre's work was addressed on *Lectures pour tous* on 19 July 1955, on 11 May 1960, on 12 February 1964, and on 15 March 1967.

36. "Lectures pour tous: Émission du 19 Juillet, 1955," 19 July 1955.

37. The lack of montage during this sequence may have resulted from technical difficulties with a second camera. Such glitches remind us that, like much early TV, this interview was broadcast live, a fact that may have helped producers evade responsibility for controversial program content.

38. See, for example,"Ephéméride Gaston Bachelard," 16 October 1968; "Rayonnement d'Albert Camus," 8 January 1962 (a nine-minute special broadcast); "Albert Camus," 7 November 1963; "Anniversaire de Camus," 11 January 1964; and "Retro Albert Camus," 3 January 1980.

39. "Rétrospective et obsèques," 9 January 1960. The archives at INA also list another obituary on 1 January 1960: "Accident Albert Camus." Its confusing date (three days *prior* to Camus's death) is due to INA's policy of attributing an arbitrary date of the first day of the month and year of production to broadcasts that failed to air.

40. "Lectures pour tous: Émission du 13 Janvier 1960," 13 January 1960; "Lectures pour tous: Émission du 17 Octobre 1962," 17 October 1962.

41. Obituaries also appeared on other book shows. For Gaston Bachelard, see "Page des lettres du 20 Octobre 1962," 20 October 1962; and *Round Up,* 21 October 1962. However, these tributes tended to mimic the style established by the television news—short clips composed of images, stock footage, and brief interviews.

42. "Lectures pour tous: Émission du 15 mai, 1957," 15 May 1957. The first discussion of a *philosopher* dates to the 19 July 1955 *Lectures pour tous* interview with Jeanson on Sartre.

43. See Monzie and Febvre, *Encyclopédie française,* vol. 19, *Philosophie, religion.* Berger is best known for his philosophical system *la prospective* (futurology) and for his work at the Centre universitaire international et des centres de prospective, which he founded and where he was director of philosophical studies. For more on *la prospective,* see Berger, *Phénoménologie du temps et prospective;* and Diagne and others, *Gaston Berger.*

44. The first televised mention of the philosopher was in 1955 on "Écouter, voir," 10 June 1955.

45. Bachelard, *Essai sur la connaissance approchée.*

46. The principal work in which Bachelard explores this transition is *Le nouvel esprit scientifique.*

47. Louis Althusser and Jacques Derrida have likewise been credited with developing this heuristic category. Michel Foucault differentiates between Bachelard's concept of the epistemological rupture and his own in "Réponse au Cercle d'épistémologie."

48. Bachelard, *La psychanalyse du feu.*

49. Bachelard, *L'air et les songes,* 72.

50. Bachelard scholars frequently comment on this. Dominique Arban, for example, describes Bachelard as a sort of "prodigious Neptune"; and Jean-Claude Margolin remarks, "The name Socrates comes naturally to mind," not merely for "facile reasons of resemblance" but for "the humor, the wit and aphorisms, the radiant optimism, the courage in the face of hardship, and above all for the sense of the concrete and the humane that he never abandoned." See Arban, quoted in Lescure, *Un été avec Bachelard,* 75; and Margolin, *Bachelard,* 103.

51. In contrast, in the succeeding twenty years (1969–89), 318 programs or 29% of the total philosophical coverage pertained to political issues.

52. Besides spots on *Lectures pour tous* in 1959, 1961, 1962, 1963, and 1964, Aron also appeared on the news and in an interview, "Études et essais politiques," 4 June 1959.

53. The quarrel, sparked by Sartre's criticism of de Gaulle during a 1947 radio broadcast, lasted until 1979, when the two *petits camerades* joined forces to support the cause of the Vietnamese and Cambodian "boat people." On Aron's relationship with Sartre, see Sirinelli, *Deux intellectuels dans le siècle.*

54. Aron, *Introduction to the Philosophy of History.*

55. Aron's *Memoirs* are essential to understanding his life and work. The most extensive study of Aron in English remains Robert Colquhoun's 1986 two-volume biography, *Raymond Aron.* A more recent biography in French is Bavarez, *Raymond Aron.* See also Judt, *The Burden of Responsibility.*

56. These include a 1981 three-part television special entitled *Raymond Aron, spectateur engagé.* In this program, journalists Jean-Louis Missika and Dominique Wolton interview Aron. See "1ère emission: La France dans la tourmente," 11 October 1981; "Démocratie et totalitarisme 1947–1967," 18 October 1981;

"3ème émission (1968) Liberté et raison," 25 October 1981. These interviews were later published as Raymond Aron, *Le spectateur engagé*. Aron also discusses the process of filming the documentary in his *Memoirs* (458–59). Missika and Wolton have each written extensively on French television and media.

57. Contat, quoted in Aron, *Memoirs*, 460. This idea is also explored at length in Sirinelli's comparative biography, *Deux intellectuels dans le siècle*.

58. Despite his anticommunism, Aron was not, however, an unstinting proponent of American capitalism or imperialism. Indeed, his *Opium of the Intellectuals* provoked such opposition on both the right and the left that it almost blocked his 1955 appointment to the Sorbonne.

59. "Lecture pour tous: Émission du 30 janvier, 1963," 30 January 1963,INA.

60. *Le développement de la société industrielle et la stratification sociale*. The monograph was reissued with the new title (*Dix-huit leçons*) in 1962.

61. Aron, *Memoirs*, 266.

62. Although the director was Michel Mitrani, not Jean Prat, the camera work is modeled on Prat's and reflects the identifiable *Lectures pour tous* style.

63. By 1965, the year of the presidential elections, the left-of-center parties had indeed united behind François Mitterrand and, although ultimately unsuccessful, posed a serious threat to de Gaulle's reelection.

64. It is worth noting that despite this association Aron was still viewed with suspicion by de Gaulle's staunchest supporters, who did not consider *La France libre* sufficiently hard-line. For his part, Aron took de Gaulle to task for personalizing the struggle of the Free French and was wary of the General's authoritarianism.

65. Aron, *Memoirs*, 258. Aron's critique of de Gaulle's 1967 statements about Israel and the Jewish people at the time of the Six-Day War, figures among the latter. Aron, *De Gaulle, Israël et les Juifs*.

66. De Gaulle, quoted in Colquhoun, *Raymond Aron*, 2:77.

67. See de Gaulle's letter to Aron, in Aron, *Memoirs*, 370.

68. See Aron, *Memoirs*, 458. On the TV series, see note 56 above.

69. Dumayet, interview with the author, 17 November 1999.

70. Aron, *Memoirs*, 372.

71. "Philosophie et sociologie," 6 February 1965; and "Un Philosophe dans le journalisme," 7 December 1969.

72. Foucault, *Les mots et les choses*. I refer to the English translation, *The Order of Things*.

73. Macey, *The Lives of Michel Foucault*, 172.

74. "Lectures pour tous: Émission du 15 juin, 1966," 15 June 1966, INA.

75. "Foucault comme des petits pains"; "Les succès du mois."

76. The Lycée Henri IV is among the most prestigious of the Parisian *lycées*, renowned for preparing its graduates for entry to the *grandes écoles*, including the ENS.

77. Foucault was not a militant and rarely attended meetings. After his departure from the PCF in 1953 (he had joined in 1950) Foucault became increasingly critical of Communist Party politics, to the point where a decade later he was often accused of having Gaullist sympathies. Nevertheless, according to Didier Eribon (*Michel Foucault*, 52), in later life Foucault claimed, "When I was in the Communist Party, Marxism as a doctrine made good sense to me."

78. "Philosophie et psychologie," 27 February 1965; and "Philosophie et vérité," 27 March 1965. Transcripts of both programs have been published; see entries

under the same titles in the first part of the bibliography. See also Foucault, *Dits et écrits, 1954–1988*, 1:438–64. An English translation of the first broadcast can be found as "Philosophy and Psychology," trans. Robert Hurley, in Foucault, *Aesthetics, Method, and Epistemology*.

79. Foucault either participated in or was discussed during at least seventy programs between his earliest appearance in 1965 and the end of the century. The 1966 interview addressed here and one given in 1976 on Bernard Pivot's book show *Apostrophes* (discussed in chapter 4) provide the emblematic television images now associated with Foucault and his work. Later programs dealing with Foucault persistently excerpt from these two shows. The only other consistently used footage on Foucault is drawn either from the interview videotaped with André Bertin at the Catholic University of Louvain's School of Criminology in 1981, or from recordings made during the series of lectures Foucault held at that institution in the spring of 1982. These lectures center on the general topic of the legal function of confession and are entitled "Mal faire, dire vrai" (Do Evil, Speak Truthfully). However, these tapes were not originally intended for broadcast. Copies of the Louvain videos can be viewed at the Bibliothèque publique d'information in Paris. The interview with André Bertin was later included in the homage to Foucault broadcast in 1988 in Pierre-André Boutang's series *Océaniques,* "Entretien avec Michel Foucault," 13 January 1988.

80. Foucault, *The Order of Things*, xi.

81. From the interview conducted with Raymond Bellours, first published in *Les Lettres françaises* 1125 (31 March–6 April 1966): 3–4, and subsequently translated and republished as Foucault, "The Order of Things," in *Aesthetics, Method, and Epistemology*, 261.

82. Foucault, *The Order of Things*, xxii.

83. Gary Gutting provides a superb summary of the major arguments of *Les mots et les choses* in *Michel Foucault's Archeology of Scientific Reason*.

84. Foucault develops his "analytic of finitude" and "empirico-transcendental doublet" in response to the paradox that the "modern" conception of man is at once finite and transcendent. James D. Faubion clarifies this complex idea in his introduction to Foucault, *Aesthetics, Method, and Epistemology*, xxxi.

85. Dumayet, interview with the author, 17 November 1999.

86. Robichon, "Desgraupes et Dumayet," 1.

87. See Brillet, "La TV ne pense pas à ceux qui doivent se lever tôt," 66; "Non à Janique," 66; and "Oui, nous voulons du football," 70–71.

88. Dumazedier and others, *Télévision et éducation populaire*, 90–91, 100.

89. "La télévision: 1ère partie," 13 April 1961.

90. Harris and Sedouy, in Dupuis and Raux, *L'O.R.T.F.*, 19–22.

91. Hercet, "Télévision et politique."

92. Lalou, *Regards neufs sur la télévision*, 112.

93. Viewer satisfaction surveys (which dropped from 80% to 53% over the same years) were more positive. For both statistics, see Peroni, *De l'écrit à l'écran*, 29.

94. The government's position privileged offer over demand and was couched in moral terms. See Missika and Wolton, *La folle du logis*, 125.

95. Ibid., 18.

96. The national educational programming developed in 1951 for Radio-télévision scolaire was an expression of this stance. On these programs, see chapter 3; see also Dieuzeide, "Place et fonctions de la télévision."

97. In the aftermath of 1968, television was one sector towards which the government proved particularly unforgiving. Reflecting back, Fouchet states, "That was because they had the greatest need of it. And because it was there that General de Gaulle met with the greatest resistance. And, you know that that man doesn't tolerate resistance from others, yes?" Fouchet, interviewed by Salachas, "Max-Pol Fouchet," 39.

## Chapter Three

1. For a complete list of the philosophy programs produced by Radio-télévision scolaire broadcast between 1965 and 1968 and a partial inventory of those broadcast through 1970 see "Inventaire des émissions de philosophie."

2. Other participants include Étienne Borne, Pierre Bourdieu (who appeared in six broadcasts, three of which were on philosophy and language), François Châtelet, François Dagognet, Elisabeth de Fontenay (the only woman), Jean Laplanche, Pierre Trotignant, Jean-Pierre Vernant, and Eric Weil.

3. For a report on the Service de la recherche by its director, Pierre Schaeffer, see Schaeffer, Le Service de la recherche. See also Schaeffer, "Le programme de prospection du Service de la recherche" and "Ce mystérieux Service de la recherche O.R.T.F."; Mayor, "Une tribu de Gibis"; Loiseau, "La bande à Schaeffer"; Challon, "Le double visage du Service de la recherche"; and, for a more recent summary, Maréchal, "Le Service de la recherche."

4. Un certain regard aired on other nights when scheduling required. From 1964 to 1966, Jean-Émile Jeannesson directed the series. After 1966, Michel Tréguer was at the helm. Between 1964 and 1967, Un certain regard also produced shows on music, theater, psychology, and psychiatry. On the inception of Un certain regard, and on Jeannesson and Tréguer, see "Une grande émission se prépare."

5. The thematic dossiers covered such topics as Leninism, Jean Monnet's Europe, race problems in the USA, the environment, machines and men, the future, and the third world.

6. Intellectual documentaries were produced on Arthur Koestler, Jacques Ellul, Jean Fourastié, Pablo Neruda, Denis de Rougement, Jean Piaget, Jean Rostand, Bertrand de Jouvenal, Rosa Luxembourg, Georges Dumézil, and William Faulkner among others.

7. See "Les savants sont parmi nous: 1ère partie," 17 October 1967; "Claude Lévi-Strauss," 21 January 1968; "Roman Jakobson," 17 March 1968; "Raymond Aron: Un philosophe dans le journalisme," 7 December 1969; "Emmanuel Mounier," 25 October 1970; "Georg Lukacs," 13 December 1970, INA; "Bertrand Russel," 21 February 1971; "Bachelard parmi nous," 2 October 1972; and the two-part feature "Jacques Lacan: 1ère Émission, Psychanalyse I," and "Jacques Lacan: 2ème Émission, Psychanalyse II," 9 and 16 March 1974. The broadcasts on Bachelard, Aron, Mounier, Picht, Lévi-Strauss, Arendt, and Jakobson were considered so important by the Institut national de l'audiovisuel that they were reissued as videos and are currently available for educational use. For information, contact www.ina.fr.

8. Like France, the United States, Great Britain, Belgium, Italy, Luxembourg, the Netherlands, Switzerland, Germany, Austria, Poland, Sweden, Czechoslovakia, India, Japan, Australia, and the USSR all experimented with educational tele-

vision. (On the international status of educational TV in the 1950s, see Strivay's 1958 coverage of the Conférence internationale de télévision scolaire et éducative in his article "Télévision et culture: La télévision scolaire en Europe".) Most of these endeavors were aimed at higher education and employed a combination of closed and open-circuit networks. The projects developed in Great Britain by the BBC and the British Open University were exemplary in this regard. American ventures began within universities. Iowa State was the first to acquire a broadcast license (in 1948). See Dirr and Pedone, *Instructional Uses of Television;* Keegan, *Foundations of Distance Education;* Murphy and Gross, *Learning by Television;* and Wood and Wylie, *Educational Telecommunications.*

9. See Tony Ballantyne's concept of "webs of empire" in his *Orientalism and Race.*

10. Gildea, *France since 1945,* 93.

11. Between 1951 and 1973, the French nation grew by almost 25%. One-third of this growth was due to immigration. Although the proportion of immigrants in the population did not change substantially (rising from 4.1% in 1954 to 6.5% in 1975), their composition did: whereas in 1954 only 13.5% of the immigrant population was North African, by 1975 one-third was North African and only 62% European. See Sa'adah, *Contemporary France,* 181, 184. For contemporary observations on the rise in student populations, see Cros, *L'explosion scolaire.*

12. Formal education in philosophy predates the French Revolution by almost six hundred years. Classes in Scholastic philosophy first manifested in the medieval universities of Paris during the twelfth century. Pedagogy matured during the sixteenth century under the double influence of Christianity and the *trivium,* a division of European classical education consisting of grammar, rhetoric, and logic, intended, according to Émile Durkheim, "to instruct the mind about the mind itself." The *trivium* and the *quadrivium* (geometry, arithmetic, astronomy, and music) were collectively known as the seven liberal arts. Knowledge in these two areas was thought essential to an encyclopedic education. Durkheim, *The Evolution of Educational Thought,* 47.

13. Of course, close relationships between states and educational systems are not unusual. However, as Bertrand Ogilvie remarks, France is unique, not in that it "deliberately and explicitly concretized the links between these institutions," but in that "it thinks itself singular and exemplary for precisely this reason." Ogilvie, "Évaluation et finalité des systèmes éducatifs," 92–93.

14. The French debate over whether both *l'instruction* and *l'éducation* should be the responsibility of the state has a long history. Hippolyte Taine, for example, was a bitter critic of the Napoleonic system precisely because he believed that it failed to incorporate the latter element. Hippolyte Taine in Ezra Suleiman, *Elites in French Society,* 23.

15. On philosophy and republicanism, see Fabiani, *Les philosophes de la République.*

16. For a history of philosophy in modern French education, see Poucet, *Enseigner la philosophie.*

17. The Sixth Section gained further power in 1975 when it acquired the name that it carries today, the École des hautes études en sciences sociales (EHESS), was made a degree-granting institution, and was given the power to grant doctoral diplomas. Derrida's appointment followed this transformation.

18. On the deleterious effects of structuralism on the primacy of philosophy, see Kauppi, *French Intellectual Nobility;* and Boschetti, *The Intellectual Enter-*

*prise*, 229–31. For a comprehensive history of structuralism in France, see Dosse, *History of Structuralism*.

19. Revel, *Pourquoi des philosophes?* The book generated so much controversy that he wrote a second book, *La cabale des dévots* in 1962 to respond to his detractors. Both texts were republished during the 1990s when the vogue for philosophy swept through France.

20. Whereas in 1930 approximately 15,000 *baccalauréats* were awarded in France, by 1965 that number had catapulted to 105,000. Between 1960 and 1970, student populations tripled, expanding from 215,000 to 736,000 over the course of a single decade. For figures, see De Certeau, "Universities versus Popular Culture," 40. In 1953 only 6% of Muslim men and 2% of Muslim women in Algeria could read French. Sa'adah, *Contemporary France*, 83.

21. Althusser, "La classe de philosophie."

22. Charles Brunold, director of secondary studies, made this observation in a 1955 note to the minister of education, quoted in Poucet, *Enseigner la philosophie*, 286.

23. M. Perret, *L'éducation nationale* 11 (13 March 1958).

24. See De Certeau, "Universities versus Popular Culture".

25. For debates over the democratization of education in the postwar period, see especially Bourdieu and Passeron, *Les héritiers, les étudiants et la culture;* Rurand-Prinborgne, *L'égalité scolaire;* Establet, *L'école est-elle rentable?;* Langouët, *Technologie de l'éducation;* Prost, *L'enseignement s'est-il démocratisé?.*

26. Martine Allaire and Marie-Thérèse Frank describe this dilemma well in the introduction to their edited volume, *Les politiques de l'éducation en France*, 13–20.

27. Dieuzeide, "Place et fonctions de la télévision," 340–341.

28. Dieuzeide, "La télévision menace-t-elle la culture?" 15.

29. On gamma rays, see the reference to *Le soir* in "Dans le cadre de la télévision éducative".

30. On reading and TV, see Brasseur, "Télévision et culture".

31. Dieuzeide, "Place et functions de la télévision," 340–41.

32. The Institut pédagogique national is now known as the Centre national de documentation pédagogique, or CNDP. The CNDP continues to coordinate the production of educational television in France.

33. Dieuzeide, "Télévision scolaire et formation du futur téléspectateur," 9.

34. Ministerial note of 1 April 1963, cited in Sublet and others, *Quand la télé entre a l'école*, 5.

35. Fouchet quoted in ibid.

36. According to a 1963 survey, an estimated 36% of lycée math teachers, 18% of chemistry teachers, and 30% of teachers in the general sciences (all disciplines undergoing rapid expansion) were insufficiently qualified. Figures from Département Radio-télévision scolaire, "Trois expériences françaises," 71–72.

37. Documentation describing how to use these programs at home can be found in "Radio-télé bac 66."

38. According to the IPN, out of 70,000 potential students, more than half requested the study guides. Students exposed to educational programming exhibited an average 23% increase in their exam results. Département Radio-télévision scolaire, "Trois expériences françaises " 84–87.

39. My knowledge of the production process owes much to an interview with Jacques Beaujean, head of the Division de la diffusion audiovisuelle at the CNDP (14 February 2001), and to Rouanet, "La grande misère d'une grande idée."

40. IDHEC was later reincarnated as the Fondation européenne de l'image et du son (FEMIS).

41. Access to the union required that the candidate had been hired for three jobs as a first assistant, or six jobs as a second assistant. Without these credentials, young directors were unable to enter the RTF. Working for Radio-télévision scolaire offered a way to circumvent these rules and get immediate experience directing one's own program. Both Rohmer and Jacques Rutman and took this route as a means of entering the more restricted and prestigious RTF. See "Entretien sur Pascal," 3 December 1965.

42. In 2000, ten of the original forty programs were in sufficiently good condition to support copying to video for viewing.

43. On the feminization of the *classe terminale* in philosophy during the 1950s, see M. Perret, *L'éducation nationale*.

44. Lévy, "L'immigration dans la production documentaire."

45. Not until the creation of the controversial if aptly named *Mosaïque* on FR3 in 1976 was a series conceived with immigrant audiences in mind. Problematically, the show's "underlying objective" was to encourage them to return to their countries of origin. Hargreaves, "Gatekeepers and Gateways," 86.

46. Biographical information on Dreyfus is drawn from my 24 May 2000 interview with Alain Badiou, and from Saint Sernin's article "Dina Dreyfus ou la raison enseignante".

47. Saint Sernin, "Dina Dreyfus," 96.

48. Saint Sernin recalls that Dreyfus's classes were highly literary, which was not surprising, he remarks, since for over fifteen years, "under a name she claimed not to remember, she published, in a foreign country and another language, more than a dozen novels." Ibid., 90.

49. Alain Badiou, interview.

50. Ibid.

51. Fléchet, "Trente ans après," 105.

52. Fléchet, "Réflexions sur les émissions de philosophie," 16.

53. Dreyfus, "L'enseignement de la philosophie et la télévision," *L'éducation nationale*.

54. Dreyfus, speaking in the broadcast "L'enseignement de la philosophie par la télévision, 4 June 1965.

55. Fléchet, speaking of Dreyfus in "Trente ans après," 107.

56. Dreyfus, in Fléchet, "Réflexions sur les émissions de philosophie," 16.

57. Dreyfus, "L'enseignement de la philosophie et la télévision," *Cahiers philosophiques,* 101.

58. Fléchet, "Réflexions sur les émissions de philosophie," 18–19.

59. "La philosophie fera son entrée a la télévision-scolaire," 19.

60. Dreyfus, "L'enseignement de la philosophie et la télévision," *Dossiers pédagogiques,* 51.

61. Dreyfus was determined to defend philosophy against all attacks. See Dreyfus and Khodoss, "L'enseignement philosophique," 1047.

62. Note that French children attend school on Saturday for a half day.

63. Four of these programs—on history, sociology, psychology, and truth—along with a fifth show on Kantian morality were later re-released on video as *Le temps des philosophes*. The original broadcasts aired as follows: "La philosophie et son histoire," 9 January 1965; "Philosophie et science," 23 January 1965; "Philosophie et sociologie," 6 February 1965; "Philosophie et psychologie," 27 Febru-

ary 1965; "Philosophie et language," 13 March 1965; "Philosophie et vérité," 27 March 1965.

64. "L'enseignement de la philosophie par la télévision: Conclusion et synthèse," 4 June 1965.

65. Alain Badiou, quoted in ibid.

66. Fléchet, "Réflexions sur les émissions de philosophie," 16.

67. Alain Badiou, interview. Fléchet also recounts this event in "Trente ans après," 109.

68. Fléchet, "Réflexions sur les émissions de philosophie," 19.

69. "Philosophie et vérité," 27 March 1965. A transcript of the program can be found in Foucault, "Philosophie et vérité."

70. Interiors were actually shot at the Institut national de recherche et de documentation pédagogique, located not far from the ENS.

71. The Owl of Minerva symbolizes Minerva, the Roman goddess of wisdom and, hence, philosophy.

72. For a similar analysis see, Harder, "Philosophie et vérité, présentation de l'émission."

73. Dreyfus, "L'enseignement de la philosophie et la télévision," *Cahiers philosophiques,* 102.

74. Responses reported in Dreyfus, "L'enseignement de la philosophie et la télévision," *Dossiers pédagogiques.*

75. Likewise, a general study on educational television in France conducted in 1966 observes, "Only a small minority of students are capable of focusing their attention [on a program] for thirty minutes. Shows that are twenty minutes in length are consequently preferable." Département Radio-Télévision scolaire, "Trois expériences françaises," 75.

76. In her defense, Dreyfus insisted that the philosophers explicitly defined technical terms. This is visible in the films when, for example, Aron gives a tripartite definition of "ideology" in "Philosophie et sociologie"; Foucault defines "cultural form" in "Philosophie et psychologie"; and Ricoeur defines "semantic," "hermeneutic," "polysemy," and "exegesis," in "Philosophie et langage."

77. See Craipeau, "Le maître irremplaçable".

78. Lavallard, in "Entretien entre les membres de l'équipe de travail," 32.

79. Dreyfus, "L'enseignement de la philosophie et la télévision," *Dossiers pédagogiques,* 50.

80. See, for example, the dialogue between Étienne Borne, Louis Guillermit, Jean-Pierre Vernant, and Eric Weil, "Philosophie et morale VI: Actualité de la morale kantienne," 5 March 1966. This program was paired with "Philosophie et morale VII: Actualité de la morale kantienne, lecture d'un texte kantien (extrait de la *Critique de la raison pratique*) par O. Chedin," 19 March 1966.

81. See "Émissions télévisées pour l'année 1965–1966." The question under examination was "To what extent are morals part of philosophy?" The Stoics, Bergson, and Kant were all featured during the 1965–66 academic year. See also "Peut-on encore être stoïcien?" 13.

82. Ross, *May '68 and Its Afterlives,* 2.

83. The precise timing of this shift is especially interesting. The shows broadcast from January to March of 1968 continue to be structured as interviews between a master and a novice. From March 1968 until the termination of the series in March 1970, the shows involve group work on philosophical texts.

84. To facilitate this process, broadcast schedules for the upcoming school year were typically published in May. An example can be found in *Bulletin de la radio-télévision scolaire* 29 (1965).

85. Alain Badiou, interview.

86. Dreyfus, "Faire vivre la philosophie par l'image."

87. Dreyfus, "L'enseignement de la philosophie et la télévision" *Cahiers philosophiques,* 105–6.

88. Born in Nancy in 1910, Schaeffer became a formidable presence in French television. His wide-ranging interests in music, philosophy, technology, and poetics were integral to his artistic vision. Trained first as a musician and then at the École polytechnique, Schaeffer was hired as a broadcast engineer by the RDF in 1936. He created a form of musical composition and theory known as *musique concrète* in the 1940s and early 1950s. Schaeffer was nominated director of the Service de la recherche in 1960. Biographical information on his extraordinary career can be found in Dallet and Brunet, *Itinéraires d'un chercheur.* See also Brunet, *Pierre Schaeffer;* Schaeffer, *Entretiens avec Marc Pierret;* and Maréchal, "Le Service de la recherche".

89. Schaeffer, quoted in "Le programme de prospection du Service de la recherche de la R. T. F." A veritable "mission statement" by Schaeffer regarding television can be found in "Ce qui est en question," his manifesto published at the beginning of the pamphlet presented by the Groupe de recherche image on the occasion of the Festival de la recherche 1960, programme des films, conferences, rencontres, held 15–28 June 1960 in Paris at the Salle des Agriculteurs, Box ORTF/ Service de la recherche, INA.

90. Dupont, "Qui parle?" 9.

91. Épin, "Au Service de la recherche".

92. The fact that training in philosophy was important enough to merit special recognition by journalists is especially interesting. Épin, "Au Service de la recherche."

93. Other important series created by the Service include André Voisin's *Les conteurs,* Jacques Rouxel's *Shadoks,* and Jean Frapat's *Tac au Tac.*

94. Jean-Claude Bringuier, interview with the author, 27 October 1999.

95. "La Recherche en matière de programmes."

96. Kuhn, *The Media in France,* 132.

97. On the distinction between cultural democratization and cultural democracy, see my introduction.

98. By 1971, advertising breaks had risen to twelve minutes per day. Although some generic advertising had existed prior to this time, it was not until 1968 that brand-name advertising was permitted. Only three categories—food, textiles, and household electrical appliances—were initially cleared for broadcast.

99. See Manigand and Veyrat-Masson, "Les journalistes et la crise."

100. "Bachelard parmi nous," 2 October 1972.

101. Bringuier, interview.

102. Ibid.

103. Maisongrande, "Gaston Bachelard faisait lui-même sa cuisine."

104. Brillet, "Bachelard."

105. Aymon, "1ere chaîne, la critique de Jean-Paul Aymon."

106. "Au bord d'une eau vive".

107. Aymon, "1ere chaîne, la critique de Jean-Paul Aymon."

108. Clavel, "Le touche-à-tout des profondeurs".

109. "Bachelard parmi nous," *L'express*, October 1972.

110. Brincourt, "Gaston Bachelard, le philosophe et son ombre."

111. Unlike most other major French intellectual figures of his time, Jacques Lacan was not trained in philosophy, but rather in medicine. However, his study of philosophy, particularly of Hegel as influenced by Alexandre Koyré and Alexandre Kojève, was crucial in helping him formulate his reinterpretation of Freud. See Roudensco, *Jacques Lacan*, especially chap. 10, "The Philosophy School: Alexandre Koyré and Others," 88–106.

112. Miller was married to Judith, Lacan's daughter with Sylvia Bataille (wife of the writer and theorist Georges Bataille).

113. Miller, "Microscopia," in Lacan, *Television*, xvii. The Service refuted this claim. See "Dans la série "Un Certain Regard" le Service de la Recherche de l'ORTF présente *Jacques Lacan*."

114. "Freud est grand et Lacan est son prophète".

115. While Miller claims that Lacan refused to edit the original film, the broadcasts do not fully correspond to the published version of the dialogue, indicating that some cuts were made before the shows were aired. Miller, in Lacan, *Television*, xvii.

116. "Jacques Lacan: 1ère Emission, Psychanalyse I," 9 March 1974; and "Jacques Lacan: 2ème Emission, Psychanalyse II," 16 March 1974.

117. The original French is as follows: *De ce qui perdure de perte pure à ce qui ne parie que du père au pire.* English translations for these broadcasts are by Denis Hollier, Rosalind Kraus, and Annette Michelson, and are taken from the W.W. Norton edition of Lacan's *Television*, (3, 7–8, 27–8, 40, 27, 46).

118. "Jacques Lacan," *Le nouvel observateur*, 11 March 1974.

119. "Jacques Lacan, psychanalyste," *Télérama*, 9 March 1974; and Achard, "Lacan, comment?"

120. "Un certain regard 'Jacques Lacan,'" *Humanité Dimanche*, 27 February 1974.

121. Chapsal, "La parole de Lacan."

122. "Jacques Lacan à la télévision."

123. Lejeune, "Psychoanalyse mon beau souci."

124. Sarraute, "Des mots, des mots."

125. Interestingly, Bernard-Henri Lévy (whose celebrity capitalizes similarly on his charisma) was among the few who downplayed Lacan's theatricality. He protested, "Lacan on television [. . .], whatever they say it is not pure circus, but an important event." Lévy, "La télévision de Jacques Lacan."

126. Baron, "Les rigolos et le psychanalyste vedettes du week-end."

127. Weyergans, "L'humeur de . . . ; Télévizer . . . "

128. Mme Arnold Tourcoing, quoted in "Ca va mieux en le disant."

129. C. M., quoted in ibid.

130. Dupont, "Qui parle?" 9–13.

131. The seven companies included three television networks, one for each channel—Télévision française 1 (TF1), Antenne 2, and France régions 3 (FR3), and one radio station, Radio France. The reform also established a production company, Société française de production (SFP), a transmission company, Télédiffusion de France (TDF), and a research institute and archive, the Institut national de l'audiovisuel (INA). On the break-up of the ORTF, see Mercillon, *ORTF l'agonie du monopole?* and Bachmann, *L'éclatement de l'ORTF*.

## Chapter Four

1. "A quoi servent les philosophes?" 18 January 1980. Jankélévitch's *Le Je-ne-sais-quoi et le Presque-rien* (republished by Seuil in 1980), has not yet been translated into English.

2. This is not to say that Jankélévitch was not publicly engaged; he appended his name to some sixty-three petitions between 1958 and 1969. Hamon and Rotman, *Les intellocrates*, 263. However, it was not until after his appearance on *Apostrophes* that Jankélévitch's philosophical oeuvre began to reach a wider public.

3. My understanding of the renewal of ethical discourse in post '68 France owes much to Julian Bourg's Ph.D. dissertation, "Forbidden to Forbid: Ethics in France, 1968-1981." Bourg outlines the contemporary history of French ethical inquiry in his introduction (1–29). He notes that "at times in France, *l'éthique* and *la morale* are used interchangeably; at other times they are opposed" (22). American dictionaries present the words as synonyms. For purposes of rhetorical simplicity, I follow this practice.

4. Among the most influential articulations of this argument is Debray's *Teachers, Writers, Celebrities*. See also Hamon and Rotman, *Les intellocrates;* Reiffel, *La tribu des clercs;* Winock, *Le siècle des intellectuels;* Bourdieu, *Homo Academicus;* Jennings, *Intellectuals in Twentieth-Century France;* and Lecourt, *The Mediocracy,* among other studies.

5. Through 1973, four book shows were airing on TF1, while Antenne 2 carried Marc Gilbert's *Italiques*. None of these managed to attract particularly large audiences.

6. Brasey, in his breezy biography *L'effet Pivot* (15), insists that cultural programs normally attracted a mere 3% of the television audience. Figures drawn from Annexe 6: Évolution du taux d'écoute d'*Apostrophes* (Moyenne Annuelle) 1975–1984, in Brasey, 362; and Nel, *À fleurets mouchetés,* 52. Percentages drawn from Brasey, 15; and Nel, 156. For a comparative perspective, Nel, 156, recounts that in 1986, when *Apostrophes* registered 10% of viewers, *Starsky and Hutch* (in translation) captured 27%.

7. In *L'effet Pivot,* Brasey mistakenly claims that only two of *Apostrophes'* broadcasts addressed philosophy between 1975 and 1987. In addition to the Jankélévitch show, cited above, the programs on philosophy include broadcasts with Foucault, "C'est de la politique ou de la littérature," 17 December 1976; with Bernard-Henri Lévy, Glucksmann, and Clavel, "Les nouveaux philosophes sont-ils de droite ou de gauche?" 27 May 1977; on Sartre, with Aron and Glucksmann, "Jean-Paul Sartre, Écrivain 1905–1980," 18 April 1980; with Bernard-Henri Lévy and Claude Lévi-Strauss, "Au carrefour des idéologies," 23 January 1981; with Serres and Huisman, "Les meilleurs," 4 January 1985; on Sartre, "Sartre et Céline," 25 October 1985; with Luc Ferry and Alain Renaut, "Sur quelques épisodes du XXeme siècle," 22 November 1985; on Heidegger and with Luc Ferry, "Doit-on les condamner?" 20 April 1988; and with Serres and René Girard, "Deux philosophes français en Californie," 21 July 1989.

8. Figures from Annexe 4: Corrélation entre meilleures ventes (source *Livres-Hebdo*) et passage à *Apostrophes* (1983 à 1986), in Brasey, *L'effet Pivot,* 349.

9. Survey from the *Syndicat de l'édition,* cited in Hamon and Rotman, *Les intellocrates,* 174.

10. Hamon and Rotman, *Les intellocrates,* 174. Nevertheless, the books *Apostrophes* featured were not as exclusively linked to particular publishing houses as

might be expected: 244 publishers (of which the 20 major houses issued 74% of the total books) were represented among *Apostrophes* literary selections between 1975 and 1986. Figures from Annexe 3: Représentativité des éditeurs à *Apostrophes*, in Brasey, *L'effet Pivot*, 345.

11. Hamon and Rotman, *Les intellocrates*, 175.

12. A sophisticated semiotic analysis of the debate structure employed on *Apostrophes* can be found in Chareaudeau and others, *La télévision*. See also Gschwind-Holtzer, "'Je vais vous presenter mes invites . . . .'"

13. See Bukowski, in "En marge de la société," 22 September 1978.

14. Debray, *Teachers, Writers, Celebrities*, 222.

15. Pivot, *Le matin*, 14 May 1979.

16. See Chevalier, *L'"expert" à la télévision*.

17. From Pivot, *Le métier de lire*, quoted in "Les années Pivot," *Lire* 296 (June 2001).

18. Brasey, *L'effet Pivot*. 66.

19. Pierre Boncenne, editor-in-chief of *Lire*, later joined Bourgnon and Bernard.

20. Barma, cited in Brasey, *L'effet Pivot*, 155.

21. Georges Ferraro (narrator), in "Du commencement de *Lecture pour tous* à la fin d'*Apostrophes*," 5 September 1990.

22. Brasey, *L'effet Pivot*, 175.

23. Bernard Pivot, interview in *Le monde*, 6 February 1977.

24. On the history of French television debates, see Nel, *À fleurets mouchetés* and his later *Le débat télévisé*.

25. Charaudeau, "Contrats de communication et ritualisations des débats télévisés," in Charaudeau and others, *La télévision*, 21.

26. Bourdieu, *On Television*, 28–29.

27. Nel, *À fleurets mouchetés*, 138.

28. "La vie intellectuelle sous l'occupation," 27 June 1975; "L'amour romanesque," 20 February 1976; "Crime et châtiment," 18 May 1979; "Les Juifs en question," 14 September 1979; "La naissance," 16 November 1979.

29. Rieffel, *La tribu des clercs*, 3:209.

30. See Chapter 9, "Le roi *Lire*," in Brasey, *L'effet Pivot*, 116–27.

31. Christofferson's excellent *French Intellectuals against the Left* is the best treatment of this phenomenon currently available.

32. Solzhenitsyn's book was available in France in Russian in December 1973. The PCF and *L'humanité* immediately attacked the book, claiming that it was attempting to undermine efforts towards détente. *Le nouvel observateur* and *Tel quel* fired back, launching the French debate over antitotalitarianism before *L'Archipel du Goulag* had even appeared in French translation (which occurred six months later). Christofferson and Hourmant both cover this history. See Christofferson, *French Intellectuals*, 89–112; and Hourmant, *Le désenchantement des clercs*, 57–88.

33. "Quel avenir pour l'homme," *Apostrophes*, Antenne 2, 17 December 1976, INA.

34. Victor Kravchenko published a damning condemnation of the Soviet camps in 1947. When the veracity of Kravchenko's work was challenged, Rousset initiated an inquiry into their existence and was also accused of falsifying evidence. See chapter 5, "From Kravchenko to Hungary via Korea, in Drake, *Intellectuals and Politics in Post-War France*, especially 65–68.

35. Christofferson makes this argument in *French Intellectuals*. See especially chapter 2, "The Gulag as Metaphor," 89–112.

36. Ibid, 91.

37. Macey, *The Lives of Michel Foucault*, 378.

38. In 1977, Foucault contrasted the media-driven success of *Les mots et les choses* in 1966 against the pitiful reception granted *Folie et déraison* in 1961, blaming the latter on the control that Marxism was then exerting over French intellectual life. Christofferson, *French Intellectuals*, 199.

39. On the former point, see Christofferson, *French Intellectuals*, 199. On the latter, see Clavel, "Vous direz trois rosaries."

40. Foucault, "Truth and Power," 114.

41. Foucault, *The History of Sexuality*, 1:151.

42. Eribon, *Michel Foucault et ses contemporains*, 64.

43. *Webster's New World Dictionary* (New York: Simon and Schuster, Inc., 1988), 1015.

44. Brasey, *L'effet Pivot*, 188. It has been suggested that Foucault's refusal to follow form was pre-planned. However, given both the personalities involved and Pivot's insistence on the importance of filming *Apostrophes* live, this idea strikes me as highly unlikely. I presume Pivot was delighted to seize on anything that might shake up an otherwise staid discussion.

45. "L'abcédaire de Gilles Deleuze," 17 September 1995.

46. Jeannette Colombel quoting Foucault, on "Spécial: 'Michel Foucault,'" 22 June 1994. See also, Foucault, "The Masked Philosopher".

47. Lévy, *Éloge des intellectuels*, 143.

48. GIP was an organization whose main goals were not prison reform but rather the collection and dissemination of information about the prison system. On this incident and Foucault's involvement with GIP, see Macey, *The Lives of Michel Foucault*, 257–89.

49. I am indebted to Julian Bourg, Michael Scott Christofferson, and Jonathan Judaken for sharing their excellent recent scholarship on the New Philosophers with me. Their conclusions inform this section.

50. "Les nouveaux philosophes sont-ils de droite ou de gauche?" 27 May 1977.

51. This is the title attributed to the broadcast in INA's archives. For ratings see Christofferson, *French Intellectuals*, 197.

52. Rieffel, *La tribu des clercs*, 1:103.

53. The New Philosophers published in "Théoriciens" and "Figures." Lévy's first book was *Bangla-Desh*.

54. See Bourg, "Forbidden to Forbid," 337.

55. Despite their periodic inclusion, work by Annie Leclerc and Françoise Lévy generally attracted less notice in the press.

56. Marxists disillusioned with the PCF generated the *gauchisme* of 1968. *Gauchisme* was inspired by the anti-Stalinist, anticapitalist, pro-proletarian democracy touted by the Trotskyists Cornelius Castoriadis and Claude Lefort in their journal *Socialisme ou barbarie;* Henri Lefebvre's critique of everyday life; Guy Debord and the Situationist International's attacks on consumer society; the mix of Marxism and anarchism developed by the Union des groupes anarchistes communistes; and the "scientific" structuralist Marxism of Louis Althusser (which many of his students later rallied in support of Maoism). Both Bernard-Henri Lévy and André Glucksmann numbered among Althusser's former pupils. Robert Gildea offers a concise explanation in English of the complex political

evolution from Marxism to *gauchisme* in France in the 1960s in his *France since 1945*, 150–52. See also Hirsch, *The French Left*. On anti-third-worldism and human rights, see Kristin Ross, *May '68 and Its Afterlives*.

57. On the ethical dimensions of the New Philosophy, see Bourg, "Forbidden to Forbid," and Pharo, "Éthique et politique." Bourg identifies the ethics of New Philosophy as characterized by four theses: "Evil is originary, there is no Sovereign Good, ethical action is rooted in culture, and ethical action is the affair of the individual" (340).

58. I am quoting Bourg (352), who cites Aubral and Delcourt's critique of these themes in *Contre la nouvelle philosophie*, 26–36.

59. A brilliant theoretical critique of the New Philosophy, placing it in dialogue with structuralism, Foucault's critique of power, and Lacanian psychoanalysis can be found in Dews, "The 'New Philosophers' and the End of Leftism." See also, Dews, "The *Nouvelle philosophie* and Foucault."

60. 'Philosophies of desire' included, of course, the work of Deleuze and Guattari in *L'anti-Oedipe*. Regarding the predilection of the New Philosophers for metaphysics, Reader, in *Intellectuals and the Left in France since 1968*, 110, comments, "Much of the hostility to the new philosophy on the Left sprang not only from the political turn-coating of many of its adherents, or their manifest media opportunism, but from a long French tradition (dating back at least to Descartes) of robust hostility to any suspicion of the metaphysical."

61. On the press coverage, see Hourmant, *Le désenchantement des clercs*, 99–102; and Christofferson, *French Intellectuals*, 192–93. The Théâtre oblique debate is covered in Bouscasse and Bourgeois, *Faut-il brûler les nouveaux philosophes?* 53–54. The radio programs were *Philosophie aujourd'hui*, aired in November 1976, and *Génération perdue*, which ran during October and November of the same year. In 1977 and '78 a series of talks called Lundis philosophiques (Philosophical Mondays) were organized at the Centre Beaubourg around the themes of "representation and power," "desire and the law" and "the reason of state and the rights of man."

62. Deleuze, "On the New Philosophers and a More General Problem," 141. Michel Foucault penned an article in support of Glucksmann's *Les maîtres penseurs* in *Le nouvel observateur*. See Foucault, "La grande colère des faits."

63. See, for example, Bernard-Henri Lévy, "La nouvelle philosophie n'existe pas."

64. Jonathan Judaken insightfully argues that the history of French intellectuals is inseparable from the history of "the Jewish question." See Judaken, "Alain Finkielkraut and the Nouveaux Philosophes."

65. Ibid., 205–6.

66. On the specific intellectual, see Deleuze and Foucault, "Les intellectuels et le pouvoir". On the evolution from the earlier Sartrean "universal" or "classic" intellectual to the later "revolutionary" model, as well as on the relationship between these and the "specific intellectual," see Drake, *Intellectuals and Politics*, especially chapter 5.

67. On Clavel, see Gachoud, *Maurice Clavel*, and Bel, *Maurice Clavel*. In English, see Bourg, "Forbidden to Forbid," 369–90.

68. Clavel was regularly associated with the New Philosophers in the media. To take just one example, on 1 August 1977, *Le nouvel observateur* published a quiz entitled "Êtes-vous un nouveau philosophe?" "Are You a New Philosopher?" that included the question, "To what inspired little hill did several New Philosophers

retire in order to meditate upon the future of the world in front of television cameras?" The correct response was "Vézelay," and the broadcast it referred to was a special on Maurice Clavel. See "Maurice Clavel," 4 July 1977. Glucksmann, Lardreau, Jambet, Foucault, and Philippe Sollers took part. The show was aired on the heels of the *Apostrophes* broadcast, when the controversy over the New Philosophy was at its height.

69. Medhi Ben Barka was a member of the Moroccan opposition and a supporter of Algerian national liberation. His mysterious disappearance in Paris in 1965, when he was purportedly captured and tortured to death by French police, provoked a national scandal.

70. The phrase is Bourg's, in "Forbidden to Forbid," 370.

71. See Ibid., 389, n. 154.

72. Bel, *Maurice Clavel*, 335.

73. Glucksmann, *La cuisinière et le mangeur d'hommes.*

74. "Alexandre Soljenitsyne," 24 June 1974.

75. Marx-Scouras, *The Cultural Politics of Tel quel*, 192.

76. For an analysis of the deployment of the term 'pleb' in Glucksmann's *La cuisinière et le mangeur d'hommes,* see Ross, *May '68 and Its Afterlives*, 178–79.

77. On the "official-dissident intellectual," see Rancière, "La bergère au goulag".

78. Figures from Marx-Scouras, *The Cultural Politics of Tel quel*,192.

79. Lévy, *Barbarism with a Human Face*, 190.

80. Quoted in Judaken, "Alain Finkielkraut and the Nouveaux Philosophes," 214.

81. Quoted in Aubral and Delcourt, *Contre la nouvelle philosophie*, 35.

82. For other politically motivated attacks on the New Philosophy, see Cohen, "La génération perdante,"; Mauriac, "Il ne faut pas tuer l'espérance"; Ribardière, "Ils nous font la leçon"; Rousset, "Un entretien avec David Rousset." Substantive critiques of the New Philosophy include Deleuze, "À propos des nouveaux philosophes et d'un problème plus general"; Lyotard, *Instructions païennes;* Debray, "Springtime Weepers," 111; Macciocchi, *De la France,* 380; and Cornelius Castoriadis, "Les divertisseurs."

83. And, indeed, Giscard's admiration went so far that in 1978 he invited the stars of *Apostrophes* to lunch at the Elysée palace. Lévy and Clavel accepted. Christofferson, *French Intellectuals,* 197. As stated earlier, the Common Program of the Left was a broad political program and electoral alliance forged in 1972 between the socialist and communist parties. It was central to French political debate throughout the 1970s.

84. Debray, *Teachers, Writers, Celebrities*, 213, 214.

85. According to INA's databases, between his first television appearance (on "Rencontre avec l'amour," 19 March 1975, in *Les grandes heures de notre vie,* a talk show about the problem of love coproduced by Claude Santelli and his boss at Grasset, Françoise Verny) and the end of 1999, Lévy either appeared or was discussed on more than 446 shows, compared to Sartre's 610 (1951–99).

86. In addition to *Ouvrez les guillemets,* mentioned above, Glucksmann appeared on "Le nouveau Dimanche, 31 March 1968, and "Han Suyin," 5 January 1969.

87. For example, in 1978, as part of his efforts on behalf of the Vietnamese "boat people," Glucksmann attracted considerable attention for coordinating the much-televised reconciliation between Sartre and Aron. See "Plateau Hai Hong," 27 November 1978.

88. "Concours les plus belles jambes," *Mini Journal,* TF1, 18 April 1985, INA.

89. For Sartre's description of this division, see his *Plaidoyer pour les intellectuels,* 421.

90. Pharo, quoted in Bourg, "Forbidden to Forbid," 339.

91. Ross, *May '68 and Its Afterlives,* 177.

92. Deleuze, "On the New Philosophers," 139.

93. Peter Dews describes this paradox in, "The *Nouvelle philosophie* and Foucault," 167.

94. On occasion, *Les idées et les hommes* is called *Des idées et des hommes.* It appears as the former in press releases, as the latter in television guides (*Télérama, Télé-7-jours*), and as both in the INA database. Huisman referred to it as *Des idées et des hommes* in the interview that I conducted with him (19 April 1999), but on the broadcasts the credit sequence appears as *Les idées et les hommes.* Research on the program requires searching under both names.

95. Lycées Turgot, Charlemagne, and Montaigne.

96. Huisman became the general director of the Société civile de l'édition littéraire française, where he was responsible to Flammarion, Gallimard, and Laffont for the recovery of the publishing rights to previously existing works of literature. As late as 1999 he was still active as series editor at Éditions Nathan, SEDES (Société d'édition d'enseignement supérieure), and Hachette in addition to being the editor of the *Dictionnaire des Philosophes* at the Presses universitaires de France, then preparing its third edition.

97. Huisman began writing philosophy manuals in 1954. For some of Huisman's many publications, see the bibliography.

98. Huisman, interview, 19 April 1999.

99. Cazeneuve, quoted in Grolleron, "TF1," 138.

100. Given the history of both the Radio-télévision scolaire's series *L'enseignement de la philosophie,* and the Service de la Recherche's *Un certain regard,* this statement was not fully accurate. Perhaps Cazeneuve was exaggerating in the enthusiasm of the moment.

101. Cazeneuve, introduction to "Dieu existe-t-il?" 5 January 1975.

102. See ibid.; "Liberté et déterminisme," 12 March 1975; "Le moi et les au tres," 24 September 1975; "Résponsabilité," 28 April 1976; "La justice," 26 November 1975; "Vérité," 19 January 1976; "L'art, le beau, et l'utile," 21 May 1975; "Le bonheur," 16 April 1975; "La mort," 22 October 1975; "L'amour," 17 December 1975.

103. Wednesday evenings were slated for cultural and educational programming. *Interrogations* alternated with programs on psychology (produced by Jacques Mousseau), medicine (produced by Igor Barrère and Étienne Lalou) and sociology. Denis Huisman, interview.

104. Marie-Agnès Malfray, the coproducer, remembers this differently. According to her, they had "complete liberty regarding choice of guests." Marie-Agnès Malfray, interview with the author, 10 May 1999.

105. Huisman, interview. Ironically, when he was awarded the Lauréat du Prix Louis Liard and made a member of the Institut de France in 1994, Huisman joined the group whose television merits he so disparaged.

106. Huisman, interview.

107. Ibid. Huisman's fascination with the physical incarnation of the philosopher eventually led to the publication of a book of photo-essays, *Visages de la philosophie* with images by Louis Monier.

108. Malfray, interview. Like Huisman, Malfray had a *licence* in philosophy. Immediately after finishing her studies in 1965, she began assisting Huisman with the books on philosophy that he produced for Éditions Nathan. She coproduced the television programs, and then acted as editorial assistant for his *Dictionnaire des philosophes*. Malfray later worked as general secretary for Huisman's École française des attachés de presse in Paris.

109. Huisman, interview.

110. Ibid. Huisman told me that, for political reasons, Cazeneuve refused to let him produce programs on either Heidegger or Sartre. In contrast, Malfray claims, the guests' "political orientation was never taken into account." Malfray, interview.

111. The featured philosophers were as follows: Alain, 27 July 1976; Camus, 4 January 1977; Pascal, 6 July 1977; Plato, 28 September 1977; Kierkegaard, 23 November 1977; Spinoza, 14 December 1977; Auguste Comte, 5 June 1978; Henri Bergson, 19 July 1978; Hippolyte Taine, 1 May 1979; Descartes, 31 August 1978; Montaigne, 31 August 1979 (rebroadcast on January 7, 1980); and Teilhard de Chardin, 1 September 1981.

112. Production information from "T.F.1 Hebdo No. 34."

113. Huisman, interview.

114. Ibid.

115. Malfray, interview.

116. "Jean-François Lyotard," 27 March 1978.

117. From 1975 to 1978, *Tribune Libre* aired at 7:40 p.m. From 1978 to 1981 it started at 6:55 p.m. Throughout the duration of its six-year run, it was directed by Yves Barbara, and produced by both Jean-Pierre Alessandri and Jean-Claude Courdy. In 1981 the program was replaced by *Liberté 3*, which ran until 1987 and aired at noon. *Tribune Libre*, Fiche collection INA.

118. See, "Vladimir Jankélévitch," 17 April 1978; "Michel Serres," 27 September 1976 and 28 November 1980; "Simone de Beauvoir et la ligue du droite des femmes," 20 January 1975; "Julia Kristeva," 15 May 1976; and "André Glucksmann," 27 June 1977. At present, only the programs on Lyotard, Jankélévitch, Kristeva, and Glucksmann are available to view.

119. Bourdon, *Haute fidélité*, 194.

120. Very little has been written about *Tribune Libre*. Raymond Kuhn's dissertation, "The Politics of Broadcasting in France, 1974–1978," contains one of the few analyses of its shows.

121. The transcript of this broadcast has been published as "A Podium with out a Podium," in Lyotard, *Political Writings*. My translation follows that of Bill Readings with a few minor alterations. Although Readings notes the unusual use of the audio track (voice-over, in sync, out of sync), he provides no images and neglects visual analysis. The philosophical impact of the program cannot be fully appreciated without this.

122. Reading offers a useful analysis of Lyotard's position concerning the intellectual's right to "speak for others." See his foreword in *Political Writings*, xxi.

123. Jean-Claude Guillebaud cited in Ory and Sirinelli, *Les intellectuels en France*, 231.

124. Max Gallo, "Les intellectuels, la politique et la modernité," *Le monde*, 26 July 1983.

125. Lyotard argues that whereas philosophers are responsible to thought and creation, "the responsibility of 'intellectuals' is inseparable from the (shared) idea

of a universal subject" and hence with the human community. Lyotard, "Tomb of the Intellectual," 6.

126. Peyrefitte, "Une nouvelle philosophie bien française," 53–54, quoted in Bourg, "Forbidden to Forbid," 411. I am indebted to Bourg's work for bringing this quotation to my attention.

127. On the "silence of the intellectuals," see Drake, *Intellectuals and Politics*, chapter 6. Drake asserts that while Deleuze, Bourdieu, and others had opposed Mitterrand's candidacy, "reservations about the new government and president were not universal." Derrida and Lyotard, for example, were among those who supported the new regime. Ibid., 168.

128. See Bourdieu, *Les héritiers* and *Homo Academicus*. Other studies include Ory and Sirinelli, *Les intellectuels en France;* Sirinelli, *Génération intellectuelle;* Charle, *Les Élites de la République*. These were followed by a number of essays, more or less academic in style, including, Debray, *Teachers, Writers, Celebrities;* Lévy, *Éloge des intellectuels;* Hamon and Rotman, *Les intellocrates;* Finkielkraut, *La défaite de la pensée;* and Ory, *Dernières questions aux intellectuels*. Despite the title of Ory's 1990 publication (Last Questions for Intellectuals"), the category of "French intellectual" remains under scrutiny a decade and more later. See, for example, Debray, *I.F. suite et fin;* Schiffer, *Grandeur et misère des intellectuels;* and Sévilla, *Le terrorisme intellectuel de 1945 à nos jours*.

129. Jennings, "Of Treason, Blindness and Silence," 75.

130. Lyotard, "Tomb of the Intellectual," 6.

131. Godechot, "Le marché du livre philosophique," 22. On the Haby reform, see also Derrida, *Who's Afraid of Philosophy;* Pinto, *Les philosophes entre le lycée et l'avant-garde;* and Lewis, *The French Education System*.

132. On GREPH, see Derrida, *Du droit à la philosophie,* especially "Qui a peur de la philosophie?" 111–78. In English, see also Derrida, *Who's Afraid of Philosophy;* Derrida, "The Institution"; and Derrida, "The Right to Philosophy." An excellent overview of the philosophical questions raised by the Haby reform is contained in Coq, "Qui a peur de la philosophie"; and Coq and others, "Table Ronde."

133. Figures from Godechot, "Le marché du livre philosophique," 22, 24.

134. Ibid., 23.

## Chapter Five

1. *Océaniques* also included programs on the arts. Glenn Gould, Salvador Dali, the ballerina Yvette Chauviré, Laurence Olivier, and Edgar Degas were all profiled. For a complete record of program titles, see the list compiled by Hellec, http://perso.wanadoo.fr/gerard.hellec/docs/oceaniques.htm.

2. The High Authority's operations were hampered by its lack of jurisdiction (commercial networks were outside its remit) and vulnerability to political bias. On its history, see especially Chauveau, *L'audiovisuel en liberté?.*

3. Given that Mitterrand had already awarded the direction of Canal Plus to his chief of staff, André Rousselet, and then allocated the "concessionary" licenses for La Cinq and TV6 on a discretionary basis to his political allies (Silvio Berlusconi and the Gaumont and Publicis advertising firm, respectively), such claims were not unfounded.

4. When the period of shared political governance known as the *cohabitation* ended in 1988, the CNCL was also deemed too susceptible to political influence. It

was replaced in 1989 (following Mitterrand's re-election), by the Conseil supérieur de l'audiovisuel (CSA), a fully independent audiovisual regulatory body responsible for broadcasting content, advertising, and the allocation and distribution of broadcasting subsidies.

5. La Cinq was delivered to the right-wing press magnate Robert Hersant (Chirac's personal friend), and the newly named M6 to the company La Lyonnaise des eaux (headed by Gaullist sympathizer Jérôme Monod).

6. France was the only European country to privatize a state channel. The CNCL selected the franchises permitted to bid on TF1 (Hachette, a media group, and the construction consortium Bouygues). Bouygues, in conjunction with the British publishing tycoon Robert Maxwell, won. The privatization of TF1 is recounted in chapters 10, 11, and 12 of Péan and Nick's history of the channel: *TF1, un pouvoir.*

7. Regourd, "Two Conflicting Notions of Audiovisual Liberalization," 31.

8. Ibid., 32.

9. Bouygues, *Le monde,* 23 June 1987.

10. Sheila Perry describes the ramifications of this complex shift in "Television."

11. Leclerc, "Antenne 2."

12. Grolleron, "TF1," 141.

13. Biographical details are from my 25 November 1999 interview with Yves Jaigu and from "Yves Jaigu" in the series *Télé notre histoire* broadcast on *Chaîne histoire,* April 1996, INA. I am grateful to Jean-Noël Jeanneney for lending me a video of this show.

14. Jaigu, "Yves Jaigu," *Télé Notre Histoire.*

15. Ibid. Many shows were rebroadcast, often at 2:00 p.m. the following day.

16. Ibid.

17. An FR3 correspondent from Marseille located the Heidegger footage. The sequence with Althusser was shot for Italian TV by RAI. The most substantive clip in the Foucault documentary came from an interview between Foucault and André Berten taped in 1981 at the Catholic University in Louvain (Brussels). Boutang, interview with the author, 17 May 2000; and Boutang, in Saintville and Cazin, "Océaniques, un essai de construction," 21.

18. Ibid, 21.

19. Boutang, interview.

20. On Pierre Boutang, see, Assaf, *Hommage à Pierre Boutang.* On the Action française, see Weber, *Action Française.*

21. The shows on Althusser were broadcast on 1 and 5 June 1992.

22. Boutang, interview.

23. Michel Cazenave, interview with the author, 24 May 2000.

24. Boutang, interview.

25. See for example, Daney, "Le pari d'*Océaniques*," 160; David, "George Steiner et Pierre Boutang face à face"; and Waintrop, "La parole au sommet de la vague."

26. Pascaud, "En pays de connaissances," 59.

27. The descriptions of Steiner are from David, "George Steiner et Pierre Boutang face à face," 150. On Steiner see, Steiner and Janabegloo, *Entretiens de George Steiner et Ramin Jahanbegloo.* For Boutang, see Brigneau, *Mon après-guerre;* Assouline, *Singulièrement libre;* and Patrick H. Hutton's description of Boutang's influence on and friendship with historian Philippe Ariès in Hutton,

"The Postwar Politics of Philippe Ariès," esp 367–70. Boutang's anti-Semitism is particularly evident in his *La république de Joinovici.*

28. David, "George Steiner et Pierre Boutang face à face," 150.

29. "Le Mythe d'*Antigone*," 21 September 1987.

30. Cazenave, interview.

31. It is worth noting that Sophocles' play was also the subject of Lacan's 1959–60 seminar on the "ethics of psychoanalysis."

32. The plot was hatched by the extreme right candidate in the 1965 presidential elections, the lawyer Jean-Louis Tixier-Vignancour. See Dumas, *La permission du maréchal.*

33. L'Association pour défendre la mémoire du Maréchal Pétain (ADMP), created in 1951, remains committed to this agenda. For Rousso's insightful analysis of the symbolic work performed by Pétain's remains, see especially pp. 40–49 and 283–95 of his *The Vichy Syndrome.*

34. Shakespeare's *Hamlet* (2.2.327–32).

35. On the history of the Cambodian genocide, see especially Kiernan, *The Pol Pot Regime.* See also, Kiernan, *How Pol Pot Came to Power,* and Chandler, *Brother Number One.*

36. In E. F. Watling's version, Zeus is translated as "God," and Antigone's speech (lines 450–55) reads as follows:

> That order did not come from God. Justice,
> That dwells with the gods below, knows no such law.
> I did not think your edicts strong enough
> To overrule the unwritten unalterable laws
> Of God and heaven, you being only a man.

Sophocles, *Antigone,* in *The Theban Plays,* 138.

37. Jaigu, "Yves Jaigu," *Télé Notre Histoire.*

38. Jaigu, interview.

39. Ibid.

40. "Le sacrifice d'Abraham," 28 September 1987.

41. Waintrop, "La parole au sommet de la vague," 54.

42. In the published transcription of this debate, *all* of Cazenave's comments are deleted, as are Boutang's responses to him. See Boutang and Steiner, *Dialogues.*

43. The *milice* was a paramilitary force created in 1943 by the Vichy government to fight the French Resistance and to participate in the roundup and deportation of Jews. The Camelots du roi was the youth group of the extreme right-wing Action française, and the Croix de feu was a French nationalist group active during the interwar period.

44. Moyn, *Origins of the Other,* 10.

45. Waintrop, "La parole au sommet de la vague," 54.

46. Rousso's classic study of France's obsession with its memories of WWII, *The Vichy Syndrome,* contains a concise section on the Barbie affair (199–216). My account relies especially on his work, on Morgan's *An Uncertain Hour,* on Marcel Ophuls's 1988 film *Hotel Terminus: The Life and Times of Klaus Barbie,* and on Susan Rubin Suleiman's excellent article "History, Memory, and Moral Judgment in Documentary Film." Erna Paris covers Barbie's early career and life in South America in *Unhealed Wounds.* See also Linklater, Hilton, and

Ascherson, *The Nazi Legacy*. On the trial's philosophical ramifications, see Finkielkraut's brilliant *Remembering in Vain*. Alice Kaplan's introduction to this latter text is especially useful.

47. These numbers are disputed (in *The Vichy Syndrome*, Rousso sets them at forty-three children and five adults) but according to the Izieu Memorial Museum, forty-four children and seven adults were deported on 6 April 1944. See www .izieu.alma.fr, the official site of the Musée-mémorial des enfants d'Izieu. For the story of the Izieu children's deportation, see Klarsfeld, *Les enfants d'Izieu*.

48. Finkielkraut, *Remembering in Vain*, 17, 19.

49. Vergès published his own version of the events as *Je defends Barbie*. Koulberg's "L'affaire Barbie" offers a potent argument against Vergès's legal machinations.

50. Given de Gaulle's role in creating this vision of France, it is no coincidence that the myth of *la France résistante* came under attack after his death. On the controversy over *Le chagrin et la pitié*, see Rousso, *The Vichy Syndrome*, 100–114. Paxton's *Vichy France* overturned the hegemonic view (proposed in Robert Aron's 1954 *Histoire de Vichy, 1940–1944*) of the Vichy state as playing a slick double game against the Germans, collaborating only insofar as such actions would protect French interests and autonomy. Touvier became the first Frenchman convicted of crimes against humanity. On the Touvier scandal, see Rousso, *The Vichy Syndrome*, 114–26. On Touvier's 1996 trial, see Golsan's "The Trial of Paul Touvier: The Law Revises History," in his, *Vichy's Afterlife*, 88–102.

51. "Le chagrin et la pitié," 28–29 October 1981.

52. For television coverage, see "C'est à lire," 12 January 1981; "Au Carrefour des Idéologies," 23 January 1981; "Déracinez-vous," 6 May 1981, INA.

53. It is staggering to note that Alain Resnais's classic 1955 film about deportations to the concentration camps, *Nuit et brouillard* (Night and Fog), fails to differentiate between those deported and their fates, and barely references either the Holocaust as a specifically Jewish experience or France's involvement in it.

54. Annette Insdorf, in *Indelible Shadows*, 5, writes that 220 million people worldwide are reported to have watched it.

55. Lanzmann's *Shoah* was broadcast on TF1 in four parts on consecutive nights at 10:30 p.m., near the end of the Barbie trial (29 June–2 July 1987). The broadcasts were discussed three times on the national news, including an interview with Lanzmann in which he directly addressed the Barbie trial. See "Shoah," 29 June 1987; "Plateau Claude Lanzmann," 2 July 1987; "Shoah," 2 July 1987.

56. De Gaulle's newsreel comment is quoted in Rousso, *The Vichy Syndrome*, 135. Rousso also covers negationism (151–61). Pierre Vidal-Naquet's *Assassins of Memory*, a stunning analysis of the motivations driving Holocaust denial, also addresses the Faurisson case. Additionally, see Igounet, *Histoire du négationnisme en France*. Lyotard's discussion of negationism in *Le différend* is especially useful. On the rise of the Front national, see Françoise Gaspard's memoir on neofascist advances in Gaspard, *A Small City in France*; and Davies, *The National Front in France*.

57. For example, Finkielkraut discussed his book *L'avenir d'une négation*, a denunciation of Faurisson's claims, on *Apostrophes* in a broadcast entitled "Attention à la marche de l'histoire" Antenne 2, 12 March 1982, INA. A year earlier, television news had covered Faurisson's trial ("Procès Faurisson," JA2 20H, Antenne 2, 25 June 1981 INA). By the late 1980s, thanks to its electoral gains, the Front national was regularly grabbing TV news headlines in such clips as "Jean

Marie Le Pen," *IT1 20H,* TF1, 14 Sept. 1987 INA and "Declaration Jean-Pierre Stirbois," *IT1 13H,* TF1, 15 Sept. 1987 INA.

58. Rousso, *The Vichy Syndrome,* 201.

59. Le Roy Ladurie, *Le Quotidien de Paris,* 7 February 1983; and Alice Kaplan, "Introduction," in Finkielkraut, *Remembering in Vain,* xvi–xvii.

60. The quotes are from Finkielkraut, *Remembering in Vain,* 25, 26, 34, 35. Finkielkraut alleges that in the context of the trial, objections to these tactics were appallingly absent. However, over time these noisome claims ironically ensured the impossibility of containing the trial discretely inside either French memories of Vichy or Jewish memories of the Holocaust, but insisted, instead, on its universal significance (36).

61. This number was derived from a web search using the key word "Barbie" in the *Le monde* database.

62. Chalandon and Nivelle's *Crimes contre l'humanité,* 13–164, includes a long section on these articles.

63. Kaplan, "Introduction," in Finkielkraut, *Remembering in Vain,* xvi.

64. Finkielkraut, *Remembering in Vain,* 69–71.

65. Justifying his cinematic approach to the material, Lanzmann proposed that the only corrective to the "obscenity of understanding" carried by the search for causal historical explanations of the Shoah was what Susan Rubin Suleiman calls (in "History, Memory and Moral Judgment in Documentary Film") "an active process of witnessing [. . .] in reverence and awe." But as Suleiman remarks, attractive as this position is, it easily leads to a kind of "sacralization of memory" that can "all too quickly degenerate into kitsch, the very opposite of critical self-reflection" (512). See also Lanzmann, "The Obscenity of Understanding"; and Cuau and others, *Au sujet de "Shoah".*

66. The proviso was broken in 2000, when some seventy hours (about half of the total footage) were broadcast on the French cable channel *Histoire,* accompanied by commentary from prominent historians. Susan Rubin Suleiman mentions that the footage aired a second time, in June and July of 2001, and observes that its "public impact has yet to be evaluated," "History, Memory and Moral Judgment in Documentary Film," 16, note 18.

67. The number is derived from searches by title, keyword, and summary in the TV databases of Inathèque de France. Philosophers frequently participated in these discussions.

68. Daney, "Le pari d'*Océaniques,*" 160.

69. "Martin Heidegger, 1ère partie," 7 December 1987.

70. There is some discrepancy regarding the date of the original German broadcast. INA's database dates the excerpt to 1969, as did Boutang in my interview with him. During the 1987 show, however, he identifies the date more vaguely as "1965 or so."

71. Farias's book appeared the following year in English. Citations here are to the French edition.

72. The Farias affair generated an inordinate amount of scholarship. In French it prompted the 1987 republication of Bourdieu's 1975 study *L'ontologie politique de Martin Heidegger,* as well as works by Fédier (*Heidegger*), Ferry and Renaut (*Heidegger et les modernes*), and Lyotard (*Heidegger et "les juifs"*). Both Derrida and Philippe Lacoue-Labarthe had already embarked on manuscripts on Heidegger, partly in response to rumors that a new set of sources about the philosopher's politics had been unearthed. See Derrida, *De l'ésprit* and Lacoue-

Labarthe, *La fiction du politique*. Thomas Sheehan's 1988 article "Heidegger and the Nazis" provides one of the best short introductions to the affair published in English. See also Richard Wolin's copious scholarship on the topic, especially his essay "French Heidegger Wars." Wolin's book motivated its own scandal when Derrida threatened to sue him and his publisher (Columbia University Press) over the inclusion of "Philosopher's Hell: An Interview," a translation of "L'enfer des philosophes," the interview Derrida granted to *Le nouvel observateur* during the height of the Farias controversy. This interview was not included in foreign editions of the journal; Wolin's 1991 book made it available to many audiences for the first time. Wolin's collection was later republished by MIT (1993) without the contentious essay. Rockmore's *Heidegger and French Philosophy* places the Farias affair within a larger critical assessment of Heidegger's importance in twentieth-century French thought.

73. See Sartre, "À propos de l'existentialisme." The PCF's attacks on Sartre's existentialism because of its alleged association with Nazism continued until at least 1948. I am grateful to David Drake for bringing this to my attention.

74. As Ferry and Renaut observe in *Heidegger and Modernity* (112, n. 9), the discussion began in 1945–46 with the publication of Maurice de Gandillac's "Entretien avec Martin Heidegger" and Frédéric de Towarnicki's "Visite à Martin Heidegger," in *Les temps modernes*. However, debate really got underway after the appearance in 1946 of Karl Löwith's "Les implications politiques de la philosophie de l'existence chez Heidegger" and Alphonse de Waelhens's "La philosophie de Heidegger et le nazisme."

75. Jean-Pierre Faye, "Heidegger et la 'révolution.'"

76. Fédier, "Trois attaques contre Heidegger," reviewed books by Guido Schneeberger, Theodor Adorno and Paul Hühnerfeld; Adorno's text was *The Jargon of Authenticity*.

77. Jean-Pierre Faye refuted Fédier's claims in "La lecture et l'énoncé." Fédier responded with "À propos de Heidegger."

78. Derrida states, "As far as the essence of the 'facts' is concerned, I still haven't found anything in this inquiry that was not already long known by those who are seriously interested in Heidegger." Derrida, "The Philosopher's Hell," 265.

79. Maggiori, "Heil Heidegger!"

80. Raymond Aron was also in the audience. Alan D. Schrift clarifies that there is no proof that Sartre attended Kojève's seminars, but adds that he was clearly familiar with Kojève's reading of Hegel. Schrift adds that Kojève's reading of the master-slave dialectic was particularly important because it betrays a turn in French thought towards the concrete and away from the idealism and spiritualism prominent, respectively, in the work of Léon Brunschvicq, Émile Boutroux, Henri Bergson, and Maurice Blondel. See Schrift, "Is There Such a Thing as 'French Philosophy'?" 28, 26.

81. Although Glucksmann fails to mention it, Heidegger's 1929 essays "What is Metaphysics?" and "On the Essence of Reason" were published in French translation in *Recherches philosophiques* in 1931, whereas his chef d'oeuvre, *Being and Time* (1927) did not appear in French translation until 1985. Since many of those working on phenomenology were similarly interested in Husserl and Hegel, it is not easy to determine precise intellectual influences, but it is generally conceded that Heidegger's impact was substantial, even prior to the availability of his works in French. On this point, see also Shrift, "Is There Such a Thing as 'French Philosophy'?" 29.

82. Heidegger's influence among postwar French philosophers extends beyond those who engage directly with his work. Foucault mentions, for example, that despite never having written on the German thinker, his "entire philosophical development was determined by [his] reading of Heidegger." Foucault, "The Return of Morality," 250.

83. Derrida continues, "The second conclusion is idiotic and dishonest. In the first, one reads the renunciation of thought and political irresponsibility." He determines that what is needed instead, is "a certain deconstruction" that will allow us to pose new questions about Heidegger. Derrida, "The Philosopher's Hell," 270.

84. Ott's work has since been published in French and in English translation as *Martin Heidegger: A Political Life*.

85. On Heidegger's interest in technology, see Ferry and Renaut, *Heidegger and Nazism*, 55–80.

86. The phrases are from Wolin, "The French Heidegger Debate," 154. On Heidegger's opinion of the relationship between national socialism and technology, see his 1966 interview "Nur ein Gott kann uns noch retten," which appeared posthumously in *Der Spiegel* on May 31, 1976. The English translation can be found in Wolin, *The Heidegger Controversy*, 91–116, especially 111.

87. How so? Andrew Feenberg, *Heidegger and Marcuse*, 2, clarifies: "A world 'enframed' by technology is radically alien and hostile. The danger is not merely nuclear weapons or some similar threat to survival, but the obliteration of humanity's special status and dignity as the being through which the world takes on intelligibility and meaning." For Heidegger's own articulation of this issue see, *The Question Concerning Technology and Other Essays*, as well as his *Introduction to Metaphysics*. For secondary sources, consult Hubert L. Dreyfus, "Heidegger on Gaining a Free Relation to Technology."

88. The 1950 "Letter on Humanism" was Heidegger's response to a series of questions posed in 1946 by Jean Beaufret subsequent to his reading of Sartre's lecture "Existentialism is a Humanism." On Heidegger's rejection of metaphysics, see his *The End of Metaphysics*. Both the timing and the meaning of a "turn" in Heidegger's thought are much debated. In *Heidegger and French Philosophy*, Rockmore, for example, notes at least ten possible "turnings," each of which is linked to a different chronological moment in Heidegger's intellectual life (102–3). However, both Derrida and Lacoue-Labarthe are adamant about distinguishing the early from the late Heidegger, arguing that the philosopher was vulnerable to the seductions of Nazism because his early work suffered from what Wolin calls "a surfeit of metaphysical thinking." Wolin labels their perspective "a brilliant piece of hermeneutical chicanery" and argues that it is intended solely to recuperate Heidegger's later work (thus purified of any residual taint of Nazism) (152–53). Derrida, *De l'esprit*; Lacoue-Labarthe, *La fiction du politique*; and Wolin, "The French Heidegger Debate."

89. Davidson, "Questions Concerning Heidegger," 424.

90. The comment on the perils of the atomic bomb is an explicit reference to Heidegger's 1949 lecture "The Thing," in which he argues that the bomb is "the grossest of all gross confirmations" of the way that modern technology destroys the essence of 'thingness.' See, Heidegger, *What Is a Thing?*

91. Steiner, *Martin Heidegger*, 121.

92. The speech was delivered in Leipzig at an election rally held by German university professors. It is translated in Wolin, *The Heidegger Controversy*, 49–52.

93. In a letter written to Herbert Marcuse in 1948, Heidegger used the same defense, arguing, "It is difficult to converse with persons [. . .] who judge the beginning of the national socialist movement from its end." Marcuse dismissed this, stating, "We knew, and I myself saw it too, that the beginning [of national socialism] already contained the end." "An Exchange of Letters. Herbert Marcuse and Martin Heidegger," in Wolin, *The Heidegger Controversy,* 152–164, especially 162–63.

94. "The Self-Assertion of the German University," translated in Wolin, *The Heidegger Controversy,* 29–39.

95. Steiner had previously argued that Heidegger was not anti-Semitic. See Steiner, *Martin Heidegger,* 124.

96. Levinas, cited in Wolin, "The French Heidegger Debate," 148.

97. The quotation is from Heidegger's 3 November 1933 appeal to German students, in which he asks for their support for Hitler's plebiscite to retroactively sanction Germany's withdrawal from the League of Nations. The text is reprinted as "German Students" in Wolin, *The Heidegger Controversy,* 46–7.

98. "Martin Heidegger, 2ème partie," 14 December 1987.

99. Glucksmann is quoting from "Neue Forschungen und Urteile über Heidegger und Nationalsozialismus" *Der Spiegel,* 18 August 1986, 169.

100. Lacoue-Labarthe, *La fiction du politique,* 58.

101. The nomination is Alexander Kojève's. The full quote appeared in Kojève's *Introduction to the Reading of Hegel,* and reads as follows: "In our times Heidegger is the first to undertake a complete atheistic philosophy." Kojève quoted in Moyn, *Origins of the Other,* 10. See also Heidegger, "Only a God Can Save Us."

102. Ferry and Renaut, *Heidegger and Modernity,* 22.

103. Some of the errors were subsequently corrected for the English and German editions of the text.

104. Daney, "Le pari d'*Océaniques*," 162. Other journalists likewise acknowledged that at the end of the programs with Steiner and Boutang there was "neither a winner nor a loser," and viewers were not asked who "was the more competent, the more convincing, the more cunning, or the more telegenic." David, "George Steiner et Pierre Boutang," 150.

105. Daney, "Le pari d'*Océaniques*," 161.

106. First published as *La pensée 68,* Ferry and Renaut's book appeared in English as *French Philosophy of the Sixties.* The book created such a splash that it prompted the young duo's first television appearance together, on Bernard Pivot's *Apostrophes.* See "Sur quelques épisodes du XXème siècle," 22 November 1985.

107. Ferry and Renaut, *Heidegger and Modernity,* 15.

108. Ott, in Rockmore, *Heidegger and French Philosophy,* 155.

109. The term "yellow journalism" is attributable to Alderman's review of Farias's *Heidegger and Nazism,*" 472–73. Rockmore describes the book in *Heidegger and French Philosophy,* as "written in the style of a criminal dossier," 157.

110. Bourdieu, "Back to History: An Interview," 275. Bourdieu's article was first published in *Libération* on 10 March 1988.

111. Cazenave, interview.

112. Emmanuel Faye, *Heidegger.* Roughly contemporaneous interventions included Janicaud's two-volume *Heidegger en France,* recounting the tempestuous history of the philosopher's reception within the Hexagon, and Francis Kaplan's feature article "Pour en finir avec *Heidegger!*" in *Le Figaro littéraire,* which attacked the German philosopher and deemed Heideggarianism "not only *not* the greatest philosophy of the twentieth century but not even philosophy."

113. In the press, see, for example, Tertulian, "Coup de tonnerre dans le ciel heideggarien," and, especially, the interview between Emmanuel Faye and Lucien Degoy, "L'urgence d'une nouvelle prise de conscience." On television, see *Campus, le magazine de l'écrit,* 4 April 2005, and "Emmanuel Faye: 'Heidegger,'" 21 April 2005.

114. "Un manifeste en 13 langues sur internet pour défendre Heidegger," *Agence France Presse,* Paris, 19 May 2005, 5:11 p.m. GMT.

115. "Texte de soutien à l'essai d'Emmanuel Faye sur Heidegger," *Agence France Presse,* Paris, June 22, 2005, 10:37 a.m. GMT.

116. Lacavalerie, "Le philosophe au menu de l'agrégation."

117. Jaigu, quoted in Leclerc, "Un Martien chez les mutants," 38.

118. Perraud, "Le vol arrêté."

119. Boutang, in Saintville and Cazin, "Océaniques," 20.

120. Boutang variably gives the audience figures at between 500,000 and 800,000 (in Pascaud, "En pays de connaissances," 59) and between 500,000 and two million (in Saintville and Cazin, "Océaniques" 20).

121. Boutang, in Saintville and Cazin, "Océaniques," 20.

122. Rousso, *The Vichy Syndrome,* 273.

123. Jaigu in Lenoir, *Le temps de la responsabilité,* 161.

124. Boutang, interview.

125. Boutang, in Pascaud, "En pays de connaissances," 58.

126. Boutang, interview.

127. Jaigu, in Lenoir, *Le temps de la responsabilité,* 159. The recent globalization of "reality shows" that has brought versions of Donald Trump's *The Apprentice* to over twenty countries is but one example of this process. See, Huff, "Meet the other 'Trumps.'"

128. Jaigu in Lenoir, *Le temps de la responsabilité,* 159.

129. Boutang, interview.

130. Jaigu, interview. Boutang, quoted in Doussot, "Et Boutang, il tourne," 8; and Jaigu, quoted in Leclerc, "Un Martien chez les mutants," 38.

131. Jaigu, interview.

132. Ahearne, *French Cultural Policy Debates,* "Introduction," 7–9.

133. Bourdieu, *Distinction,* and Bourdieu, "Inequality at School," 62–69.

134. Pascaud, "En pays de connaissances," 58.

135. Boutang, interview.

136. Boutang realized that there weren't "thousands of solutions" to this dilemma: "Either you needed a place where the shows were available to view, or you needed a system of commercialization that made it possible to rent or purchase videocassettes of the shows." Boutang, in Saintville and Cazin, "Océaniques," 22.

137. Honecker was the communist leader of the German Democratic Republic.

138. Perraud, "Le vol arrêté," 60–61. By December the two-part broadcast on Heidegger was among the most requested of these cassettes.

139. Ibid.

140. Boutang, interview.

141. Jaigu, interview.

142. Maurice Papon was an official in the Vichy government, a collaborator, and an influential politician after the war. He was tried and convicted for crimes against humanity in 1997–98. Elderly and sick, he was released from his life sentence in 2002. Paul Touvier was head of the *milice* under Klaus Barbie and later a regional head of the Vichy government. In 1994, he was likewise tried and convicted for crimes against humanity. Touvier died in prison in 1996. René

Bousquet, the French chief of police from 1942 to 1943, played an important role in organizing mass deportations of Jews from France to the concentration camps. The third Frenchman accused of crimes against humanity, Bousquet was assassinated in 1993, prior to his trial.

143. During the 1989 *affaire du foulard*, two Muslim schoolgirls were expelled from their lycées for wearing traditional headscarves to school—an action purportedly prompted by concerns over protecting the separation of church and state (enshrined in French law since 1905). After more than a decade of debate, on 15 March 2004, President Jacques Chirac signed into effect a law on secularity banning the ostentatious display of religious symbols in French primary and secondary schools. Although not specifically identified as such, the law is presumed to have targeted the Islamic headscarf and the veil. As a result, its passage attracted considerable national and international attention.

144. C. Collman usefully deploys Lévi-Strauss's concept of *bricolage* to explain how Deleuzian theories of desire affected the way in which these "rationalist promises" were constructed. See his unpublished paper "From Descartes to Deleuze via Lévi-Strauss: Desiring Machines, Baroque Promises and the Architecture of Rationalization," proceedings of the first annual meeting of La petite societé de l'architecture, Honfleur, France, August 2006.

145. Daney, "Le pari d'*Océaniques*," 162.

146. Boutang, interview.

147. Excerpted from the July 1959 decree defining the responsibilities of the newly established Ministry of Cultural Affairs, cited in Lebovics, *Mona Lisa's Escort*, 89. Despite Malraux's reticence about television's cultural potential, his work in the culture industry supported the televising of philosophy by promoting a national climate favorable to the expansion of cultural discourse. Lebovics interprets Malraux's statement both as predicting a passive relationship to culture for the majority of the French population, and as suggestive of an interest in expanding cultural appreciation beyond the Hexagon. Interestingly, television has often been accused of fostering identical responses.

148. Missika and Wolton, *La folle du logis*, 18.

## Conclusion

1. The eight series were *Grain de Philo, Les mots de la philosophie, Pas si vite, Cogito, L'abécedaire de Gilles Deleuze, Philosophies, Télé qua non,* and *La philo selon Philippe* (a sit-com). *Inventer demain, Bouillon de culture,* and *Le cercle de minuit* regularly featured philosophy.

2. By 1997 one could philosophize in this fashion in more than fifty French cafés, half of them located in Paris. For numbers, see "Categorical Aperitif," 92. Philosopher Marc Sautet started the first *café-philo* at the Café des Phares on the Place de la Bastille in Paris. Sautet, *Un café pour Socrate,* and www.philos.org. Like philosophy on television, the *café-philo* generated concern about the vulgarization of the discipline. See Portevin and Ariane Poulantzas, "Les gens préfèrent aller au café-philo qu'acheter Kant."

3. Sautet founded the Cabinet de philosophie de France in 1992.

4. *Le temps des philosophes,* vols. 1-5.

5. These festivals were produced in conjunction with the Centre national du livre and have continued to the present day. The most recent *citéphilo* was held 4-24 November 2006. See http://www.citephilo.org.

6. "Philosophie: La nouvelle passion."

7. Comte-Sponville, *A Small Treatise on the Great Virtues,* back cover copy.

8. Jostein Gaarder, *Le monde de Sophie.* Sales figures from Catinchi, "Autopsie d'une inflation sémantique," 35.

9. "Le retour de la philo," 6, 8, 9 January 1997.

10. The very title, "Why is Philosophy So Popular?" of Bernard Pivot's 1996 show on *Bouillon de Culture* (a series that Pivot hosted for fifteen years after *Apostrophes* went off the air), both interrogated and confirmed the discipline's importance. "Pourquoi la philosophie est-elle si populaire?" 20 December 1996.

11. Mewshaw, "The Existential Burger."

12. "Categorical aperitif."

13. Christopher Phillips, the founder of www.philosophers.org, a website dedicated to what he calls "philosophical outreach," published *Socrates Café: A Fresh Taste of Philosophy* and runs a regular philo-café in San Francisco. Lou Marinoff, the author of *Plato, Not Prozac,* a professor of philosophy at City College, New York, and the founding president of the American Philosophical Practitioners Association, promotes philosophical counseling.

14. For a variety of reasons, these figures probably underestimate the number of shows dealing with philosophy that aired. First, the totals do not include reruns. Second, my statistical results (both here and throughout this book) are necessarily dictated by keyword searches conducted in files prepared by archivists over a fifty-year period in which standards for data collection and entry were regularly revised. Third, despite the fact that, until its dissolution in 1974, the ORTF attempted to catalogue all broadcasts produced prior to and during its mandate, and that INA continues this laborious task, before 1995 no provisions were made for documenting programs produced outside of INA's supervision, meaning that some records for La Cinqième, M6, Canal Plus, and ARTE are absent from the database. Fourth, through 2000, INA made no arrangements to document cable productions, and the data reflect this gap. Despite these discrepancies, as evidence for 90% of the field during the recent past, and virtually 99% for the preceding period, quantitative results derived from INA's database remain statistically useful. As cable is concerned, INA archivist Rachel Denoeud argues that because of its limited success, cable TV exerted a minimal impact on French television through the end of the century, and hence its absence is of negligible importance. Denoeud, interview with the author, 12 October 2000.

15. The French television production company La Sept was founded in Paris in 1986. Initially broadcast on TDF 1-2 Satellite and then, after 1990 on FR3, in 1992 it began sharing airtime with ARTE. To reflect this partnership, ARTE was renamed La Sept-ARTE in 1993. After 1994, La Cinquième filled the daytime schedule. La Sept-ARTE's appellation was changed again in 2000 to ARTE France.

16. Catinchi, "Autopsie d'une inflation sémantique."

17. Cavada, interviewed in Labé, "La philo dans une lucarne."

18. "Enfin, la philosophie sort des boudoirs!" 68. See also "Dossier Cogito"; Kerviel, "Le clip du professeur Field"; Fouilleron, "Philosophie"; "Nouvelle philosophie pour La Cinquième"; Sébert and Paulin, "Télégenie de la philo"; "À propos d'un abécédaire"; "Jackie Berroyer, un parfum de philo."

19. Lyotard, interviewed by Truong, "Élaborer des questions," 47.

20. "La Philosophie," 30 January 1996.

21. Luc Ferry, interview with the author, 23 November 1999; André Comte-Sponville, interview with the author, 9 November 1999.

22. Pierre-André Boutang, interview with the author, 17 May 2000.

23. Yves Jaigu, interview with the author, 25 November 1999.

24. Andreu, "Les philosophes crèvent l'écran," 27.

25. The series was later published in book form. See Bernard-Henri Lévy, in "Les aventures de la liberté," 13, 20, 27 March, and 3 April 1991; and Lévy, *Adventures on the Freedom Road*. He has also written and produced movies, some of them starring his wife, the actress Arielle Dombasle.

26. The fifty-six-minute monthly broadcast was divided into four sequences: a theme, often chosen for its contemporary ethical relevance; an exposé on the real-world jobs held by people with formal training in philosophy who had not pursued scholarly careers; a report on the places in which philosophy is practiced (cafés, clubs, libraries, etc.); and current events in philosophy (coverage of publications, seminars, critical dates). Alain Etchegoyen, interview with the author, 10 November 1999.

27. Luc Ferry, quoted in Sébert and Paulin, "Télégenie de la philo."

28. "Le progrès," 22 March 1997.

29. "L'effet Serres," 6 February 1991; Pinto, "Le journalisme philosophique," 36.

30. Luc Ferry, interview; and Emanuel, "Cultural Television," 146.

31. Bourdieu, "Le fonctionnement du champ intellectuel," 11.

32. Foucault, "The Masked Philosopher," 323.

33. The "contaminated blood affair" was a scandal that broke when it was revealed that the Centre national de transfusion sanguine had knowingly distributed blood carrying the AIDS virus to hemophiliacs in 1991. See "La notion de responsabilité," 14 February 1998; and "Procréation ou reproduction," 17 May 1997.

34. These include "Le sexe homocide," 16 March 1990 INA; "Ex Libris," 7 March 1991 INA; "Michel Piccoli," 5 January 1992.

35. Éribon, *Michel Foucault,* 324.

36. Roger-Pol Droit, "Philosophie populaire," *Le monde* 27 February 2004.

37. Godechot, "Le marché du livre philosophique," 25.

38. Michel Serres's *Le tiers instruit* sold more than 100,000 copies within a month of its release. Ibid., 25.

39. By 2006, the Université populaire had inspired imitators in Lyon, Arras, Picardie, and Narbonne, as well as in Mans in Belgium.

40. Michel Onfray, quoted in "Pivot . . . fermez les guillemets."

41. Doug Ireland, "Michel Onfray on Jean Meslier," http://direland.typepad .com/direland/2006/03/michel_onfray_o.html. Consulted 24 November 2006.

42. Badiou, "The Adventure of French Philosophy," 67, 71–72, 77.

43. Paulin, "Phil, Sophie, Flo et les autres,"; Fouilleron, "Philosophie."

44. Meunier, "France's Double-Talk on Globalization," 20.

45. Gordon and Meunier, "Globalization and French Cultural Identity," 25.

46. Strode, "French Identity in the Information Society," 322.

47. De Gaulle, quoted in a press conference at the inauguration of the ORTF, 14 December 1963.

48. Lecomte, "La liberalization de la télévision des années Mitterrand, 1981–1995," 58.

49. "France launches world TV channel," BBC News, http://news.bbc.co.uk/ go/pr/fr/-/2/hi/europe/6215170.stm, 6 December 2006.

50. Strode, "French identity in the Information Society," 325.

51. Hare, "Towards Demassification of French Television in the 21st Century?" 315.

52. Even Denis Huisman's appropriately titled, *Socrate sur Internet,* fails to complete this task.

## Printed Sources

"À propos d'un abécédaire." *Cahiers du cinema* 510 (February 1997): 20–21.
Achard, Maurice. "Lacan, comment?" *Télérama*, 30 March 1974.
Adorno, Theodor, and Max Horkheimer. *The Dialectic of Enlightenment.* Translated by John Cumming. New York: Herder and Herder, 1972.
———. *The Jargon of Authenticity.* Translated by Knut Tarnowski and Frederic Will. Evanston: Northwestern University Press, 1973.
Aguhlon, Maurice. *The French Republic, 1879–1992.* Translated by Antonia Nevill. Oxford: Blackwell, 1995.
Ahearne, Jeremy, ed. *French Cultural Policy Debates: A Reader.* London: Routledge, 2002.
Alderman, Harold. Review of Farias, *Heidegger and Nazism.* American Historical Review 96, no. 2 (April 1991): 472–73.
Allaire, Martine, and Marie-Thérèse Frank, eds. *Les politiques de l'éducation en France, de la maternelle au baccalauréat.* Paris: La documentation française, 1995.
Althusser, Louis. "La classe de philosophie" *Esprit*, June 1954: 858–64.
Anderson, Benedict. *Imagined Communities: Reflections on the Origin and Spread of Nationalism.* Rev. ed. London: Verso, 1991.
Andreu, Anne. "Les philosophes crèvent l'écran." *Le monde de l'éducation* 224 (January 1997): 27.
Aron, Raymond. *De Gaulle, Israël et les Juifs.* Paris: Plon 1968.
———. *Dix-huit leçons sur la société industrielle.* Paris: Gallimard, 1962. Originally published as *Le développement de la société industrielle et la stratification sociale,* vol. 1. Paris: Centre de documentation universitaire, 1956.
———. *The Elusive Revolution: Anatomy of a Student Revolt.* Translated by Gordon Clough. New York: Praeger, 1969.
———. *Introduction to the Philosophy of History.* Translated by George J. Irwin. New York: Beacon Press, 1961.

————. *Memoirs: Fifty Years of Political Reflection.* Translated by George Ho-
loch; foreword by Henry A. Kissinger. New York: Holmes and Meier, 1990.
————. *The Opium of the Intellectuals.* Translated by Terence Kilmartin. New
York: Doubleday, 1957.
————. *Paix et guerre entre les nations.* Paris: Calmann-Lévy, 1962. Translated
as *Peace and War: A Theory of International Relations.* Garden City, NY:
Doubleday, 1966.
————. *Le spectateur engagé: Entretiens avec Jean-Louis Missika et Dominique
Wolton.* Paris: Presses Pocket, 1982.
Aron, Robert. *Histoire de Vichy, 1940–1944.* Paris: Fayard, 1954.
Asline, Jacques. *La bataille de 20 heures: Quarante ans de journaux télévisés.*
Paris: Acropole, 1990.
"Au bord d'une eau vive." *Hebdo TV,* 12 October 1972.
Assaf, Antoine-Joseph. *Hommage à Pierre Boutang.* Paris: F.-X. de Guibert, 1998.
Assouline, Pierre. *Gaston Gallimard: Un demi-siècle d'édition française.* Paris:
Balland, 1984.
————. *L'épuration des intellectuels, 1944–1945.* Brussels: Complexe, 1985.
Assouline, Pierre, and Raoul Girardet. *Singulièrement libre: Entretiens.* Paris:
Perrin, 1990.
Aubral, François, and Xavier Delcourt. *Contre la nouvelle philosophie.* Paris: Gal-
limard, 1977.
Aymon, Jean-Paul. "Première chaîne, la critique de Jean-Paul Aymon." *France
Soir,* 4 October 1972.
Bachelard, Gaston. *L'air et les songes: Essai sur l'imagination des forces.* Paris:
José Corti, 1943.
————. *Essai sur la connaissance approchée.* Paris: Vrin, 1928.
————. *Le nouvel esprit scientifique.* Paris: Alcan, 1934.
————. *La psychanalyse du feu.* Paris: Nouvelle revue française, 1938.
"Bachelard parmi nous." *L'express,* October 1972.
Bachmann, Sophie. *L'éclatement de l'ORTF: La réforme de la délivrance.* Paris:
Harmattan, 1997.
Badiou, Alain. "The Adventure of French Philosophy." *New Left Review* 35
(September–October 2005): 67–77.
————. "Definition of Philosophy." In *Manifesto for Philosophy,* followed by two
essays, "The. Return of Philosophy Itself" and "Definition of Philosophy,"
edited, translated, and with an introduction by Norman Madarasz. Albany:
State University of New York Press, 1999.
Baker, Keith Michael. "On the Problem of the Ideological Origins of the French
Revolution." In *Modern European Intellectual History: Reappraisals and
New Perspectives,* edited by Dominick La Capra and Steven L. Kaplan,
197–219. Ithaca: Cornell University Press, 1982.
Ballantyne, Tony. *Orientalism and Race: Aryanism in the British Empire.* New
York: Palgrave Macmillan, 2002.
Barbier-Bouver, Christine, and others. "Catalogue des collections littéraires à la
télévision française." In *Littérature et Télévision,* vol. 7, edited by Pierre Bey-
lot and Stéphane Benassi, 221–31. Paris: Corlet-Télérama / Centre national du
cinéma.
Baron, Marie-Guy. "Les rigolos et le psychanalyste vedettes du week-end."
*France-Soir,* 12 March 1974.
Barthes, Roland. *The Death of the Author: Image, Music, Text.* Edited and trans-
lated by Stephen Heath. New York: Hill, 1977.

Baudrillard, Jean. *Simulacra and Simulation*. Translated by Sheila Faria Glaser. Ann Arbor: University of Michigan Press, 1994.

Bauman, Serge, and Alain Écouves. *L'information manipulée*. Paris: Éditions de la RPP, 1981.

Bavarez, Nicolas. *Raymond Aron: Un moraliste au temps des idéologies*. Paris: Flammarion, 1993.

Beaulieu, Jacqueline. *La télévision des réalisateurs: Pour la création, ils témoignent*. Paris: La documentation française, 1984.

Beauvoir, Simone de. *Force of Circumstance: The Autobiography of Simone de Beauvoir*. Translated by Richard Howard, with an introduction by Toril Moi. New York: Paragon House, 1992.

Bel, Monique. *Maurice Clavel*. Paris: Bayard, 1992.

Benda, Julien. *La trahison des clercs*. Paris: Grasset, 1927.

Bennington, Geoffrey, and Jacques Derrida. *Jacques Derrida*. Translated by Geoffrey Bennington. Chicago: University of Chicago Press, 1993.

Benoist, Paul. "La télévision et le télé-club en milieu rural." *Cahiers d'études de radio-télévision* 11 (1956): 207–15.

Berger, Gaston. *Phénoménologie du temps et prospective*. Foreword by Edouard Morot-Sir. Paris: Presses universitaires de France, 1964.

Berger, Yves. "L'éditeur ne doit pas donner des cours de maintien" *Les écrits de l'image* 6 (Spring 1995): 138–39.

Bersani, Jacques, and others. *La littérature en France de 1945 à 1961*. Paris: Bordas, 1982.

Bertholet, Denis. *Sartre*. Paris: Plon, 2000.

Birchall, Ian H. *Sartre against Stalinism*. New York: Berghahn Books, 2004.

Blum, Carol. *Rousseau and the Republic of Virtue: The Language of Politics in the French Revolution*. Ithaca: Cornell University Press, 1986.

Boschetti, Anna. *The Intellectual Enterprise: Sartre and "Les Temps Modernes."* Translated by Richard C. McCleary. Evanston: Northwestern University Press, 1985.

Bosséno, Christian. *200 téléastes français*. Paris: CinémAction–Corlet / Télérama, 1989.

Botton, Alain de. *The Consolations of Philosophy*. London: Hamish Hamilton, 2000.

Bourdieu, Pierre. "Back to History: An Interview." In Wolin, *The Heidegger Controversy* (see below), 274–81.

———. *Distinction: A Social Critique of the Judgement of Taste*. Translated by Richard Nice. Cambridge, MA: Harvard University Press, 1984.

———. "Le fonctionnement du champ intellectuel." *Regards sociologiques* 17–18 (1999): 5–27.

———. *Homo Academicus*. Translated by Peter Collier. Stanford: Stanford University Press, 1988.

———. "Inequality at School as the Key to Cultural Inequality (1966)." In Ahearne, *French Cultural Policy Debates* (see above), 62–69.

———. *L'ontologie politique de Martin Heidegger*. Paris: Éditions de minuit, 1987.

———. *Sur la télévision*, followed by *L'emprise du journalisme*. Paris: Liber, 1996.

———. *On Television*. Translated by Priscilla Parkhurst Ferguson. New York: New Press, 1998.

Bourdieu, Pierre, and Jean-Claude Passeron. *Les héritiers, les étudiants et la culture*. Paris: Éditions de minuit, 1964.

Bourdon, Jérôme. "Pour une histoire des programmes de la télévision." *Bulletin du Comité d'histoire de la télévision* 8 (1983): 32–42.

———. *Haute fidélité: Pouvoir et télévision, 1935–1994.* Paris: Éditions du Seuil, 1994.

———. *Histoire de la télévision sous de Gaulle.* Paris: Anthropos/INA, 1990.

———. "Old and New Ghosts: Public Service Television and the Popular—a History." *European Journal of Cultural Studies* 7 (August 2004): 283–304.

———. "Les techniques: Une complexité sans cesse croissante." In Bourdon and others, *La grande aventure du petit écran.*

Bourdon, Jérôme, and others. *La grande aventure du petit écran.* Paris: Musée d'histoire contemporaine / BDIC / INA, 1997.

Bourdon, Jérôme, and François Jost. *Penser la télévision: Actes du colloque de Cerisy.* Médias Recherches. Paris: Nathan/INA, 1998.

Bourg, Julian. "Forbidden to Forbid: Ethics in France, 1968–1981." Ph.D. diss., University of California at Berkeley, 2000.

Boutang, Pierre. *La république de Joinovici.* Paris: Amiot-Dumont, 1949.

Boutang, Pierre, and George Steiner. *Dialogues: Sur le mythe d'Antigone, sur le sacrifice d'Abraham.* Paris: Jean-Claude Lattès, 1994.

Bosséno, Christian. *200 téléastes français.* Paris: CinémAction–Corlet, 1989.

Bouscasse, Sylvie, and Denis Bourgeois. *Faut-il brûler les nouveaux philosophes? Le dossier du "procès."* Paris: Nouvelles éditions Oswald, 1978.

Brasey, Edouard. *L'effet Pivot.* Paris: Ramsay, 1987.

Brasseur, H. "Télévision et culture." *T.V.* 24 (April 1957): 7–10.

Brillet, Janine. "Bachelard." *Télé 7 Jours.* 14 October 1972.

———. "Non à Janique, oui à la Maison-Rouge." *Télé 7 Jours* 162 (27 April 1963): 66.

———. "Oui, nous voulons du football, mais aussi des pièces de Beckett." *Télé 7 Jours* 180 (31 April 1963): 70–71.

———. "La TV ne pense pas à ceux qui doivent se lever tôt." *Télé 7 jours* 136 (27 October 1962): 66.

Brigneau, François. *Mon après-guerre.* Paris: Éditions de Présent, 1985.

Brincourt, André. "Gaston Bachelard, le philosophe et son ombre." *Le Figaro littéraire* 30 (September 1972).

Brochand, Christain. *Histoire générale de la radio et de la télévision en France.* Paris: La documentation française, 1994.

Broglie, Gabriel de. "'Hors antenne' avec Pierre Desgraupes." *Les cahiers du Comité d'histoire de la télévision* 9 (1 April 1995): 7–20.

Brubaker, Rogers. *Citizenship and Nationhood in France and Germany.* Cambridge, MA: Harvard University Press, 1992.

Brunet, Sophie. *Pierre Schaeffer.* Paris: Richard-Masse, 1969.

Brunswic, Anne. "Pierre Dumayet et Robert Bober." *Téléscope* 9 (1995): 8–9

Brusini, Hervé, and Frances James. *Voir la vérité: Le journalisme de télévision.* Paris: Presses universitaires de France, 1982.

*Bulletin de la radio-télévision scolaire* 29 (1965).

Bussière, Michèle de, and others. *Radio et télévision au temps des "Événements d'Algérie," 1954–1962.* Foreword by Jean-Noël Jeanneney. Paris: Éditions de l'Harmattan, 1999.

Buxton, David, and others. *Télévision: La vérité à construire.* Paris: L'Harmattan, 1995.

"Ca va mieux en le disant." *Télérama,* 3 March 1974.

Camus, Albert. *The Outsider.* Translated by Joseph Laredo. London: Penguin Books, 2000.

Cardinal, Pierre. *Réalités,* April 1963, pp. 99–100.

Carey, John. *The Intellectuals and the Masses: Pride and Prejudice among the Literary Intelligentsi, 1880–1939.* London: Faber and Faber, 1992.

Cassirir, Ernst. "The Mind of the Enlightenment." In *The Philosophy of the Enlightenment,* translated by Fritz C. A. Koelln and James P. Pettigrove. Princeton: Princeton University Press, 1968.

Castoriadis, Cornelius. "Les divertisseurs." *Le nouvel observateur,* 20 June 1977. Translated as "The Diversionists." *Telos* 33 (Fall 1977): 102–6.

"Categorical Aperitif." *Economist* 342 (8 February 1997): 92.

Catinchi, Philippe-Jean. "Autopsie d'une inflation sémantique." *Le monde de l'éducation,* 24 January 1997: 35–36.

Cazenave, François, ed. *Jean d'Arcy parle: Pionnier et visionnaire de la télévision.* Paris: La documentation française, 1984.

"Ce mystérieux Service de la recherche O.R.T.F." *L'Aurore,* 13 September 1968.

Chalaby, Jean K. *The de Gaulle Presidency and the Media: Statism and Public Communications.* New York: Palgrave Macmillan, 2002.

Challon, Robert-G. "Le double visage du Service de la recherche: La critique institutionelle." *Le Figaro,* 18 March 1971.

Chalandon, Sorj, and Pascale Nivelle. *Crimes contre l'humanité: Barbie, Touvier, Bousquet, Papon.* Paris: Plon, 1998.

Chandler, David P. *Brother Number One: A Political Biography.* Rev. ed. Boulder, CO: Westview Press, 1999.

Chaniac, Régine. *La télévision de 1983 à 1993: Chronique des programmes et de leur public.* Paris: La documentation française, 1994.

Chapsal, Madeleine. "La parole de Lacan." *L'express,* 25 March 1974.

Charaudeau, Patrick. "Contrats de communication et ritualisations des débats télévisés." In *La télévision* (see next entry).

Chareaudeau, Patrick, and others, eds. *La télévision: Les débats culturels "Apostrophes."* Paris: Didier érudition, 1991.

Charle, Christoph. *Les élites de la République, 1880–1900.* Paris: Fayard, 1987.

Chartier, Roger. *The Cultural Origins of the French Revolution.* Translated by Lydia G. Cochrane. Durham: Duke University Press, 1991.

Chauveau, Agnès. *L'audiovisuel en liberté? Histoire de la Haute Autorité, 1982–1986.* Paris: Presses de Sciences Po, 1997.

Chevalier, Yves. *L' "expert" à la télévision: Traditions électives et légitimité médiatique.* Paris: CNRS Éditions, 1999.

Christians, Clifford G., and others. *Media Ethics.* New York: Longman, 1987.

Christofferson, Michael Scott. *French Intellectuals against the Left.* New York: Berghahn, 2004.

Clavel, Maurice. "Le touche-à-tout des profondeurs." *Le nouvel observateur,* 9 October 1972.

———. "Vous direz trois rosaries," *Le nouvel observateur* 633 (27 December 1977): 55.

Clément, Catherine. *La nuit et l'été: Rapport sur la culture à la télévision.* Paris: Éditions du Seuil / La documentation française, 2003.

Closets, Sophie de. *Quand la télévision aimait les écrivains.* Brussels: De Boeck / INA, 2004.

Cohen, Olivier. "La génération perdante." *Libération,* 27 May 1977.

Cohen-Solal, Annie. *Sartre: A Life*. Translated by Anna Cancogni; edited by Norman Macafee. New York: Pantheon Books, 1987.

Colquhoun, Robert. *Raymond Aron*. Vol. 1: *The Philosopher in History, 1905–1955;* Vol. 2: *The Sociologist in Society, 1955–1983*. Beverly Hills: Sage Publications, 1986.

Comte-Sponville, André. *Petit traité des grandes vertus*. Paris: Presses universitaires de France, 1995. Translated by Catherine Temerson as *A Small Treatise on the Great Virtues*. New York: Henry Holt, 2001.

Comte-Sponville, André, and Luc Ferry. *La sagesse des Modernes: Dix questions pour notre temps*. Paris: Robert Laffont, 1998.

Coq, Guy. "Qui a peur de la philosophie?" *Esprit* 38 (February 1980): 52–59.

Coq, Guy, and others. "Table Ronde." a transcript from the États Généraux de la philosophie, with Guy Coq, Roland Brunet, Jacques Derrida, Vladimir Jankélévitch, and Olivier Mongin. *Esprit* 38 (February 1980): 60–75.

Corbett, Anne, and Bob Moon. *Education in France: Continuity and Change in the Mitterrand years, 1981–1995*. London: Routledge, 1996.

Corbett, James. *Through French Windows*. Ann Arbor: University of Michigan Press, 1994.

Craipeau, Maria. "Le maître irremplaçable." *Les cahiers de la télévision* 9 (1963): 13–19.

Cros, Louis. *L'explosion scolaire*. Paris: Publication du comité universitaire d'information pédagogique, 1961.

Cuau, Bernard, and others, eds. *Au sujet de "Shoah": Le film de Claude Lanzmann*. Paris: Belin 1990.

Dallet, Sylvie, and Sophie Brunet. *Itinéraires d'un chercheur / A Career in Research*. Paris: Éditions du CERPS, 1997.

"Dans le cadre de la télévision éducative et scolaire en France, 2e partie." *T.V.* 32 (February 1958): 8–12.

"Dans la série "Un Certain Regard" le Service de la recherche de l'ORTF présente Jacques Lacan." Box Un Certain Regard, documentation écrite, INA.

Daney, Serge. "Le pari d'Océaniques." In *Le salaire du zappeur*, 160–63. Paris: P.O.L. Éditeur, 1993.

David, Catherine. "George Steiner et Pierre Boutang face à face." *Le nouvel observateur*, 21–27 September 1987.

Davidson, Arnold I. "Questions Concerning Heidegger: Opening the Debate." *Critical Inquiry* 15 (Winter 1989): 407–26.

Davies, Peter. *The National Front in France: Ideology, Discourse and Power*. London: Routledge, 1999.

Debord, Guy. *La société du spectacle*. Paris: Buchet-Chastel, 1967.

Debray, Régis. *L'état séducteur: Les révolutions médiologiques du pouvoir*. Paris: Gallimard, 1993.

———. *I.F. suite et fin*. Paris: Gallimard, 2000.

———. "Les pleureuses du printemps." *Le nouvel observateur*, 13 June 1977. Translated as "Springtime Weepers." *Telos* 33 (Fall 1977).

———. *Le pouvoir intellectuel en France*. Paris: Ramsay, 1979.

———. *Teachers, Writers, Celebrities: The Intellectuals of Modern France*. Translated by David Macey. London: NLB, 1981.

De Certeau, Michel. "Les sciences humaines et la mort de l'homme." *Études* 326 (March 1969): 344–60. Translated as "The Black Sun of Language: Foucault." in *Heterologies*, translated by Brian Massumi, with a foreword by Wlad Godzich. Minneapolis: University of Minnesota Press, 1997.

———. "Universities versus Popular Culture." In *Culture in the Plural,* edited and with an introduction by Luce Giard, translated and with an afterword by Tom Conley, 39–52. Minneapolis: University of Minnesota Press, 1997.

Dehée, Yannick. "Les magazines littéraires." In Jeanneney, *L'écho du siècle* (see below), 417–20.

Delacampagne, Christian. "Bilan d'un siècle de philosophie." *Magazine littéraire* 339 (January 1996): 27–28.

Delbos, Victor. *La philosophie française.* Paris: Librarie Plon, 1919.

Deleuze, Gilles. "L'homme, une existence douteuse." *Le nouvel observateur,* 1 June 1966, pp. 32–34.

———. "A propos des nouveaux philosophes et d'un problème plus général." *Minuit* (Supplément) 24 (5 June 1977). Translated as "On the New Philosophers and a More General Problem." *Discourse* 20, no. 3 (Fall 1998).

———. *Negotiations, 1972–1990.* New York: Columbia University Press, 1995.

Deleuze, Gilles, and Michel Foucault. "Les intellectuels et le pouvoir." *L'arc* 49 (1972).

Deleuze, Gilles, and Félix Guattari. *L'Anti-Oedipe.* Paris: Éditions de minuit, 1972.

———. *What is Philosophy?* New York: Columbia University Press, 1994.

Département radio-télévision scolaire, Institut pédagogique national, Paris. "Trois expériences françaises en matière d'enseignement direct." In *L'enseignement direct par la télévision, rapport du Séminaire européen, Rome 1966,* 69–87. Strasbourg: Conseil de la coopération culturelle du Conseil de l'Europe, 1967.

Derrida, Jacques. *De l'esprit: Heidegger et la question.* Paris: Galilée, 1987.

———. *Du droit à la philosophie.* Paris: Galilée, 1990.

———. "L'enfer des philosophes." *Le nouvel observateur,* 6–12 November 1987.

———. "The Institution." In Bennington and Derrida, *Jacques Derrida* (see above).

———. "The Philosopher's Hell." In Wolin, *The Heidegger Controversy* (see below), 264–73.

———. "The Right to Philosophy." In *Deconstruction in a Nutshell: A Conversation with Jacques Derrida,* edited with a commentary by John D. Caputo, 49–70. New York: Fordham University Press, 1997.

———. *Who's Afraid of Philosophy? Right to Philosophy I.* Translated by Jan Plug. Stanford: Stanford University Press, 2002.

Derrida, Jacques, and Bernard Stiegler. *Echographies of Television.* Translated by Jennifer Bajorek. Cambridge, UK: Polity Press, 2002.

Descartes, René. *Discourse on Method and Meditations* (1637). Translated and with an introduction by Laurence J. Lafleur. New York: Macmillan, 1988.

Descombes, Vincent. *Modern French Philosophy.* Cambridge: Cambridge University Press, 1996.

Desgraupes, Pierre. *Hors antenne: Entretiens avec Annick Peigné-Giuly et Marion Scali.* Paris: Quai Voltaire, 1992.

Dews, Peter. "The 'New Philosophers' and the End of Leftism." In *Radical Philosophy Reader,* edited by Roy Edgley and Richard Osborne, 361–84. London: Verso, 1985.

———. "The *Nouvelle philosophie* and Foucault." *Economy and Society* 8, no. 2 (May 1979): 127–71.

Diagne and others. *Gaston Berger: Introduction à une philosophie de l'avenir.* Dakar: Les nouvelles éditions africaines du Sénégal, 1997.

Diderot, Denis, and Le Rond d'Alembert. *Encyclopédie, ou Dictionnaire raisonné des sciences, des arts, et des métiers.* Facsimile of first edition of 1751–80.

Vol.12. Stuttgart–Bad Cannstatt: Friedrich Frommann Verlag / Günther Holalboog, 1967–67.

Dieuzeide, Henri. "Place et fonctions de la télévision et le système éducatif français." *Cahiers d'études de radio-télévision* 20 (1958): 338–55.

———. "La télévision menace-t-elle la culture?" *T.V.* 36 (June 1958): 14–17.

———. "Télévision scolaire et formation du futur téléspectateur." *T.V.* 52 (February 1960): 8–12.

Dirr, Peter, and Ronald Pedone. *Instructional Uses of Television by State and Land-Grant Colleges and Universities.* Washington DC: National Center for Education Statistics, Department of Health, Education and Welfare, September 1979.

Domenach, Jean-Marie. *Enquête sur les idées contemporaines.* Paris, Éditions du Seuil, 1981.

D'Ornano, Michel. *La manipulation des médias.* Paris: Le Figaro, Albatros / Veyrier, 1983.

Dosse, François. *History of Structuralism.* Translated by Deborah Glassman. Vol. 1: *The Rising Sign, 1945–1966;* Vol. 2: *The Sign Sets, 1967–present.* Minneapolis: University of Minnesota Press, 1997.

"Dossier Cogito." *Téléscope* 102 (27 May–2 June 1995): 6–9.

Dostoevsky, Fyodor. *The Devils* and *The Possessed.* Translated by David Magarshack. Harmondsworth: Penguin Books, 1971.

Doussot, Michel. "Et Boutang, il tourne." *Téléscope* 126 (23–29 March 1996): 8–9.

Drake, David. *Intellectuals and Politics in Post-War France.* Houndmills, UK: Palgrave, 2002.

Dreyfus, Dina, "L'enseignement de la philosophie et la télévision." *L'éducation nationale* 36 (10 December 1964).

———. "L'enseignement de la philosophie et la télévision: Sythèse des émissions de l'année 1964–1965." *Dossiers pédagogiques de la radio-télévision scolaire* 17 (1965): 49–52.

———. "L'enseignement de la philosophie et la télévision." *Cahiers philosophiques* 55 (June 1993): 99–104.

———. "Faire vivre la philosophie par l'image." *Bulletin de la radio-télévision scolaire* 76 (1968): 35–36.

Dreyfus, Dina, and F. Khodoss. "L'enseignement philosophique." *Les temps modernes* 21 (1965): 1001–47.

Dreyfus, Hubert L. "Heidegger on Gaining a Free Relation to Technology." In *Technology and the Politics of Knowledge,* edited by Andrew Feenberg and Alastair Hannay, 97–107. Bloomington: Indiana University Press, 1995.

Droit, Roger-Pol. *Philosophie et démocratie dans le monde.* Paris: UNESCO, 1995.

———. "Philosophie populaire: Avantages, inconvénients." *Le monde,* 27 February 2004.

Dumas, Michel. *La permission du maréchal: Trois jours en maraude avec le cercueil de Pétain.* Paris: Albin Michel, 2004.

Dumayet, Pierre. "L'interview télévisuelle." *Communications,* 1966. Record #480 in INA database.

Dumazedier, Joffre, and others. Report in "Les émissions littéraires amènent-elles les spectateurs à lire davantage?" *Le monde,* 30 November 1967.

———. *Télévision et éducation populaire: Les télé-clubs en France.* Paris: UNESCO, 1955.

Dupont, Alain. "Qui parle? Et dit: quoi? A qui? Comment? Pourquoi? Et avec quels effets?" *Télérama* 1065 (14 June 1970): 9–13.

Dupont, Pierre. "Des lectures pour tous au temps de lire: Pierre Dumayet retrouve le monde des livres à la télévision." *Le Figaro,* 27 January 1970.

Dupuis, George, and Jean Raux. *L'O.R.T.F.* Paris: Armand Colin, 1970.

Durkheim, Émile. *The Evolution of Educational Thought: Lectures on the Formation and Development of Secondary Education in France.* Translated by Peter Collins. London: Routledge and Kegan Paul, 1977.

Emanuel, Susan. "Cultural Television: Current French Critiques." *French Cultural Studies* 5 (1994): 139–50.

"Émissions télévisées pour l'année 1965–1966." *Bulletin de la radio-télévision scolaire* 31 (1965): 65–66.

"Enfin, la philosophie sort des boudoirs!" *Les écrits de l'image* 14 (Spring 1997): 68–72.

Épin, Stéphane. "Au Service de la recherche cent artistes et techniciens travaillent pour la TV de demain." *Télé 7 Jours* 253 (23 January 1965).

Eribon, Didier. *Michel Foucault.* Translated by Betsy Wing. Cambridge, MA: Harvard University Press, 1991.

———. *Michel Foucault et ses contemporains.* Paris: Fayard, 1994.

Esquenazi, Jean-Pierre. *Télévision et démocratie: Le politique à la télévision française, 1958–1990.* Paris: Presses universitaires de France, 1999.

Establet, Roger. *L'école est-elle rentable?* Paris: Presses universitaires de France, 1987.

Establet, Roger, and Georges Felouzis. *Livre et télévision: Concurrence ou interaction?* Paris: Presses universitaires de France, 1992.

Estienne, Henri. *Traité de la conformité du langage françois avec le grec.* Geneva: Slatkine Reprints, 1972. Originally published in Geneva in 2 volumes in 1565 and 1576, and in Paris in 1579.

"Êtes-vous un 'nouveau philosophe'?" *Le nouvel observateur,* 1 August 1977.

Ewald, François. "Une philosophie pour notre temps." *Magazine littéraire* 320 (August 1994): 18–26.

Fabiani, Jean-Louis. *Les philosophes de la République.* Paris: Éditions de Minuit, 1988.

Faye, Emmanuel. *Heidegger: L'introduction du nazisme dans la philosophie.* Paris: Albin Michel, 2005.

Faye, Emmanuel, and Lucien Degoy. "L'urgence d'une nouvelle prise de conscience." *L'humanité,* 28 April 2005, p. 22.

Faye, Jean-Pierre. "Heidegger et la 'révolution.'" *Médiations* 3 (1961).

———. "La lecture et l'énoncé." *Critique* 237 (February 1967).

Farias, Victor. *Heidegger et le Nazisme.* Translated from the Spanish by Myriam Benarroch and Jean-Baptiste Grasset. Paris: Verdier, 1987.

Faubion, James D. "Introduction." In Foucault, *Aesthetics, Method, and Epistemology* (see below).

Fédier, François. "À propos de Heidegger: Une lecture dénoncée." *Critique* 242 (July 1967).

———. *Heidegger: Anatomie d'un scandale.* Paris: Robert Laffont, 1988.

———. "Trois attaques contre Heidegger." *Critique* 234 (October 1966).

Feenberg, Andrew. *Heidegger and Marcuse: The Catastrophe and Redemption of History.* New York: Routledge, 2005.

Ferry, Luc, and Alain Renaut. *French Philosophy of the Sixties; An Essay on Anti-humanism*. Translated by Mary Schnackenberg Cattani. Amherst: University of Massachusetts Press, 1990.

———. *Heidegger et les modernes*. Paris: Grasset, 1988. Translated by Franklin Philip as *Heidegger and Modernity*. Chicago: University of Chicago Press, 1990.

———. *Philosopher à 18 ans*. Paris: Grasset, 1999.

Finkielkraut, Alain. *L'avenir d'une négation: Réflexion sur la question du géno-cide*. Paris: Éditions du Seuil, 1982.

———. *La défaite de la pensée*. Paris: Gallimard, 1987. Translated by Judith Friedlander as *The Defeat of the Mind*. New York: Columbia University Press, 1995.

———. "Préface." In *Le XXe siècle en France: Art, politique, philosophie*. Edited by Alexandre Abensour. Paris: Berger-Levrault, 2000.

———. *Remembering in Vain: The Klaus Barbie Trial and Crimes against Humanity*. Translated by Roxanne Lapidus with an introduction by Alice Y. Kaplan. New York: Columbia University Press, 1992.

Fléchet, Jean. "Réflexions sur les émissions de philosophie, du point de vue de leur réalisation." *Bulletin de la radio-télévision scolaire* 30 (October 1965): 16–19.

———. "Trente ans après, entretien avec Jean Fléchet." *Cahiers philosophiques* 55 (June 1993): 105–12.

Fouché, Pascal, ed. *L'édition française depuis 1945*. Paris: Editions du Cercle de la librairie, 1998.

"Foucault comme des petits pains." *Le nouvel observateur*, 10 August 1966, p. 29.

Foucault, Michel. *Aesthetics, Method, and Epistemology*. Edited and with an introduction by James D. Faubion, translated by Robert Hurley and others. New York: New Press, 1998.

———. *Dits et écrits, 1954–1988*. Vol. 1: *1954–1969*; vol. 2: *1970–1975*; vol. 3: *1976–1979*; vol. 4: *1980–1988*. Paris: Gallimard, 1994.

———. *Folie et déraison: Histoire de la folie à l'âge classique*. Paris: Plon, 1961. Translated and abridged by Richard Howard as *Madness and Civilization*, with an Introduction by José Barchilon. New York: Pantheon, 1964.

———. "La grande colère des faits." *Le nouvel observateur*, 9 May 1977.

———. *The History of Sexuality*. Vol. 1: *An Introduction*. Translated by Richard Hurley. New York: Vintage Books, 1990.

———. "The Masked Philosopher." In *Michel Foucault: Ethics, Subjectivity and Truth*, edited by Paul Rabinow, translated by Robert Hurley and others, 321–28. New York: New Press, 1997.

———. *Les mots et les choses: Une archéologie des sciences humaines*. Paris: Gallimard, 1966. Translated as *The Order of Things: An Archeology of the Human Sciences*. New York: Vintage Books, 1994.

———. *La naissance de la clinique*. Paris: Presses universitaires de France, 1963.

———. "Philosophie et psychologie." *Dossiers pédagogique de la radio-télévision scolaire*, 27 February 1965, pp. 65–71. Translated by Robert Hurley as "Philosophy and Psychology," in Foucault, *Aesthetics, Method, and Epistemology* (see above).

———. "Philosophie et vérité." *Dossiers pédagogiques de la radio-télévision scolaire*, 27 March 1965, pp.1–11. Revised version in Foucault, *Dits et écrits* (see above), 1:438–64.

———. "Radioscopie de Michel Foucault." Reprinted in *Dits et écrits*, vol. 2.

————. "Réponse au Cercle d'épistémologie." *Cahiers pour l'analyse* 9: *Généalogie des sciences*, Summer 1968, pp. 9–40.

————. "The Return of Morality." In *Foucault, Politics, Philosophy, Culture: Interviews and Other Writings, 1977–1984*, edited and with an introduction by Lawrence Kritzman, translated by Alan Sheridan and others, 242–54. New York: Routledge, 1990.

————. "Truth and Power." In *Power/Knowledge: Selected Interviews and Other Writings, 1972–1977*, edited by Colin Gordon, 109–33. New York: Pantheon Books, 1980.

————. "What is Enlightenment?" In *The Foucault Reader*, edited and translated by Paul Rabinow. Harmondsworth: Penguin Books, 1984.

————. "What is an Author." In *Language, Counter-memory, Practice: Selected Essays and Interviews by Michel Foucault*, edited and with an introduction by Donald F. Bouchard, translated by Donald F. Bouchard and Sherry Simon. Ithaca: Cornell University Press, 1996.

Foucault, Michel, with Raymond Bellours. "The Order of Things," translated by John Johnston, in *Aesthetics, Method, and Epistemology*, 261–67. First published in *Les lettres françaises* 1125 (31 March–6 April 1966): 3–4.

Fouilleron, Charlotte. "Philosophie: La télévision prend le temps de penser." *La croix*, 14 February 1997, p. 23.

"Freud est grand et Lacan est son prophète." *Paris Match*, 9 March 1974.

Fumaroli, Marc. *L'état culturel: Essai sur une religion moderne*. Paris: Fallois, 1992.

Gaarder, Jostein. *Le monde de Sophie*. Paris: Éditions du Seuil, 1995.

Gachoud, François. *Maurice Clavel: Du glaive à la foi*. Paris: Presses universitaires de France, 1982.

Gans, Herbert J. *Popular Culture and High Culture: An Analysis and Evaluation of Taste*. Rev. ed. New York: Basic Books, 1999.

Gaspard, Françoise. *A Small City in France*. Translated by Arthur Goldhammer. Cambridge, MA: Harvard University Press, 1995.

Gildea, Robert. *France since 1945*. Oxford: Oxford University Press, 1996.

Glucksmann, André. *La cuisinière et le mangeur d'hommes: Essai sur l'État, le marxisme, les camps de concentration*. Paris: Éditions du Seuil, 1975.

————. *Les maîtres penseurs*. Paris: Grasset & Fasquelle, 1977. Translated by Brian Pearce as *The Master Thinkers*. New York: Harper and Row, 1980.

Godechot, Olivier. "Le marché du livre philosophique." *Actes de la recherche en sciences sociales* 130 (1999): 11–28.

Golsan, Richard. *Vichy's Afterlife: History and Counterhistory in Postwar France*. Lincoln: University of Nebraska Press, 2000.

Gordon, Dan. *Citizens without Sovereignty: Equality and Sociability in French Thought, 1670–1789*. Princeton: Princeton University Press, 1994.

Gordon, Philip H., and Sophie Meunier, "Globalization and French Cultural Identity." *French Politics, Culture and Society* 19, no. 1 (Spring 2001): 22–41.

Greenfeld, Liah. *Nationalism: Five Roads to Modernity*. Reprint. Cambridge, MA: Harvard University Press, 2003.

Grolleron, Anne. "TF1." In Jeanneey, *L'écho du siècle* (see below), 138–43.

Gschwind-Holtzer, Gisèle. "'Je vais vous presenter mes invites . . . ,' ou Apostrophes et l'acte de presentation." *La médiacritique littéraire, Semen* 5, GRELIS, edited by Jean Peytard. Paris: Annales littéraires de l'Université de Besançon, 1990.

Guérin, Jean-Yves. *Camus: Portrait de l'artiste en citoyen.* Paris: François Bourin, 1993.

Guérin, Jean-Yves, ed. *Camus et la politique.* Paris: Harmattan, 1986.

Gutting, Gary. *French Philosophy in the Twentieth Century.* Cambridge: Cambridge University Press, 2001.

———. *Michel Foucault's Archeology of Scientific Reason.* Cambridge: Cambridge University Press, 1989.

Habermas, Jürgen. *The Structural Transformation of the Public Sphere.* Translated by Thomas Burger and Frederick Lawrence. Cambridge, MA: MIT Press, 1996.

Hall, Catherine. *Civilising Subjects: Colony and Metropole in the English Imagination, 1830–1867.* Chicago: University of Chicago Press, 2002.

Hamon, Hervé, and Patrick Rotman. *Les intellocrates: Expédition en haute intelligentsia.* Paris: Ramsay, 1981.

Hanley, L., and others, eds. *Contemporary France: Politics and Society since 1945.* London: Routledge, 1989.

Harder, Yves-Jean. "Philosophie et vérité, présentation de l'émission," documentation insert for *Philosophie et vérité,* 4–11, in the video series *Le temps des philosophes.* Paris: CNDP/Nathan, 1993.

Hare, Geoff. "Towards Demassification of French Television in the 21st Century?" *Modern & Contemporary France* 7, no. 3 (1999): 307–17.

Hargreaves, Alec G. "Gatekeepers and Gateways: Post-colonial Minorities and French Television." in *Post-Colonial Cultures in France,* edited by Hargreaves and Mark McKinney, 84–98. London: Routledge, 1997.

Hayman, Ronald. *Sartre: A Life.* New York: Simon and Schuster, 1987.

Heidegger, Martin. *The End of Metaphysics.* Translated by Joan Stambaugh. New York: Harper and Row, 1973.

———. *Introduction to Metaphysics* (1935). Translated by Gregory Fried and Richard Polt. New Haven: Yale University Press, 2000.

———. "Letter on Humanism." In *Basic Writings,* 2nd ed. (1964), edited and with an introduction by David Farrell Krell, 213–66. San Francisico: Harper, 1993.

———. "Nur ein Gott kann uns noch retten." *Der Spiegel,* 31 May 1976. Translated by Maria P. Alter and John D. Caputo as " 'Only a God Can Save Us': *Der Spiegel*'s Interview with Martin Heidegger," in Wolin, *The Heidegger Controversy* (see below), 91–116.

———. *The Question Concerning Technology and Other Essays.* Translated by William Lovitt. New York: Harper and Row, 1977.

———. *What Is a Thing?* Translated by W. B. Barton Jr, and Vera Deutsch. Chicago: Regnery, 1968.

Hercet, G. "Télévision et politique." *Tribune socialiste,* 20 February 1969. Reprinted in Georges Dupuis and Jean Raux, *L'O.R.T.F.,* 13–15. Paris: Armand Colin, 1970.

Hirsch, Arthur. *The French Left: A History and Overview.* Montreal: Black Rose Books, 1982.

Hobsbawm, Eric. *Nations and Nationalism since 1970.* 2nd ed. Cambridge: Cambridge University Press, 1990.

Honderich, Ted, ed. *Oxford Companion to Philosophy.* Oxford: Oxford University Press, 1995.

Hourmant, François. *Le désenchantement des clercs: Figures de l'intellectuel dans l'après-mai 68.* Rennes: Presses universitaires de Rennes, 1997.

Huff, Richard. "Meet the other 'Trumps.'" *New York Daily News,* 23 February 2005.

Huisman, Denis. *Dictionnaire des 1000 oeuvres-clés de la philosophie universelle.* Paris: Nathan, 1994.

———. *Le guide de l'étudiant en philosophie.* Foreword by Georges Davy. Paris: Presses universitaires de France, 1955.

———. *Socrate sur Internet.* Paris: De Fallois, 1997.

———. *Visages de la philosophie.* Photographs by Louis Monier. Paris: Arléa, 2000.

Huisman, Denis, ed. *Dictionnaire des philosophes.* 2 vols., 4000 entries. Paris: Presses universitaires de France, 1984.

———. *Histoire de la philosophie française.* Paris: Perrin, 2002.

———. *Intégrales de Philo.* Separate editions on Plato, Aristotle, Kant, Machiavelli, Descartes, Spinoza, Rousseau, Hegel, Comte, Nietzsche, and others. Paris: Nathan.

Huisman, Denis, and G. Deledalle. *Les philosophes français d'aujourd'hui.* Paris: SEDES, 1959.

Huisman, Denis, and A. Vergez. *Histoire des philosophes illustrée par les textes.* Paris: Nathan, 1996.

———. *La philosophie contemporaine en cent textes choisis.* Paris: Nathan, 1973.

Huisman, Denis, and Alfred Weber. *Histoire de la philosophie européenne.* 2 vols. Paris: Fischbacher, 1957.

Huisman, Denis, and Marie-Agnès Malfray, eds. *Les pages les plus célèbres de la philosophie occidentale.* Paris: Perrin, 1989.

———. *Les plus grands textes de la philosophie orientale.* Paris: Albin Michel, 1992.

Huret, Marcel. *Ciné actualités: Histoire de la presse filmée, 1895–1980.* Paris: Henri Veyrier, 1984.

Hutton, Patrick H. "The Postwar Politics of Philippe Ariès." *Journal of Contemporary History* 34, no. 3 (1999): 365–81.

Igounet, Valérie. *Histoire du négationnisme en France.* Paris: Éditions du Seuil, 2000.

Insdorf, Annette. *Indelible Shadows: Film and the Holocaust.* Foreword by Elie Wiesel. 3rd edition. Cambridge: Cambridge University Press, 2002.

"Inventaire des émissions de philosophie produites et diffusées par la Radio-télévision scolaire entre janvier1965 et mars 1968." *Cahiers philosophiques* 55 (June 1993): 143–49.

"Jackie Berroyer, un parfum de philo." *Le monde,* 25–26 January 1998, p. 4.

"Jacques Lacan, psychanalyste." *Télérama,* 9 March 1974.

"Jacques Lacan." *Le nouvel observateur,* 11 March 1974.

"Jacques Lacan à la télévision." *Psychologie,* April 1974.

Jambet, Christian, and Guy Lardreau. *L'ange: Pour une cynégétique du semblant.* Paris: Grasset, 1976.

Janabegloo, Ramin. *Entretiens de Georges Steiner et Ramin Jahanbegloo.* Paris: Éditions du Félin, 2000.

Janicaud, Dominique. *Heidegger en France.* 2 vols. Paris: Albin Michel, 2001.

Jankélévitch, Vladimir. *Le je-ne-sais-quoi et le presque-rien.* Rev. ed. Paris: Éditions du Seuil, 1980.

Jay, Martin. *Downcast Eyes: The Denigration of Vision in Twentieth-Century French Thought.* Berkeley: University of California Press, 1994.

Jeanneney, Jean-Noël. *Une histoire des médias, des origines à nos jours.* Paris: Éditions du Seuil, 1996.

Jeanneney, Jean-Noël, ed. *L'écho du siècle: Dictionnaire historique de la radio et de la télévision en France.* Paris: Hachette littératures, 1999.

Jeanson, Francis. *Sartre par lui-même.* Paris: Éditions du Seuil, 1955.

Jennings, Jeremy. "Of Treason, Blindness and Silence: Dilemmas of the Intellectual in Modern France." In *Intellectuals in Politics: From the Dreyfus affair to Salman Rushdie,* edited by Jeremy Jennings and Anthony Kemp-Welch, 65–85. London: Routledge, 1997.

Jennings, Jeremy, ed. *Intellectuals in Twentieth-Century France: Mandarins and Samurais.* New York: St Martin's Press, 1993.

Judaken, Jonathan. "Alain Finkielkraut and the Nouveaux Philosophes: French-Jewish Intellectuals, the Afterlives of May '68 and the Rebirth of the National Icon." *Historical Reflections / Reflections Historiques* 32, no. 1. (2006): 193–223.

Judt, Tony. *The Burden of Responsibility: Blum, Camus, Aron, and the French Twentieth Century.* Chicago: University of Chicago Press, 1998.

———. *Past Imperfect: French Intellectuals, 1944–1956.* Berkeley: University of California Press, 1992.

Julliard, Jacques, and Michel Winock, eds. *Dictionnaire des intellectuels français.* Paris: Éditions du Seuil, 1997.

Kant, Immanuel. "What is Enlightenment?" In *The Portable Age of Reason Reader,* edited and with an introduction by Crane Brinton, 298–307. New York: Viking, 1956.

Kaplan, Alice. *The Collaborator: The Trial and Execution of Robert Brasillach.* Chicago: University of Chicago Press, 2000.

———. "Introduction." In Finkielkraut, *Remembering in Vain* (see above), ix–xxxvi.

Kaplan, Francis. "Pour en finir avec Heidegger!" *Le Figaro littéraire,* November 27, 2003, p. 6.

Kauppi, Niilo. *French Intellectual Nobility: Institutional and Symbolic Transformations in the Post-Sartrian Era.* Albany: State University of New York Press, 1996.

Keegan, Desmond. *Foundations of Distance Education.* New York: Routledge, 1996.

Kellner, Douglas. *Television and the Crisis of Democracy.* Boulder, CO: Westview Press, 1990.

Kelly, Michael. *The Cultural and Intellectual Rebuilding of France after the Second World War.* New York: Palgrave Macmillan, 2004.

Khilnani, Sunil. *Arguing Revolution: The Intellectual Left in Postwar France.* New Haven: Yale University Press, 1993.

Kiernan, Ben. *The Pol Pot Regime: Race, Power, and Genocide in Cambodia under the Khmer Rouge, 1975–79.* New Haven: Yale University Press, 1996.

———. *How Pol Pot Came to Power: Colonialism, Nationalism and Communism in Cambodia, 1930–1975.* 2nd ed. New Haven: Yale University Press, 2004.

Kerviel, Sylvie. "Le clip du professeur Field." *Le monde,* 22–23 September 1996.

Klarsfeld, Serge. *Les enfants d'Izieu: Une tragédie juive.* Paris: A. Z. Repro, 1984.

Klibansky, Raymond, and David Pears, eds. *La philosophie en Europe.* Compiled and published at the request of UNESCO. Paris: Gallimard, 1993.

Koulberg, André. "L'affaire Barbie: Stratégie de la mémoire et justification du mal dans les années quatre-vingt en France." *Les temps modernes* 495 (October 1987): 100–116.

Kubler, Thierry, and Emmanuel Lemieux. *Cognac-Jay 1940.* Paris: Plume, 1990.

Kuhn, Raymond. "The Politics of Broadcasting in France, 1974–1978." Ph.D. diss., University of Warwick, 1980.

———. *The Media in France.* London: Routledge, 1995.

Kuisel, Richard F. *Seducing the French: The Dilemma of Americanization.* Berkeley: University of California Press, 1993.

Labé, Yves-Marie. "La philo dans une lucarne." *Le monde de l'éducation,* 24 January 1997.

Lacan, Jacques. *Television.* Translated by Denis Hollier, Rosalind Kraus, and Annette Michelson; edited by Joan Copjec. New York: Norton, 1990.

Lacavalerie, Xavier. "Le philosophe au menu de l'agrégation: Heidegger est déterré." *Télérama,* 2891 (8 June 2005).

Lacoue-Labarthe, Philippe. *La fiction du politique.* Paris: Christian Bourgeois, 1987.

Lacouture, Jean. *De Gaulle: The Ruler, 1945–1970.* Translated by Alan Sheridan. New York: Norton, 1992.

Lakanal, Joseph. *Rapport fait au Conseil des cinq-cents, par Lakanal, un de ses membres, sur les livres élémentaires présentés au concours ouvert par la loi du 9 pluviôse, an II.* Paris: De l'Imprimerie nationale, brumaire, an IV [1795].

Lalou, Étienne. *Regards neufs sur la télévision.* Paris: Tardy, 1957.

Lamy, Jean-Claude. *René Julliard.* Paris: Julliard, 1992.

Langouët, G. *Technologie de l'éducation et démocratization de l'enseignement: Méthodes pédagogiques et classes sociales.* Paris: Presses universitaires de France, 1982.

Lanzmann, Claude. "The Obscenity of Understanding: An Evening with Claude Lanzmann." In *Trauma: Explorations in Memory,* edited by Cathy Caruth, 200–220. Baltimore: Johns Hopkins University Press.

Lavallard, M. H., and others. "Entretien entre les membres de l'équipe de travail." *Bulletin de la radio-télévision scolaire* 36 (1966): 31–32.

Lebovics, Herman. *Mona Lisa's Escort: André Malraux and the Reinvention of French Culture.* Ithaca: Cornell University Press, 1999.

———. *True France: The Wars over Cultural Identity, 1900–1945.* Ithaca: Cornell University Press, 1992.

Leclerc, Thierry. "Antenne 2: La puissance ou la gloire?" *Télérama* 1991 (9 March 1988): 49–52.

———. "Un Martien chez les mutants." *Télérama* 2013 (10 August 1988): 38–39.

Lecomte, Monia. "La libéralization de la télévision des années Mitterrand, 1981–1995," *Modern & Contemporary France* 6, no. 1 (1998): 49–59.

———. "La mission culturelle de la télévision française." *French Cultural Studies* 10 (1999): 39–50.

Lecomte, Patrick. *Communication, télévision et démocratie.* Lyon: Presses universitaires de Lyon, 1993.

Lecourt, Dominique. *The Mediocracy: French Philosophy since the mid-1970s.* Translated by Gregory Elliott. London: Verso, 2001.

Lejeune, Claude. "Psychoanalyse mon beau souci." *Combat,* 30 March 1974.

Lenoir, Frédéric. *Le temps de la responsibilité: Entretiens sur l'éthique.* Paris: Fayard, 1991.

Le Roy Ladurie, Emmanuel. *Le quotidien de Paris,* 7 February 1983. Cited in Rousso, *The Vichy Syndrome* (see below), 210n80.

"Les succès du mois." *L'express,* 8–14 August 1966, p. 32.

Lescure, Jean. *Un été avec Bachelard.* Paris: Luneau Ascot, 1983.

Lévy, Bernard-Henri. *Adventures on the Freedom Road.* Translated by Richard Veasey. London: Harvill Press, 1995.

————. *Bangla-Desh: Nationalisme dans la révolution.* Paris: Maspéro, 1973.

————. *La barbarie à visage humaine.* Paris: Grasset & Fasquelle, 1977. Translated by George Holoch as *Barbarism with a Human Face.* New York: Harper and Row, 1979.

————. *Éloge des intellectuels.* Paris: Grasset, 1987.

————. *L'idéologie française.* Paris: Grasset, 1981.

————. "Les Nouveaux Philosophes." *Les nouvelles littéraires,* 10 June 1976.

————. "La nouvelle philosophie n'existe pas." *La nef* 66 (1977).

————. "La télévision de Jacques Lacan." *France quotidien,* March 1974.

Lévy, Marie-Françoise. "La création des télé-clubs: L'éxpérience de l'Aisne." In Lévy, *La télévision dans la République* (see below).

————. "L'immigration dans la production documentaire, le magazine, la fiction française: Variations autour d'un thème, 1975–1991." In *Télévisions d'Europe et immigration,* edited by Claire Frachon and Marion Vargaftig, 57–65. Paris: INA / Association dialogue entre les cultures, 1993.

————. "Jean D'Arcy." In Jeanneney, *L'écho du siècle* (see above), 283–84.

Lévy, Marie-Françoise, ed. *La télévision dans la République: Les années 50.* Paris: Complexe 1999.

Lévy-Bruhl, Lucien. *History of Modern Philosophy in France* (1899). Translated by G. Coblence and W. H. Carruth. New York: Lenox Hill Publishing, 1971.

Lewis, H. D. *The French Education System.* London: Croom Helm, 1985.

Linklater, Magnus, Isabel Hilton, and Neal Ascherson. *The Nazi Legacy: Klaus Barbie and the International Fascist Connection.* New York: Holt, Rinehart and Winston, 1985.

Loiseau, Jean-Claude. "La bande à Schaeffer." *L'express,* 22–28 February 1971.

Löwith, Karl. "Les implications politiques de la philosophie de l'existence chez Heidegger." *Les temps modernes* 2 (1946): 346–60.

Lustière, Colette. "Le journal télévisé: L'évolution des techniques et des dispositifs." In Marie-Françoise Lévy, *La télévision dans la République* (see above).

Lyotard, Jean–François. *La condition postmoderne: Rapport sur le savoir.* Paris: Les Éditions de Minuit, 1979.

————. *Le différend.* Paris: Les Éditions de Minuit, 1983.

————. *Heidegger et "les juifs."* Paris: Galilée, 1988.

————. *Instructions païennes.* Paris: Galilée, 1977.

————. "A Podium without a Podium." In *Political Writings* (see below), 90-95.

————. *Political Writings.* Translated by Bill Readings and Kevin Paul Geiman, with a foreword by Bill Readings. Minneapolis: University of Minnesota Press, 1993.

————. *La postmoderne expliqué aux enfants: Correspondance 1982–1985.* Paris: Galilée, 1986.

————. "Tombeau de l'intellectuel." *Le monde,* 8 October 1983. Translated as "Tomb of the Intellectual," in Lyotard, *Political Writings* (see above), 3–7.

Macciocchi, Maria-Antoinetta. *De la France.* Paris: Éditions du Seuil, 1977.

Macey, David. *The Lives of Michel Foucault.* New York: Vintage, 1995.

Maggiori, Robert. "Heil Heidegger!" *Libération,* 16 October 1987.

Mah, Harold. "The Epistemology of the Sentence: Language, Civility, and Identity in France and Germany, Diderot to Nietzsche." *Représentations* 47 (1994).

Maisongrande, Henri. "Gaston Bachelard faisait lui-même sa cuisine et son marché." *Télé 7 Jours,* 2 October 1974.

Manigand, C., and I. Veyrat-Masson, "Les journalistes et la crise." In *Comité d'histoire de la télévision, Mai 68 à la ORTF.* Paris: La documentation française, 1987.

Maréchal, Denis. "Le Service de la recherche." In Jeanneney, *L'écho du siècle* (see above), 137–38.

Margolin, Jean-Claude. *Bachelard.* Paris: Éditions du Seuil, 1974.

Martin, Marc. "La télévision." In *La France d'un siècle à l'autre, 1914–2000,* edited by Jean-Pierre Rioux and Jean-François Sirinelli, 418–25. Paris: Hachette littératures, 1999.

Marinoff, Lou. *Plato, Not Prozac: Applying Eternal Wisdom to Everyday Problems.* New York: HarperCollins, 1999.

Marx-Scouras, Danielle. *The Cultural Politics of Tel Quel: Literature and the Left in the Wake of Engagement.* University Park: Pennsylvania State University Press, 1996.

Mathy, Jean-Philippe. *Extrême Occident: French Intellectuals and America.* Chicago: University of Chicago Press, 1993.

Mauriac, Claude. "Il ne faut pas tuer l'espérance." *Le monde,* 6 June 1977.

Mayor, Francis. "Une tribu de Gibis: Le Service de la recherche." *Télérama* 1065 (14 June 1970).

Mercier, Arnaud. *Le journal télévisé: Politique de l'information et information politique.* Paris: Presses de Sciences Po, 1996.

Mercillon, H., ed. *ORTF l'agonie du monopole?* Paris: Plon, 1974.

Mermet, Gérard. *Démocrature: Comment les médias transforment la démocratie.* Paris: Aubier, 1987.

Meunier, Sophie. "France's Double-Talk on Globalization." *French Politics, Culture and Society* 21, no. 1 (Spring 2003): 20–33.

Mewshaw, Michael. "The Existential Burger: A nation of Sartres ponders life's meaning. An American asks, 'Where are the fries?' " *New York Times,* 6 April 1997.

Michel, Hervé. *La télévision en France et dans le monde.* Paris: Presses universitaires de France, 1989.

Miège, B., and others. *Le J.T. mise en scène de l'actualité à la télévision.* Paris: La documentation française, 1986.

Miller, Jacques-Alain. "Microscopia: An Introduction to the Reading of Television." In Lacan, *Television* (see above).

Miller, James. *The Passion of Michel Foucault.* New York: Doubleday, 1993.

Missika, Jean-Louis, and Dominique Wolton. *La folle du logis: La télévision dans les sociétés démocratiques.* Paris: Gallimard, 1983.

Mongin, Olivier. "L'inquiétude éthique." In *Le XXe siècle en France: Art, politique, philosophie,* edited by Alexandre Abensour with a foreword by Alain Finkielkraut. Paris: Berger-Levrault, 2000.

Monzie, Antatole de, and Lucien Febvre, eds. *Encyclopédie française.* Vol. 19: *Philosophie, religion,* edited by Gaston Berger. Paris: Société de gestion de l'Encyclopédie française, 1957.

Morgan, Ted. *An Uncertain Hour: The French, the Germans, the Jews, the Klaus Barbie Trial and the City of Lyon, 1940–1945.* New York: Morrow, 1990.

Mortley, Raoul. *French Philosophers in Conversation.* London: Routledge, 1991.

Mourgeon, Jacques. "Comment apprendre à lire." *L'éducation*, 23 March 1972.

Mousseau, Jacques. "Le livre à la télévision." *Les cahiers du Comité d'histoire de la télévision*, 4 June 1999, pp. 54–72.

Mousseau, Jacques, and Christian Brochand. *L'aventure de la télévision*. Paris: Nathan, 1987.

Moyn, Samuel. *Origins of the Other: Emmanuel Levinas between Revelation and Ethics*. Ithaca: Cornell University Press, 2005.

Murphy, James, and Randall Gross. *Learning by Television*. New York: Academy for Educational Development, 1966.

Nel, Noël. *À fleurets mouchetés: 25 ans de débats télévisés*. Paris: La documentation française, 1988.

———. *Le débat télévisé*. Paris: Armand Colin, 1990.

Nora, Pierre, ed. *Lieux de mémoire*. Vol. 2: *La nation*. Paris: Gallimard, 1986.

"Nouvelle philosophie pour La Cinquième." *Le Figaro*, 24 February 1997.

Ogilvie, Bertrand. "Évaluation et finalité des systèmes éducatifs." In *L'enseignement de la philosophie à la croisée des chemins*, edited by Laurence Cornu and others, 89–112. Paris: Centre national de documentation pédagogique, 1994.

Onfray, Michel. *Traité d'athéologie*. Paris: Grasset, 2005.

Ory, Pascal, ed. *Dernières questions aux intellectuels*. Paris: Olivier Orban, 1990.

Ory, Pascal, and Jean-François Sirinelli. *Les intellectuels en France, de l'affaire Dreyfus à nos jours*. Paris: Armand Colin, 1986.

Ott, Hugo. *Martin Heidegger: A Political Life*. Translated by Allan Blunden. NY: Basic Books, 1993.

Parinaud, André. *Bachelard*. Paris: Flammarion, 1996.

Paris, Erna. *Unhealed Wounds: France and the Klaus Barbie Affair*. New York: Methuen, 1985.

Pascaud, Fabienne. "En pays de connaissances." *Télérama* 1991 (9 March 1988): 58–59.

Patriat, Claude. *La culture, un besoin d'État*. Paris: Hachette, 1998.

Paulin, Catherine. "Phil, Sophie, Flo et les autres." *Téléscope* 115, November 25–December 1, 1995.

Paxton, Robert O. *Vichy France: Old Guard, New Order*. New York: Knopf, 1972.

Péan, Pierre, and Christophe Nick. *TF1, un pouvoir*. Paris: Fayard, 1997.

Peroni, Michel. *De l'écrit à l'écran: Livre et télévision*. Paris: Centre Georges Pompidou, Bibliothèque publique d'information, 1991.

Perraud, Antoine. "Le vol arrêté." *Télérama* 2077 (1 November 1989): 60–61.

"Peut-on encore être stoïcien?" *Bulletin de la radio-télévision scolaire* 37 (1966).

Perry, Sheila. "Television." In *Aspects of Contemporary France*, edited by Sheila Perry, 114–33. London: Routledge, 1997.

Peyrefitte, Alain. "Une nouvelle philosophie bien française." *La Nef* 66 (January–April 1978).

Pharo, Patrick. "Éthique et politique, ou les intellectuels dans l'histoire." *L'année sociologique* 30 (1979–80).

Phillips, Christopher. *Socrates Café: A Fresh Taste of Philosophy*. New York: Norton, 2002.

"Philosophie: La nouvelle passion." *Magazine littéraire* 339 (January 1996).

"La Philosophie fera son entrée a la télévision-scolaire." *Bulletin de la radio-télévision scolaire* 16 (1964): 19.

Pinto, Louis. "Le journalisme philosophique." *Actes de la recherche en sciences sociales* 101–2 (1994): 25–38.

———. *Les philosophes entre le lycée et l'avant-garde.* Paris: L'Harmattan, 1987.

Pisanias, Jean-Philippe. "Un philosophe de marque: A la télé, Michel Serres fait la promo de SFR." *Télérama* 2670 (14 March 2001): 24.

Pivot, Bernard. "Les années Pivot." *Lire* 296 (June 2001).

———. *Le métier de lire: Réponses à Pierre Nora.* Paris: Gallimard, 1990.

"Pivot . . . fermez les guillemets." *Télérama* 2683 (13 June 2000): 84–92.

"Plusieurs idées importantes." in "Ça va mieux en le disant." *Télérama,* 3 March 1974.

Popper, Karl, and John Condry. *La télévision: Un danger pour la démocratie.* Translated by Claude Orsoni. Paris: Éditions 10/18 Anatolia, 1994.

Portevin, Catherine, and Ariane Poulantzas, "Les gens préfèrent aller au café-philo qu'acheter Kant." *Télérama* 2664 (31 January 2001): 58–60.

Poucet, Bruno. *Enseigner la philosophie: Histoire d'une discipline scolaire, 1860–1990.* Paris: CNRS Éditions, 1999.

Poujol, Geneviève. "The Creation of a Ministry of Culture in France." *French Cultural Studies* 2 (1991): 251–60.

"Le programme de prospection du Service de la recherche de la R.T.F." *Correspondance de la Presse* #2774, 19 July 1961. Box ORTF / Service de la recherche, INA.

Prost, Antoine. *L'enseignement s'est-il démocratisé?* Paris: Presses universitaires de France, 1986.

"Radio-télé bac 66, pour une meilleure préparation des candidats à la deuxième session du baccalauréat." *Dossiers pédagogiques de la radio-télévision scolaire,* supplement, 1966, pp. 7–15.

Rancière, Jacques. "La bergère au goulag." *Révoltes logiques* 1 (Winter 1975): 96–111.

Reader, Keith A. *Intellectuals and the Left in France since 1968.* New York: St. Martin's Press, 1987.

Reading, Bill. "Foreword." In Lyotard, *Political Writings* (see above), xiii–xxvi.

"La recherche en matière de programmes." Paris: O.R.T.F Documentation de la Direction générale, 1971. Te IV AT 6 Box Service de la Recherche, INA.

Regourd, Serge. "Two Conflicting Notions of Audiovisual Liberalization." In *Television Broadcasting in Contemporary France and Britain,* edited by Michael Scriven and Monia Lecomte, 29–45. New York: Berghahn, 1999.

Revel, Jean-François. *La cabale des dévots.* Reprinted in *Pourquoi des philosophes?* Paris: Robert Laffont, 1997.

———. *Pourquoi des philosophes?* Paris: Julliard, 1957.

Ribardière, Diane. "Ils nous font la leçon." *Courrier de parlement,* n.d.

Rieffel, Rémy. *La tribu des clercs: Les intellectuels sous la Ve République, 1958–1990.* 3 vols. Paris: Calmann-Lévy, 1993.

Riffard, Pierre. *Les philosophes: Vie intime.* Paris: Presses universitaires de France, 2004.

Rigaud, Jacques. *L'exception culturelle: Culture et pouvoirs sous la Ve république.* Paris: Grasset, 1995.

Rigby, Brian. *Popular Culture in Modern France.* London: Routledge, 1991.

Rigby, Brian, and Nicholas Hewitt, eds. *France and the Mass Media.* Houndmills, UK: Macmillan, 1991.

Rioux, Jean-Pierre, and Jean-François Sirinelli, eds. *La France d'un siècle à l'autre, 1914–2000.* Paris: Hachette littératures, 1999.

————. *Histoire culturelle de la France*. 4 vols. Paris: Éditions du Seuil, 1997–98.

Robichon, Jacques. "Desgraupes et Dumayet: Terroristes de l'interview." *Nouvelles littéraires*, 17 December 1964.

Rockmore, Tom. *Heidegger and French Philosophy: Humanism, Antihumanism and Being*. London: Routledge, 1995.

Ross, Kristin. *May '68 and Its Afterlives*. Chicago: University of Chicago Press, 2002.

Rouanet, Anne. "La grande misère d'une grande idée." *Les cahiers de la télévision*, special issue, "La télévision scolaire existe," 9 (October1963): 9–12.

Roudensco, Elisabeth. *Jacques Lacan*. Translated by Barbara Bray. New York: Columbia University Press, 1997.

Rousset, David. "Un entretien avec David Rousset." *Le quotidien de Paris*, 29 November 1977.

Rousso, Henry. *The Vichy Syndrome*. Translated by Arthur Goldhammer. Cambridge, MA: Harvard University Press, 1991.

Rurand-Prinborgne, C. *L'égalité scolaire: Par le coeur et par la raison*. Paris: Nathan, 1988.

Sa'adah, Anne. *Contemporary France: A Democratic Education*. Lanham, Maryland: Rowman and Littlefield, 2003.

Sabbagh, Pierre. *Encore vous, Sabbagh*. Paris: Stock, 1984.

Salachas, Gilbert. "Max-Pol Fouchet: La culture n'est pas de savoir que Mozart existe, c'est de recommencer Mozart." *Téléciné* 159 (June 1969): 38–46.

Saint Sernin, Bertrand. "Dina Dreyfus, ou la raison enseignante." *Cahiers philosophiques* 55 (June 1993): 85–98.

Saintville, Dominique, and Sylvie Cazin. "Océaniques: Un essai de construction de la mémoire." *Les dossiers de l'audiovisuels* 30 (November 1990): 20–22. INA Bry-sur-Marne.

Sapiro, Gisèle. *La guerre des écrivains, 1940–1953*. Paris: Fayard, 1999.

Sartre, Jean-Paul. "À propos de l'existentialisme: Mise au point." *Action* 17 (29 December 1944).

————. *The Communists and Peace, with a reply to Claude Lefort*. New York: G. Braziller, 1968.

————. *Critique de la raison dialectique*, preceded by *Questions de méthode*. Paris: Gallimard, 1960.

————. *The Devil and the Good Lord*. Translated by Kathy Black. New York: Vintage Books, 1960.

————. "Existentialism is a Humanism." In *Existentialism from Dostoevsky to Sartre*, edited, translated, and with an introduction by Walter Kaufmann. New York: Penguin Books, 1989.

————. *Plaidoyer pour les intellectuels. Situations VIII: autour de 68*. Paris: Gallimard, 1972.

————. "Situation of the Writer in 1947." in *"What is Literature?" and Other Essays*, with an introduction by Steven Ungar. Cambridge, MA: Harvard University Press, 1988.

————. *Situations* Paris: Gallimard, 1964–1976.

Sarraute, Claude. "Des mots, des mots." *Le monde*, 12 March 1974.

Sautet, Marc. *Un café pour Socrate*. Paris: Robert Laffont, 1995.

Schaeffer, Pierre. "Le programme de prospection du Service de la recherche de la R.T.F." *Correspondance de la presse*, no. 2774 (19 July 1961). Box ORTF / Service de la recherche, INA.

———. "Ce mystérieux Service de la recherche O.R.T.F." *L'aurore,* 13 September 1968.

———. *Le Service de la recherche de l'O.R.T.F.* Paris: Editions Michel Brient, 1968.

———. *Entretiens avec Marc Pierret.* Paris: Belfond, 1969.

Schiffer, Daniel Salvatore. *Grandeur et misère des intellectuels: Histoire critique de l'intelligentsia du XXe siècle.* Paris: Éditions du Rocher, 1998.

Schrift, Alan D. "Is There Such a Thing as 'French Philosophy'? or Why Do We Read the French So Badly?" In *After the Deluge: New Perspectives on the Intellectual and Cultural History of Postwar France,* edited by Julian Bourg, 21–48. Lanham, Maryland: Lexington Books, 2004.

———. *Twentieth-Century French Philosophy: Key Themes and Thinkers.* Malden, MA: Blackwell, 2006.

Scriven, Michael. "Sartre and the Audiovisual Media, 1968–1975." *French Cultural Studies* 1 (1990): 213–31.

———. *Sartre and the Media.* New York: St. Martin's Press, 1993.

Sébert, Isabelle, and Catherine Paulin. "Télégenie de la philo." *Téléscope* 55 (5–28 March 1997): 6–7.

Serres, Michel. *Éloge de la philosophie en langue française.* Paris: Flammarion, 1997.

———. *Le tiers-instruit.* Paris: Gallimard-Jeunesse, 1992.

Sévilla, Jean. *Le terrorisme intellectuel de 1945 à nos jours.* Paris: Librarie académique Perrin, 2000.

Sheehan, Thomas. "Heidegger and the Nazis." *New York Review of Books* 35, no. 10, (16 June 1988).

Simonin, Anne. *Les Éditions de Minuit, 1942–1955.* Paris, Éditions de Minuit, 1994.

Sirinelli, Jean-François. *Génération intellectuelle: Khâgneux et Normaliens dans l'entre-deux-guerres.* Paris: Fayard, 1988.

———. *Intellectuels et passions françaises.* Paris: Fayard, 1990.

———. *Deux intellectuels dans le siècle: Sartre et Aron.* Paris: Fayard, 1995.

Sophocles. *Antigone.* In *The Theban Plays,* translated by E. F. Watling. Harmondsworth: Penguin Books, 1978.

Soulié, Charles. "Anatomie de goût philosophique." *Actes de la recherches en sciences sociales* 109 (1995): 3–28.

Steiner, George. *Martin Heidegger.* Chicago: University of Chicago Press, 1978.

Stoekl, Allan. *Agonies of the Intellectual.* Lincoln: University of Nebraska Press, 1992.

Strivay, Renaud E. "Télévision et culture: La télévision scolaire en Europe." *T.V.* 50 (December 1959).

Strode, Louise. "French Identity in the Information Society: The Challenge of the Internet." *Modern and Contemporary France* 7, no. 3 (1999): 319–28.

Sublet, Françoise, and others. *Quand la télé entre à l'école.* Poitiers: CNDP/ CRDP, 1983.

"Les succès du mois." *L'express* (8–14 August 1966): 32.

Suleiman, Ezra. *Elites in French Society: The Politics of Survival.* Princeton: Princeton University Press, 1979.

Suleiman, Susan Rubin. "History, Memory and Moral Judgment in Documentary Film: On Marcel Ophuls's *Hotel Terminus: The Life and Times of Klaus Barbie.*" *Critical Inquiry* 28, no. 2 (Winter 2002): 509–41.

Sullerot, Evelyne. "Télévision et culture traditionnelle." *Télévision et éducation,* 18 May 1966, pp. 34–37.

"T.F.1 Hebdo N° 34: Programmes du samedi 16 au vendredi 22 août 1980, Les idées et les hommes" (51–52). *Bulletins de presse,* 1980, INA.

Taine, Hippolyte. *Les philosophes classiques du XIXe siècle en France.* 3rd ed. Paris: Hachette, 1868.

Taviollot, Pierre-Henri. "L'invention de la classe de philosophie." in Ferry and Renaut, *Philosopher à 18 ans* (see above).

Tertulian, Nicolas. "Coup de tonnerre dans le ciel heideggarien." *L'humanité,* 28 April 2005, 22.

Todd, Olivier. *Albert Camus: A Life.* Translated by Benjamin Ivry. New York: Knopf, 1997.

"Trois expériences françaises en matière d'enseignement direct." In : *Rapport du Séminaire européen, Rome 1966,* 69–87. Strasbourg: Conseil de la coopération culturelle du Conseil de l'Europe, 1967.

Truong, Nicolas. "Élaborer des questions." *Le monde de l'éducation* 224 (January 1997): 47.

Ulmann-Maurait, Caroline. "Le critique de télévision, initiateur et témoin." In Marie-Françoise Lévy, *La télévision dans la République* (see above).

"Un certain regard 'Jacques Lacan.'" *L'humanité dimanche,* 27 February 1974.

"Une grande émission se prépare: es émissions du Service de la recherche de l'ORTF." *Fiche de télévision* 37 (March 1967), supplement to *Télévision et éducation populaire,* 2–29.

UNESCO. *L'enseignement de la philosophie: Enquête internationale de l'Unesco.* Paris: UNESCO, 1953.

Vergès, Jacques. *Je defends Barbie.* Paris: Picollect, 1988.

Vermeren, Patrice. *La philosophie saisie par l'UNESCO.* Paris: UNESCO, 2003.

Veyrat-Masson, Isabelle. *Quand la télévision explore le temps: L'histoire au petit écran.* Paris: Fayard, 2000.

Vidal-Naquet, Pierre. *Assassins of Memory: Essays on the Denial of the Holocaust. Translated and with a foreword by Jeffrey Mehlman. New York: Columbia University Press, 1993.*

Waelhens, Alphonse de. "La philosophie de Heidegger et le nazisme." *Les temps modernes* 3 (1947–48): 115–27.

Waintrop, Edouard. "La parole au sommet de la vague." *Libération,* 28 September 1987, p. 54.

Weber, Eugen. *Action Française.* Stanford: Stanford University Press, 1962.

———. *Peasants into Frenchmen: The Modernization of Rural France.* Stanford: Stanford University Press, 1976.

Weyergans, François. "L'humeur de . . . ; Télévizer . . . " *Le Figaro,* 24–25 March 1974.

Williams, Raymond. *Communications.* 2nd ed. New York: Barnes and Noble, 1967.

———. *Television: Technology and Cultural Form.* Introduction by Lynn Spigel. Hanover: Wesleyan University Press, 1992.

Winock, Michel. "L'âge d'or des intellectuels." *L'histoire* 83 (November 1985): 22–34.

———. *Le siècle des intellectuels.* Paris: Éditions du Seuil, 1997.

Winock, Michel, and Jacques Julliard, eds. *Dictionnaire des·intellectuels français.* Paris: Éditions du Seuil, 1997.

Wolin, Richard. "The French Heidegger Debate." *New German Critique* 45 (Autumn 1988): 135–61.

———. "French Heidegger Wars." In Wolin, *The Heidegger Controversy* (see below), 282–310.

Wolin, Richard. ed. *The Heidegger Controversy: A Critical Reader.* New York: Columbia University Press, 1991.

Wolton, Dominique. *Éloge du grand public: Une théorie critique de la télévision.* Paris: Flammarion, 1990.

Wood, Donald N., and Donald G. Wylie. *Educational Telecommunications.* Belmont, CA: Wadsworth, 1977.

Wright, Gordon. *France in Modern Times.* 4th ed. New York: Norton, 1987.

Yvoire, Jean d'. Retranscription of "L'enseignement de la philosophie par la télévision: Conclusion et synthèse." *L'enseignement de la philosophie,* Antenne 1, 4 June 1965, RTS, in *Cahiers philosophiques Hors Série,* June 1993, pp. 96–107.

## Television and Radio (organized by date of broadcast)

"100ème de 'Le diable et le bon dieu' de Jean-Paul Sartre fêtée au Claridge." *JT 20H,* Channel 1, 22 November 1951, INA.

"Prix Goncourt et Renaudot." *JT 20H,* Channel 1, 6 December 1954, INA.

"Écouter, voir." Channel 1, 10 June 1955, INA.

"Lectures pour tous: Émission du 19 Juillet, 1955." *Lectures pour tous,* Channel 1, 19 July 1955 INA.

"Diplôme *Honoris Causa* en Belgique." *JT 20H,* Channel 1, 15 December 1956, INA.

"Lectures pour tous: Émission du 15 mai, 1957." *Lectures pour tous,* Channel 1, 15 May 1957, INA.

"Madame Oswald et ses enfants." Channel 1, 17 June 1957, INA.

"Lectures pour tous: Émission du 23 octobre, 1957." *Lectures pour tous,* Channel 1, 23 October 1957, INA.

"Interview de M. Albert Camus, Prix Nobel 1957." *Journal National, Actualités françaises* 23 October 1957, INA.

"Conférence de presse André Malraux." *JT 13H,* Channel 1, 25 June 1958, INA.

"Que veut la jeunesse d'aujourd'hui." *Liberté de l'esprit,* Channel 1, 14 November 1959, INA.

"Que veut la jeunesse d'aujourd'hui: 2ème partie." *Liberté de l'esprit,* Channel 1, 20 November 1958, INA.

"Études et essais politiques." *Liberté de l'esprit,* Channel 1, 6 April 1959, INA.

"Albert Camus." *Gros plan,* Channel 1, 12 May 1959, INA.

"Discorama: Émission du 22 mai 1959." *Discorama,* Channel 1, 22 May 1959, INA.

"Études et essais politiques." *Liberté de l'esprit,* Channel 1, 4 June 1959, INA.

"Lectures pour tous: Émission du 1 juillet 1959." *Lectures pour tous,* Channel 1, 1 July 1959, INA.

"Albert Camus présente 'Les possédés'." *JT nuit,* Channel 1, 24 January 1959, INA.

"Lectures pour tous: Émission du 28 janvier 1959." *Lectures pour tous,* Channel 1, 28 January 1959, INA.

"Retrospective et obsèques d'Albert Camus, Le Prix Nobel." *JT Nuit,* Channel 1, 9 January 1960, INA.

"Lectures pour tous: Émission du 13 Janvier 1960." *Lectures pour tous,* Channel 1, 13 January 1960, INA.

"Attribution du Prix Paul Pelliot." *JT 13H,* Channel 1, 25 February 1960, INA.

"À la recherche de: Albert Camus: Documents sur la guerre d'Espagne." *L'art et les hommes,* Channel 1, 21 February 1961, INA.

"La dévotion à la croix," Channel 1, 21 February 1961, INA.

"Portrait d'un philosophe." *Cinq colonnes à la une,* Channel 1, 1 December 1961, INA.

"Anniversaire de la mort de Camus." *JT 20H,* Channel 1, 4 January 1961, INA.

"La télévision: 1ère partie." *Faire face,* Channel 1, 13 April 1961, INA.

"Plastic chez Jean-Paul Sartre." *JT 13H,* Channel 1, 8 January 1962, INA.

"Rayonnement d'Albert Camus." Channel 1, 8 January 1962, INA.

"Séquence Bachelard Gaston." *JT 20H,* Channel 1, 16 October 1962, INA.

"Prix des ambassadeurs." *JT 20H,* Channel 1, 17 October 1962, INA.

"Lectures pour tous: Émission du 17 Octobre 1962." *Lectures pour tous,* Channel 1, 17 October 1962, INA.

"Page des Lettres du 20 Octobre 1962." *Page des Lettres,* Channel 1, 20 October 1962, INA.

*Round Up,* Channel 1, 21 October 1962, INA.

"Vente charité enfance orpheline." *JT 13H,* Channel 1, 8 November 1962, INA.

"Un cas intéressant," Channel 1, 15 January 1963, INA.

"Lecture pour tous: Émission du 30 janvier, 1963." *Lectures pour tous,* Channel 1, 30 January 1963, INA.

"Louis Le Grand a 500 ans." *L'avenir est à vous,* Channel 1, 15 May 1963, INA.

"Prix Hachette et Larousse." *JT 13H,* Channel 1, 19 October 1963, INA.

"Albert Camus." *JT 13H,* Channel 1, 7 November 1963, INA.

"Jean-Paul Sartre à Prague." *JT 13H,* Channel 1, 18 November 1963, INA.

"Les séquestrés d'Altona de Jean-Paul Sartre." *JT 13H,* Channel 1, 26 November 1963, INA.

"Varese; Lipchitz; J. Villon; Camus." *L'art et les hommes,* Channel 1, 1 January 1964, INA.

"Anniversaire de Camus." *JT 20H,* Channel 1, 11 January 1964, INA.

"À propos d'un crime." *À propos de,* Channel 2, 23 February 1964, INA.

"À Propos de *L'étranger* d'Albert Camus." *À propos de,* Channel 2, 23 February 1964, INA.

"Hommes et caméras." *Un certain regard,* Channel 1, March 1964, INA.

"Extraits de 'Caligula' et de 'Le journal d'un fou.'" *Page théâtre,* Channel 1, 14 June 1964, INA.

"Extrait de 'Le Malentendu' d'Albert Camus." *Page théâtre,* Channel 1, 9 August 1964, INA.

"Les jeux de l'image et du hazard." *Un certain regard,* Channel 1, 14 September 1964, INA.

"Monsieur Jean-Paul Sartre Prix Nobel." *JT 20H,* Channel 1, 22 October 1964, INA.

"Le refus de Sartre." *JT 20H,* Channel 1, 23 October 1964, INA.

"Sartre et le Nobel." *JT 13H,* Channel 1, 23 October 1964, INA.

"L'interview." *Un certain regard,* Channel 1, 15 November 1964, INA.

"Rétrospective Albert Camus." *JT 13H,* Channel 1, 4 January 1965, INA.

"La philosophie et son histoire." *L'enseignement de la philosophie*, Channel 1, 9 January 1965, RTS.

"Philosophie et science." *L'enseignement de la philosophie*, Channel 1, 23 January 1965, RTS.

"Philosophie et sociologie." *L'enseignement de la philosophie*, Channel 1, 6 February 1965, RTS.

"Philosophie et psychologie." *L'enseignement de la philosophie*, Channel 1, 27 February 1965, RTF.

"Philosophie et langage." *L'enseignement de la philosophie*, Channel 1, 13 March 1965, RTS.

"Philosophie et vérité." *L'enseignement de la philosophie*, Channel 1, 27 March 1965, RTF.

"L'enseignement de la philosophie par la télévision: Conclusion et synthèse." *L'enseignement de la philosophie*, Channel 1, 4 June 1965, RTS.

"Rétrospective Nobel." *Journal de Paris*, Channel 1, 17 June 1965, INA.

"Théâtre: 'Gigi' et 'Huis-Clos.'" *Page théâtre*, Channel 1, 27 June 1965, INA.

"Extrait Les séquestrés d'Altona." *Page théâtre*, Channel 1, 9 September 1965, INA.

"L'homme de télévision." *Un certain regard*, Channel 1, 12 September 1965, INA.

*Huis Clos*, Channel 1, 12 October 1965, INA.

"Entretien sur Pascal." *L'enseignement de la philosophie*, Channel 1, 3 December 1965, RTS.

"L'âge d'or de Saint-Germain-des-Prés." *A la vitrine du libraire*, Channel 1, 4 December 1965, INA.

"Extraits de 'Les justes,' 'Du vent dans les branches de Sassafras.'" *Page théâtre*, Channel 1, 16 January 1966, INA.

"Philosophie et morale VI: Actualité de la morale kantienne." *L'enseignement de la philosophie*, Channel 1, 5 March 1966, RTS.

"Philosophie et morale VII: Actualité de la morale kantienne. Lecture d'un texte kantien (extrait de la *Critique de la raison pratique*) par O. Chedin." *L'enseignement de la philosophie*, Channel 1, 19 March 1966, RTS.

"Lectures pour tous: Émission du 15 juin, 1966." *Lectures pour tous*, Channel 1, 15 June 1966, INA.

"Festival de Marvejols. Lozere (extrait de 'Les Bouches Inutiles')." *Page théâtre*, Channel 1, 7 August 1966, INA.

"Mariage de la fille d'Albert Camus." *JT Nuit*, Channel 1, 23 August 1966, INA.

"Débat sur le Viêt Nam." *JT 13H*, Channel 1, 29 November 1966, INA.

"Un souvenir de Camus." *Panorama*, Channel 1, 24 February 1967, INA.

"Cinéma: Émission du 28 Septembre 1967." *Cinéma*, Channel 1, 28 September 1967, INA.

"Les savants sont parmi nous: 1ère partie." *Un certain regard*, Channel 1, 17 October 1967, INA.

"Claude Lévi-Strauss." *Un certain regard*, Channel 1, 21 January 1968, INA.

"Roman Jakobson." *Un certain regard*, Channel 1, 17 March 1968, INA.

"Film 'L'écume des jours." *JT Nuit*, Channel 1, 18 March 1968, INA.

"Le nouveau dimanche: Émission du 31 mars, 1968." *Le nouveau dimanche*, Channel 2, 31 March 1968, INA.

"24 Heures avec Robert Kennedy." *Panorama*, Channel 1, 17 May 1968, INA.

"Commission des affaires culturelles et interview Peyrefitte." *JT 20H*, Channel 1, 20 September 1968, INA.

"Miguel Angel Asturias: Un Maya à la cour du Roi Gustave." *Images et idées*, Channel 2, 6 October 1968, INA.

"Ephéméride Gaston Bachelard." *JT 13H*, Channel 2, 16 October 1968, INA.

"Ce jour-là: Camus Prix Nobel." *JT 13H*, Channel 1, 17 October 1968, INA.

"Spectacles de la semaine du 17 novembre 1968." *Spectacles de la semaine*, Channel 1, 17 November 1968, INA.

"Extrait de 'Le diable et le bon dieu,'" *Les trois coups*, Channel 1, 30 November 1968, INA.

"Han Suyin." *L'invité du dimanche*, Channel 2, 5 January 1969, INA.

"Le malentendu du 2ème sexe." *Lire et comprendre*, Channel 1, 5 October 1969, INA.

"Raymond Aron: Un philosophe dans le journalisme." *Un certain regard*, Channel 1, 7 December 1969, INA.

"L'affaire de Song My: Jean-Paul Sartre." *Panorama*, Channel 1, 11 December 1969, INA.

"Emmanuel Mounier." *Un certain regard*, Channel 1, 25 October 1970, INA.

"Georg Lukacs." *Un certain regard*, Channel 1, 13 December 1970, INA.

"Bertrand Russell." *Un certain regard*, Channel 1, 21 February 1971, INA.

"Bachelard parmi nous." *Un certain regard*, Channel 1, 2 October 1972, INA.

"Jacques Lacan: 1ère émission, Psychanalyse I." Channel 1, 9 March 1974, INA.

"Jacques Lacan: 2ème émission, Psychanalyse II." Channel 1, 16 March 1974, INA.

"Alexandre Soljenitsyne." *Ouvrez les guillemets*, Channel 1, 24 June 1974, INA.

"Dieu existe-t-il?" *Interrogations*, TF1, 5 January 1975, INA.

"Simone de Beauvoir et la ligue du droit des femmes." *Tribune Libre*, FR3, 20 January 1975 INA.

"Liberté et déterminisme." *Interrogations*, TF1, 12 March 1975, INA.

"Rencontre avec l'amour." *Les grandes heures de notre vie*, TF1, 19 March 1975, INA.

"Le bonheur." *Interrogations*, TF1, 16 April 1975, INA.

"L'art, le beau, et l'utile." *Interrogations*, TF1, 21 May 1975, INA.

"La vie intellectuelle sous l'occupation." *Apostrophes*, Antenne 2, 27 June 1975, INA.

"Le moi et les autres." *Interrogations*, TF1, 24 September 1975, INA.

"La mort." *Interrogations*, TF1, 22 October 1975, INA.

"La justice." *Interrogations*, TF1, 26 November 1975, INA.

"L'amour." *Interrogations*, TF1, 17 December 1975, INA.

"Vérité." *Interrogations*, TF1, 19 January 1976, INA.

"L'amour romanesque." *Apostrophes*, Antenne 2, 20 February 1976, INA.

"C'est de la politique ou de la littérature." *Apostrophes*, Channel 2, 12 March 1976, INA.

"Résponsabilité. *Interrogations*, TF1, 28 April 1976, INA.

"Julia Kristeva." *Tribune libre*, FR3, 15 May 1976, INA.

"Michel Serres." *Tribune libre*, FR3, 27 September 1976, INA.

"Quel avenir pour l'homme." *Apostrophes*, Antenne 2, 17 December 1976, INA.

"Les nouveaux philosophes sont-ils de droite ou de gauche?" *Apostrophes*, Antenne 2, 27 May 1977, INA.

"André Glucksmann." *Tribune libre*, FR3, 27 June 1977, INA.

"Maurice Clavel." *La part de la vérité,* TF1, 4 July 1977, INA.
"Soeren Kierkegaard." *Les idées et les hommes,* TF1, 11 November 1977 INA.
"Jean-François Lyotard." *Tribune libre,* FR3, 27 March 1978, INA.
"Vladimir Jankélévitch." *Tribune libre,* FR3, 17 April 1978, INA.
"En marge de la société." *Apostrophes,* Antenne 2, 22 September 1978, INA.
"Plateau Hai Hong." *Questions de temps,* Antenne 2, 27 November 1978, INA.
"Simone de Beauvoir." *Les rendez-vous du dimanche,* TF1, 7 January 1979, INA.
"Crime et châtiment." *Apostrophes,* Antenne 2, 18 May 1979, INA.
"Les Juifs en question." *Apostrophes,* Antenne 2, 14 September 1979, INA.
"La naissance." *Apostrophes,* Antenne 2, 16 November 1979.
"Retro Albert Camus." *Soir 3,* FR3, 3 January 1980, INA.
"À quoi servent les philosophes?" *Apostrophes,* Antenne 2, 18 January 1980, INA.
"Jean-Paul Sartre, écrivain 1905–1980." *Apostrophes,* Antenne 2, 18 April 1980, INA
*Sartre par lui-même, première partie.* TF1, 21 April 1980, INA.
*Sartre par lui-même, deuxième partie.* TF1, 22 April 1980, INA.
"Michel Serres." *Tribune libre,* FR3, 28 November 1980, INA.
"C'est à lire: L'idéologie française." *Soir 3,* FR3, 12 January 1981, INA.
"Au carrefour des idéologies." *Apostrophes,* Antenne 2, 23 January 1981, INA.
"Déracinez-vous." *La rage de lire,* TF1, 6 May 1981, INA.
"1ère emission: La France dans la tourmente." *Raymond Aron, spectateur engagé,* Antenne 2, 11 October 1981, INA.
"Démocratie et totalitarisme 1947–1967." *Raymond Aron, spectateur engagé,* Antenne 2, 18 October 1981, INA.
"3ème émission (1968) Liberté et raison." *Raymond Aron, spectateur engagé,* Antenne 2, 25 October 1981, INA.
*Le chagrin et la pitié.* FR3, 28–29 October 1981, INA.
"La réalité, 1945 –1958." *Paris Paris, ou Le temps d'une génération,* A2, 11 September 1983, INA.
"Simone de Beauvoir." *Témoins,* FR3, 15 January 1984, INA.
"Les meilleurs." *Apostrophes,* Antenne 2, 4 January 1985, INA.
"Sartre et Céline." *Apostrophes,* Antenne 2, 25 October 1985, INA.
"Sur quelques épisodes du XXe siècle." *Apostrophes,* Antenne 2, 22 November 1985, INA.
"Shoah." *IT1 20H,* TF1, 29 June 1987 INA.
"Plateau Claude Lanzmann." *IT1 13H,* TF1, 2 July 1987 INA.
"Shoah." *IT1 20H,* TF1, 2 July 1987 INA.
"Le mythe d'Antigone." *Océaniques,* FR3, 21 September 1987, INA.
"Le sacrifice d'Abraham." *Océaniques,* FR3, 28 September 1987, INA.
"Martin Heidegger: La parole et le silence, 1ère partie." *Océaniques,* FR3, 7 December 1987, INA.
"Martin Heidegger: La parole et le silence, 2ème partie." *Océaniques,* FR3, 14 December, 1987, INA.
"Entretien avec Michel Foucault." *Océaniques: Des idées,* FR3, 13 January 1988, INA.
"Doit-on les condamner?" *Apostrophes,* Antenne 2, 20 April 1988, INA.
"Deux philosophes français en Californie." *Apostrophes,* Antenne 2, 21 July 1989, INA.
"Le sexe homocide." *Apostrophes,* Antenne 2, 16 March 1990, INA.

"Du commencement de *Lectures pour tous* à la fin d'*Apostrophes:* Quarante ans de lecture à la télévision." *La belle mémoire,* FR3, 5 September 1990, INA.

"L'effet Serres." *La marche du siècle,* FR3, 6 February 1991.

"Ex Libris: Émission du 7 mars 1991." *Ex Libris,* TF1, 7 March 1991 INA.

*Les aventures de la liberté,* Four parts. Antenne 2, 13 March 1991, 20 March 1991, 27 March 1991, April 1991, INA.

"Michel Piccoli." *Bouillon de Culture,* Antenne 2, 5 January 1992.

"Avant-propos de Pierre Dumayet." *Lectures pour tous,* special series, September 1992, INA.

*Le temps des philosophes* (videos). Paris: CNDP/Nathan, 1993.

"À vous Cognac Jay." *Notre télévision,* France 2, 15 July 1993, INA.

"Les Buttes." *Notre télévision,* France 2, 19 August 1993, INA.

"Dossier: Aron, Sartre: Cinquante ans d'histoire." *Les brûlures de l'histoire,* France 3, 12 October 1993, INA.

"Spécial: 'Michel Foucault.'" *Le cercle de minuit,* France 2, 22 June 1994, INA.

"Spécial: Philosophie." *Le cercle de minuit,* France 2, 6 December 1994, INA.

"Jean-Paul Sartre, écrivain." *Un siècle d'écrivains,* France 3, 17 May 1995, INA.

"L'abcédaire de Gilles Deleuze." *Metropolis,* ARTE, 17 September 1995, INA.

"La philosophie." *Le cercle de minuit,* France 2, 30 January 1996.

"Pourquoi la philosophie est-elle si populaire?" *Bouillon de culture,* France 2, 20 December 1996, INA.

"Procréation ou reproduction." *Grain de philo,* France 3, 17 May 1997, INA.

"Le progrès." *Philosophies,* La cinquième, 22 March 1997.

"Le retour de la philo." *France Culture,* 6, 8, 9 January 1997.

"La notion de responsabilité." *Grain de philo,* France 3, 14 February 1998, INA.

"Droits d'auteurs: Émission no. 22." *Droits d'auteurs,* La Cinq, 14 February 1999, INA.

*Le siècle des intellectuels.* France 3, 20 October 1999, INA.

*Philosophy: A Guide to Happiness.* Six-part series hosted by Alain de Botton, Channel 4, Spring 2000, BBC.

"Philosophical Implications." *Weekend Edition,* Saturday, interview with Alain de Botton by host Scott Simon, National Public Radio, 2 December 2000.

*Campus, le magazine de l'écrit.* France 2, 4 April 2005, INA

"Emmanuel Faye: 'Heidegger: L'introduction du nazisme dans la philosophie,'" *Un livre,* France 2, 21 April 2005, INA.

### Internet Sources

"France launches world TV channel." BBC News, http://news.bbc.co.uk/go/pr/fr/-/2/hi/europe/6215170.stm, published 6 December 2006.

Institut national de l'audiovisuel. http://www.ina.fr.

Ireland, Doug. "Michel Onfray on Jean Meslier," http://direland.typepad.com/direland/2006/03/michel_onfray_0.html. Consulted 24 November 2006.

### Interviews

Laure Adler (24 May 2000); Alain Badiou (24 May 2000); Jean Beaujean (14 February 2001); Marie-Anne Bernard (1 December 1999); Pierre-André Boutang

(17 May 2000); Jean-Claude Bringuier (October 27, 1999); Michel Cazenave (24 May 2000); André Comte-Sponville (9 November 1999); Rachel Denoeud (12 October 2000); Pierre Dumayet (17 November 1999); Alain Etchegoyan (10 November 1999); Frédéric Ferney (10 December 1999); Luc Ferry (23 November 1999); Denis Huisman (19 April 1999); Paula Jacques (19 November 1999); Yves Jaigu (25 November 1999); Jean-Noël Jeanneney (11 October 1999); Tony Judt (7 February 2000); Marie-Agnès Malfray (10 May 1999); Louis Pinto (12 May 1999); Michel Winock (1 December 1999).

*À armes égales,* 137, 149
*L'abécédaire de Gilles Deleuze,* 186, 227
"Abraham's Sacrifice" broadcast on *Océaniques,* 179, 187–88, 195–99, 220
Académie de Paris, 87, 101
Académie française, 162
accessibility. *See* clarity and accessibility of French philosophy
Action française, 185, 196
*Actualités de Paris,* 54
*Les actualités françaises,* 37, 38, 250n89
Adler, Laure, 230–31
Adorno, Theodor, 205
advertising, 13, 53, 115, 264n98
Aeschylus, 39
*affaire du foulard,* 224, 282n143
Agacinski, Sylviane, 165, 230
Ahearne, Jeremy, 221–22
Alain de Lille, 24, 160, 272n111
"Albert Camus" on *Gros plan,* 44–47, 252n131
Alembert, Jean Le Rond d', 24–25
Alessandri, Jean-Pierre, 272n117
Algerian War, 2–3, 41–42, 169, 200, 251n116; Camus on, 48, 252n133; Evian accords and independence, 88–89; Front de libération nationale, 89; "Manifesto of the 121," 42; Organisation de l'armée secrète (OAS), 42–43
Alleg, Henri, 251n116

Althusser, Louis, 76, 146, 175, 256n47, 268–69n56; biography of, 185; *Océaniques* series, 179, 199, 274n17; on problems in philosophy, 92–93
American philosophy series, 227, 245n10
*L'amour en vogue* (Pivot), 134
analytic of finitude, 77–80, 258n79
Antenne 2, 132, 254n11, 265n131, 266n5; funding of, 181–82; Holocaust miniseries, 201; *La marche du siècle,* 231. *See also* Channel 2, France 2
*Antigone* (Sophocles): Lacan's seminar on, 275n31; *Océaniques* broadcast on, 174, 179, 187–95, 220, 275n36, 277n60; Peyrefitte's views on, 174
anti-Semitism, 180, 197, 201–2; Dreyfus affair, 12, 21, 244n38; Jewish question, 147–48; "Martin Heidegger" broadcast on *Océaniques,* 204–19; New Philosophy's examination of, 148, 201. *See also* Vichy regime
antitotalitarianism, 147–54
*Apostrophes,* 13, 52, 83, 130, 132–59, 177, 253n3; audience of, 133, 145, 166, 266n6; critical responses to, 134; debate format of, 133–34; ethical themes on, 138; Foucault's appearances on, 130, 138–44, 258n79, 268n44; hosting style of Pivot on, 133–36, 144; impact on book sales, 130, 133, 233; Jankélévitch's appear-